CAMBRIDGE SOUTH ASIAN STUDIES

THE EMERGENCE OF PROVINCIAL POLITICS

The Madras Presidency 1870–1920

CAMBRIDGE SOUTH ASIAN STUDIES

These monographs are published by the Syndics of Cambridge University Press in association with the Cambridge University Centre for South Asian Studies. The following books have been published in this series:

1 S. GOPAL: *British Policy in India, 1858–1905*

2 J. A. B. PALMER: *The Mutiny Outbreak at Meerut in 1857*

3 A. DAS GUPTA: *Malabar in Asian Trade, 1740–1800*

4 G. OBEYESEKERE: *Land Tenure in Village Ceylon*

5 H. L. ERDMAN: *The Swatantra Party and Indian Conservatism*

6 S. N. MUKHERJEE: *Sir William Jones: A Study in Eighteenth-Century British Attitudes to India*

7 ABDUL MAJED KHAN: *The Transition in Bengal, 1756–1775: A Study of Saiyid Muhammad Reza Khan*

8 RADHA SHYAM RUNGTA: *The Rise of Business Corporations in India, 1851–1900*

9 PAMELA NIGHTINGALE: *Trade and Empire in Western India, 1784–1806*

10 AMIYA KUMAR BAGCHI: *Private Investment in India, 1900–1939.*

11 JUDITH M. BROWN: *Gandhi's Rise to Power: Indian Politics, 1915–1922*

12 MARY C. CARRAS: *The Dynamics of Indian Political Factions*

13 P. HARDY: *The Muslims of British India*

14 GORDON JOHNSON: *Provincial Politics and Indian Nationalism*

15 MARGUERITE S. ROBINSON: *Political Structure in a Changing Sinhalese Village*

16 FRANCIS ROBINSON: *Separation among Indian Muslims: The Politics of the United Provinces' Muslims, 1860–1923*

17 CHRISTOPHER JOHN BAKER: *The Politics of South India 1920–1937*

THE EMERGENCE
OF PROVINCIAL POLITICS

The Madras Presidency
1870–1920

D. A. WASHBROOK
Lecturer in History, University of Warwick

CAMBRIDGE UNIVERSITY PRESS
CAMBRIDGE
LONDON · NEW YORK · MELBOURNE

Published by the Syndics of the Cambridge University Press
The Pitt Building, Trumpington Street, Cambridge CB2 1RP
Bentley House, 200 Euston Road, London NW1 2BD
32 East 57th Street, New York, NY 10022, USA
296 Beaconsfield Parade, Middle Park, Melbourne 3206, Australia

First published 1976

Photoset and printed in Malta by Interprint (Malta) Ltd

Library of Congress Cataloguing in Publication Data

Washbrook, D. A.
The emergence of provincial politics.

(Cambridge South Asian studies; no. 18)
Bibliography: p.
Includes index.
1. Madras (Presidency) – Politics and government.
I. Title. II. Series.
DS485.M28W37   320.9'54'8203   75–36292
ISBN 0–521–20982–X

For S.T.W., A.C.W.
AND S.W.

CONTENTS

PREFACE

This book has evolved out of a fellowship dissertation presented at Trinity College, Cambridge in 1971 and a Ph.d. dissertation presented at Cambridge University in 1974. The research was financed by a Pre-research linguistic studentship (1969–70) and a Research Fellowship (1971–5) from Trinity College, Cambridge, and by a Hayter Studentship (1970–1) from the Department of Education and Science.

In the course of my research, I have incurred enormous debts to a great many people. Firstly, I would like to thank, for their time and trouble in finding material for me, the directors and staffs of the Cambridge University Library, the India Office Library (London), the Madras University Library, the National Archives of India (New Delhi), the Nehru Memorial Museum Library (New Delhi), the Tamil Nadu Archives (Madras) and the Theosophical Society Archive and Library (Adyar, Madras).

I also owe a great deal to the many friends and colleagues who have given their time to read and comment on this manuscript in one or other (and usually more than one) of its many avatars. In particular, I would like to thank Dr Christopher Bayly, Dr Carolyn Elliott, Professor John Gallagher, Dr Gordon Johnson, Dr John Leonard, Mr Peter Musgrave, Dr Tapan Raychaudhuri, Dr Francis Robinson, Professor Eric Stokes, Ms Lucy Carroll and Dr Brian Tomlinson for their help and kindness.

My greatest debt, however, is to the three people with whom I have worked most closely and but for whose encouragement the following pages would certainly have remained blank. Dr Christopher Baker has shared many of my South Indian and English hours and has given generously of his own allied material and ideas. Dr Anil Seal, my research supervisor, has been a major source of strength and inspiration since my undergraduate days. My wife, Angela, has enabled me to survive the unconscionably long period of this book's gestation.

Needless to say, however, responsibility for the sentiments and arguments of this book is mine.

Coventry   *D. A. Washbrook*
June 1975

ix

ABBREVIATIONS, NOTES ON REFERENCES AND SPELLING

A.I.C.C.	All India Congress Committee
C.L.A.	Central Legislative Assembly
D.C.C.	District Congress Committee
I.N.C.	Indian National Congress
I.O.L.	India Office Library, London
L and M, L. or M, or Leg.	Local and Municipal Department, Local, or Municipal, or Legislative Branches
M.D.G.	Madras District Gazetteer
M.L.A.	Member of the Legislative Assembly
N.A.I.	National Archives of India, New Delhi
N.M.M.L.	Nehru Memorial Museum Library, New Delhi
P.C.C.	Provincial Congress Committee
P & J	Public and Judicial Department, India Office
P.P.	Parliamentary Paper
R.N.P.	Reports on the Native Press (*see* Bibliography)
S.A.H.	State Archives, Hyderabad
S.I.L.F.	South Indian Liberal Federation
S.I.P.A.	South Indian People's Association
T.N.A.	Tamil Nadu Archives, Madras
T.S.A.	Theosophical Society Archives, Adyar (Madras)

References to the proceedings of the Government of Madras are given as follows: G[overnment] O[rder], Number, Department, Date, Place (T.N.A. or S.A.H.). References to the proceedings of the Government of India are given as follows: Department, Branch, Date, File Number, Place (N.A.I.).

Note on spelling: All proper names are given in the spelling which was most common at the time.

Introduction

In 1917, the political life of Southern India appeared to undergo a massive transformation. Madras, known for thirty years as the most 'benighted' and conservative of the presidencies, suddenly exploded into political activity. The Home Rule League, organised from a suburb of Madras city, confronted the British with the most serious and largest movement of dissidence which their rule had faced anywhere in India since the Mutiny. The non-Brahman movement, also organised from the provincial capital, spread a wave of racial hatred across the presidency and threatened to tear Southern society apart into mutually antagonistic political communities. Both the Home Rule League agitation and the non-Brahman movement represented extremely new phenomena in Madras politics. Contemporaries never tired of pointing out how, just five years before they appeared, there was not the slightest sign of their imminence.[1] And even a casual glance at the political debates and postures of 1912 would support this conclusion. In that year, the men (and women) who were to lead the Home Rule League were recognised generally as the most loyal supporters of the British *raj*;[2] the later arch-ideologue of the non-Brahman cause was presenting to a Parliamentary Commission evidence which not even his enemies considered to show a trace of communal bias;[3] and the provincial government of Madras was steadfastly denying to its superiors in London and New Delhi the existence of anything resembling communal conflict within its territories.[4] One of the main purposes of this book is to explain how and why the novel issues of politics in the years 1917 to 1920 arose.

But it was not just the issues of political controversy at this time which were so new: it was also the forms of expression, of 'agitation' and 'movement', and of political organisation. In 1912, campaigns to unite the whole of the province against its British rulers or to unite the millions of non-Brahmans against their Brahman 'oppressors' had

---

[1] See, for example, E. S. Montagu, *An Indian Diary* (London, 1930), pp. 113–14.
[2] Mrs Annie Besant, C. P. Ramaswami Iyer, and G. A. Natesan, all of whom had been instrumental in defeating the Extremist challenge of 1906–9.
[3] T. M. Nair. See *Hindu* 5 April 1913.
[4] See G. O. 916 (L and M,L) dated 12 July 1911. *T.N.A.*

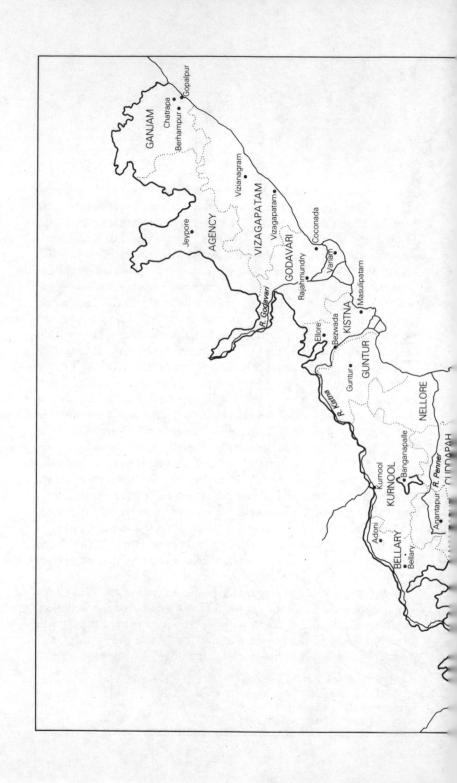

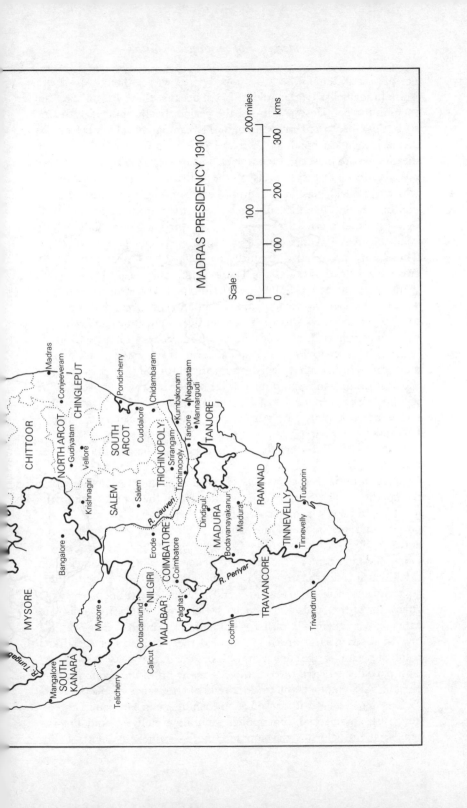

MADRAS PRESIDENCY 1910

not appeared, simply because nobody had as yet thought of them. More fundamentally, they did not exist because there was no place for them in the political structure of the period. In the context of the institutions, forces and interests of 1912, campaigns which set out to create ideological bonds of their species would have been politically meaningless to most contemporaries. The linkages of interest and purpose between different levels of the political system, the means by which the ideologies were communicated to and understood by the political actors and the circumstances which made apparent ideological conflict a crucial element in the political system, all of which conditioned the events of 1917 to 1920, were not present in 1912. There were profound differences in the political structures of the two adjacent periods, and the Home Rule and non-Brahman movements were at least as much the products of new structures as they were of new ideas. A second, and much larger, interest of this book is to uncover the ways in which the political institutions and relationships of Southern India were changing to produce the new forms of politics. In order to do so, it will wander over a wide range of matters and a broad time-span. It will examine the nature of change in many of the institutions through which political power was exercised and it will push back its inquiries to the point in time (the 1870s) from which it sees the changes which were crucial to the events of 1917 to 1920 beginning to emerge.

Chapter 1 outlines briefly the main social, economic and political contours of the Madras Presidency during the period of study. Chapter 2 initiates the analysis of political change by investigating the operations of government. It is natural that the concept of government should form a major organising theme of this book, for the powers and privileges of government did much to determine the entire political structure. The Government of Fort St George was much closer in type to the oriental despotisms which previously had ruled South India than it was to the circumscribed and constitutional governments of its European masters' homeland. It was not simply the guarantor of the peace and security which would allow its subjects to carry on with their own business but it directly ordered their lives in a myriad of ways. It granted and denied the legitimacy of social and political positions right down to the level of village society; it extracted (and partially redistributed) a large proportion of the economic surplus; it gave employment to hundreds of thousands of people in its various departments; it worked as an economic entrepreneur, controlling vast commercial monopolies, building railways and digging canals; and it helped to develop and, more significantly, control educational and cultural facilities and the learned professions. The influence of government pervaded social life to a degree unknown outside Asia. Its shape and organisation must be taken as the beginning of any examination of the political system. Moreover, of course, the British government of Madras was an alien, colonial government whose structure and policies were determined, to a considerable extent, by events in other parts of the world. It was not simply the reflection of a ruling class thrown up by indigenous economic and social pressures. In consequence, when analysing the nature and causes of political change in South India, government has to be treated in part as an autonomous agent which was capable of altering both itself and the forms of South Indian political life for reasons which had nothing to do with South Indian society – it was an exogenous factor in the politics of Madras. The purpose of Chapter 2 is to determine the locations in the governmental structure from which effective power was exercised and to trace over time changes in both the location and nature of this power.

Although extremely influential, however, government by no means controlled directly the distribution of all the economic resources in Madras nor did it possess a monopoly of all political authority. Indeed, in many ways the British deliberately had weakened the position which they had inherited from previous regimes and had permitted power over several important social institutions to slip from their hands. In consequence, in order to continue their government, the British were obliged to rely on the support and co-operation of a relatively small number of South Indians who exercised considerable political influence independently of them. Chapter 3 examines the institutions of 'indigenous' political organisation, which gave these men their power, and attempts to assess the changes which were taking place within these institutions. As its main purpose is to explain how order was maintained and how conflicts were settled, the chapter concentrates particularly on problems of social control.

The organisation of Chapters 2 and 3 implies a dichotomy between the governmental and the 'indigenous' or 'social' political systems. Obviously, however, this dichotomy is artificial, for although governmental and social power can be separated analytically, in reality they were inextricably enmeshed. Chapter 4 attempts to put them together again in order to show how their changing relationship, between 1870 and 1920, was beginning to produce new types of political construct. As the argument of these chapters will have developed, a further conceptual dichotomy will have emerged. A very clear difference is noticeable between the principles on which 'state-' or 'provincial-level' politics and on which 'local-level' politics were organised. Chapters 2, 3 and 4 concentrate largely on the local level and try to show how a variety of changes within it were producing connections between the local and the provincial levels. Perhaps their most important finding is that the virtually autonomous political arenas of 1870 were becoming fused into a much more broadly based political structure. Chapters 5 and 6 explore the nature of the provincial political system and attempt to show how changes there were generating their own set of linkages to the locality. Political behaviour at the provincial level was being modified heavily by the new relationship to the localities. In Chapter 7, the argument reaches the events of 1917 to 1920 which it has set out to explain. The behaviour of the central political actors is placed within the changing context of the political system.

Several questions are raised by the writing of this book: Why a regional study; why this region; why this time and these events? The author's answer would be that he believes that, in the present state of Indian historiography, a regional study of Madras in the later nineteenth and early twentieth centuries can improve our knowledge of both modern Indian and British colonial political history. By selecting a region, an author does not have to pretend that he has chosen an entity which exists in complete isolation from everything outside it. Clearly, for example, Madras was part of a larger country, of a greater civilisation and of an international empire. The influences which stem from these wider contacts need not be excluded from study. Indeed, in this book they form a major area of investigation. But if concentration is placed only on the higher and larger categories of activity and existence, many of the nuances of historical development will be missed and a great many events will remain inexplicable. Bengal, for example, shared the relationships of Madras to country, civilisation and empire but its reaction to those relationships was very different and its political history notably distinct. There was a level at which the character of the social and political institutions of Madras and Bengal diverged sharply. The regional study, when compared to other regional studies, helps us to see the depth at which this level lay and the materials of which the different levels were composed. The regional study facilitates our understanding of the points of contact between greater and lesser institutions and hence our understanding of the processes of politics and of political change. As British colonial and Indian history contain so many points of contact between larger and smaller socio-political structures, it must aid our appreciation of them.

Introduction

A casual glance at the library shelves suggests one reason why South India is a peculiarly fitting subject for a regional study. In spite of its size, wealth and contemporary importance, very little of its colonial history has been written. It represents a vast gap on the historical map of India. A second glance, this time at the contents of the shelves, reveals a second and more substantial reason for its selection. Many of the analytical tools which have been used to carve the political history of modern India appear very blunt when they are applied to the South. Unquestionably, for example, the Madras Government was the most financially and bureaucratically oppressive of all Indian provincial governments. Unquestionably too, its administration and laws were designed to interfere more deeply in the economic and social institutions of indigenous life than were those of any of its neighbours. These factors ought to have made Madras a turbulent and dangerous presidency. Yet so far from meeting with the angry reactions of its subjects and having to face constant outbreaks of hostility, Fort St George governed the quietest and, in colonial terms, the most successful of provinces. Equally, Madras was among the leading presidencies in the development of western education which, we are used to being told, was the primary cause of the development of an Indian nationalist movement. Yet South India's overall performance in the nationalist stakes was, to put it kindly, not unduly noticeable. However, on two occasions Madras did break at the seams with nationalist fervour. For a few years in the 1880s and again between 1917 and 1920, it was in the forefront of the nationalist movement. But the people who took it there were certainly not the western-educated alone and their interest in the movement proved to be more pragmatic than intellectual or cultural. Moreover, in Indian history, we read much about the politics of communal conflict. Members of different castes, religions and races sometimes are seen to belong to separate political communities which jockey against one another for place, power and status. Before about 1915, however, almost no significant event in British South Indian history could possibly be understood in communal terms alone. And when overt communal conflict appeared, it did so in the most remarkable of forms. One community, representing 98 per cent of the population and possessing the vast bulk of wealth and effective political power, denounced another community, which consisted of less than two per cent of the population and was possessed of nothing like the same economic and political resources, for oppressing it. Superficially examined with many of the tools which are supposed to be part of the Indian historian's trade, South India appears to consist of nothing but paradoxes. By a closer examination, we may not only reconcile

7

these paradoxes but also change our view on the utility of some of the tools.

The significance of the years 1917 to 1920 has not been missed in previous political studies of modern India. It was from this time that the Indian national movement took on its mass persona, that communal politics extended their appeal beyond tiny elites, and that the history of the British in India becomes the history of a retreat. Few historians would disagree that the road along which India would march to Independence and Partition was opened in these years. Yet, until recently, the historical reasons why the period should have been so important have remained obscure. Historians have preferred to see the wartime agitations as the beginning of 'modern' politics and to proceed forward from them towards the later achievements of nationalism and communalism. Naturally, this starting point has limited their appreciation of the period. Most of their accounts of the origins of the political movements of 1917–20 centre on such features as the pressures of the war and the characters of Tilak, Mrs Besant and Gandhi. While adequate on the nature of the issues which divided political life, these accounts fall far short as explanations of the qualitatively new forms of politics which were making the divisions apparent. It was not just that people were expressing new views but that they were acting politically in new ways. Demands made at the capitals of government were earning the support and hostility of men who previously had given no indication that they knew where the capitals were. Provincial and national political conflicts were concerned with a range of issues which had been very remote from them before. By looking at the bed-rock institutions of politics and by tracing the changes which had been taking place within them over the previous forty years, it is possible to approach the problem of 1917–20 from a more satisfactory angle. The Home Rule League and non-Brahman movements may then be seen not as the semi-inexplicable beginning of a chain of events but as the culmination of a long-term process of change. Moreover, the new structure of political relationships which had brought the movements into existence also may stand clearly revealed. It was the changes in structure, which remained long after the sparks and fumes of agitational invective had dispersed, which more truly heralded the end of British rule than did the mere issues of politics during the First World War. If we allow the events of 1917–20 to have had an important role in the evolution of modern India, then how much more important must have been the processes of institutional change which began in the 1870s and which made those events?

Introduction

The central concern of this book, therefore, is the changing political system of South India between about 1870 and 1920. In consequence, it may be necessary to warn the reader that the political history which he will find here will not look like that which he is used to finding in most of the historical literature on Indian politics at this time. Indian political history has tended to concentrate heavily on the analysis of particular political movements and agitations. This is hardly surprising, for India's independence and partition – her greatest modern events – were won through these movements and agitations, and the historian, whatever his protestations, can but be drawn to the past through the present. The questions which have underlain this historical writing have been how did the Indian people oppose and eventually defeat British imperialism and how and why did the communal tensions, which colour South Asia's experience in the twentieth century, arise. The perspective which it has adopted has been designed to illuminate the changes in values, ideas and political associations, which increased the hostility of Indians to the British and to members of other races and religions.

The present book, however, is written from a different perspective and seeks to uncover an essential but hitherto neglected area of South Indian history. While it is certainly true that nationalism and communalism were important political forces, it is also true that they did not succeed in tearing India out of her imperial connection nor in dividing the subcontinent into antagonistic ethnic and religious communities until the later 1940s. In consequence, throughout the period from 1870 to 1920 and beyond, there remained a viable colonial political system through which power was distributed and conflicts were contained and compromised. Indeed, it was only by destroying this system that nationalism and communalism came to achieve their later positions as dominant political themes. This book has chosen its particular standpoint in order to illuminate the salient features of the colonial political system. The questions which underlie its inquiries are how did this system function, why did it operate successfully for as long as it did and how and why did it change. Its perspective facilitates particularly an analysis of the relationships of power and authority in South Indian society: it examines changes in the disposition of sanctions, the location of forces and the distribution of resources. Naturally, given its unusual angle of vision, when the argument of this book touches nationalism and communalism, it will be attempting to make points of a different character to those which would be made from the other, more orthodox, viewpoint. It will be obliged to treat those phenomena only as they related to the

9

political system and not as they stood apart from it: it will see them only as reactions to and influences on its own subject matter.

The author's justification for asking his particular questions and for following his particular approach is easily made. The triumph of nationalism and communalism has for too long provided the context of the present out of which the historian has drawn his questions to the past. But this triumph itself is no longer a feature of the present. India's contemporary problems and conflicts are the seed-beds from which ideas for the development of Indian historiography now must come. Of these problems and conflicts, as political scientists and sociologists have not been slow to see, the nature and locations of power in the political system have been crucial. Unfortunately, however, our historical understanding of the organisation of political power in the late colonial period, which the Indian Republic inherited in 1947 and which has conditioned her situation ever since, is remarkably poor. So dominant in the historical literature have been the themes of nationalism and communalism that we know almost nothing about the Indian political structure and its development. Indeed, we have less of the political fabric of the India of Their Majesties than we do of that of the East India Company or even of the Grand Moghul. This hiatus in understanding can be seen clearly in much of the literature of political science, where 1947 has been taken as a cata-clysmic year in which the whole basis of Indian political activity switched from the high ideals of the movements for independence and partition to the low practices of a struggle over the distribution of power and resources. Without arguing that idealism had nothing to do with nationalism and communalism, it must be obvious that the struggle for power and resources in Indian society had been going on long before 1947 and that, in part at least, it had determined the course of nationalism and communalism. The political scientists' wonderment at the effects of independence and partition owes more to the deficiencies of the historical literature which they have been obliged to receive than to the scale of the transformation actually achieved by those events. It is to bring to the past some of the issues raised by India's present, and hence to extend the process by which the past can be historically understood, that this book has been written.

I

The Madras Presidency

By 1800, the British had acquired most of what was to become their presidency of Madras. They found themselves in possession of a collection of territories which covered about 140,000 square miles and which, between 1870 and 1920, came to contain a population of some 30 to 40 millions. The province was certainly the most artificial of all those held by the British in India. Its administrative and formal political unity masked enormous economic, linguistic and cultural diversities. The presidency was composed of seven clearly distinct geophysical regions, each with its own economy. Around the Cauveri and the Kistna–Godavari deltas, there were two areas of intensive rice cultivation. From the Kistna and Godavari hills, south and west through the Ceded Districts (Anantapur, Bellary, Kurnool and Cuddapah) and hinterland Tamilnad (North and South Arcot, Salem, Coimbatore, Madura, Trichinopoly and Tinnevelly districts) stretched a region which, though giving way to cattle-breeding on higher ground and to rice cultivation along the banks of occasional rivers and tanks, was mainly under systems of 'dry' cultivation. The basic produce were grains of the combu, cholum and ragi varieties, and cotton and groundnut cash crops – all grown without sophisticated irrigation works. In the south-west and north-east of the presidency, ranges of hills broke up the plains and plateaux: in the former area, the Nilgiri and Palnad hills attracted European tea and coffee planters who came to dominate the local economies; in the latter, the 'Agency tracts' of Ganjam, Vizagapatam and Godavari districts continued to be populated by tribal groups with only the most primitive forms of settled agriculture. In the extreme south-west of the province lay the coastal strip of Malabar, along which a heavy rainfall made possible rice and coconut cultivation without recourse to extensive irrigation works. The many regional economies of Madras, with their own settlement patterns, crops, marketing arrangements and agricultural seasons, naturally produced a variety of regional social and political structures.[1]

---

[1] See O. H. K. Spate, *India and Pakistan: A General and Regional Geography* (London, 1954).

In Bengal and Bombay presidencies, some of the centrifugal tendencies created by the diversity of local economies were corrected by
the growth of great commercial centres. Calcutta and Bombay city
handled between 95 and 99 per cent of their provinces' external trade
and developed as major financial and manufacturing complexes. Their
influence touched the economy of every district in their administrative
hinterlands. The long coastline of the Madras Presidency, however,
guaranteed that its capital could not develop a similar role. The
products of its regions could easily find their own local export outlets.
Harbours at Cocanada and, later, Vizagapatam, served the north-
east; at Negapatam, Danushkodi and Tuticorin the south-east and
south; at Calicut, Mangalore and Cochin the west. In spite of the
effects of early railway building which, by following administrative
and military rather than commercial convenience, had made it a route
centre, Madras city was no more than one, albeit the largest, port and
commercial centre among many. During our period it handled only
about 40 per cent of the presidency's external trade.[2] Its exports – cotton,
groundnut and hides – were drawn only from its immediate hinterland.
Even the European business houses, which had made the city their
headquarters, were rivalled by other European and Indian firms which
preferred to operate entirely from the various regional bases.

To add to economic disunities, there were five major linguistic
divisions in the presidency. In 1921 Tamil was the largest single first
language, spoken by about $17\frac{1}{2}$ million people in the south and
south-east. Telugu was used nearly as widely, by about 16 million
people, mostly in the north-east. Approximately $3\frac{1}{4}$ million Malayalam
speakers lived in the south-west, $1\frac{1}{2}$ million Canarese speakers in the
north and north-west and $1\frac{1}{2}$ million Oriya speakers in the extreme
north-east. In addition, Islamic and Maratha conquests had left
nearly a million Hindustani and a quarter million Marathi speakers
dotted around the province, while tribal groups in the hills continued
to speak a variety of tribal languages.[3] These divisions were further
exacerbated by radical differences in dialect and, more importantly
for mass communication, by the divorce of written and spoken Tamil
and Telugu in the three centuries prior to British rule.

The vast majority of the population was Hindu by religion. But this
should not be taken to mean that it followed the same pattern of worship or adhered to the same formal system of morals or recognised a
common religious authority. There was the usual theological division

---

[2] *Review of the Sea-borne Trade of the Madras Presidency* (Madras, Annual Series,
1880 to 1920).

[3] *Census of India. Madras. 1921. Volume XIII. Part 2* (Madras, 1922), pp. 79–83.

between the worshippers of Siva and of Vishnu and a multiplicity of
further divisions between the many philosophical schools which had
grown up among each body of worshippers. Probably the most savage
religious controversy in the South was that between the Vadagalai
and Thengalai schools – or castes as they had become – of Vaishnav-
ism. More pertinently, perhaps, the main linguistic divisions also
mapped out major cultural divisions. Although, at some level of
abstraction, Tamils, Telugus and Malayalis may all be seen to be the
inheritors of a single religious tradition, their separate vernacular
cultures, as well as the sharply differing circumstances of their
societies, meant that in practice they tended to understand different
things by this tradition. The types of issue, over religious reform and
orthodoxy, which split intellectual society on the banks of the Godavari, for example, were virtually unintelligible to educated Tamil
society along the Cauveri.[4] Similarly, the debate on the relationship
between Aryan and Dravidian cultures, which began to heat the Tamil
districts towards the end of our period, was viewed with a mixture of
incomprehension and incredulity in Andhra.[5] Of course, to point to
these divisions is not to argue that any other Indian province was
perfectly united in its religious culture. Obviously, every province
had its parochialisms. But some areas were better able to negotiate
these obstacles than were others. Across most of Northern India, for
example, the links of religio-cultural unity were extremely strong.
Political movements, such as the Arya Samaj, cow-protection and
Sanatan Dharm movements, which made use of these links, swept the
plains of Hindustan and its adjacent regions and found the means of
communicating their various messages to audiences from Gujerat to
Bengal.[6] In the South, by contrast, the parochialisms proved too
great and no religio-political movement of the Arya Samaj, Sanatan
Dharm or any other type managed to bridge the gap between
vernacular cultures. Moreover, the bulk of the 'Hindu' population
of each vernacular region had never been drawn into the mainstream
of high theological Hinduism. In sharp contrast to Northern India,
the temple centres were isolated and had few social contacts with the
peoples of their surrounding villages, where Brahmans were few and

---

[4] For example, K. Viresalingam's Widow Remarriage movement. See J. G. Leonard,
'Kandukuri Viresalingam: A Biography of an Indian Social Reformer 1848–1919',
unpublished Ph.D. dissertation, University of Wisconsin, 1970.
[5] Literary anti-Brahmanism made only a very limited impact on the Telugu-speak-
ing districts.
[6] See C. A. Bayly, 'The Development of Political Organisation in the Allahabad
Locality 1880–1925', unpublished D.Phil dissertation, University of Oxford,
1970.

the Vedas barely known. Except along the Cauveri and Kistna–Godavari deltas and in coastal Malabar, the peasant population tended to follow local and clan gods which were often throwbacks to pre-Aryan tribal days.[7] This, of course, further limited the scope of religio-cultural contacts and movements.

In 1921, approximately 7 per cent of the population was Muslim, mostly of the Sunni faith.[8] By far the largest proportion of these were low-caste converts to Islam – weavers and artisans in the Telugu areas, petty merchants and traders in Tamil Nad and peasants in Malabar – who were much nearer in language and customs to their various Hindu neighbours than they were to the custodians of Islamic culture. There were, however, a few Persian or Urdu Muslim families in the presidency, who had been rulers and administrators under previous regimes. Some of these, like the family of the Nawab of Arcot, still held considerable lands and were attracted into government service and the liberal professions. Others became important merchants in Madras city and at Vanniyambadi, in Salem district, which was one of the centres of Islam in the South. About 3 per cent of the inhabitants of Madras were Christians of various kinds.[9] The largest concentration in the region was in Tinnevelly district where about 10 per cent of the population followed the religion of Christ. Most of these were low-caste Shanars and Bharatha fishermen but a handful came from important peasant stock. The other main area of Christian activity was in the north-east where again success was obtained mostly at the bottom of the social scale.

In comparison to the United Provinces, where widespread religio-cultural homogeneities underlay the boundaries of the province, or Bengal and Bombay, in which economic linkages tied together the various regions, the Madras Presidency was a peculiar collection of autonomous territories. No Madrasi could speak his language to half his fellows; particular institutions of religion and movements of religious revivalism were relevant to only a small fraction of the population; market connections integrated only small, regional groups of producers and consumers. After independence, the heterogeneity of the province was rationalised by its partition into five separate states.[10] But, during our period, the presidency was an arbitrary conglomerate held together only by the fiat of an imperial power.

[7] See *M.D.G.*, Francis, *Madura* (Madras, 1906), p. 84; F. W. Hemingway, *Trichinopoly* (Madras, 1907), pp. 88–9; C. F. Brackenbury, *Cuddapah* (Madras, 1916), pp. 64–5.

[8] *Census of India. 1921. Madras. Volume XIII. Part 2*, pp. 27–9.

[9] *Ibid.*

[10] Orissa, Andhra, Tamilnad, Mysore and Kerala.

Lines of social, economic and cultural distinction, however, did not only divide Madras into regional components. They also ran through each region, separating one social group from another. While, as in all societies, South Indians may have shared certain social and cultural perceptions, as in all societies also, they did not share the same social and political roles, the same recognised behavioural models, the same boundaries of social action and the same levels of material culture. The drawing of these lines of social definition is a difficult task and the questions of where they should be placed and how precisely they must be marked depend very much on the purpose which an author has in making them. Obviously, the dichotomies which command the attention of the anthropologist are not necessarily those which will catch the sight of the student of political, economic or religious history; nor will the nib of the student of a province or region need to be as fine as that of the student of a village. Our purpose here is that of provincial political history and consequently the clearest conceptual distinction which we have to make, for it extends through the length and breadth of our subject matter, is that between 'local-' and 'state-levels' of political culture. This distinction will be seen to match partially, although by no means wholly, those frequently made by anthropologists and culturologists of South Indian between Left and Right hand castes, between the Great and the Little Traditions and between Aryan and Dravidian cultures. However, its intention is to facilitate the study of politics rather than of religious culture, and so the phenomena which it seeks to distinguish between are of a somewhat different order.

Social groups of 'local-level' political culture may be taken to be those whose political orientation was almost entirely towards the control and use of resources, particularly land and its labour, within very restricted physical localities. By occupation, they tended to be closely involved with the processes of agricultural production, whether as the directors of farming operations, as farmers themselves, as farm labourers or as the providers of a variety of menial services to those who worked the land. Their commitment to land and the locality was evidenced in a number of ways. Their kinship patterns extended over only extremely small territories and were used to reinforce economic or social positions within the locality.[11] Their religious worship emphasised heavily the gods of the locality or the clan segment rather than those of Brahmanic Hinduism. They were

[11] See, for examples, B. Beck, *Peasant Society in Konku* (Vancouver, 1972), pp. 229–32 on the Gounder Vellalas; E. K. Gough, 'Caste in a Tanjore Village', in E. Leach (ed.), *Aspects of Caste in South India, Ceylon and North-West Pakistan* (Cambridge, 1960), pp. 45–6 on lower castes in Tanjore.

almost entirely illiterate and hence cut off from many of the channels of wider social communication. In short, their political culture was parochial and inward-looking and they paid scant attention to relationships which were not immediate or face-to-face.

Groups of 'state-level' political culture, by contrast, may be taken to be those whose orientation was towards political activity in much broader spatial categories – usually several districts but also, occasionally, the cultural region and the cultural nation. By occupation, they tended to be state administrators or members of the liberal professions, merchants, manufacturers in territorially organised handicraft industries or the religious and artistic servants of those in these occupations. They possessed a highly literate culture which supported their supra-local transactional needs. Their kinship patterns emphasised the breadth rather than depth of their connections: marriages were made to safeguard or pass resources along greater territorial networks.[12] Their religious worship centred on gods of the Hindu pantheon and drew them into a relationship with higher all-Indian theology. The reference points of their perception of the political world were set altogether much wider and were much more likely to encompass abstractions and generalities than were those of groups of 'local-level' political culture.[13]

Few of the social mega-categories in which the British organised their census data, and with which historians have tended to discuss the social history of India, help us to put names to 'local-' and 'state-level' groups. Caste is particularly useless: obviously most Brahmans would be of state-level culture but all other large caste categories would be split in half. The Velamas, Vellalas and Maravars, for example, included great *zamindar* chiefs whose interests undoubtedly lay at the state-level and hosts of petty cultivators and labourers who were buried in parochialism. Equally, religion offers us little aid: according to the census, all those who were neither Muslim nor Christian nor Buddhist were classified as 'Hindu'. Even economic categorisation can have its difficulties. The fact that local-level groups were interested in the possession and control of land does not mean that state-level groups were landless: in Tanjore and Malabar and in most *zamindari* areas they held legal titles to land and sometimes directed its cultivation. The difference between the two lay largely in the activities which they used the resources of the land to pursue.

---

[12] *Ibid.* on castes of the left hand and Brahmans respectively.

[13] The dichotomy between state- and local-levels is brought out clearly in the different descriptions of social organisations among Brahmans and Komatis, on the one hand, and Reddis, on the other, in N. Gopalakrishnamah Chetty, *A Manual of the Kurnool District in the Presidency of Madras* (Madras, 1866).

The social parameters of the distinction become clearer, however, if we turn to the history of South India. From the fourteenth century, arguably from the seventh century, the South Indian political system had centred on a series of warrior kingdoms, each seeking to establish a rulership over parcels of land and the people who worked it, and each seeking to participate in a higher, almost diplomatic, regional political system which was conducted between warrior states.[14] Even the later Muslim conquests did not radically alter this situation for the Muslim empires more or less contented themselves with holding the ring around the higher regional system and leaving the warriors to their own devices within their territories. Golconda's attempts to accomplish more than this seem to have been short lived and to have ended with the Moghul invasion;[15] the great expectations of Hyder Ali and Tipu Sultan were thwarted by constant harassment and ultimately defeat at the hands of the East India Company.

The warriors themselves clearly required a variety of services from other social groups if they were to succeed in their purposes as territorial governments and as participants of the regional system. They needed administrators, diplomats, financiers, merchants and artisans. They also needed priests and poets who controlled the means of (cultural) communication in the regional system. The social groups which were drawn into providing these services naturally became connected to the same politico-cultural framework as the warriors. Their own destinies were bound up with the extension of warrior government and with the continuation of the higher regional system. This is not to say, of course, that their own interests were identical to those of the warriors: administrative families, for example, would tend to be more interested in the profits and security of administrators than in the power of their employers; priests may have been more concerned to honour the deities than to publicise their warrior patrons. But, obviously, there was a point at which the interests of the warriors and of the groups which served them coincided: administrators could not work if their warriors had no power and priests could not live without patronage and protection. In consequence, the social organisations of these 'service' groups developed around the warrior states, supporting both their own needs and those of the warriors. Administrative groups developed (often kinship) contacts between court and village within the boundaries of a single warrior

---

[14] See B. Stein, 'Integration of the Agrarian System of South India', in R. E. Frykenberg (ed.), *Land Control and Social Structure in Indian History* (Madison, Milwaukee and London, 1969), pp. 175–216; also, T. V. Mahalingam, *Administration and Social Life under Vijayanagar* (Madras, 1940).

[15] See J. F. Richards, 'Mughal Rule in Golconda 1687–1724', unpublished Ph.D. dissertation, University of California, 1970.

state and court-to-court contacts across the regional system.[16] These contacts acted as ties of government, as links of diplomacy and as sinews holding a region together as a single politico-cultural unit. Similarly, priestly groups (and temples) accepted a warrior's patronage, which took them out of his court and into the countryside where they attested to his glory, or which enabled them to project his image to other courts as a worthy and respectable prince.[17] Merchants, financiers and artisans also organised themselves in relation to the warriors' needs both in his kingdom and in his wider world.

The whole of this warrior edifice, however, was imposed from above on the variety of primitive tribes, agrarian settlements and defeated warriorships which had inhabited the region before it was built. These tribes and settlements, whether because they had not developed beyond the stage of basic husbandry or whether, through invasion and conquest, because they had been driven back to simple cultivation, were primarily involved in the production of agricultural commodities. The warriors, and the social groups associated with them, lived by the expropriation of this production. In consequence, there was a very clear dichotomy between the political purposes of the 'cultivators' and of the 'rulers': the one seeking to defend the wealth which it had produced, the other seeking to take it. This dichotomy suggests one reason for the local political orientation of the cultivators. Obviously, the social organisations which facilitate the development and protection of a resource such as land will be much more concerned with the depth of local power than will those which facilitate an extensive, expropriatory rulership. In many areas also, this distinction of political purpose was overlaid by a wider cultural division. Over much of Tamilnad, the warriors, brought down by the Vijayanagar empire, were of a foreign Telugu culture and they had imported many 'service' groups of their own. Telugu and Maratha Brahmans, Komatis and Telugu Kammalas staffed the agencies of many warrior governments. Moreover, even where the warriors were of the same vernacular as their subjects, their own religious culture was often very different. In most of southern Andhra and hinterland Tamilnad

---

[16] This can be seen, for example, in the spread of Sri Vaishnava Brahman families, brought into Tamil districts by the Telugu warriors of Vijayanagar. See R. E. Frykenberg, *Guntur District 1788–1848: A History of Local Influence and Central Authority in South India* (Oxford, 1965), pp. 13–17; Stein, 'Integration of the Agrarian System of South India', p. 195

[17] See G. W. Spencer, 'Religious Networks and Royal Influence in Eleventh Century Tanjore' in *Journal of the Economic and Social History of the Orient*, XII, 45–56; B. Stein, 'Economic Functions of a Medieval South Indian Temple' in *Journal of Asian Studies*, IX: 2 (1960).

(the 'dry' zone), the subject peoples may best be described as Dravidian in that their customs owed much more to pre- or non-Aryan tribal forms than to the recognised 'codes' of pan-Indian Hinduism. The regional cultures in which their rulers (and associated groups) participated, however, were at least variants of pan-Indian Hinduism. Cultural differentiation, perpetuated by political hostility, further kept warriors and subjects apart. Tied to their localities in order to protect their resources, lacking incentives to participate in the alien politico-cultural system of the warriors, often never having possessed a wider, territorial system of their own or having seen it smashed by warrior government,[18] these subject groups had few reasons to be other than parochial in their political ambitions and outlooks.

In political terms, the line between local- and state-level groups has to be drawn at different points in different places. The extent to which the state-level penetrated the locality depended on a variety of factors, most of which we shall be discussing later. A brief survey of South India, however, indicates that groups of state-level culture dominated landed society only in Malabar, the central eastern seaboard of Tamilnad and, to a much lesser extent, the Kistna–Godavari deltas. Here not only had state-level groups gained control of agrarian production by means of state action but their presence in great strength had attracted into the state-level category many powerful landed groups whose previous culture had been of the local level. The leading Kallar families of Tanjore district, for example, were full participants of state-level culture; Kallars over most of the rest of South India were semi-tribals of the local-level.[19] The line of division in these areas would have to be drawn below the point of land control and would confine to the local level a collection of slaves, labourers and hereditary thieves who, nonetheless, formed the majority of the

[18] Many of the local-level systems of South India were clan-based and so, at one time, contained political institutions which were supra-local. However, the impact of warrior government tended to break down most of these institutions: the function of integrating dispersed settlements being performed by the warrior court rather than the clan head. In southern Andhra, almost all relationship between clan and local political power disappeared. In Konkunad, the relationship was severely modified: state servants held land in clan territories to which they did not belong; clan and lineage no longer clearly demarcated areas of political control; uxorilocal residence (the death of a patrilineal clan political system) became an unexceptional practice. Only in the deep South, where Vijayanagar warriors established few kingdoms, did broad clan organisations continue to play the political role which they possessed over most of North India at this time.

[19] See L. Dumont, *Une Sous-Caste de l'Inde du Sud: organisation sociale et religieuse des Pramalai Kallar* (Paris and The Hague, 1957).

population. Elsewhere in South India, in the hills of the north-east and south-west and across the plateaux and plains of south Andhra and hinterland Tamilnad (that is over most of South India), the line would have to be placed very much higher. State-level culture was more or less confined to the principal towns, which housed the courts of the warriors, and to 'urban' groups. Its spread over the countryside was extremely thin and it had little control over direct landed power. Brahman priests and administrators, Vaishya trading castes and literate Sat-Sudras were few in number and, consequently, were unable to form the focal points of and the agents of direction in local culture. To a considerable extent they remained outsiders, and potentially hostile outsiders, to the social elements which dominated the land.

In reality, of course, the dichotomy between state- and local-levels was not as complete as we have pictured it. There was some shading down from one to the other. Politically dominant groups of the local-level perforce had some contact with the state which was attempting to govern them. For example, they might be contracted by their warrior prince to keep the peace and to help in revenue collection. Their internal political organisation could be altered if they accepted this contract.[20] In the Indian context, relationships of this type were likely to leave religious and cultural as well as purely political marks. Elements of the state-level might enter the culture of dominant local groups and percolate through them to their subordinates, gradually becoming weaker and weaker until they disappeared. In this sense, it is arguable that the state- and local-levels were but different points of register on the same spectrum. Such an admission would destroy the value of the distinction if our purposes were anthropological: the concepts of state- and local-level would then obscure more than they clarify. But, within South Indian political history, the distinction still retains its usefulness.

In South India, much more than in the North, the great bulk of the population fell clearly into either the state- or the local-level category and the middle ground between them was very poorly populated. Outside the ricelands of Malabar, Coromandel and Andhra, as we have seen, local-level culture began at the point of land control and with the elite which dominated agrarian production. As over 80 per cent of the population was involved in the processes of the agrarian economy, this would put at least 80 per cent of the population somewhere below the local-level line. Moreover, the cultural contacts which linked the locally dominant 'peasant' elite to state-culture in

[20] Beck, *Peasant Society in Konku*, pp. 40–9.

the first instance were extremely loose. In contrast to, say, Hindustan where peasant elites participated directly in Brahmanic Hinduism, by patronising village Brahmans, attending in person many of the great festivals of the Sanskrit calendar and keeping records of their familiar activities in the sacred centres of Hinduism, the participation of South Indian peasant elites tended to be more indirect and much more distant. Although many of their temples, their ceremonies and their priests may have been related, at some remove, to authorities in Brahmanic Hinduism, in local patterns of activity there were few traces of this relationship. South Indian peasants in the 'dry zone', for example, were seldom married by Brahman priests, seldom attended major festivals or visited sacred pilgrimage sites (unless those festivals and sites were in their immediate physical vicinity) and seldom worshipped with Sanskritic forms of ritual. Even where Brahmanic institutions had an immediate presence in the locality, they did not play a central social role. Thus, for example, Brenda Beck writes of a *kirāmam* (revenue village) in Konkunad:

> First and foremost, each *kirāmam* has its own Civa temple.... Furthermore, most *kirāmams* have a Visnu temple, a KariyakaLiyamman (locally Pat-tirakaLi) temple, and at least one temple dedicated to Murukan. All of these are cared for by Brahmans, and left- and right [caste] division groups worship at them. However, none of them is central to the religious activity of the local population at large, especially to that of members of the right-hand division. They serve rather to tie the NaTu to the leading deities of literary Hinduism. Their presence satisfies formal requirements rather than emotional ones, to judge from the mild popular interest which they are generally accorded.[21]

Included in this right-hand division were the Gounder Vellalas, who constituted the politically dominant peasant elite of the region, and most of the subordinate agricultural community. In two recent studies, the sharp differences between the politico-cultural orientations of peasant groups occupying very similar local economic and political positions in Northern and in Southern India have been highlighted. While what is striking about the Jats of Vilyatpur is the breadth of the social context in which they operated,[22] what is striking about the Gounders of Konkunad is the narrowness of the base of their social activities. For the Gounders, actual rather than mythical social relationships beyond the locality would seem to be rare.[23] If, then, when studying North India it is the features of continuity

[21] *Ibid.*, p. 111.
[22] T. G. Kessinger, *Vilyatpur 1848–1968* (Berkeley, Los Angeles and London, 1974).
[23] Beck, *Peasant Society in Konku*.

between cultural levels which command attention, by the same process, in South India it is the features of dislocation.

Yet not only is the dichotomy between state- and local-level cultures very clear in most of South India, it is also of vital consequence to the study of political history. The single most important fulcrum around which South Indian political history revolves is that of land control and the point at which the dichotomy becomes apparent over most of South India is at that of land control. The groups on both sides of the divide were locked in battle for control of the same agrarian surplus. But, being in different relationships to the modes of production and operating within very different politico-cultural frameworks, the way in which they perceived and conducted this battle, and the resources which they called in to aid them, were very different. For one, victory meant closing off the locality to outside intrusion and exercising a deep and direct control; for the other, it meant fully integrating the locality into a wider political system. It is impossible to render intelligible the political history of nineteenth-century South India unless this difference in purpose and meaning is recognised.

The arrival of the British, of course, changed many of the relationships of the South Indian political system. Everywhere warriors lost their military power and, where *zamindaris* were abolished, much of their economic power as well. As Burton Stein has argued, the British dismantled the machinery of the warrior states. They also destroyed the higher regional system in which the warriors had participated. Administrative groups had to accommodate themselves to working for new masters within a new political context. Priests and many types of artisans were cut adrift from the state. Merchants and financiers were obliged to concentrate less on the needs of governments and more on those of the consumer population. The core around which state-level cultural groups had organised themselves for so long had been removed and replaced by one of a completely different shape. Naturally their social organisations began to change to fit the new circumstances. Nonetheless, the remains of the older system, embodied in certain attitudes, deferences and cultural interests, continued to exist throughout the nineteenth century and beyond. Indeed, as the new system developed the dichotomy between state- and local-levels was in some ways reinforced and given new and even more important meanings. Reference to it will help to illuminate our passage through some of the darker areas of South Indian social and political history.

2
The governance of Madras

'Government' was omnipresent in the life of colonial South India. Whether we examine the newspapers, the letters, the autobiographies, the pamphlets or the books of the period, repeatedly we find references to the power, promise or peculiarities of the entity known as government. The avaricious begged its favour, the ambitious its confidence, the pious its protection and the nationalistic its self-destruction. By the standards of contemporary Europe, Madras society was obsessed by the notion of government. If, however, we try to define what precisely was meant by the term 'government' and of what social material it was made we encounter an improbably complex series of problems. Government in Madras was both a great deal more and a great deal less than the hundred or so Europeans who composed its senior civil service. Involved in it, in one way or another, were the British Parliament, sitting six thousand miles away and concerned with the affairs of an international empire; barely literate peasants, on salaries of four shillings a month and concerned with the taxation of a few barren acres; and the broad spectrum of people and interests which lay between them. Men whose outlooks were bounded by the village, the town, the district, the province, the nation and the empire all were locked together in the chain of government in Madras. Depending on the position from which it is viewed, therefore, 'government' can be seen to form many different patterns and to be composed of many different substances in different places. If we are to obtain any real idea of the nature of this government and of its relationship to political society, our initial task must be to take the chain to pieces and to assess the strengths and weaknesses of its various links.

At its highest levels, Madras was governed by three separate policy-making bodies: the Secretary-of-State-in-Council in London, the Government of India in Calcutta (later Delhi) and the Government of Fort St George in Madras city. Each of these institutions pursued its own ends, judged the results it obtained by different standards and overlapped scarcely at all in personnel. It is not surprising that the occasions of antagonism between the three were frequent

23

and bitter as each sought advantage at the expense of the others. Every initiative coming from London and Calcutta was obstructed by Fort St George which insisted that its superiors had no knowledge of the problems of the Southern presidency. Ripon's local self-government reforms, the 1892 and 1909 Councils Acts and, above all, the constitutional proposals of Montagu and Chelmsford were pushed through in Madras in spite of the opposition of Fort St George.[1] The allocation of taxes raised in Madras between Calcutta and Fort St George was another point of contention.[2] During most of our period 65 to 70 per cent of the total income of Madras disappeared into the Government of India's treasury, crippling the ability of the local government to conduct any form of ambitious social or economic policy.[3] To the Government of India, Madras appeared a bottomless purse which could be looted whenever need arose; and, as the political situation in other provinces made it increasingly difficult to find more revenue in them, need did arise with growing regularity. The greed of the Government of India was of crucial importance in determining many of the characteristics of government in Madras: it considerably limited the ability of Fort St George to pay for staff and services out of a central provincial treasury and consequently forced the provincial government to execute some of the most advanced measures of financial decentralisation in India. Financial friction between the provincial and national governments of Madras was not merely a negative force but had a profound influence on the political development of the presidency.

If we were to decide which of the several governments of Madras was the most politically important in Madras, however, the answer must be Fort St George. Except for the rare occasions when it altered the framework of government by promoting major constitutional reform, the influence of the Secretary of State and the Government of India was felt in Madras in only two ways. London and Calcutta possessed powers of veto on legislation and of demand on the revenue. But they left Fort St George to conduct its own administration –

[1] *Report of the Committee on Local Self-Government in Madras 1882* (Madras, 1883), p. 3; Home Public A. October 1908, Nos 116–46. *N.A.I.*; Letter No. 57, Home Department (Reforms), Government of India to Secretary of State, in P & J (Reforms), File 77. *I.O.L.*

[2] See G. Slater, *Southern India. Its Political and Economic Problems* (London, 1936), pp. 50–1.

[3] Under the 1882 contract, the Government of India took 67.14 per cent of the revenues of Madras; under the 1897 contract, it took 71.40 per cent. Lord Ampthill to Lord George Hamilton, 11 June 1902. Ampthill Papers. *I.O.L.* See also, *Report of the Committee Appointed by the Secretary of State for India on the Question of the Financial Relations between the Central and Provincial Governments in India. P.P.* 1920. Vol. xiv.

to enforce the law and to collect taxation – which was much the most potent of political tools. In general, provincial governments in India were administering rather than legislating governments: they sought to hold their positions and to promote such social reorganisation as they saw fit through their bureaucracies rather than their legislatures. The assessment of land revenue, the distribution of government jobs and contracts and the construction of irrigation works were of far greater political weight than any paper statutes, while the importation of the English legal system guaranteed that at least as much law would be made in the courts as in the legislatures. Certainly, from the later nineteenth century, there was an increasing tendency to use legislation to solve social problems – as in the Punjab Land Alienations Act, the Bombay Agricultural Indebtedness Act and the various Bengal and U.P. tenancy laws. But it would be difficult to see these laws, at least before 1920, as more than individual aberrations in the political system, and most of them broke down in administrative practice. If anything, Fort St George was the least aberrant of provincial governments and its legislative attempts at social engineering amounted to very little. The Malabar Tenancy Acts of 1885 and 1898, which affected only one area, failed to secure tenant rights in the courts,[4] and the much lauded Estates Lands Act of 1908, which was thirty years in the writing, was designed to return tenancy law to the state it had been in before a High Court decision of 1870 had wrecked it. Moreover, Fort St George was paralysed from interfering in social and religious affairs by Calcutta's outright ban on efforts to alter native custom. The Government of India's rights in legislative matters, therefore, were not of much consequence when legislation was not central to the way that government was conducted.

Equally, the large share of Madras revenues which the Government of India sucked off was instrumental less in drawing attention to itself than in turning it back towards Fort St George's administration. The Government of India was committed to an enormous expenditure on its army and had little surplus to redistribute to the provinces. The Madras Government was committed to supplying Calcutta's inordinate demands and also found little left over to use in the development of the projects and interests of its subjects. The centres of any spoils system of politics, therefore, had to be at the points where revenue was collected rather than where it was redistributed. Money, once it was allowed to become revenue, was lost. Those who wished to divert public funds to their own pur-

---

[4] D. Kumar, *Land and Caste in South India. Agricultural Labour in the Madras Presidency during the Nineteenth Century* (Cambridge, 1965), p. 89; G.O. 2374 (Judicial) dated 1 October 1894. *T.N.A.*

poses, whether noble or ignoble, were best served by policies of influencing the administrators who were gathering it. The Government of India's financial gluttony helped to keep the village and the *tahsil* as the most important political arenas in the presidency.

The government of Fort St George was, *par excellence*, an administering government, using its bureaucracy both to make and to enforce policy. The centre of its administration was its revenue department which raised the money without which it could not exist and, in doing so, moulded native society by reorganising the major resources of the economy. Three-quarters of the Madras Presidency was under the *ryotwari* system of revenue administration which had been devised by Colonels Read and Munro in the 1790s but much reformed in the 1820s.[5] The government stripped away intermediary layers of authority between itself and the cultivating peasant and undertook to measure and assess for land revenue every field in the presidency. After the harvest, government officers toured their charges collecting the taxation due and remitting payment on lands on which the crops had failed.[6] The task which government set itself was mammoth, for it took officials into the very heart of village India and gave them vast responsibilities. The proximity of revenue administrators to the ground allowed, and to some extent forced, the government to carry its other jurisdictions to an equally local level. Revenue officials were also magistrates, the supervisors of the machinery of local self-government and the informal agents of every other department from excise to public works and from police to agriculture. They possessed colossal powers to match their responsibilities and everywhere formed the natural centres of local politics. Of course, this system meant that the number of people employed in the revenue department was huge, stretching from the departmental Secretary in Madras city to hosts of minor stipendiary officials in every village – a choking bureaucracy to be compared in the style of its government to imperial Russia or the Prussian state.

Clearly, the way in which the bureaucracy ordered its powers provides an important clue to the way it worked in practice and to the places within it where greatest power lay. The virtual omnicompetence of the revenue department meant that Fort St George could not develop a system of departmental checks and balances whereby officials in one department were circumscribed in their activities by officials in another, who were subject to different superiors. The divisions of authority in the Madras bureaucracy were essentially by

[5] See N. Mukherjee, *The Ryotwari System in Madras* (Calcutta, 1962).
[6] For a detailed description of the burden of revenue work, see Note signed F. A. Nicholson in G.O. 173 (Revenue) dated 20 February 1902. *T.N.A.*

territory and by the scope of primary jurisdiction. At the head of the district administration was the Collector whose role was well summarised by the Royal Commission on Agriculture in 1928:

The powers and duties of the Collector embrace almost every subject which comes within the functions of modern government. In fact, in the eyes of the cultivator, he is the supreme authority, the *ma bap* (literally mother and father) who is expected to interest himself in all that affects the well-being of the people under his control.[7]

He supervised the work of all the subordinates in his district and was responsible in the first instance for cases of revenue and law enforcement which were of great importance. Beneath him were a company of sub-, deputy-, and assistant collectors, each of whom enjoyed similar overall responsibility in two or three *taluks*, supervised their subordinates and arbitrated in cases of moderate importance. Below them came a cohort of *tahsildars* whose territory was a single *taluk* and whose primary jurisdiction lay in matters of less weight. Below them was a legion of *gumastahs* and revenue inspectors who operated in circles of thirty or so villages. And, finally, below them came an army of village officers.[8] The district administration consisted of a series of despotisms within despotisms from the village to the district capital and beyond. The districts were linked to Fort St George through the Board of Revenue and the Secretariat which in turn were subject to the Government of India and the Secretary of State. An extraordinarily elaborate pyramid had been constructed which guaranteed the passing of huge quantities of paper from one layer to the next and the presence of intrigue at every stage.

Throughout our period the Madras bureaucracy was perched precariously on the edge of breakdown. For the administrative system to work efficiently it was necessary that territorial charges should be of manageable proportions, that the primary duties of superior officers should not be so heavy that they were unable to supervise inferiors and that information about the conduct of inferiors should be freely available. At no time before 1920 were any of these requirements remotely practicable. The basic territorial division, the revenue district, was enormous and often contained a population of between $1\frac{1}{2}$ and 2 millions.[9] Territorial divisions below the district were equally

[7] *Report of the Royal Commission on Agriculture in India* (H.M.S.O., 1928), XIV, 231.

[8] The chain of command is laid out in W. S. Meyer, *Report on the Constitution of Additional Districts, Divisions and Taluks in the Madras Presidency, and on Other Connected Matters* (Madras, 1904).

[9] Letter No. 1033 (Revenue) dated 13 September 1884. Government of Madras (Revenue) to Government of India (Financial and Commercial) in P & J File 249 of 1885. *I.O.L.*

massive: a Rs 200 a month *tahsildar* might be the lord of 250 villages. The *tahsildar*, the deputy collector and the Collector were all expected to spend a considerable period of time – in the case of *tahsildars* as much as six months – away from their offices on tour.[10] Until 1885, Collectors also were supposed to conduct *jamabundi* in their home *taluks* – a job considered full-time for any other officer. In addition to their duties as revenue gatherers, magistrates, local politicians and policemen, they had to spend hours filling in forms and answering questionnaires for their superiors. The problem of providing effective supervision in their charges was insurmountable and was exacerbated by the mountain of red-tape in which the British wrapped their administrative practices. Each set of village revenue records was kept in 24 separate accounts, one of which alone had 115 separate columns.[11] It was a life's work to check the addition and a generation's work to attempt to see how closely the result corresponded to reality.[12] The Secretariat was well aware of the difficulties inherent in its own administration:

> Under the present system of large divisional charges, however, Divisional Officers, and for that matter Tahsildars, are often so tied to their desks as to be not much more than post offices, and their subordinates are left with so little supervision as to constitute a serious danger to public administration.[13]

Yet, even presupposing that superior officers had the time and possessed the capabilities to watch over the activities of their inferiors, it is by no means clear that they could obtain sufficient independent information to interfere effectively. They relied upon their subordinates for information and, given the union of powers within the administration, they had no independent sources upon which to draw. Revenue accounts, for example, came up through the regular hierarchy of the bureaucracy from the village to the district capital: if the inferior officials of the department agreed that they were correct, the Collector had no means and no outside evidence against which to check them. In 1899, following the Shanar–Maravar riots, one of the periodic breakdowns of government in Madras, Sir Denzil Ibbetson

---

[10] Meyer, *Report on the Constitution of Additional Districts, Divisions and Taluks in the Madras Presidency*, p. 2.

[11] Evidence of J. N. Atkinson in *Minutes of Evidence Taken before the Royal Commission upon Decentralization in India*, II, 189. *P.P.* 1908. Vol. XLIV.

[12] In one *taluk* in 1882, a *tahsildar* was responsible for issuing and collecting 12,870 forms; and, supposedly, for checking the veracity of the returns. J. H. Garstin, *Report on the Revision of the Revenue Establishments in the Madras Presidency* (Madras, 1883), p. 21.

[13] G.O. 173 (Revenue) dated 20 February 1902. *T.N.A.*

in the Government of India commented sourly of the Tinnevelly Collector in whose charge they had occurred: 'Passage after passage of Mr Scott's explanation shows him to imagine that the whole duty of a district officer is to receive such information as his subordinates choose to give him.'[14] Scott was no more than a classic adherent to the Madras school. Of course, internal factional warfare in the lower levels of the bureaucracy might throw up to senior officials information which at least one faction would have preferred to leave buried. Most successful prosecutions for corruption were based on evidence so derived. Equally, specific and detailed investigations by the Board of Revenue, as in Guntur in 1845, might bring to light specific instances of governmental breakdown.[15] But both checks came from outside the regular and general system of administration.

The lack of co-ordination and control between the levels of government in Madras was very obvious. Possibilities existed everywhere for officials to practise their own private and discretionary government regardless of the orders of their superiors and of policy emanating from London, Calcutta and even Fort St George. Indeed, in the 1880s, a number of scandals revealed that the problem of control began at the connection between Fort St George itself and the Government of India. The rules of service in the I.C.S. notwithstanding, a Chief Secretary was found taking bribes to provide for his forthcoming retirement;[16] the First Member of the Governor's Executive Council was caught in a lie to the Secretary of State and in land speculation;[17] 35 civilians, including the whole of the Board of Revenue and half of the Governor's Executive Council, were discovered speculating in plantation and gold shares in the native states;[18] two leading officials, D. Carmichael and W. Huddleston, were accused publicly of nepotism;[19] a Collector was dismissed for bribery[20] and another just escaped a trial for attempting to murder an enemy who was a member of the

---

[14] Note signed D. Ibbetson dated 6 January 1900, in Home Police A, March 1900, Nos 1–8. *N.A.I.*

[15] See Frykenberg, *Guntur District 1788–1848.*

[16] M. E. Grant Duff to Sir Arthur Godley, 29 October 1883. Kilbracken Papers. *I.O.L.*

[17] 'Case of H. E. Sullivan, Report of the Special Committee dated 25 November 1886' in P & J File 1886 of 1886. *I.O.L.*

[18] 'Copy of Extracts from the Correspondence respecting alleged Participation of British Officials in Mysore Gold Mining Transactions and respecting Alienation of State Domains in Mysore' in P & J File 1095 of 1887. *I.O.L.*; 'Special Register showing the particulars of land held by Civil Officers' in P & J File 1095 of 1887. *I.O.L.*

[19] Home Public A July 1884, Nos 260–5. *N.A.I.*

[20] *Hindu* 28 May and 6 June 1884.

Board of Revenue.[21] To the utter dismay of the Secretary of State and the Viceroy, Fort St George, rather than admitting contritely the faults of its senior members, attempted in most cases to use its influence to prevent action being taken against the offenders, and only the First Member and the corrupt Collector suffered for their sins.[22]

The major connection between Fort St George and its districts was through the Collector's office. In most cases, the Collector was wholly ignorant of the affairs of his charge. In addition to the impossible size of his district and the workload he was expected to complete, he was seldom allowed to remain in one post long enough to learn the names of his subordinates. Madras' chronic shortage of I.C.S. officers forced the civilian service into playing a grotesque game of musical offices as it tried to fill in the gaps left by illness and vacation. Between 1880 and 1914, for example, there were 44 different postings to the Salem Collectorate[23] and 38 to that of Tinnevelly,[24] while between 1880 and 1905, there were 27 to Madura.[25] Where the average length of posting was less than a year, the Collector had little chance to be more than an administrative cypher.

Occasionally, however, through long acquaintance with a single district or through the possession of personal interests in the area, a Collector might come to acquire sufficient knowledge to do justice to the powers of his office. The problem then faced by the Board of Revenue was how to make him do its will rather than his own. One of the classic cases of the independent *raj* of a Collector was that of C. S. Crole in Madura in the 1880s. Much of Crole's early service had been spent in the district and he was on friendly terms with the administrators of the great Ramnad *zamindari*, having been taught Tamil by the son of Subbayya Iyer, the estate's *vakil*.[26] Subbayya already possessed close contacts with the subordinate bureaucracy. One of his sons, Ramaswami, was *huzur sheristidar* (head clerk) for a number of years, while another, Subramania, had managed to acquire the public prosecutorship at the age of twenty, before he had even studied law, and had become a *tahsildar* at twenty-six.[27] The family was also involved in temple and municipal politics in alliance with Kotaswami Thevar, the 'prime minister' of the Ramnad *zamindari* and a cousin of the

[21] The case concerned C. S. Crole, Collector of Madura, and J. H. Garstin, Member of the Board of Revenue. P & J File 2057 of 1886. *I.O.L.*
[22] See P & J Files 1886 of 1886 and 1095 of 1887. *I.O.L.*
[23] *M.D.G.* F. J. Richards, *Salem* (Madras, 1918), 1, pt 2, 71.
[24] *M.D.G.* H. R. Pate, *Tinnevelly* (Madras, 1917), 1, 319.
[25] *M.D.G.* Francis, *Madura*, 1, 209.
[26] S. M. Raja Rama Rao, *Sir Subramania Aiyer. K.C.I.E. D.L.* (Trichinopoly, 1914), pp. 7, 10—11.   [27] *Ibid.*

zamindar.[28] In 1882, Crole was made Collector of Madura and turned over his administration to his friends. S. Subramania Iyer became municipal vice-chairman;[29] Kotaswami Thevar vice-president of the Local Board;[30]Sankara, another son of Subbayya Iyer, obtained the valuable receivership of the Sivaganga *zamindari*;[31] R. Ramasubba Iyer, Subbayya's nephew, became public prosecutor. Crole allowed this clique to use the revenue department bureaucracy to collect money for its private purposes, such as a Public Park and a Union Club.[32] He moved his subordinates round at its wishes[33] and battled with the Board of Revenue to lower the land revenue demand in its interests.[34] In many ways, he was the raja of Madura, making his own policy and using his friends as his own administrators. He received presents and bribes from all and sundry and treated the temple elephants as his private property.[35] He also conducted his own 'foreign' diplomacy: it was alleged, though never proved, that he employed the *zamindar* of Bodayanayakanur, another of his local allies, to ambush and kill J. H. Garstin, a member of the Board of Revenue who was snooping into his affairs;[36] and he was instrumental in obtaining the dismissal of the First Member of the Governor's Executive Council for attempting to force the Bodayanayakanur *zamindar* to buy a tea plantation.[37] Yet so weak was Fort St George in controlling its districts that Crole escaped prosecution, as the mass of evidence raised against him by an official inquiry was removed from the Collector's office and destroyed by his allies.[38] Indeed, a decade later Crole was made a member of the Governor's Executive Council and, shortly afterwards, S. Subramania Iyer (later Sir S. Subramania Iyer) was nominated to a vacant High Court Judgeship.

Few other Collectors achieved Crole's depth of local interest but many used their vast resources of patronage – Collectors were responsible for all district appointments below the deputy collector cadre – and their influence to push forward the careers of proteges and to aid

[28] *Ibid.*, pp. 12–13.   [29] *Ibid.*, p. 14.
[30] H. S. Thomas, *Report on Mr Charles Stewart Crole. Collector of Madura* (Madras, 1886), p. 49.
[31] *Hindu* 7 March 1884.
[32] Thomas, *Report on Mr Charles Stewart Crole*, pp. 2–5.
[33] *Hindu* 29 October 1885.   [34] *Hindu* 29 April 1885.
[35] *M.D.G.* Francis, *Madura*, I, 264.
[36] P & J File 2057 of 1886. *I.O.L.*; G.O. 723 (Public) dated 5 April 1886. *T.N.A.*
[37] P & J Files 701 and 707 of 1887 and File 1476 of 1886. *I.O.L.*
[38] Letter No. 144 (Confidential), H. S. Thomas, Senior Member, Board of Revenue, to C. F. Webster, Chief Secretary to the Government of Madras, in P & J File 189 of 1886. *I.O.L.*

temporarily favoured social groups. Sometimes these activities might appear to be part of a farce, as when Sir Henry Montgomery appointed his butler, Muthuswami Naicker, a *tahsildar*,[39] but at other times they were deadly serious. Many of the communal rumblings which were reverberating through the presidency during our period can be traced to the independent service policies of district revenue officials. In Salem in 1882, for example, the Collector's avowed sympathy with and support of Muslims was a contributing factor to religious rioting. Collector Macleane, appointed only the year before, was an Urdu scholar with many friends among the large Islamic population of the Ceded Districts where he had spent most of his service.[40] When he moved to Salem he brought with him a number of Muslim acquaintances whom he placed in favoured positions in the local bureaucracy.[41] Already there was considerable tension in Salem between Muslim merchants, who recently had raised a mosque in a predominantly Hindu area, and Komati trading rivals. Macleane's arrival sparked off a series of anti-Muslim riots in which several people were killed. Local Hindu officials, whose prospects had been damaged, connived at the Komatis' plot and kept Macleane so ignorant of the dangers that he left Salem for the Bangalore races on the day that the second and most serious riot took place.[42] Policies to prevent communal conflict, framed by the Secretariat and Board of Revenue, had little relevance while immediate district subordinates were in a position to ignore them and supplant them with their own.

Beneath and, more often than not, alongside the Collector, other government servants also carried on their own discretionary rule. Even elementary information about the nature and extent of cultivation in the presidency was poor: surveys made in the 1820s and 1830s were not re-examined until the 1870s and 1880s and the cumbersome machinery of *jamabundi* guaranteed that many obvious facts could be hidden. Everywhere government subordinates, often at the lowest village and *tahsil* levels, usurped the powers of the revenue settlement officer in order to alter demands and payments. In 1886–7, the re-

[39] *Indian Statesmen, Dewans and Prime Ministers* (Madras, n.d.), p. 195.
[40] Macleane was regarded in the Secretariat as an expert on Islam. He was made president of the Madras Mohammedan Education Endowments Committee in 1886 and sent to attend the Calcutta session of the Central Mohammedan Association. G.O. 12 (Education) dated 7 January 1886; G.O. 539 (Education) dated 22 July 1886. *T.N.A.*
[41] 'Mr Macleane in introducing into his own office many of his favourite Mahomedans in the place of many innocent clerks ...' Further, one of his men, 'Kadir Bahadur Sahib brought in many of his own men from Vellore and Krishnagiri and distributed them as Karnams and Munsiffs.' *Hindu* 28 November 1883.
[42] G.O. 353 (Judicial) dated 10 February 1883. *T.N.A.*

settlement of the Nilgiri Wynaad raised revenue payments in some areas by as much as 10,000 per cent:

These startling increases were explained to be chiefly due to the great extent of concealed cultivation which had been brought to light, [and] to the manner in which Government demand had been whittled down by the lower subordinates.[43]

A few years earlier, the resettlement officer in the Godavari district, at the other end of the presidency, described the cultivation changes that had occurred in the previous forty years, 'as far as can be ascertained':

I say as far as can be ascertained, for it is impossible to find out with any accuracy the rates really paid for certain descriptions of land. In the first place the areas are incorrect. . . . So much dry land is entered as wet; so much wet as dry; there has been such continual readjustments of the *shist* on the whole rented area; so many additions have been made to the joint-rent in the lump, which additions have afterwards been distributed in the field more with reference and circumstances of the positions of the Ryots than to the value of the fields.[44]

The 1905 South Kanara resettlement raised the assessment by 150 per cent in one *taluk* and by 64 per cent overall, due to the discovery of concealed cultivation and misclassification of land;[45] the mid-1870s resettlement of Salem raised the assessment by 4 per cent for the same reasons;[46] the Madura resettlement of 1885 found that, although the total revenue demand was correct, much of it had been shifted gradually from the rich wet to the poorer dry lands.[47] Sometimes whole villages appeared as from nowhere in the revenue accounts,[48] while others disappeared no less suddenly. In 1870, one South Arcot revenue officer found thirty-five villages paying a rent reduced by a Board of Revenue rule which had been obsolete for forty years.[49]

The lower levels of the revenue department were riddled with bribery and corruption. One member of the Board of Revenue officially estimated that 20 per cent of the revenue remissions granted every

[43] *M.D.G.* W. Francis, *The Nilgiris* (Madras, 1908), I, 281.

[44] *Selections from the Madras Records. XXII* (Madras, 1870), p. 18.

[45] *M.D.G.* J. F. Hall, *South Kanara* (Madras, 1938), II, 28.

[46] *M.D.G.* Richards, *Salem*, I part 2, 35–6.

[47] *M.D.G.* Francis, *Madura*, I, 203–4.

[48] For example, 23 villages 'appeared' in Coimbatore in 1870. 'Report on Coimbatore', p. 8 in *Report on the Settlement of the Land Revenue in the Districts of the Madras Presidency for Fasli 1280 (1870–1)* (Madras, 1871). Hereafter this annual series as *Land Revenue. . . .*

[49] 'Report on South Arcot', p. 23 in *ibid.*

year were the result of outright fraud which could never be detected or stopped.[50] In 1902, in a letter to the Secretary of State, Lord Ampthill, the Governor, neatly summarised the technique of revenue-gathering current in his presidency:

What happens is this: All the lands on which the crops have failed have to be inspected by subordinate agency which, as you know is very amenable to bribery in this country. The consequence is that the well-to-do ryot who can afford to bribe the village officers or the revenue inspectors gets them to report that his crops are withered or totally lost so as to entitle him to remission. . . . Again it is by no means infrequent that the remissions granted never reach the ryots for whom they are intended as the village officers deceive the ryots by telling them that no remissions were granted collect the full assessment and pocket the money themselves.[51]

Ampthill was not the only senior official to be disarmingly frank about the administration. In 1908 J. A. Cumming, the Collector of Godavari, shocked the Whitehall and Calcutta members of the Decentralization Commission by telling them: 'No doubt there is a great deal of corruption goes [sic] on in the tahsildar's office, and there is a great deal of corruption goes [sic] on in my office.'[52] But Fort St George was unlikely to be able to effect sweeping changes through the mere consciousness of its problems.

The independence of the official was not the prerogative of the revenue department alone; the many other departments of government had followed in its wake deep into the village and were closely related to it in personnel and activities. In the Andhra deltas, Public Works Department men controlled the supply of piped water, which was crucial to second cropping, and were notoriously corrupt.[53] The Excise Department operated an individual tax on each palmyra tree and gave its lower subordinates ample opportunity to develop private administrations, for supervision was impossible. The police were in a similar state: the Superintendent of Tanjore reported in 1883:

Bribery is rife in the District so much so that it is only surprising that more cases are not reported against the Police. When such cases do occur it is with the greatest difficulty that any really reliable evidence can be obtained.[54]

[50] H. S. Thomas, *Report on Tanjore Remissions in Fasli 1294 (A.D. 1884–5)* (Madras, 1885), pp. 45–6.
[51] Lord Ampthill to Lord George Hamilton, 6 August 1902. Ampthill Papers. *I.O.L.*
[52] Evidence of J. A. Cumming in *Minutes of Evidence taken before the Royal Commission upon Decentralization in India.* II, 293. *P. P.* 1908. Vol. XLIV.
[53] See N. G. Ranga, *Fight for Freedom* (New Delhi, 1968), pp. 8–9.
[54] *Administration Report of the Madras Police for the year 1883* (Madras, 1884), p. 91. Hereafter this annual series as *Madras Police* . . .

Twenty years later, Lord Curzon appointed a commission to examine the working of the Madras police. It found: 'Dishonesty in investigation is, we are told, prevalent everywhere.'[55] Nor was judicial administration any better. In 1886, the Collector of North Arcot reported:

Holy places like Tripati [sic], where there is an abundance of other people's money in the hands of priests and where debauchery, intrigue and extortion are chronically rife, prove the ruin of most of the native subordinates who serve in them. Next to these holy places come Zamindary. Of both North Arcot has a large share, and to this is doubtless partly due the lamentably low standard of official morality that exists among our subordinate Magistracy. . . . There are three or four Sub-Magistrates in this district who rarely do an official act save on corrupt inducement.[56]

While the Madras government pretended to exercise such vast powers – far greater in theory than any other provincial government – without the information or the machinery to fulfil the duties they implied, the development of interlocking systems of private and discretionary rule by its subordinates was inevitable. Village officers, clerks, revenue and police inspectors and *tahsildars* were of far greater consequence in deciding the vital questions of who paid what and whose grievances were redressed than the Governor or departmental Secretaries. Of course, such an administrative system, if it can be so called, would tend to border on the anarchic as the authority of every official would be countermanded by his subordinates. To some extent this was the case: ultimate authority always lay at the lowest possible level. Yet certain factors within district administrations led to the growth of channels of influence and authority between the layers of the bureaucracy, which amounted to structures of government although they had nothing to do with Fort St George, and seldom anything to do with the Collector.

R. E. Frykenberg, in his absorbing study of Guntur district in the first half of the nineteenth century, has shown how groups of Maratha Brahmans, through their control of information and appointments, were able to recruit and set up a virtually parallel government inside the British bureaucracy.[57] By the later nineteenth century, the excesses of such private systems had been curbed: administrative reforms, improved information following the resettlements of revenue in the 1870s and 1880s and the growth of a scandal-hungry press made it

---

[55] *Statement of the Police Committee on the Administration of the District Police in the Madras Presidency* (Madras, 1902), p. 50.

[56] *Madras Police 1886.* Appendix C, p. v.

[57] Frykenberg, *Guntur District 1788–1848.*

more difficult for secret combinations to extend as widely and to operate for as long as those in Frykenberg's Guntur. Yet the basic causes which had led to the rise of parallel administrations were not treated, and the organised bureaucratic clique remained an important feature of government in Madras.

Below the cadre of deputy-collector, of which there were only fifty members in 1880, there was no regular provision for the movement of government officials between the districts. Most were recruited and served to retirement within the same district and, if they early became a *tahsildar* or *huzur sheristidar*, often spent many years in the same post.[58] As late as 1920, 70 per cent of Madras *tahsildars* were serving in the districts in which they had been recruited fifteen or twenty years before.[59] *Tahsildars* and *huzur sheristidars*, with their very considerable powers, were given every chance to acquire knowledge and interests in their charges. The agency which supervised them, however, possessed no similar opportunity. Yet it was this agency, and the Collector in particular, who possessed the power of appointment to all the non-provincial offices. It is not surprising that most Collectors were under the thumb of their permanent establishments:

In the distribution of patronage in the District – the appointments of Tahsildars, Sub-Magistrates, Divisional Offices' Head Clerks, Revenue Inspectors and numerous other appointments, be in the gift of the Collector. The Collector is practically guided by his Sheristidar.[60]

The *huzur sheristidar* thus came to have great influence throughout the revenue bureaucracy and could make or break the careers of a great many officers beneath him in rank. He could use his position to build up his own administration. Although family and caste were not the only means by which the *huzur sheristidar* recruited, their presence helps to give some idea of his scope. From Coimbatore in 1884 came the cry:

The office is filled with men who are all members of one and the same family. These men fill the places of important offices such as Huzur Sheristidars, Head Writers, Tahsildars, Sub-Magistrates, Taluk Sheristidars and Munshis of Collectors, while men are shut up from promotion for years and years owing to the influence of the family to which the present officials belong

---

[58] For example, by 1884, G. N. Chinnathambi Pillai had been the *tahsildar* of Tinnevelly *taluk* for fourteen consecutive years. *Hindu* 23 June 1884.

[59] G.O. 1435 (Revenue) dated 17 June 1920. *T.N.A.*

[60] *Hindu* 13 September 1894; see also *Hindu* 25 September 1901.

with the Collectors. The members of one family may be seen in all the Taluks and the Head-quarters of the district filling from the post of Karnam to the place of Head Writer and Tahsildar.[61]

The Governor, M. E. Grant Duff, once wrote to Sir Arthur Godley: 'It may interest you to know that in two divisions of one Madras District, Cuddapah, I heard there were over eighty members of one Brahmin family in Government employ, forty in one and forty odd in the other.'[62] In fact, Grant Duff underestimated the problem: D. Krishna Rao, the Cuddapah *huzur sheristidar* had 117 relatives in the district service; prior to his appointment in Cuddapah he had been *huzur sheristidar* in neighbouring Anantapur and had brought in another 108 there.[63] Evidence from South Kanara, North Arcot, Kistna, Godavari, Kurnool and Chingleput indicates that each also had its bureaucratic caste clique.[64]

In certain, though rare, circumstances, the families who were successful practioners of this sub-imperialism in the district and *tahsil* offices could direct their own form of government right down to the village level. Where the social groups which held higher bureaucratic posts were also those which held village posts, particularly those of *kurnam* (accountant), and large quantities of land, the conditions were created for centrally organised rural kingdoms to be established. Through the discipline of caste institutions and through ties of 'primordial' sentiment, district bureaucrats could draw local powers under their authority and dictate decisions to them. Conspiracies based on these connections always were the most tightly welded. The British, ever watchful of the ramifications of caste, endeavoured to weaken the local role of the *kurnam* and to strengthen that of the headman who was drawn from the major peasant castes which had little presence in the higher bureaucracy. In areas where this move achieved its ends (as it did generally), the domination of conspiracies from above was ended. However, the conspiracies themselves certainly did not cease to occur. All that happened was that peasant headmen took a greater share in them and tilted the balance in the distribution of power within them more towards local interests. The conspiracies

[61] *Hindu* 22 February 1884.
[62] M. E. Grant Duff to Sir Arthur Godley, 31 July 1884. Kilbracken Papers. *I.O.L.*
[63] *Hindu* 17 September 1892 and 4 May 1893; see also Anon., *The Ways and Means for the Amelioration of the Conditions of the Non-Brahman Races* (Bangalore, 1893), pp. 18–19.
[64] *Hindu* 13 November 1893; *Hindu* 14 May 1897; *Hindu* 2 March 1887; *Hindu* 30 May 1887; *Hindu* 22 June 1895. Also, *Andhrapatrika* 2 December 1918 and *Kistnapatrika* 21 February 1920. *R.N.P.*

were bound to continue while British supervision of the administration remained weak and while Indian bureaucrats and local landowners could still find mutual advantage in altering revenue payments to suit themselves.

Several of the most noteworthy cliques uncovered in our period were entirely the result of non-kinship, 'professional' contacts and the balancing of reciprocal interests. In Vizagapatam in the 1880s, for example, the Board of Revenue discovered a conspiracy in salt manufacture worth many *lakhs* of rupees, which involved European Assistant Salt Commissioners as well as native contractors.[65] In Palladum *taluk* of Coimbatore in 1907, a cross-communal network, including the *tahsildar*, police inspectors and sub-registry clerks, was found at work. Investigations showed that this clique extended into the Collector's office where district records were rewritten at its command.[66]

Perhaps the greatest conspiracy case of our period was that in Tanjore in 1884, investigated by H. S. Thomas of the Board of Revenue. It demonstrates the breadth and depth of such connections and the inevitable failure of government attempts to break them up simply by tinkering with the mechanisms of communal recruitment. In the Tanjore remissions scandal, the participants included non-Brahmans and Tamil and Maratha Brahmans, and several of the principals were deputy collectors who, by the nature of their post, had no personal ties with Tanjore.[67] Heavy rains in the winter of 1883 had damaged severely the paddy crop in several parts of the district. Following an inspection of the disaster area by revenue subordinates, claims for a remission of revenue totalling Rs 8,21,900 were sent to the Collector, Mr Pennington, who accepted them and passed them on to the Board of Revenue in Madras. The Board, stung by the heaviness of the claim, was stirred from its usual lethargy. It deputed as investigator H. S. Thomas, a recent ex-collector of the district, who had a deep knowledge of the area and many personal contacts in the subordinate bureaucracy. His investigation revealed that Rs 4,07,322 of the claim were fraudulent:

This report places beyond doubt that there was a widespread and organised conspiracy amongst those natives of the district, to whom the inspection of the crops, etc. and the preparation of the accounts for the annual settlement

---

[65] Proceedings of the Board of Revenue, No. 187 (Misc.) dated 24 January 1883. *T.N.A.*

[66] *Hindu* 11 May 1907.

[67] G.O. 218 (Revenue) dated 22 March 1886. *T.N.A.*

were entrusted, to defraud the Government of a sum almost equalling that for which remission could be claimed.[68]

The brain behind the plot was that of the new *huzur sheristidar*, R. Venkatarama Iyer, who had not yet been confirmed in his appointment. So carefully executed was his scheme that he had warned all his subordinates to fill in their returns in pencil so that alterations might be made with ease later.[69] Involved with him were subordinates at all levels:

> Turning now to the subject of the conduct of the officials condemned by Mr Thomas, Government have to observe that fraud was present at the primary inspection; that it again, and in the worst form, characterised the action of the officials, whose duty it was to check the results of the inspections and to examine the accounts drawn up by the subordinate staff; and that, as this fraud was not only winked at, but actually planned and arranged beforehand by the higher officers, vis. the Deputy Collector, Acting Huzur Sheristidar, sundry Tahsildars, Taluk Sheristidars, and the principal employees of the Collector's office, Mr Pennington was induced to accept as true the misconceptions and false accounts and returns, which were placed before him by those on whom he had every right to believe that he could repose trust.[70]

Although the revelations of the Tanjore remissions investigation appeared to come as a shock to the government, nobody in the Board of Revenue or the districts of the presidency was the least surprised. As H. S. Thomas said himself, the events in Tanjore were no more than a particularly noisy orchestration of a theme being played in every district all the time.[71] If the Board of Revenue had not taken the unwonted step of sending an investigator, and if that investigator had been other than Thomas with his local connections, it is unlikely that the sounds from Tanjore would have broken through the heavy proofing which surrounded them. The enormous powers of the revenue bureaucracy and the way in which they were structured promoted the development of conspiratorial cliques between the village and the higher offices of district government. That was how the administration worked. Tanjore was a paradigm of the practice of British administrative theory.

Fort St George was not a government to concern itself much with promoting rapid social or political reform but, had it been, the nature

[68] G.O. 122 (Revenue) dated 15 February 1886. *T.N.A.*
[69] G.O. 218 (Revenue) dated 22 March 1886. *T.N.A.*
[70] *Ibid.*
[71] Thomas, *Report on Tanjore Remissions*, pp. 45–6.

of its bureaucracy would have prevented its policies from being translated into reality. In the most elementary ways, it lacked the machinery to do anything more than survive. Due to the local nature of recruitment and the usurpation of the powers of appointment by permanent district officials, it could not even control its own employment policy. In 1851, the Board of Revenue issued Standing Order No. 128 (2), which precluded the appointment in the same government office of members of the same family. As we have seen from examples in the 1880s, this had had very little effect. In fact, the much-acclaimed First Communal Order of 1921, by which government in collaboration with the non-Brahman Justice Party sought to limit the number of Brahmans in government service, was no more than the re-issuing of this standing order which had been ignored for seventy years.[72] Naturally, the personal and social interests of these uncontrolled local bureaucrats coloured the performance of government more brightly than did the distant Secretariat. Repeated attempts by Fort St George to raise the position of untouchables, for example, were rendered nugatory for its predominantly high-caste executive refused to enforce them: land set aside for *panchama* resettlement disappeared from the records and a High Court ruling of 1917 revealed that slavery still existed in Malabar, eighty-four years after it had been outlawed.[73] The capital's direct influence in the locality was largely notional.

Yet although Fort St George may appear hopeless and incompetent by the standards that are expected of a modern state, it was, in fact, perfectly tuned to the needs of the mid-nineteenth-century British Empire. For Parliament in London and for the Government of India, it existed to provide a high yield of revenue and to guarantee its own security. Both of these tasks it performed admirably, indeed better than any other provincial administration. This may seem a paradox but when we begin to examine the political relationships implied by the administrative system, the reasons for Fort St George's success become obvious. Its government was carried on by or in the interests of men who independently possessed a large share of political authority in native society.

In much nationalist fiction, the rule of British officials and their native subordinates has been characterised as tyrannical and autocratic. Recently, this judgment has been lent academic respectability by scholars who have weighed the political importance of various

[72] E. F. Irschick, *Politics and Social Conflict in South India* (Berkeley and Los Angeles, 1969), p. 236.
[73] G.O. 1675 (Home, Misc.) dated 2 December 1919. *T.N.A.*

Indian communities by the number of government jobs which they held[74] or who have argued that Brahman and Sat-Sudra groups rose to power in British South India by capturing and using in their private interests the mechanisms of the administration.[75] A careful scrutiny of the nature of government in Madras, however, suggests that these views, at least as they relate to the period from 1870 to 1920, are very difficult to substantiate. If association with the administration of Fort St George immediately and of itself produced the force with which officials could smash the hegemonies of non-officials and establish their own rule, then that administration must have been very powerful and must have been able to command in society an overwhelming preponderance of force. To draw parallels from history, its practice must have matched that of a Peter the Great, a Robespierre or a Stalin for only in the type of state system operating under those men was power so concentrated as to make rulership of this sort possible. In the early years of the British settlement of South India, a case for government by terror could perhaps be made. With the rules of law uncertain, the direction and volume of the flow of resources to the state undecided and large quantities of armed men available to support the judgments of Company servants, bureaucrats and their hangers-on were often in a position to seize what they liked. This epoch of violence and rapid change, however, certainly was over by the 1850s, if not the 1830s. It was replaced by a period of slow and paralysingly inefficient government. Much as the Viceroy Lord Curzon may have envied Peter the Great, the administration which he inherited was not the kind of weapon which he or his bureaucrats could use for the creation of terror and the expropriation of property. It was more 'a mighty and magnificent machine for doing absolutely nothing'.

It would be a truism, of course, to say that ultimately the British were able to stay in India only because of their military resources. But when looking at the *modus operandi* of government in Madras what is most noticeable is the degree of force which the British did *not* have to apply to keep their administration running. Although sitting on a reserve of armed might and punitive police, which could in theory be applied to any area in which the rule of government had broken down, the British in fact were extremely loath to treat their Madras subjects heavy-handedly. In the first place, and obviously, as strong as they were they could not spare the troops from wider imperial duties to rule by the sword everywhere all the time. Secondly, and more

[74] See, for example, A. Seal, *The Emergence of Indian Nationalism* (Cambridge, 1968).
[75] Stein, 'Integration of the Agrarian System of South India', pp. 202–4, 211.

relevantly, the internal use of troops cost the Government of India more money than it cared to spend. The severe castigation which Fort St George received for calling out the army to avert a riot situation in Rajahmundry in 1907 indicates very clearly the limits of military force available to provincial governments.[76] For all except the wildest outbreaks of famine or Moplah violence, soldiers were out of the question. The alternative was to send in punitive police who possessed the virtue of being paid for by the people whom they were punishing. Yet this method of coercion also had its problems. Punitive police were difficult to control, provoked the anger of innocent and otherwise loyal subjects and tended to exacerbate already delicate situations. It was general policy to use them as sparingly and for as little time as possible. The great hammer of force which appeared to back Fort St George's political position, therefore, was by no means easy to swing; and, as if to make this position clear to its subordinates in the localities, when it did swing the hammer it often hit the local subordinates who had allowed their charges to run out of control as hard as it hit more formally designated troublemakers. At Salem in 1882, Tinnevelly in 1899 and Cocanada in 1907,[77] Fort St George decimated the district bureaucracy for its failure to cope with its own problems.

For all practical purposes, government servants in the *mofussil* could not rely on Fort St George for the coercive force necessary to fulfil their potential roles. They had to find resources of power within their localities. Yet the independent resources available to them were extremely limited. In particular, they could place no faith in the ability of the police department to provide them with support. Following the revelations of the Torture Commission (1855), the Madras police had been constituted into an agency separate from the revenue department.[78] *Tahsildars* who wished to use the powers of the police now had at least to satisfy officials in another bureaucracy of their *bona fides*. More importantly, however, even were lower revenue subordinates to succeed in obtaining police power, it is not clear that they could achieve very much with it. The portion of the police department which was under direct bureaucratic control, and capable of being seen as an independent force in society, was very small indeed.

[76] Home Police A August 1907 Nos 10–11; Home Police A October 1907, No. 123. *N.A.I.*

[77] G.O. 353 (Judicial) dated 10 February 1883. *T.N.A.*; Home Police A March 1900, Nos. 1–8. *N.A.I.*; G.O. 1266 (Judicial) dated 16 July 1907. *T.N.A.*

[78] See *Report of the Commissioners for the Investigation of Alleged Cases of Torture in the Madras Presidency* (Madras, 1855).

At no time before 1900 was the ratio of district policemen to district population better than 1:2000; outside the main towns it was nearer 1:4000.[79] The police department proper was only intended to provide a service of secondary investigation. All primary investigation was carried out by the village police who were under the control of local powers — village headmen who, as we shall see, were local landowners, and *zamindars*. Using only the powers of the district police, a *tahsildar* could have little hope of cowering his *taluk* into mute obedience. Moreover, against village-level resistance, he could not use the police courts for the village police were just as much of a legal force as were his district police and, more significantly, were much nearer to the source of evidence. The only way in which he could continue his government was by enlisting the support of men under the prior control of village headmen and *zamindars*. While this could give him some room for manoeuvre, by playing the ambitions of one local power off against those of another, it did not give him an independent basis for despotism. If he wished to retain power he had to keep some of the 'big men' in his charge on his side all the time.

In spite of, or perhaps because of, the elaborateness of the bureaucracy, the lower government official was no better placed to use the slower processes of administrative coercion to strengthen his rule. In theory, he could order the sale of land of any man whom he deemed to be a revenue defaulter; in practice, he could neither legally describe the defaulter's land nor find buyers for it without the co-operation of the village-based revenue office.[80] In theory, he was in a position to 'arrange' legal cases against any local inhabitant of whom he disapproved and have him convicted; in practice, the rules of evidence required under British law were so rigorous and the ability of rich local men to conceal evidence or hire witnesses was so great that he could seldom obtain a conviction against, or even take to trial, any man of substance.[81] In theory, he could raise the taxes on whom he liked, interfere in trade as much as he pleased and distribute his patronage wherever he chose; in practice, he had to balance the use of his powers between the various contending political groups of his locality or he would foment riots, strikes and *hartals* and render his

---

[79] See *Madras Police 1900*.

[80] *Report of the Indian Famine Commission. Appendix. Volume III. Condition of the Country and People*, p. 416. *P.P.* 1881. LXXI, part 2; *Madras Provincial Banking Enquiry Committee. Evidence* (Madras, 1930), III, 679. Hereafter, these volumes as *MPBC*. . . .

[81] See below pp. 44, 109–10.

charge ungovernable.[82] The regularity with which local protests and uprisings occurred during our period indicates clearly the strength of non-official society's resistance to the overzealous and incautious bureaucrat.

Indeed, influential local subjects were very well placed not only to resist but to destroy their titular government masters. Their ability to control information both inside and outside the bureaucracy was often greater than that of their chief local official. Mothey Venkataswami, a millionaire merchant of Ellore, for example, had a large number of debtors and dependents inside the Ellore Sub-Collectorate. Twice reports on his more dubious activities were despatched from Ellore to the Godavari Collectorate in Cocanada and twice they were intercepted and destroyed *en route*.[83] Should a magnate take to the offensive and prepare a corruption charge against his local *tahsildar* or sub-judge, the official could find himself acutely embarrassed even if there were no substance to the charges. Against hundreds of bought and rehearsed witnesses, his pleas of innocence sounded hollow. In 1896, Mothey Venkataswami broke the Ellore sub-judge, I. N. Swaminatha Iyer, whose main defence was that he had found against the Mothey interest in several suits and was now the victim of a revenge plot.[84] In Bellary in 1890, another sub-judge, who also had alienated some of the local notability, was forced to plead the same defence and go the same way. In this second case the sessions judge remarked that it was passing strange that the accusations emanated from a pauper who, somehow, had managed to retain the best lawyers in town to act on his behalf.[85] Corruption trials were as much a part of life in British South India as mangoes; and although the number of officials who actually were dismissed and imprisoned may have been small, the number who were transferred after acquittal (a satisfactory solution from the local magnate's point of view) was considerable. If the corruption trial failed, there were many other ploys: large-scale public meetings,[86] letters to the newspapers and petitions would draw the at-

---

[82] See, for example, the strike of bazaarmen organised against municipal taxation in Madura in 1880 in Raja Rama Rao, *Sir S. Subramania Aiyer*, p. 12; or in Bellary in 1908 against municipal bye-laws, G.O. 2120 (L and M, M), dated 19 December 1908. *T.N.A.*; or in Trichinopoly in 1886 against municipal maladministration, *Vettikodayan*, 23 October 1886. *R.N.P.*; or in Anantapur in 1896 against income-tax assessments, *Hindu* 18 September 1896.

[83] Marginal notes of Collector of Godavari on A. R. Banerji, Assistant Collector, Ellore, to Collector of Godavari, 29 March 1901 in G.O. 1011 (L and M, M) dated 17 July 1901. *T.N.A.*

[84] *Hindu* 5 June 1896.

[85] *Hindu* 15 October 1890.

[86] As at Salem in 1893, *Hindu* 15 December 1893.

tention of his superiors to the trouble which the official was causing. Again, although these seldom led to dismissal, they often produced investigations and transfers.

The notion that subordinate government servants, and by implication the social groups from which they were drawn, came to exercise great power through their connection with the British administration in South India, then, would seem to be untenable. It confuses the potential powers of office with the ability to fulfil them and, moreover, the ability to draw considerable financial rewards with the ability to exercise direct power. At best, the government servant was an intermediary, acting between Fort St George and the greater non-official powers in his locality. Fort St George used him to extract as much as he could from his charge without disturbing its peace; the magnates used him to negotiate the minimum for which Fort St George would settle before it had to use its reserve powers and send in troops, punitive policemen and Board of Revenue investigators. The whole system, and his position within it, hinged on the fact that both sides sought an amicable compromise with as little fuss and interference as possible. The successful servant had to rely as much on the confidence of the non-officials around him as he did on the government. The occasions on which he could act independently came only when both of his masters were confused and weak. These were quite common in his relationships with his 'superiors' but, in those with his 'inferiors', were confined to the periods when he could choose between two or more equally balanced 'big men' or factions composed of 'big men'. Local symmetries of this type were rare; and the moment that he committed himself to one side or the other they ended. Certainly, as a middle-man he obtained great rewards, receiving a salary from the government and 'bribes' from local inhabitants, but it makes little sense to regard his prosperity as a sign of his personal power. As R. E. Frykenberg ultimately saw in Guntur: 'The corruption of authority in Guntur (and in other districts) ought not to blind us to the fact that the Maratha Brahmans [administrators] were go-betweens.'[87]

At worst, and most usually, however, the government servant's possible independence had been sold away the instant that he donned his government cap. The fragmentation of the administration disconnected him from Fort St George and forced him, whether willingly or not, to give or sell his services to the men who controlled local methods of coercion. He became an employee of the powers within his charge and served their interests to the exclusion of Fort St George's. This

[87] Frykenberg, *Guntur District 1788–1848*, p. 234.

can be seen clearly when we examine the background of the people in the administration and the ways in which they operated.

In the first place, many local bureaucrats were already local powers when they took their seats in their government office. In Chapter 4, we shall be looking closely at the nature of the village officers who occupied the lowest and most critical stratum of the governmental pyramid. Here we need only point out that they were drawn from the wealthiest and most influential families in their village. Above the village officers, up to the 'provincial' post of deputy-collector, some of the servants of government also were recruited from the major economic powers in the district and exercised a strong social control based upon this wealth. In Tanjore in 1885, H. S. Thomas found:

> Many of the Tanjore officials are largely interested in land in the district, and there is thus thrown about a Collector a network of men interested, both personally and through their relatives, in obtaining remissions on lands. . . . Tanjore officials are interested in land in their own district to an extent which covers 73 square miles, pays an annual assessment of about two lakhs and may be valued at Rs 97,71,000 say close on a crore of rupees.[88]

This development was also particularly noticeable in Malabar, where the social groups who served in the upper reaches of the district bureaucracy were also those who dominated landed resources.[89]

Secondly, whenever a government officer took a bribe, he signed a contract by which he placed his influence at the disposal of his non-official paymaster. He became the paid agent of the magnate whom he was supposed to govern. Frykenberg noted this inversion of the sources of supposed authority in Guntur: 'Village money spread a corrupting influence into even higher levels of the hierarchy, and the administration became caught in the webs of village influence.'[90] It was implied by Ampthill in his description of *jamabundi*, which we quoted earlier, and lay at the heart of Thomas' findings in Tanjore. Further examples of it litter the history of the South. A Collector of North Arcot stormed at his judiciary: 'Zamindars, Poligars, Jaghidars, Gurus – *anybody* with power or command of money, simply used the Sub-Magistrates as weapons of offence.'[91] In 1916, the Revenue Department considered placing an I.C.S. officer in Devakottai division

[88] Thomas, *Report on Tanjore Remissions*, p. 37.
[89] Namely, the Nairs.
[90] Frykenberg, *Guntur District 1788–1848*, p. 230.
[91] *Madras Police 1886*. Appendix C, p. v.

of Ramnad district, the home'of the Nattukottai Chetty international bankers: 'Devakottai is very exceptionable. There is any number of extremely wealthy Nattukottai Chetties who buy up any officials they can.' The department greatly appreciated 'the danger of subservience to the Chetties'.[92] In Rajapalaiyam at about the same time, the landed magnate A. K. D. Dharma Raja 'procured' the services of his *tahsildar* T. S. Ramaswami Iyer to keep his private market free from the avaricious gaze of government.[93] Following the Salem riots of 1882, the *huzur sheristidar* A. Venkatasubba Iyer was dismissed less for his part in the riots than because 'I [the Collector] have come to the conclusion from the conduct of work before me during the last six months that he has unduly exposed himself to the influence of the Mittadars, which means corruption.'[94] In 1906, the deputy-collector Raja Rama Rao, who came from one of the most illustrious service families in Madras, was dismissed for receiving presents from the raja of Ramnad for services rendered while he was in the Ramnad division.[95] In some *zamindari* areas it was difficult to tell the difference between the estate and the government bureaucracy. Not only did local bureaucrats switch between the two[96] but many had relatives permanently in the service of both.[97] Indeed in Kistna district at the turn of the century, the distinction had altogether disappeared and the *zamindar* of Munagala was giving away government revenue inspectorships.[98] The influence of local magnates on local bureaucrats can be gauged again from the part the former played in harassing central investigations.[99]

As the structure of government actually touched Madras society, it was moulded and shaped by that society. Indigenous, non-official powers, by one means or another, absorbed and controlled the functions of the state in the locality. This happened not simply because bureaucrats were weak or put personal interest before that of the

---

[92] G.O. 349 (Home, Misc.) dated 4 April 1917. *T.N.A.*

[93] G.O. 1984 (L.S.G.) dated 7 September 1923. *T.N.A.*

[94] Note signed C. D. Macleane in G.O. 353 (Judicial) dated 10 February 1883. *T.N.A.*

[95] *Andhraprakasikha* 5 December 1906. *R.N.P.*

[96] For an example in the Pithapuram estate, see *Hindu* 22 August 1910.

[97] Such as the 'Koka' family of Audi-Velamas, see *Hindu* 26 March 1920.

[98] A. Kaleswara Rao, *Na Jivita Katha—Navya Andhramu* (Vijayawada, 1959), p. 19. (Telugu).

[99] For example, H. S. Thomas' investigations in Tanjore stirred an agitation led by the prominent landowner S. A. Saminatha Iyer who, presumably, had some interest at stake. *Hindu* 19 January, 13 March, 25 May and 13 October 1885. Equally, in Cuddapah in 1884, Assistant Collector Farmer tried to break a Collectorate clique and was sued by a variety of local landowners for libel and property damage. *Hindu* 19 January and 13 March 1885.

state but because the social material from which the British had built their administrative machine, the design of that machine and the purposes which the machine was intended to serve virtually guaranteed that it would happen. Although it is possible to find few British civilians of the period who were prepared openly to admit that their government rested on the personal power of their greater subjects, many acts of British administrative practice make it clear that this position was at least tacitly recognised by them. No systematic effort was made to prevent local landholders from becoming bureaucrats in their own districts. The interchange of personnel between *zamindari* and district bureaucracies, and the consequent confusion of loyalties between *zamindars* and government, was actively encouraged. Moreover, a great deal of the administration was farmed out and left to the responsibility of local notables. The legal system recognised a number of independent authorities of which it made use at every opportunity: Fort St George appointed *Kazis* to administer Islamic civil law to the Muslim population, allowed its courts to refer disputes between members of the same caste to caste headmen and *panchayats* and, in the countryside, gave village headmen the right to try small cases. In order to improve sanitation and communications, it brought together urban and rural notables in municipal committees and local fund boards, and asked them to take over responsibility for these affairs. It appointed Honorary Magistrates from among its most prominent citizens to try petty criminal cases. During times of riot and civil strife it sought the authority of wealthy and powerful men to help it calm the storm. And, more informally of course, its administrative system allowed many local leaders a large say in the actual apportionment and distribution of taxation. In every locality, the government of Fort St George was based on a series of alliances and tacit understandings with men of substance and power who thus had an interest in the continuation of that government.

The existence of a tight web of local connections between government and society helps to explain Fort St George's success in raising revenue, keeping the peace and preserving its own political security. In return for a fixed tribute, set high by historical accident,[100] and for the promise of order, it agreed to stay out of the localities and allow them to find their own political balances. It set the rules of the game and, through the threat of its reserve powers, could make sure that

---

[100] A century of continuous warfare, Hyder Ali's government, and the Maratha depredations had destroyed local society's ability to resist a high revenue demand at the time of the British conquest.

they were kept; but it did not look too carefully at what was happening in the scrimmages and placed at least half the field on its blind side. It gave to those non-officials who were prepared to take them, chances to develop and use their existing powers without interference. It thus established alliances in every *taluk* and town with men who had an incentive to abide, or to appear to abide, by its regulations and to do its work for it. Revenue continued to flow and order to be maintained although, by any standard, there was little formal government.

Of course, misguided policies and economic and social pressures were bound to upset the balances sometimes: local officials might alienate strong magnates and famine or communal rioting fracture the networks of magnate control.[101] But the highly decentralised nature of the political sytem guaranteed that these disturbances never threatened Fort St George with a Mutiny situation. In the nineteenth century, Madras achieved the reputation of a 'benighted' province in which political lethargy was general. While this description certainly would fit its provincial politics, it would be wholly false of its local politics. Every agitational technique to be found in the twentieth-century nationalist movement, from stone-throwing to *satyagraha* and from assassination to newspaper scandal, was well established in Madras by 1870. Magnates and political leaders battled for the ear of government, rent strikes were organised, huge anti-British and anti-government demonstrations were arranged and policies of non-co-operation were offered. However, the arenas in which these campaigns took place were always those of the locality, in which the critical level of government decision-making lay. As virtually no two *taluks*, or even *firkas*, need be subject to the same governmental problems, and as the same social forces in two adjacent areas could be accommodated by governmental authorities in different ways, it was extremely difficult for dissidences to spread.

In these conditions, Fort St George's political position was safe. In every district it had hosts of collaborators only too eager to attach themselves to it and to carry on its revenue and police duties for it. Most local conflicts stemmed not from opposition to the government but from rivalry to become associated with it.[102] Even when violent disturbances did break out, they were isolated and could be handled with disdain. The British, before the second decade of the twentieth century at the earliest, were not challenged at the state level because there was no state-level arena in which an important challenge

---

[101] See below, Chapter 3.
[102] As for jobs in the bureaucracy or for control of local administrative institutions.

could be made. Political satisfaction was a matter to be sought as near to the ground as possible.

Yet, obviously, the price Fort St George paid for its revenue and its security was high. Once it had created a political system which kept it remote from the daily affairs of its subjects, it could not initiate a general policy of interference without destroying that system and promoting upheaval. This debility was of little consequence while the society it governed and the ends it pursued remained constant. But changes in either could present it with great problems. From the 1870s, both its society and its ends began a process of significant change, which forced it to undertake a major reorganisation of the resources of the state. In doing so it had to modify severely the political system on which it rested.

Fort St George was fortunate in that violent social change was confined to a few areas which, because of the segmented nature of the state, did not impinge heavily on the presidency as a whole. Equally, it was lucky in not having to cope with the permanent, growing and organised hostility of its educated society. The economic problems of the Bengali *bhadralok* and the cultural difficulties of *bhadralok* and Chitpavan Brahman revivalism were not repeated in the South. Moreover, the press was small and limited in its influence and job competition between traditional and 'newly' literate groups was not to develop until the 1930s.[103] It was less social than economic change which steadily undermined Fort St George's position of *quieta non movere*. From their earliest settlements, the British had sought to collect revenues in cash. Between the 1820s and the 1860s, this revenue flow – this tribute from the localities – had remained constant and had become a fixed part of the bargain between Fort St George and its local indigenous powers. For most of the period the British had had the better of the bargain because commodity prices had tended to fall.[104] During the latter four decades of the nineteenth century, however, prices began to rise at first steadily but from the 1890s with alarming rapidity.[105] Fort St George simply had to find new sources of revenue and to cultivate new resources of wealth if it were even to stay still. It had to interfere in

---

[103] For dicussions of these and other factors, which lay behind the development of the nationalist movement in other provinces, see L. A. Gordon, *Bengal: The Nationalist Movement 1870–1940* (New York and London, 1974); Seal, *Emergence of Indian Nationalism*; G. Johnson, *Provincial Politics and Indian Nationalism* (Cambridge, 1973).

[104] Kumar, *Land and Caste in South India*, p. 91.

[105] *Ibid.*

the long-standing arrangements which it had made with its subjects.

Moreover, it soon found that staying still was not going to be enough. Ultimately, the ends which Fort St George pursued were determined by the British Parliament and the Government of India whose horizons were much wider than its own. Madras served the purposes of the British Empire and, during our period, those purposes themselves were changing. Competition in Europe and America challenged the industrial supremacy of Britain and made her increasingly reliant on Indian markets and on Indian commodity surpluses to meet her balance of payments deficits;[106] extended imperial commitment, particularly in Africa, and the threat of Russian expansion in Central Asia threw a new weight onto the Indian army;[107] international currency difficulties squeezed the imperial economy and forced Britain to seek more real wealth through taxation in India.[108] An administrative system which had been tuned to the needs of 1830 began to look rather fragile when faced with the needs of 1900. Fort St George was ordered to find more money, to streamline and cheapen its government, to develop communications and economic resources, to prevent the worst effects of famine and disease, which periodically devastated its economic and revenue performance, and to stimulate trade and industry. Its masters ordered, and sometimes whipped, it into activity.

Four sets of reforms which Fort St George was forced to undertake in response to these new pressures were of crucial importance in altering political relations in the presidency. The first three served to weld the bureaucratic capital much more firmly to the base of the localities and to make local notables consider the centre of government more seriously when planning their political strategies. The fourth actually 'extended' the locality into a larger arena, composed not of a few adjacent villages or suburbs but of whole towns and districts. This extended locality produced more complex patterns of political interaction and also was more easily seen and interfered in by the capital of government.

Firstly, Fort St George was impelled to intervene more regularly in the operations of the economy in order to raise more revenue and to promote commerce and economic development. In seeking cash, it

---

[106] See E. J. Hobsbawm, *Industry and Empire: and economic history of Britain since 1750* (London, 1969).

[107] See J. Gallagher and R. Robinson, 'The Imperialism of Free Trade' in *Economic History Review*, VI: 1 (1953), 4–5; also *Imperial Gazetteer of India* (Oxford, 1907), IV, 186.

[108] *Imperial Gazetteer of India* IV, 194–6, 518.

soon discovered that it could not count on an infinite series of increases in the assessment on land. Its land revenue resettlements provoked agitations and disturbances on an unparalleled scale; on several occasions it had to substitute political discretion for financial valour and reduce or even postpone indefinitely the implementation of resettlements.[109] Moreover, its reliance on rich rural inhabitants for the force on which its government rested meant that it lacked a coercive arm when attempting to expropriate rural wealth. The rise in the land revenue did not nearly match the rise in prices and in governmental costs. It was obtained only by uncovering and bringing into the tax system land previously concealed or newly cultivated or newly irrigated, not by increasing significantly the rate of assessment per acre. Between 1886–7 and 1925–6, the rate of assessment per acre rose only by 12 per cent in the case of wet land and by 7 per cent in the case of dry.[110] Fort St George had to look elsewhere for its money and the proportion of total revenues represented by the land revenue dropped rapidly from 57 per cent in 1880 to 28 per cent in 1920.[111]

To compensate for the rigidities of its land revenue system, the Government of Madras turned away from the major source of wealth in its society and concentrated its attention on more peripheral areas of the economy. In the internal sector, its eye fell immediately on trade and commerce. Beginning in 1886, it administered for the Government of India a tax on non-agricultural incomes which came to yield Rs 2 *crores* p.a. by 1920.[112] On its own behalf, it undertook a rigorous campaign of taxation and control against the huge native liquor industry. Prior to 1880, the influence of government in this field had been small. It had licensed the manufacture of spirits and sold rights to the monopoly of liquor distribution in certain areas but it had left the speculators and contractors who bought the licences and monopolies to provide their own administrations and, consequently, government profits from the trade had been limited. In 1882–3, its entire excise revenue reached only Rs 60 *lakhs*.[113] Over the next forty

---

[109] In the face of fierce local agitation in Tanjore in 1892–3, the government was forced to reduce the rate of assessment increase in its resettlement of the district. *Hindu* 17 July 1896. The Malabar resettlement of 1883 was still unenforced in 1903. Lord Ampthill to Broderick. 12 November 1903. Ampthill Papers. *I.O.L.*

[110] Calculated from *Land Revenue 1885–6* and *1925–6*.

[111] *Report on the Administration of the Madras Presidency during the year 1880–1* (Madras, 1881), pp. cxxvii–viii; *ibid.*, 1920–1, p. 80.

[112] *Report on the Administration of Income Tax under Act II of 1886 in the Madras Presidency for the year 1920–1* (Madras, 1921). Hereafter this series as *Income Tax*...

[113] *Report on the Administration of the Abkari Revenue in the Presidency of Fort St George for the year 1882–3* (Madras, 1883). Hereafter this annual series as *Abkari*.

years, however, Fort St George's drive for more money forced it to interfere much more closely in the industry. It built a new bureaucracy solely for excise administration and clamped down heavily on licensees and monopolists. By 1920, it had increased its excise revenue ninefold to Rs 5.4 *crores* or to 21 per cent of its total income.[114]

New measures of taxation, however, were not enough. What was needed also were measures to protect economic resources, to foster economic growth and to remove the social obstacles to material prosperity. In pursuit of these ends, Fort St George launched an administrative crusade which carrried it into the countryside and led it to interfere in many of the basic economic activities and relationships of its inhabitants. In 1878, it passed laws to arrest the alarming denudation of the forest reserves which played a large part in the economy of the 'dry' areas.[115] At about the same time, it began to consider legislation to clarify the nature of contract between landlords and tenants and to bring the administration of *zamindari* estates under better bureaucratic and legal control.[116] Following the disasters of the famine of 1876–8, it elaborated a new famine code which brought relief more speedily to the distressed.[117] In addition to saving life and land, this code had the effect of interposing government between the weaker and stronger elements of rural society during periods of acute agrarian crisis. By the early 1890s, Fort St George was even setting itself to solve two of the most profound problems of the economy. In the main *mirasi* areas of the province, it sought to break the slave-like dependence of landless labourers on landlords by providing land and house-sites for *pariahs*.[118] And it deputed one of its most knowledgeable civilians, Frederick Nicholson, to report on the possibilities of providing cheaper and more flexible systems of rural credit than then existed.[119] In 1904, some of Nicholson's suggestions were incorporated into a Co-operative Credit Societies Act which sought to promote state-backed mutual lending associations among cultivators.

[114] *Report on the Administration of the Madras Presidency during the year 1920–1* (Madras, 1921), p. 80.

[115] *Report on the Administration of the Forest Department of the Madras Presidency 1882–3* (Madras, 1883).

[116] Such as the Zamindari Village Officers Act of 1894, which was first discussed in the Legislative Council in 1883.

[117] *Report of the Indian Famine Commission. 1880. Volume II. P.P.* 1881. Vol. LXXI.

[118] G.O. 1675 (Home, Misc.) dated 2 December 1919. *T.N.A.*

[119] F. A. Nicholson, *Report regarding the possibilities of introducing Agricultural Banks into the Madras Presidency* (Madras, 1895 and 1897), 2 vols. Hereafter, these volumes as Nicholson, *RAB*.

Fort St George's initiatives in matters of taxation and economic planning produced two important alterations in the relationship between government and society. In the first place, government came into contact with and began to affect the interests of economic groups which previously it had left alone. Merchants, businessmen, contractors, industrialists, cattle-breeders, moneylenders and landlords found themselves under a new pressure from the intrusion of the bureaucracy into many areas of their lives. Naturally, they responded to this pressure by organising movements of resistance. In the years leading up to the First World War, violent opposition on the ground between government officials and various local economic powers grew in intensity until it threatened to destroy much of the machinery of administration.[120] Moreover, it fed into the wider currents of the nationalist movement and immeasurably strengthened the power of nationalist leaders. Several of the more conspicuous local victories of Gandhi's non-co-operation campaign of 1920–2 were the result of support from merchants, eager to lower the income-tax on themselves; liquor traders, attempting to cut excise revenue; and cattle-breeders, pursuing their long-standing conflict with the forest department.[121]

Secondly, the character of the taxation and economic policies helped to shift the attention of various economic groups away from the locality and fixed it firmly on the institutions of the capital. In sharp contrast to the land revenue system, the excise and income-tax administrations stressed the role of Madras city in the making of important decisions. Under the *ryotwari* system, as we have seen, the effective apportionment of revenue demand lay with local officials of one kind or another. The only time that revenue payers could gain anything by approaching the Secretariat or Board of Revenue was immediately after resettlement operations when Fort St George was considering the expediency of implementing the recommendations of its resettlement officers. As resettlements were made district by district at thirty- or forty-year intervals and as the rates of commutation and payment were set by local circumstance rather than provincial fiat, it is not surprising that the constant pressure exercised by land revenue payers on Fort St George was not great. Fierce as may have

---

[120] By 1914, illicit distilling and prosecutions for offences against the excise laws were reaching mammoth proportions, see *Abkari, 1914–15* and *1915–16*; evasions of forest laws and attacks on forest subordinates had grown hugely, see *Report on the Working of the Forest Department of the Madras Presidency 1915–16* (Madras, 1916); in certain areas, the village police and revenue services were in open revolt, see below pp. 152–9.

[121] C. J. Baker, 'Noncooperation in South India' in C. J. Baker and D. A. Washbrook (eds.), *South India: Political Institutions and Political Change* (New Delhi, 1975).

been the reactions of individual districts to their own resettlements, there was no standing provincial association of *ryotwari* landholders in Madras until 1918 and, apart from vague murmurings about the desirability of a permanent settlement, no general political lobby in the interest of *ryotwari* landholders.

The economic interests touched by Fort St George's new excise and income-tax policies, however, came to be organised very differently. Certainly, at no time before 1920 was it impossible for them to bribe local excise and income-tax officials in order to wring concessions out of the administration. But they could also serve their interests in significant ways by going to the centre. Fort St George itself set the general rates of demand on the liquor industry and had sufficient freedom over the Government of India's income-tax to decide the categories in which payers should be placed and the ways in which they should pay. Sometimes the favours to be had from Fort St George far outmatched the rewards buyable in the locality. The Nattukottai Chetty bankers, for example, acquired the right for each of their family banks to be assessed for income-tax as a single unit rather than as a number of separate branches. This enabled them to write off the losses of one branch against the profits of another and thus saved them thousands of rupees a year.[122] Equally, chit lottery banking proprietors succeeded in having their businesses moved from a 'private' to a 'company' classification which enabled them also to cut the taxation burden.[123] In the liquor industry, various groups mounted demands to Fort St George for a lowering of excise duty and for a reorganization of the excise administration. Often they were successful, as in the 1890s when Malabar sweet-toddy traders persuaded the excise department to redesign completely its bureaucratic machine in the district.[124]

Similarly, the economic interests influenced by Fort St George's economic policies could not avoid going to the capital when seeking certain types of redress. Again, cattle-breeders could bribe local

---

[122] The Nattukottai Chetties maintained a standing *vakil* in the Legislative Council to look after their affairs. For most of the period between 1904 and 1920, he was P. S. Sivaswami Iyer. See S. R. Rm. A. Annamalai Chetty to P. S. Sivaswami Iyer, 11 June 1920; N. Sivaramakrishnan to P. S. Sivaswami Iyer, 22 June 1920. P. S. Sivaswami Iyer Papers. *N.A.I.*

[123] *Income Tax, 1899–1900*. For a list of provincial bye-laws passed by Fort St George to the Government of India's Act II of 1886, see *An Income Tax Manual being Act II of 1886 with Rulings and Orders issued by the Governments of India, the Madras Government and Board of Revenue and the Circular Instructions issued by the Accountant-General Madras upto 31st January 1900* (Madras, 1900).

[124] *Abkari, 1892–3* and *1893–4*.

forest guards, *zamindars* pay their local government officials to turn a blind eye to many practices and *mirasidars* heavily influence the humanitarian measures being extended to their *pariah* serfs. But it was only at Fort St George, from which the policy initiative emanated, that they could obtain other substantial concessions. By campaigning before the Secretariat in Madras city, the forest interest managed to alter entirely the technique of forest administration which had been established in 1878;[125] the *zamindari* interest managed to switch the burden of local cess taxation from itself to government;[126] and the *mirasidar* interest managed to persuade Fort St George to dilute its *pariah* policy.[127] By forming permanent associations,[128] organising petitions and, most importantly, using the new breed of educated Indian publicist who was growing up around the capital at this time, mercantile and industrial interests forged new political links with Fort St George. They helped to turn an administrative system, which was becoming ever broader and more provincial in its scope, into the basis of a political system in which the widely dispersed parts were held together through their connection to a common centre of decision- making.

Once the Madras Government had begun to seek an improvement in the performance of its bureaucracy, it soon come to recognise the desperate need for a reorganisation of the bureaucratic agency itself. From the early 1880s, Fort St George pursued this end along two parallel paths. Firstly, it attempted to break down the administrative omnicompetence of the revenue department, which had given revenue subordinates a stranglehold on the information which reached it. The dangers of concentrating full bureaucratic powers in one man had been appreciated by the Torture Commission of 1855, which had recommended that *tahsildars* be relieved of their police functions.[129] Although this reform was accomplished in the late 1850s, natural inertia and lack of pressure from outside combined to prevent any further measures of departmentalisation in the administration for thirty years. In 1885, however, in order to provide an executive arm for its aggressive excise policy, Fort St George created a new *Abkari* and Excise Department and removed powers of supervision over excise matters from the ordinary revenue staff. In 1892, in order to

---

[125] *Report of the Forest Committee 1913* (Madras, 1913), Vol I.

[126] From about 1908, Fort St George was paying the majority share of village officer's stipends in *zamindari* areas. Home Judicial, File 931 of 1922. *N.A.I.*

[127] Home Political 'Deposit' April 1917 No. 61. *N.A.I.*

[128] Such as the Nattukottai Nagaratha Association (1904), the Madras Landholders Association (1890) and the Southern Indian Chamber of Commerce (1911).

[129] *Report of the Commissioners for the Investigation of Alleged Cases of Torture.*

improve its magisterial service, it withdrew common magisterial powers from *tahsildars* who were on tour and appointed a series of 'stationary submagistrates' who took over magisterial duties at *taluk* headquarters.[130] From the 1880s, the steady increase in the number of subordinate civil courts gradually whittled away the general arbitrational functions which revenue subordinates had served: disputes which once might have been about revenue rights became increasingly about property rights. From 1909, the revenue department was pulled back from the rural boards through which it had supervised the provision of local facilities such as roads, wells and drains. Moreover, at this time, separate agencies for the promotion of agricultural improvement, industrial development and social welfare began to make their own investigations into the conditions of local life. Certainly by the second decade of the twentieth century, Fort St George could expect to receive information and to have its governmental duties performed by several men in the same administrative division. It was thus in a much better position to know and to control what its subordinates were doing.

The second path of bureaucratic reform which it followed led towards the breakdown of the domination which the locality possessed over government appointments. From about 1880, Fort St George began to enlarge the cadre of deputy-collector, appointments to which were made in the Secretariat rather than the district and members of which were not allowed to serve in districts in which they had personal interests. Between 1880 and 1920, the number of deputy-collectors rose from 50 to 160.[131] This enabled Fort St George to replace completely the influence of the 'local' *huzur sheristidar* with that of men whom it was better able to control. Spurred on by this success, in 1910 it took away the rights to appoint *tahsildars* from the Collector's office and vested them in the Board of Revenue.[132] This allowed it to make provision for the regular movement of *tahsildars* from *taluk* to *taluk* in order to prevent the build-up of local commitments among them. In 1911, it proposed a complete reorganisation of all appointments to the revenue department. Only men who were appointed by the centre, after examination or vetting by an appointments board, could ever aspire to hold revenue offices carrying a salary of more than Rs 100 per month – that is to be *tahsildars* or high-grade clerks.[133] Beneath

[130] Meyer, *Report on the Constitution of Additional Districts, Divisions and Taluks*, p. 2.
[131] *History of the Services of Gazetted and Other Officers in the Civil Department in the Madras Presidency, Corrected to 1st July 1885* (Madras, 1885); *ibid., 1920.*
[132] G.O. 1435 (Revenue) dated 17 June 1920. *T.N.A.*
[133] G.O. 682 (Revenue, Confidential) dated 11 March 1911. *T.N.A.*

the central revenue department proper, Fort St George also attempted to reform the village establishment – by giving its immediate superiors more powers to punish it, by clipping many of its prerogatives and even by considering an eradication of hereditary rights to appointment in it.[134] Similar developments were taking place at this time also in the judicial and police departments. The swelling importance of formal judicial process, to be seen in the rapid growth of litigation, gave the law courts an ever larger place in local life. The officers who controlled the courts, the District Judges, sub-judges and district *munsiffs*, all were appointed directly from the capital. Moreover, the personal despotisms which some of these officials had exercised in the past also were circumscribed: *vakil* certificates from the High Court steadily replaced the pleadership certificates, issued at the discretion of judges, which previously had provided entry to local bars. In the police department, reforms following the report of Curzon's police committee established a new cadre of centrally appointed sub-inspectors to fill the yawning gap between the local village police and the existing provincial police 'umbrella'. This move brought agents of the central government very nearly into the heart of village India.

Of course, the political effects of the progressive centralisation of the bureaucracy were not as straightforward nor as immediate as the British would have liked. Shortages of men, money and time prevented Fort St George from fulfilling wholly the new role which it had set itself. Although by 1920, for example, it had managed to move revenue officials around so that only eight *tahsildars* and eleven deputy *tahsildars* had served in their posts for more than three years, little had been done to turn *tahsildars* into members of a truly provincial cadre. Seventy per cent of them continued to serve in the districts in which they had been recruited and which were their homes.[135] Moreover, local society's almost infinite capacity for obstruction and resistance was never completely overcome. As we shall see in Chapter 4, the theoretical revolution in government did not become fully actual at the local level. Nonetheless, certain important political changes did follow in the wake of the reforms. In the first place, some areas of decision-making were shifted to higher levels in the bureaucracy. Local notables could no longer rely on their ability to deal with officials who were detached from the bureaucratic chain but had to negotiate with officials who were firmly linked to Madras city. Naturally, they had to redirect their efforts to influencing their new masters' home base. Secondly, and of much greater importance in

[134] See below pp. 152–9.
[135] G.O. 1435 (Revenue) dated 17 June 1920. *T.N.A.*

58

the short term, the career structure in which bureaucrats themselves worked was drastically altered. For all those social groups interested in careers in government service, the Secretariat rather than the *huzur sheristidar's* verandah became the centre around which they had to turn. This meant that the career structure of the civil service was put on a provincial basis and that men from every district had to compete against each other for jobs. It greatly broadened the field of conflict for places in the government and provoked wider patterns of alliance and opposition than could have been seen in the 'office cliques' of old. Interestingly, however, the political techniques used to influence the nodes of the appointments system did not change for the principles of appointment themselves had not changed. In spite of the hard facade of efficiency which it now put to the world, the Madras Government did not replace appointment by personal discretion and favouritism with appointment by impersonal ability. During the years of the Statutory Civil Service (1883–93), for example, it consistently preferred candidates who had done poorly in the civil service examination to candidates who had done well.[136] Equally, after 1912 it happily ignored the results of its 'competitive' revenue inspector examination; between 1912 and 1917, $87\frac{1}{2}$ per cent of the men appointed as revenue inspector had not even sat the papers.[137] Fort St George's liking for 'the old ways' left the centre of the appointments industry wide open for anybody who captured it to use as he pleased. With control of jobs across the whole province rather than one district at stake, by 1916 the fighting around the centre had become bitter indeed.

A third set of reforms which drew native society towards Fort St George was that which concerned the 'Indianisation' of the policy- and decision-making centre. As we have hinted before, the Madras Government was always chronically short of the resources necessary to complete its task. Not the least of these shortages was that of British manpower; it never had sufficient 'trusted' imperial officials to go around. As the centre of the administration expanded and the number of Britons willing to undertake a career in the Indian civil service actually declined, it was inevitable that Indian subjects should move

---

[136] 'The plan is quite unintelligible, it is based neither upon the principle of competition nor upon the old system of personal favouritism. If the appointment is to be made according to the results of the competition, the candidate that stood first in the examination should get it; or if it is ultimately to rest upon the favour of someone in the Secretariat Council, there was no honest purpose that the competitive examination was intended to serve.' *Hindu* 30 January 1885.

[137] Proceedings of the Board of Revenue No. 113 (Confidential) dated 23 October 1917. *T.N.A.*

to positions higher and higher in the bureaucratic machine. As early as the 1860s, Madras civilians had found themselves confronted with the (for them) terrible prospect of an Indian who was a full member of the I.C.S.[138] By 1890, the percolation of Indians into the higher grades of service, both through the I.C.S. and the Statutory Civil Service, had produced its first native Collector.[139] Over the next thirty years, Indian bureaucrats reached towards the heart of government and took over dominant posts in Madras city. In 1914, L. D. Swammikannu Pillai became Director-General of Registration; in 1915 R. Ramachandra Rao became a full departmental secretary; in 1918 Mahommed Bazlullah was appointed to the Board of Revenue. A similar process was taking place in the judicial administration. The first Indian High Court Judge was appointed in 1880 and by 1920 approximately half of the senior bench was composed of natives. The Attorney-Generalship, Solicitor-Generalship and Provincial Public Prosecutorship were all in Indian hands by the 1890s.

The lack of British alternatives, however, was not the only reason for this development. Secretaries-of-State and the Government of India, although not Fort St George, were acutely aware of the need to temper the advance of their administration with political concessions to their subjects. They were sensitive to the dangers both of rebellion and mistake which could follow from driving forward policies without the advice and consent of some of the people who were affected by them. From 1861, the provinces had possessed Legislative Councils on which natives sat, but in 1892 these were widened and provided with an elected element. In 1909 they were enlarged yet again and in 1920 their elected members become a majority. London and Calcutta, however, were not satisfied to leave natives only in advisory roles. From the time of Ripon and Dufferin, with occasional pauses, they pushed the provinces into providing natives with senior executive appointments in the government itself. In the 1880s, the idea for an Indian Statutory Civil Service, parallel to the I.C.S. proper, came from the Government of India;[140] in 1909, Lord Morley insisted that a native be appointed to every Governor's Executive Council and given control of a number of departmental portfolios;[141] in 1920, Edwin Montagu turned more than half of every provincial government over to Indian ministers.[142] Just as Fort St George was coming

[138] Pulicat Ratnavelu Chetty.
[139] Madhavan Raja, who was a member of the family of the Zamorin of Calicut.
[140] See Seal, *Emergence of Indian Nationalism*, pp. 117–19.
[141] Home Public A October 1908 Nos 116–46; Home Public A February 1909, Nos 205–44. *N.A.I.*
[142] *Report on Indian Constitutional Reform. P.P.* 1918, vol. VIII.

to take control of its presidency, so that control was coming to be exercised more and more by men who were indigenous to the presidency. By the 1910s, the classic colonial model of imperial master and native subject was rapidly losing its appropriateness in the context of the Madras state system. Indians were involved actively as well as passively in the highest processes of government.

The fourth strand of administrative reform which was being spun during this period also served to increase the scope of political power available to Indians. This time, however, the area of its operation was not the province as a unit but a series of localities. The task which Fort St George had been set of raising more money naturally took it to considering ways of developing the resources of the country and of limiting the impact of famine and disease. Ideally it could simply bump up taxation and order its bureaucracy to execute its orders. But such an option was never available to it. It could not afford to enlarge its bureaucracy sufficiently to undertake a whole new set of duties which would include everything from clearing prickly pear to planning railway lines. Moreover, an attempt to raise the huge sums necessary for development by methods of direct taxation would have led, as it was finding with other forms of direct taxation, to a further deterioration of its political position. The economic and human conditions of Madras could not be improved by an administrative change. Luckily, however, it was not necessary that they should be. While in the other fields of reform which we have examined, Fort St George had to exercise a greater personal control over the making and enforcement of policy, in the matter of local government it was not so restricted. As long as somebody could be persuaded that his interests lay in improving the transport systems, sanitation, water resources, educational facilities and general living standards of the locality it did not have to be government itself; although, of course, government would have to remain in a position from which it could see that these ends were being accomplished.

Since the 1840s, Fort St George had possessed some administrative institutions for the maintenance of roads in the countryside and defence against major health hazards in the towns but, following Lord Ripon's local government initiative in 1882, these were expanded out of all recognition.[143] Under the Madras District Municipalities and District Boards Acts of 1884–5, the foundations of a new administrative system was laid. In most large conurbations, municipal councils were formed to allow local non-officials to come together with officials and participate in local government. Similarly, out-

[143] *Report of the Committee on Local Self-Government in Madras. 1882.*

side the towns, a system of district boards was devised to bring important local notables into institutions of formal administration. Slowly – in some cases painfully slowly – the bureaucracy was withdrawn from these councils and boards and its place taken by electorates and elected executive officers. The result was to leave behind a series of crucially important political institutions, with considerable powers of taxation and enormous powers of administrative interference, which spanned large areas of Madras and in which control, for good or evil, could be achieved by manipulating the machinery of primitive democracy.[144]

In other fields of government also Fort St George was forced, by financial pressure or political expediency, to transfer aspects of its administration to committees of local notables. Between the 1890s and the 1920s, local committees to enforce forest conservation, to control the siting and size of liquor shops, to hear appeals against the income-tax, to select policemen, to settle communal disputes and to control the distribution of water from irrigation schemes were set up in many areas. According to the Royal Commission on Agriculture in India (1928), Fort St George relied far more on the help of *panchayats* to run its administration than did any other provincial government.[145]

Technically, this handing-over of government powers to councils, boards and committees was termed the decentralisation of the administration because the centralised bureaucracy no longer played a part in it. Politically, however, its effects were the reverse of decentralisation. Whatever the theoreticians of British rule might have thought, the bureaucracy proper had never been able to establish its control over much of the administration which was being transferred to the new institutions. Even where government officials had possessed some influence, as over urban sanitation or forest laws, they had had to exercise it through the local notables to whom they were connected and on whose power they rested. The networks which these notables operated tended to be very small and personal and, consequently, the arenas in which these powers had been exercised were highly restricted. What happened when the government had finished its institution-building, however, was that the powers passed to a common district or town centre, decisions in which affected a much broader hinterland. The fragmented, personal empires of the local notables became welded together at the point where they all jostled for power on the same district board, municipal council or *taluk* committee. The locality of their operations had to be extended. Moreover, their empires began to be pulled out even farther to touch Fort St

---

[144] See below pp. 166–73.
[145] *Royal Commission on Agriculture in India* (H.M.S.O., 1928), XIV, 256–8.

George. When important political decisions were made at the level of village and neighbourhood by notables who could count on their local officials to protect them from the capital, the central influence of government was minimal. Fort St George could not see what was happening. When these same decisions were made in large-scale institutions which the Secretariat itself had designed, however, the opportunity for central influence to make itself felt obviously was much greater. Fort St George wrote the rules by which politics in the new institutions were played. As we shall see, it came to bear down heavily on the life and times of many important local notables.

3

The political economy of Madras

In our discussion of the nature and organisation of government in Madras, we have noted the enormous reliance of the bureaucracy on local notables. Lacking an effective coercive arm in the locality, Fort St George's rule rested on the empires of control and authority operated independently of it by some of its subjects. In this chapter, we shall be concerned to probe the character of these empires; our purpose will be to discover who ran them, how they were run and how their internal structure and external relations were changing over time. Clearly, such an undertaking is fraught with difficulty for we are asking no less than why did some South Indians obey others. A complete answer, if it were possible, would have to follow Aristotle and travel from the household to the nation and from the family to the culture and beyond. Such an answer could have no end. Nor, more importantly, could it have a beginning. Some social relationship would have to be examined first and hypothesised as the base on which the other relationships are seen to act. If a base itself were not defined, the relationships could then be seen only as reacting to each other without priority and no specific point about them could be explained. Indeed explanation would have to give way to description alone. Yet to choose a base, be it religious culture or economics, is to make an assumption about behaviour which can never be tested but which determines the whole answer. Abstract arguments about why Indian society operates in the way that it does by their nature cannot be satisfactory.

The answers which we may offer to the question of obedience, however, are not conceived in the abstract but generated by a concrete historical problem. We are looking for the men who could exercise a sufficient measure of control over the behaviour of others to support the tasks of government. Control, while it may be exercised through the medium of persuasion or informal influence, is most readily observable and most secure only when it is backed up by sanctions. Our first task, then, becomes an investigation of the types of sanctions available in non-official South Indian society. Given that some sanctions can be demonstrated to have been more powerful and to have been used more regularly than others, we at least have the possibility of finding objectively a set of relationships which can be seen to be primary and with which other sets of relationships (other sanctions) may be said to interact. Of course, this model of sanctions will help us to see only the mechanics of social control, not the reasons why men may have wanted to control others. It will be purely instrumentalist in approach. Of course, also, it will slant the interpretation of social structure its own way. South India could look very different if analysed to answer a different set of questions. The virtue of the model lies only in its ability to provide answers to the specific problems of government at this time.

The economic foundations of political organisation

The society of Madras was, by any standard, one of extreme poverty. Its economic problems concerned questions not only of relative affluence but also of starvation. In looking for systems of control in political life, the systems of production and distribution must be taken as primary for when they collapsed, as for example during a long period of famine, they took with them most of the political order. Servants commandeered the property of their masters;[1] markets were looted and moneylenders murdered;[2] ancient factional and caste rivalries, which had been suppressed for decades, flared up in open warfare;[3] religious antagonisms, which had been expressed in symbolic rivalries, provided the ignition point for riots;[4] the crime rate rose and outbreaks of banditry became common.[5] Many of the social relationships, the inferiorities and superiorities, which could be seen in times of normality were overturned once grain pits became empty and money worthless. Famines provided the occasions for the most serious challenges to the stability of the Madras state. During the shortages of 1918, most of the markets in Madras city were looted, one quarter of the town was burnt down and the government had to call

---

[1] *Fourteenth Annual Report of the Sanitary Commissioner for Madras. 1877* (Madras, 1878), p. 10.
[2] As after the poor harvests of 1890–2, G.O. 57 (Judicial), dated 17 January 1890, G.O. 613 (Judicial) dated 25 May 1892. *T.N.A.*; and of 1918, Home Police B June 1918, Nos 158 and 241–2; Home Police B September 1918, Nos 274–83. *N.A.I.*
[3] As between Komatis and Koyas, *Madras Police 1896*, p. 4; and Maravars and Nadars, *ibid., 1918*.
[4] As between Hindus and Muslims in Nellore, *Hindu* 18 October 1893; and in Cuddapah, G.O. 1538 (Judicial) dated 1 July 1918. *T.N.A.*
[5] See *Madras Police 1877*.

out troops to deal with disturbances in the *mofussil* no fewer than five times.[6] By contrast, in 1920, in spite of Gandhi's non-co-operation campaign, troops were not required at all.[7] Given the devastating political consequences of economic breakdown, the best way in which we can begin to analyse the socio-political structure of the presidency is by examining the bases of economic organisation.

Agrarian society

The economy of Madras was dominated by the land. More than three-quarters of the province's population followed directly agrarian occupations, while most of the rest were involved in the administration of the land or the commerce and manufacture of its products. The government drew most of its wealth from the countryside and, if it were to rule at all, it had to accommodate itself to the organisations of rural society. Let us start our examination of economic relations, therefore, by looking at the conditions of agrarian production.

Unfortunately, our knowledge of the economic history of South India under Company *raj* is extremely fragmentary: we possess few systematic economic surveys from this period and have to rely largely on the random comments of administrators. It seems likely, however, that the economy was subject to severe pressure during the whole of this epoch. Government revenue assessments were pitched more or less at the monetary levels which they had attained during the wars of the eighteenth century. Yet, with the coming of peace, grain prices were falling dramatically.[8] The effective demand of the state on the surplus of the village was thus very high and, as N. Mukherjee has shown, the economy stagnated.[9] Moreover, famines savaged the province with monotonous regularity.[10] Between the late 1850s and 1876, however, there is evidence of an improvement in agrarian conditions. Grain prices began to rise slowly, government revenue demands were progressively lightened, road transport facilities were improved, large irrigation works completed, new cash crops introduced and cultivation extended.[11] But famine remained a frequent visitor and its arrival in the central area of 'dry' cultivation in 1876 terminated this brief interlude of progress. By the most conservative

[6] G.O. 2303 (Judicial) dated 11 October 1918; G.O. 444 (Public) dated 12 July 1921. *T.N.A.*

[7] G.O. 444 (Public) dated 12 July 1921. *T.N.A.*

[8] Kumar, *Land and Caste in South India* p. 91.

[9] Mukherjee, *The Ryotwari System in Madras*, pp. 253–313.

[10] *Ibid.*, pp. 314–53.

[11] Kumar, *Land and Caste in South India*, pp. 115–16, 118–19.

estimate, $3\frac{1}{2}$ million people died of starvation between 1876 and 1878 and the cultivated area in several districts was driven back by twenty years.[12]

The years between 1880 and 1920, on which this book concentrates, fit into the period of recovery and slow growth which the agrarian economy enjoyed between the end of the great famine and the beginning of the depression. Many of the strands of development which had emerged in the 1860s and 1870s were picked up again and drawn out much further than before. Although the threat of scarcity never disappeared, and brief famines broke out in 1896 and 1918, there was no sudden devastation on the scale of 1876–8. Nor was there any sign of a serious rise in the human pressure on economic resources. Between 1884–5 and 1921, the population increased by about 32 per cent and the productive area grew by almost the same amount.[13] Certainly, some of this new land brought under the plough may have been of marginal utility but changes in irrigation, crop patterns and crop prices very much more than compensated for it. Although there were no new projects to match the Kistna–Godavari irrigation works of the 1850s, the area of wet land under *ryotwari* tenure (the only form of tenure for which accurate statistics are available) increased by 25 per cent.[14] On the basis of rough revenue accounts, wet land was expected to be at least five times as productive as dry. Improvements in the transportation system, particularly through the building of railways, linked the provinces more closely to national and international markets. Cash cropping in cotton, oil-seeds, tobacco and sugar developed more quickly than before and raised the profitability of agriculture. Cotton and oil-seeds were especially important because they flourished in soils capable of producing only the poorest quality grains. Between 1884–5 and 1920–1, the acreages under the two crops rose by 60 and 160 per cent respectively and came to cover 15–18 per cent of the entire cropped area.[15] Better transport facilities also freed food crops from local restrictions on sales and enabled them to find their best prices in larger markets. Between the 1880s and the late 1910s, the increase in dry grain prices averaged between 80 and 100

---

[12] *Land Revenue 1874–5* and *1879–80*; W. R. Cornish, 'The Influence of Famine on Growth of Population' in *Fifteenth Annual Report of the Sanitary Commissioner for Madras, 1878* (Madras, 1879), pp. lxv–xci.

[13] Calculated from Dharma Kumar's estimate of population in 1884–5, *Land and Caste in South India*, p. 116; *Census of India. 1921. Madras. Volume XIII. Part 2* (Madras, 1922), pp. 2–4; *Land Revenue 1884–5 and 1921–2*.

[14] Calculated from *Land Revenue 1885–6* and *1920–1*.

[15] 'Area under Crops' in *Agricultural Statistics of British India* (Calcutta, 1884–5 and 1920–1), Vol. I.

per cent, and in rice prices between 60 and 80 per cent.[16] As increases in the costs of manufactured and other non-agricultural commodities were much lower than this, the real wealth of rural producers must have increased. Moreover, the state was unable to take a large share of the new profits in land taxation; as we saw, the antique revenue system prevented it from raising its land revenue to keep pace with inflation.

Of course, the prosperity of the period was not shared evenly between the many geophysical regions which comprised the presidency. Different climates, soil types and transport facilities produced a great variety in the methods of production and in the commodities produced. Equally, an increase in the wealth of any one region did not mean the fair distributing of it among all the inhabitants. In order to obtain an accurate idea of the political implications of economic progress, it is necessary to examine the social and political structures which controlled the creation and disbursement of wealth. Naturally, these structures differed from region to region.

The dry zone. In the large central zone of dry cultivation (upland Kistna, Godavari, Guntur and Nellore districts, the Ceded Districts and hinterland Tamilnad), the most distinctive feature of agrarian society was the economic dependence of the mass of the rural population on a tiny elite of rich peasants. Brian Murton, in a recent article on Salem and Coimbatore districts, has pointed to the fundamental role in agrarian decision-making, which a few wealthy villagers possessed at the time of the British conquest.[17] Although we lack a detailed study of rural society between the conquest and the later nineteenth century, there can be little doubt from the evidence available for the period of our concentration that no major structural change had been wrought in the intervening years. In general, the agrarian society of the 'dry' zone was as stratified in 1900 as it had been in 1800; and, in some ways, the stratification was even more clearly defined.

According to various censuses of the time, the proportion of the workforce classified officially as 'landless labourer' and reliant entirely on employment in the fields of others was from 10 to 20 per cent of the total.[18] Such landless labourers were seldom more than predial serfs who depended for their survival on the wages paid to them by

[16] 'Statement on Grain Prices' in *Land Revenue 1880–1* to *1915–16*.
[17] B. J. Murton, 'Key People in the Countryside: Decision Makers in Interior Tamilnad in the late eighteenth century' in *Indian Economic and Social History Review* x: 2 (1973).
[18] See *A Statistical Atlas of the Madras Presidency* (Madras, 1895, 1908 and 1924).

local landowners. The true number of economic dependents in the rural areas, however, was very much higher than even these figures imply. In 1900, under the *ryotwari* tenure which covered most of the dry zone, 70 per cent of all the *pattas* issued by government were for the payment of less than Rs 10 per annum in land revenue.[19] The average payment in *pattas* of this class was Rs 4 per annum. As many *pattas* represented the joint holdings of more than one *ryot*, the actual proportion of 'landowners' involved in this smallholding agriculture was about 85 per cent.[20] Few of these small cultivators could expect to subsist on the products of their land alone. In the 1890s, a senior government official estimated that eight acres of medium quality dry land were required to keep a family through a good agricultural season.[21] The payment of Rs 4 per annum in land revenue represented the ownership of only about four acres and, in the dry region, many seasons were bad.[22] In order to survive, the great majority of the landowning population needed extra resources, over and above those produced by its land.

These small cultivators also required a variety of facilities which they could not provide for themselves if they were to work their own lands. They needed water throughout the year in order to supplement the miserable rainfall; and they did not have the capital to dig their own wells.[23] In many areas, they needed heavy ploughing equipment to break up the soil; and again, they were unlikely to be able to afford it themselves.[24] As revenue demands fell heaviest immediately after the harvest, they needed a market near at hand; they did not have the cash-flow to meet their commitments while holding their crops for storage and transportation.[25] Perhaps most profoundly, however, they needed credit facilities. Regular, albeit minor, crop failures wiped out their long-term profits; the replacement of stock and seed necessitated the immediate spending of sums which it would take them years to save; and social conventions, such as dowries and wedding feasts, required of them occasional, lavish expenditure. In most cases,

[19] 'Statement of the Rent-Roll' in *Land Revenue 1900–1*.
[20] F. Nicholson, *RAB*, I, 232.
[21] S. Srinivasa Raghavaiyangar, *Memorandum on the Progress of the Madras Presidency During the Last Forty Years of British Administration* (Madras, 1892), p. 75.
[22] Srinivasa Raghavaiyangar's own statistics indicated that rather more than 75 per cent of Madras landholders held less than 5 acres. *Ibid.*
[23] *M.D.G. F. A. Nicholson and H. Stuart, Coimbatore* (Madras, 1898), pp. 191–93.
[24] C. H. Benson, *An Account of the Kurnool District based on an Analysis of Statistical Information Relating Thereto and on Personal Observation* (Madras, 1889), p. 65.
[25] *Reports of the Provincial Banking Enquiry Committees* (Calcutta, 1931), 'Madras', p. 106. Hereafter, this volume as *RPBC*.

petty *ryots* 'could not begin to cultivate without borrowing seed, cattle, grain for maintenance, etc.'[26]

In the dry economy, the provision of these vital services rested almost wholly with a small group of rich peasants. The theory of the *ryotwari* settlement, which stressed a rough equality of peasant land-ownership, had never become practice. In every district and every 'rural locality', there were families who paid the government upwards of Rs 50 per annum in land revenue and whose broad acres contrasted with the miserable plots of their neighbours. In 1900, the $7\frac{1}{2}$ per cent of *pattas* paying more than Rs 50 p.a. met 43 per cent of the total revenue demand; and the 1 per cent paying more than Rs 100 met 14 per cent.[27] The men who held these large *pattas* and possessed landed resources twelve or more times greater than the average, stood at the centre of the agrarian economy. They supplemented employment by letting out lands on unprotected tenancies: in the villages of Bellary district, which were investigated by the Cotton Commission(1925–8), as many as 35 per cent of the local landholders were also the tenants of other landholders.[28] They also hired labourers. *Ryots* with a considerable surplus had the capital to sink wells and to buy heavy ploughs, which they made available to small cultivators.[29] At the harvest, they bought much of the village produce on the spot and put it into large storage pits.[30] Above all, they had the cash and grain to pump into village credit in order to keep the economy turning over. In 1895, F. A. Nicholson estimated that wealthy peasants were responsible for at least 90 per cent of rural loans and pointed out that *ryots* held more than 75 per cent of even written mortgages.[31] Forty years later, the Banking Enquiry's investigations indicated that there had been no basic change.[32] The Cotton Commission's examinations also supported Nicholson's findings. Even on a cash crop like cotton in the immediate vicinity of Adoni, the largest cotton-buying town in the Ceded Districts, landlords were responsible for the majority of loans to cultivators.[33]

By providing these facilities for the continuation of agricultural production, richer peasants gained a large measure of control over

---

[26] Nicholson, *RAB*, I, 232.

[27] 'Statement of the Rent-Roll' in *Land Revenue 1900–1*.

[28] *Indian Central Cotton Commission. General Report on Eight Investigations into the Finance and Marketing of Cultivators' Cotton. 1925–8* (Bombay, n.d.), p. 50.

[29] Benson, *Account of the Kurnool District*, p. 65.

[30] *RPBC*, p. 106; *MPBC*, III, 658, 946; 'Report on Kurnool' in *Land Revenue 1902–3*.

[31] Nicholson, *RAB*, I, 230.

[32] *RPBC*, pp. 30, 79.

[33] For 56 per cent. Only 27.3 per cent of the loans came directly from urban sources. *Indian Central Cotton Commission*, pp. 14–16.

the economy of their localities. Their dominance was particularly tight because their own numbers were so small and because they faced few rivals from outside offering similar services in the village. As we saw, only $7\frac{1}{2}$ per cent of *pattadars* paid more than Rs 50 per annum. To make the point again but more concretely, we may take the evidence of a witness before the Banking Enquiry. In his opinion, only *ryots* who held a minimum of twenty acres of dry land were in a position to market their own crops and to preserve some economic independence.[34] This was presumably good quality dry land, paying, say, Rs 1.5 per annum per acre in land revenue (against the average of Rs 1.18). If independence were possible at or above the level of Rs 30 p.a. in land revenue, then only between 5 and 10 per cent of the landholders of each dry district were independent. Further, the number of *ryots* who were large enough to go beyond mere self-preservation and actively into rural moneylending and crop-buying must have been even smaller still. Allowing for the fact that only about 70 per cent of the rural workforce could be classified as a landholder at all, the rich peasants were probably no more than 2–3 per cent of the working population. In any village, clients seeking the facilities which they offered did not have many patrons to choose between.

Moreover, non-village-based credit and trading groups had failed to penetrate the dry regional economy and to mount a challenge to the rich peasant's village hegemony. This failure was caused by several factors. In the first place, there was no high volume of trade to sustain specialist mercantile groups. The precariousness of agriculture and of prices in international markets inhibited crop specialisation.[35] Most villages harvested a variety of produce – grains and vegetables as well as cotton and oil-seed. Most trade was localised between small circles of adjacent villages and only a fraction of the produce of any one 'rural locality' was ever exported.[36] Similarly, the demand for commodities from the outside was limited to a few luxury goods and cattle.[37] With so little scope for the development of broad trading relations between the village and larger marketing structures, there was little room in the village for the specialised merchant. In the immediate vicinity of big towns, of course, urban merchants, seeking supplies for their shops, might establish some more permanent village connection.[38] But beyond this, the most usual relationship which

---

[34] *MPBC*, II, 298.   [35] *RPBC*, p. 14.

[36] *Ibid.*, p. 107; *Royal Commission on Agriculture in India*, XIV, 270.

[37] Benson, *Account of the Kurnool District*, pp. 15–16, 90.

[38] Such as the Nadar merchants around the Tinnevelly–Ramnad cotton towns, the Komati merchants around the centres of trade in the Ceded Districts, the Devanga merchants around the Salem and Coimbatore towns and the Vannigas around urban North Arcot.

mercantile groups had with the countryside was only through the carts which they sent out at harvest time to pick up the loose fraction of the crop. In a basically subsistence economy, they were too far removed from the sources of production to exercise any considerable influence.

Secondly, although important merchant and moneylending communities were attracted to those towns and railheads which were expanding under the cotton and later oil-seed trades, the presidency's failure to develop impersonal systems of credit prevented them from pursuing these cash crops far into the hinterland. The poverty of the soil in all but a few *taluks*, the *ryotwari* revenue system (under which the state always had first call on the produce of the land), the joint family property system and the delays of between three and five years in effecting litigation combined to make land unviable as a form of security.[39] Few moneylenders would risk their moneys in loans to people whom they did not know to be creditworthy or to have assets more readily realisable than land. Obviously, few cultivators were likely to be known as creditworthy, or at all, outside their immediate circle of villages or to have assets other than land. Mercantile groups working out of towns with their own resources of credit, therefore, tended to approach rural localities through the larger landholders whose existing capital and likely surpluses made them good risks.[40] In this way, although they can be seen to reach the village in some areas, they were doing so only through the rich peasant who was established there already. Their influence ran horizontal to and helped to increase his own; it did not lead to the development of a parallel and rival system of primary economic control in the countryside.

Without serious competition, the rich peasant could charge heavily for his services. His tenants were unprotected and their rent was invariably high and taken in kind.[41] His labourers' wages, though difficult to calculate in money terms, were never seen by contemporaries as higher than subsistence level.[42] When he bought in the harvest market, the temporary glut of produce guaranteed that he did so at rock-bottom prices.[43] When he lent grain and money, he obtained extortionate interest rates and could often force on the debtor an option to buy his whole harvest at a prearranged, low price.[44] In effect,

---

[39] *RPBC*, pp. 78–81, 173–82.   [40] *Ibid*, pp. 87–9.

[41] Customarily, between a half and two-thirds of the gross produce.

[42] *Fourteenth Annual Report of the Sanitary Commissioner for Madras. 1877* (Madras, 1878), pp. 7–9.   [43] *RPBC*, p. 106.

[44] Nicholson, *RAB*, I, 232; *RPBC*, pp. 79, 106; Benson, *Account of the Kurnool District*, p. 116.

individual rich peasants operated networks which ran through the village economy and held large numbers of their neighbours in a variety of conditions from simple client to debt-bonded serf.[45] Often, in a single lifetime, a villager would pass from the higher links in this chain, where he had some freedom to manoeuvre, to the lower, where he had none at all:

The Sahukar charges his own rates of interest as the ryot can no longer bargain with him: what is worse the ryot has next to plough the lender's field gratis and to do any other work at his bidding. The younger members of the family, the sons and brothers, are sometimes engaged as the private servants of the Sahukar without payment and in partial payment of the amount borrowed.[46]

Through his network, the rich peasant came to dominate the poor, disorganised producers of his village and to enjoy the fruits of many more fields than those nominally his own.

The nature of agrarian organisation in the dry zone raises several serious terminological problems. According to Eric Wolf's classic definition, one of the basic conditions of a peasant economy is that economic decisions are made by and in the interests of separate family-households of small cultivators.[47] From what we have seen of the dry region, this condition may well have been absent during the nineteenth and the early part of the twentieth centuries. Through a variety of 'informal' economic relationships, the large resident landholder, with a considerable surplus above his own subsistence needs, had at his disposal means which he could use to direct the agricultural production of most of his poorer neighbours. His will could determine the economic decisions made by many separate family-households. Whether or not he did make use of the powers available to him, of course, is another matter and can be settled satisfactorily only by further research using materials more local than those presented here. Yet a number of contemporary commentators were convinced that he was operating in this fashion. Sir Frederick Nicholson, for example, noted how small landholders, deeply sunk in debt, 'are thus in the worst cases little more than tenants of the lender who prescribes what crops they shall grow and demands what terms he pleases'.[48]

[45] 'Under each rich ryot there will be a set of ordinary ryots who depend on him for money. When once a ryot goes to a particular rich ryot for money then a convention is established that the poor ryot is the client of the rich ryot.' *MPBC*, III, 664.

[46] *Ibid.*, p. 699. See also *Report on the Famine in the Madras Presidency during 1896 and 1897* (Madras, 1898), I, 50.

[47] E. Wolf, *Peasants* (Englewood Cliffs, 1966), p. 14.

[48] Nicholson, *RAB*, I, 232; also, Benson, *Account of the Kurnool District*, p. 116.

Certain paradoxes in the performance of the dry economy at this time also support the case.

In a recent dissertation, Michelle McAlpin has shown that between 1860 and 1900, there was no significant correlation between the annual price and the annual acreage of cotton in many districts of Bombay and the U.P.[49] Her explanation of this fact is that peasant cultivators regarded their first priority as the building-up of a grain store to keep them through a bad season and that only when they had sufficient grain would they consider planting cotton. The price and the acreage of cotton at any one time were thus but distantly related. McAlpin's only analysis of a Madras district, however, revealed a unique case of some correlation. Working on the statistics of cotton price to acreage in Madras for a somewhat later period (1900 to 1940), Dharm Narain also has noted the exceptional tightness of their relationship. Indeed: 'The overall fit of the two curves, plotted to scale so chosen that their amplitudes of fluctuation about agree, is in fact so close that the price factor alone would seem to account for most of the change in area.'[50] As our period lies across those of McAlpin and Narain, Table 1 represents an attempt to calculate the coefficient of correlation between changes in cotton price and cotton acreage, and Figure 1 an attempt to plot their relationship in the districts of Bellary, Coimbatore and Tinnevelly during the years 1884 to

Table 1

Partial correlation coefficients (zero order partials).

Bellary		Coimbatore		Tinnevelly	
1	2	1	2	1	2
1. 1.0000	0.6937	1. 1.0000	0.5794	1. 1.0000	0.4465
S=0.001	S=0.001	S=0.001	S=0.001	S=0.001	S=0.007
2. 0.6937	1.000	2. 0.5794	1.000	2. 0.4465	1.000
S=0.001	S=0.001	S=0.001	S=0.001	S=0.007	S=0.001

(A value of 99.0000 is written if a coefficient cannot be computed)
Columns 1 = percentage of acreage under cotton.
Columns 2 = price of cotton.

[49] M. B. McAlpin, 'The Impact of Railroads on Agriculture in India: A Case Study of Cotton', unpublished Ph.D. dissertation, University of Wisconsin, 1973.
[50] D. Narain, *Impact of Price Movements on Areas under Selected Crops in India. 1900–1939* (Cambridge, 1965), p. 40.

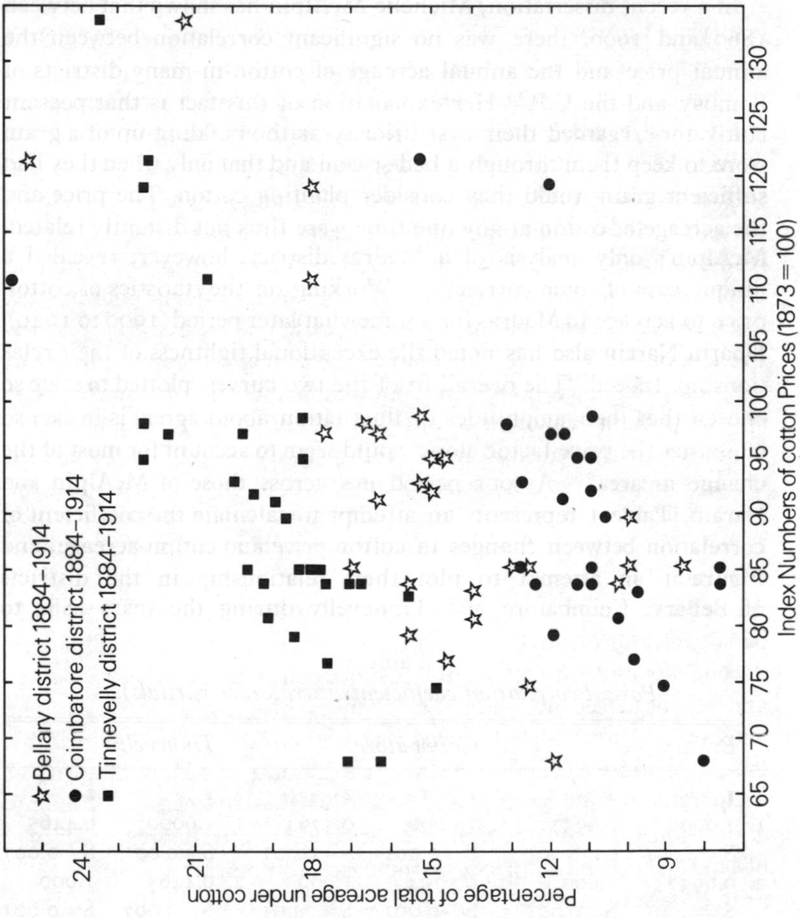

Figure 1: Scatter diagram of relationship of price to cotton acreage in selected districts 1884–1914

Legend:
- ☆ Bellary district 1884–1914
- ● Coimbatore district 1884–1914
- ■ Tinnevelly district 1884–1914

Y-axis: Percentage of total acreage under cotton

X-axis: Index Numbers of cotton Prices (1873 = 100)

1914.[51] As can be seen, the correlation is very high and the elasticity of acreage under the influence of price quite remarkable. As with Narain's statistics, they 'begin by enlarging the hope, and end up in justifying the reflection, that price bears in an usually large degree on the variations of Madras cotton area'.[52]

This correlation cannot be accounted for simply by removing the grain storage model from agrarian operations. The cotton districts of Madras were at least as, if not more, likely to suffer from bad seasons as those of Bombay and the U.P. Landholders grew grain on most of their land and many tried to keep three or four years' supply ready to hand.[53] The occasional, sudden drops in cotton production, displayed in the figure, mark years of recovery after a poor harvest when stocks of grain had to be replenished. The greater price responsiveness of Madras can be explained, however, if the implications of the non-peasant economy are followed up. Obviously, in localities of true peasant economic conditions, where virtually all cultivating families participated in deciding the quantity of grain to be stored, the interests of virtually every family would be represented in the store. The amount of land kept under grain would then have to be sufficiently large to feed everybody through a bad season. But in conditions in which the large landholder made decisions for his dependents, the interests of every cultivating family were unlikely to be so well represented. The claims of some of the large landholder's dependents undoubtedly would be more marginal than those of others and all his decisions would be taken in his general interests. The amount of land which he was prepared to allocate to grain in his locality could well ignore the needs in famine of a large minority of the population and hence could be smaller than in a peasant economy. A decision made in this light would free a relatively greater acreage of land to respond to prices in the cash crop market.

If this were how economic decisions were made in the dry zone, it would also go a long way to explaining the terrible devastation of the Great Famine. After a series of fairly good years, between 20 and 25 per cent of the population of the Ceded Districts was wiped out by the failure of just two seasons' crops.[54] This savage loss of life cannot

---

[51] Calculated from 'Area under Crops' in *Agricultural Statistics of British India* (Calcutta, 1884–5 and 1914–15) and *Index Numbers of Indian Prices 1861–1918* (Calcutta, 1919). The price of cotton in the year previous to the cotton harvest was used to determine the correlation.

[52] Narain, *Impact of Price Movements*, p. 42.

[53] Cornish, 'The Influence of Famine on Population Growth' in *Fifteenth Annual Report of the Sanitary Commissioner for Madras, 1878*, p. lxxi.

[54] *Ibid.*, pp. lxviii–xci.

be attributed to some supposed surplus of people over production needs, which had built up in the area over previous decades and was waiting for a calamity to burn it off. The acreage under cultivation and the yield of land revenue (indices of productive capacity) also fell by between 20 and 25 per cent.[55] The only way that it is possible to reconcile this startling human catastrophe with what we know of economic organisation is to suppose either that the peasant cultivators of these districts were extraordinarily indigent and careless of the threat of famine under which they lived; or, more reasonably, that they were not peasant cultivators at all but dependents and workers of a small rural elite which treated some of them as expendable.

If we accept the likely hypothesis of the dominant decision-making role of the larger landholder in dry Madras, we must also abandon the terminology of the peasant economy. In the rest of this book, the rich peasant of the dry districts will be termed the 'rural-local boss' – a vague term but one which the complexity of its subject demands. Poorer peasants will be known as 'agrarian dependents'.

Between 1880 and the late 1920s, the rise in grain prices and in the demand for cash crops served greatly to increase the profitability and the scope of the rural-local boss' empire. Having obtained cheap grain from his estates and debtors and in the harvest market, he possessed the capital resources to play the roulette wheel of price fluctuation with success. Although improvements in transport were levelling out seasonal and local price fluctuations, they had by no means eradicated them. Even in a good year, such as 1892–3, grain prices differed from month to month by as much as 30 per cent;[56] the annual average of prices paid in bazaars in adjacent *taluks* could differ by more than 15 per cent.[57] By storing and moving grain, the rural-local boss took full advantage of these market distortions.[58] He was also in a position to increase the value of his cash crops. The best prices for cotton and groundnut were obtained only by those sellers who processed the raw produce, carried it to the main railheads and drove a hard bargain with the *dallals*, through whom the purchasing companies worked and

---

[55] Calculated from *Land Revenue 1874–5* and *1880–1*.

[56] G.O. 581 (Revenue) dated 9 August 1894. *T.N.A.*

[57] *M.D.G.* K. N. Krishnaswami Ayyar, *Statistical Appendix. Together With a Supplement, to the District Gazetteer (1917) for Tinnevelly District* (Madras, 1934), pp. 106–8.

[58] For the role of the Reddi (peasant) caste in the grain trade of the Ceded Districts, see *Appendix to the Report of the Indian Famine Commission, 1898, being Minutes of Evidence, etc. Volume II. Madras Presidency*, p. 101. P.P. 1899, Vol. XXXII; *Report on the Famine in the Madras Presidency during 1896 and 1897* (Madras, 1898), I, 48; II, 139.

who combined to keep down prices.[59] Obviously, the agrarian dependent was too poor and too weak to manage these feats. His cash crops, if they were still his own at harvest time, were sold in the village or in the ground for a minimal return.[60] But the rural-local boss, with money for processing and carting and with the market power lent him by the tons of cotton or groundnut which he could bring to or withhold from the town auction block, was able to maximise his profits. Indeed, by the 1920s, some of the wealthiest *ryots* were investing in their own cotton presses and groundnut decorticating machines in their villages, and cutting out the *dallals* by selling directly to factories and Bombay city through their own agents.[61]

By gaining entry to the world of urban and inter-district commerce, the large landlord-moneylender-trader also derived a further range of benefits. Once he became known as 'creditworthy' in the towns, he could tap the relatively cheap supplies of urban credit to channel more resources through his village network and thereby deepen his local control.[62] Alternatively, he could diversify his operations out of simple village commerce and into more profitable ventures which he might see from his town perch. Rural-local bosses financed mica mining[63] and railway, military and civil contracting for the government[64] and aided the development of provincial banking facilities, particularly after the Cooperative Credit Act of 1904.[65] They were also behind the explosion of cotton mills in the Tinnevelly–Ramnad–Coimbatore cotton belts in the late 1920s.[66]

Our investigation of the mechanics of production and marketing,

---

[59] *RPBC*, pp. 112, 123; *Royal Commission on Agriculture in India*, XIV, 268.

[60] *Indian Central Cotton Commission*, p. 21.

[61] *RPBC*, pp. 108, 112, 123; *MPBC*, II, 36, 50–51, 62, 298–9; III; 319, 750, 966, 972.

[62] *RPBC*, pp. 87–9; *MPBC*, II, 62, 124, 210, 318, 593.

[63] See biography of K. Audinarayana Reddi in Reforms (Franchise) B, March 1921, Nos 34–99. *N.A.I.*

[64] For example, A. Dhanakoti Mudaliar, who came from a rich Palli landowning family in North Arcot, became one of the largest railway contractors in South India. By the 1880s, he was a member of the Madras city Corporation. Also see biography of M. Venka.araghavulu Reddiar in *Hindu* 19 May 1919.

[65] See biographical notes on G. Eswara Reddi (p. 751), C. S. Ratnasabhapati Mudaliar (p. 609) in V. L. Sastri (ed.), *Encyclopaedia of the Madras Presidency and the Adjacent States* (Cocanada, 1920); also on P. S. Kumaraswami Raja (p. 144), V. K. Palaniswami Gounder (p. 196) and K. A. Nachiappa Gounder (p. 176) in *Directory of the Madras Legislature* (Madras, 1938).

[66] For example, the family of A. K. D. Dharma Raja in Ramnad district and of V. C. Vellingiri Gounder in Coimbatore district. See A. K. D. Venkata Raja, *A Brief Life Sketch of P. S. Kumaraswami Raja* (Rajapalaiyam, 1964); N. Perumal, *Talented Tamils* (Madras, 1957), p. 82.

therefore, strongly suggests that the rise in grain prices and the development of cash-cropping led to the increasing stratification of rural society in the dry zone. Large landholders were able to take advantage of the new market situation in ways denied to their poorer neighbours and, indeed, to reap the profits from many of these neighbours' cultivation. But against what statistical evidence can we test these findings? Of course, it is by now a cliche that Indian economic statistics of this period are notoriously unreliable. Indeed, it is for the reason of their difficulty that this chapter has thus far largely proceeded by deducing behaviour from a model derived from the written evidence of contemporaries. Nonetheless, the statistics do exist and unless an argument can square them with its conclusions, or at least explain why they cannot be squared, it cannot be a satisfactory contribution to economic history. The statistics of agrarian activity in the Madras Presidency are among the least useful of all those taken by provincial governments – they contain no data on actual landholding or tenancy, only on revenue payment, and have few categories of commercial information. By examining them carefully, however, we may see that even they would lend some support to our findings.

Changes in the ownership of land would only begin to give us an accurate gauge of the movement of wealth if individuals tended to express their economic progress in the accumulation of legal titles to land. Yet, with land usually worth no more than the crops and people on it (which the large landholder controlled already), with litigation difficult and with better ways available of using money than pursuing formal landed possessions, there was little incentive to demonstrate wealth in this way. It was important for the large landholder to continue to hold some land but less important for him that this was 300 rather than 200 acres in extent. The fact that the vast majority of rural loans were unsecured indicates that the constant acquisition of land did not motivate the vast majority of rural creditors.[67] Nonetheless, in the course of his transactions some land was bound to come the large landholder's way and such change as there was in landownership between 1886–7 and 1925–6 favoured the growth of the larger proprietor at the expense of the smaller. Of course, the number of wealthy landowners involved in commerce was so small that this development, in terms of the total landholding, may seem insignificant. In the period, the minute fraction of *pattas*

[67] In fact, legal land transfers were among the lowest in British India and seldom amounted to more than 1 to $1\frac{1}{2}$ per cent of the cropped area per annum. See 'Land Transfers' in *Agricultural Statistics of British India*, Vol. i.

paying more than Rs 250 per annum increased its share of revenue from 4.3 to 6.7 per cent of the total, or by about 50 per cent.[68] Yet in the context of Madras landholding this was important. The division of *pattas* between heirs, the growth in population and the extension of cultivation by carving small plots of land out of the jungle and obtaining *pattas* for them all had led to a reduction in the average size of *pattas*. Revenue per *patta* fell from Rs 14.9 to Rs 10.6 and acreage from 7.3 to 4.9.[69] That large *pattas* should not only hold themselves against this trend but actually move in the opposite direction indicates the growing wealth of the large landholder. Moreover, *patta* figures include only the lands held in one revenue village. They, therefore, conceal the total holdings of men with land in two or more revenue villages. As the large landholder, operating within a broader marketing and credit structure, was much more likely to have lands widely dispersed than the agrarian dependent, these statistics would tend to minimise his real landed possessions.

We also may turn to data on wages for a second support to our conclusions about the movement of rural wealth. As Morris D. Morris has shown, the figures of the agrarian wage censuses are much too fragile to build upon them grand theories.[70] As wages were composed of a multiplicity of gifts, moneys, foods and services and as the sampling techniques of the day were so defective, the official census of rural wages was highly inaccurate. Nonetheless, hardly any of the censuses taken in the dry zone indicated that wages were rising.[71] Moreover, from other sources, there are few grounds for us to believe that the level of wages in the dry zone did increase and some to suggest that it fell. The origins of any supposed increase in wages must have been the development of more labour intensive crops, such as cotton, and of migration possibilities which reduced labour supply, for human and land variables otherwise remained in remarkable equilibrium. However, although cotton was an important crop in this area, the acreage under it was never very large. The highest percentage of a district's land put under it was 25 per cent, during the 1917 cotton boom, and the average for most cotton-growing districts was seldom above 18 per cent.[72] Its influence on the overall use of labour, therefore, was limited. Moreover, the other major cash crop of the region, ground-

---

[68] Calculated from 'Statement of the Rent-Roll' in *Land Revenue 1885–6* and *1925–6*.

[69] *Ibid.*

[70] M. D. Morris, 'Economic Change and Agriculture in Nineteenth Century India' in *Indian Economic and Social History Review*, III: 2 (1966).

[71] Kumar, *Land and Caste in South India*, pp. 163–7.

[72] See Fig. 1.

nut, was labour extensive and the acreage under it came to surpass that under cotton.[73]

The question of migration can be divided into two parts – overseas movements and internal movements. Overseas migration reached significant proportions in Madras as a whole and must have cut back on the labour supply. Yet the bulk of migrants at this time came from the southern coastal districts of which only Tinnevelly and Ramnad were in the dry zone.[74] The effects on the southern fringes of Madras, therefore, are worth considering but, on the economy of the dry region as a whole, must have been strictly marginal. Internal migration also was of limited consequence. Except in the Tinnevelly–Ramnad cotton belt, there were very few towns[75] and those that there were did not grow fast. Between 1881 and 1921, the urban population of the presidency increased by only 55 per cent.[76] Most of this expansion was concentrated in the narrow Andhra deltas and Tinnevelly–Ramnad cotton belt and, again, although it may have influenced the fringes of the dry zone did not affect the region as a whole. Over most of the dry area, towns grew little faster than the total population. Migration between rural areas, which probably had been large in the pre- and early British periods, was noticeably small at the end of the nineteenth century: on the night of the 1881 census, the astonishing proportion of 95.6 per cent of the presidency's inhabitants were recorded as living in the districts in which they had been born.[77] Once more, the bulk of the mobile sector was to be found on the coastal fringes not in the dry heartland.

Although we must discard the wage censuses, other official evidence indicates that if wages were moving at all, they were moving downwards. Several district officials noted that rural employers increasingly were paying their labourers' grain wages at price-fixed rather than custom-fixed rates.[78] During a period of rising prices, this change could only be to the advantage of the employers.

In our present state of ignorance, exact statistical measurement of alterations in the distribution of wealth may well be impossible to make. However, there are good reasons for thinking that the economic inequalities which existed when the British arrived in Madras widened under their rule. Those who possessed large landholdings and an agrarian surplus were perfectly placed to take advantage of new

[73] 'Area under Crops' in *Agricultural Statistics of British India*, vol. I.
[74] Kumar, *Land and Caste in South India*, pp. 137–43.
[75] *Census of India. 1881. Madras. Volume IV* (Madras, 1883), p. 430.
[76] *Census of India. 1921. Madras. Volume XIII. Part 2* (Madras, 1922), pp. 8–12.
[77] *Census of India. 1881. Madras. Volume I* (Madras, 1883), p. 170.
[78] *Land Revenue 1908–9.* p. 74; *Land Revenue 1911–12*, p. 71.

marketing opportunities. But those without much land or surplus before the expansion of the market economy were able to derive little benefit from it: subject to the constant threat of famine and shortage, they remained poor and were drawn progressively into greater dependence on their rural-local bosses. The political implications of this economic situation are not difficult to see. The rural-local boss' control over many of the staples of life permitted him to exercise a pervasive social power. He could rely on his agrarian dependents to provide him with servants, retainers and an army for use in local political squabbles and 'all kinds of litigation'.[79] Their existence enabled him to commandeer many of the public resources of the rural economy, such as grazing rights and irrigation channels, which he could add *de facto* to his estate.[80] He thus brought further sections of the rural population under his shadow. Also, it was essentially his wealth, or the wealth which he controlled, which maintained many of the non-productive groups in village society: priests, musicians, barbers, temple-servants and festival functionaries ultimately were dependent for their livelihood on his largesse and sufferance.[81] The provision of this patronage gave him influence over the ceremonial and religious features of life in his locality. The central political position of the rural-local boss is obvious from two simple facts: firstly, it was to him that the vast majority of his neighbours brought their petty disputes for arbitration;[82] and secondly, it was often on, or in deference to, the rituals of his caste group that subordinate social groups modelled their own customs.[83]

In many ways, it was to maintain and extend this social control that the economic activities of the rural-local boss were aimed. Our emphasis on the economic mechanics of his empire ought not to be taken to mean that he was a crude creature of profit to whom the social dimensions of power were *adiaphora*. That would be to confuse our discussion of means with one of ends. There can be little doubt that the rural-local boss used his economic position as an instrument of his political power and made his decisions more on the grounds of the people who would be brought under his sway than of the rupees

[79] *MPBC*, III, 699.

[80] In the dry areas, *pettandar* rights of supervision over communal village resources were almost uniformly in the hands of the wealthiest 'cultivators' of each village. See *Report of the Forest Committee. 1913* (Madras, 1913), II, 164, 309, 400, 440–1, 555.

[81] That is to say he controlled a large part of the grain heap from which they lived.

[82] See *Report of the Forest Committee. 1913*, II, 148, 156.

[83] See, for example, F. A. Nicholson, *The Coimbatore Manual* (Madras, 1887), pp. 57–61.

he would be able to put in the bank. In the words of a contemporary: 'His power and prestige must at all costs be secured by having a large number of village people at his disposal. Considerations of his importance influence the advance of money rather than profit from usurious rates of interest.'[84] This commitment, to his role and status as a leader of men, naturally put limitations on the things which he could do. In famine times, for example, he could not sell off all his grain store even when prices reached absurdly high levels. If he emptied his grain pits, he destroyed the means as well as the visible sign of his power and was liable to be faced with a mutiny of his dependents.[85] Equally, he could not sacrifice his local involvements entirely to the lucrative commercial opportunities of the market towns without losing his social position. Richer though he might become, his grasp on the network which converted riches into social power would have weakened. Consequently, it is not surprising that it is not until the period of the depression (1930–3), when economic catastrophe had already smashed the network, that we find rural-local bosses switching their interests completely to the towns rather than using urban resources largely for the extension of their local businesses.[86] Economic considerations always were subordinate to and an instrument of political activity.

Nonetheless, the nature and shape of instruments greatly condition what can be done with them and changes in the organisation of the Madras 'dry' economy certainly altered the social and political relations which they served. The large landholder's wealth increased, separating him further from the poorer cultivators of his neighbourhood. In the context of the rural locality, his advance may scarcely seem worthy of notice: he had been dominant before 1800 and his position in 1900 was only marginally stronger. Yet in wider context, the greater development of the commercial economy was important for it changed his economic character. Unlike his agrarian dependents, he was no longer trapped in an economy bounded by the rural locality but was reaching out to district, national and international markets. He was in some senses a different economic being. Naturally,

---

[84] The quotation continues: ' ... Nevertheless, the lifelong dependence of the borrower upon the landlord and a variety of free services to be rendered to the latter during agricultural seasons are features closely associated with the system. It is not unusual that the smaller agriculturist borrowers are obliged to sell the produce to the apparently obliging landlord.' *MPBC*, III, 1034.

[85] *Fourteenth Annual Report of the Sanitary Commissioner for Madras, 1877* (Madras, 1878), p. 10.

[86] C. J. Baker, *The Politics of South India, 1920–1937* (Cambridge, 1976), ch. 3.

these economic changes also affected his social and political personality.

The rural-local bosses whom we have been examining were almost invariably participants of 'local-level' cultures, that is to say of cultures characterised by their extreme physical restriction. Typically, the rural-local boss belonged to a 'peasant' caste and was illiterate. The wives he married came from villages only a few miles from his own. Social interaction between members of the rural-local boss elite barely existed beyond the level of adjacent localities. Before the early twentieth century, of course, there had been little reason and few means for this interaction to take place. Once clans had settled an area, the processes of agricultural production and the lack of a major market economy had tended to take them apart.[87] Except for occasional gatherings for ritual purposes, their lineages had no need of each other. Moreover, subsequent political conquests of their territories, particularly by Vijayanagar warriors, did not alter this situation greatly. The warrior 'integrations,' of which Burton Stein has written,[88] seldom involved men from the local level. They were carried out in the locality much more by connection to or importation of social groups who shared the warriors' own 'state-level' culture. Although subjects within these larger integrations, rural-local bosses (or agrarian decision-makers) were passive rather than active members of them. State-level culture was strong only in the court centres (the towns).

The growth of market opportunities broadened the framework of rural-local operations. Wealthy landowning families slowly were drawn out of their petty localities and towards the principal marketing centres. They met to do business and their progressive economic enmeshment provided a basis for political and social connection. By the 1910s, for example, groups of rural-local bosses in some areas had begun to identify among themselves common political interests and to act as pressure groups on rural government for the improvement of commercial facilities.[89] Equally, marriage networks among them began to extend – thereby also extending the means by which they could mobilise credit and other economic resources.[90] Many of them

---

[87] For discussions on the effect of settled agriculture on the lineage organisation of the Kallars, see Dumont, *Une Sous-Caste de l'Inde du Sud*, pp. 7–9; also, *M.D.G.* Francis, *Madura*, I, 92–3.

[88] Stein, 'Integration of the Agrarian System of South India' in Frykenberg (ed.), *Land Control and Social Structure in Indian History*, pp. 175–216.

[89] *Hindu* 1 February and 17 May 1915.

[90] Towns became the focal points of marriage brokerage. *Royal Commission on Agriculture in India*, XIV, 233. For discussions of the economic and political uses

set up houses in the towns and became more open to urban influences. They started to send their children to school and college and to pursue the learned professions.[91] Some of them even became involved in Sanskritic culture, for social status in the towns tended to be expressed through the forms of the Hindu religion.[92] As we shall see later, these tendencies came to be developed also and more fully by administrative change.

Admittedly, by 1920 this process was in its infancy and many of its wider implications were hardly foreseeable. Yet what was happening was slowly changing the face of South Indian society in this region. Groups whose cultural-orientation had been local before were beginning to participate directly in a larger 'regional' system. This participation did not end the existence of purely local-level culture: agrarian dependent groups were still held inside it. Nor, importantly, did it simply lead to the absorption of the rural-local boss element into state-level culture. The regional culture of the rural elite came to be a hybrid which contained features of both: it brought Hindu gods into the village and village gods into the towns, and mixed the symbols of both cultures promiscuously. Indeed, the regional culture's contacts were better with the locality for, following its progenitors' economic and, as we shall see, administrative methods, it really used the resources of the town to strengthen its rural position. As a hybrid, however, it was not only sympathetic to both cultural levels but also antagonistic to them. Its existence challenged the autonomy of each. By the 1930s, under the pressure of economic calamity and rising population, its development was to lead to fierce clashes with all prevailing forms of South Indian culture. The spearhead of the Self-Respect movement was formed out of young members of the 'regionalising' and 'urbanising' rural elite.

The Cauveri delta and Malabar. Along the Cauveri economic stratification and the development of a 'regional' rural elite were both much

of marriage alliance among South Indian peasant castes, see C. M. Elliot, 'Caste and Faction Among the Dominant Caste: the Reddis and Kammas of Andhra' in R. Kothari, *Caste in Indian Politics* (New Delhi, 1970), pp. 129–71; also J. Manor, 'The Evolution of Political Areas and Units: the Lingayats and Vokkaligas of Princely Mysore.' Privately circulated paper.

[91] For example, the Kasu Reddi family of upland Kistna. See K. Kasipathi, *Tryst with Destiny* (Hyderabad, 1970).

[92] For example, although Gounder Vellala local culture may not pay much attention to Aryan expressions of social status, in 1921 certain Gounder rural-local bosses established a caste association to claim Kshatriya *varna* status for their caste. Beck, *Peasant Society in Konku*, pp. 154–81; *Hindu* 12 August 1921, 28 January 1922, 18 December 1923, 10 and 27 May and 16 July 1924.

farther advanced than in the dry zone. Cauveri rice had been intensively cultivated for the market for centuries when the British first established their *raj*. The delta provided an agrarian surplus which had made possible sophisticated regional government from the time of the Cholas. These economic and political factors conspired to vest effective land control over large areas in the hands of a few families. In spite of avowals to the contrary, the East India Company did little to alter the arrangements which it found. It recognised the hereditary rights of the great *mirasidar* families to the ownership of their estates under the *ryotwari* system and it allowed them in practice if not in theory, to control wastelands.[93] The number of large landholders was much higher in the Cauveri area than elsewhere in *ryotwari* Madras. In 1918 in Tanjore district, the heart of the delta, there were 3321 landlords paying more than Rs 250 p.a. in revenue, compared to a district average of about 200 in the rest of the presidency and of less than 80 in the dry region.[94] Of these 3321, 421 also paid more than Rs 1000 p.a. compared to a dry district average of 5.[95] In 1918, *pattas* worth more than Rs 250 met 30 per cent of Tanjore's total revenue demand. In the dry zone, they met 6 per cent.[96]

The *mirasidar's* domination of agrarian production was complete. At least in other *ryotwari* areas, the poorer peasant could carve a few acres of land out of the jungle and establish some, be it only a nominal, basis for independent existence; if he were not totally sunk in debt, he might also manage to play off one rural-local boss against another in order to reduce the terms of his dependency. In Tanjore, however, neither of these two options was open to him. Land shortage and *mirasidar* control of most known wastes prevented the mass of village society from possessing even the sites of their own huts and long-term debt bondage had reduced most cultivators to the status of hereditary serfs.[97] The *mirasidar* worked his fields through hired labourers and unprotected, crop-sharing tenants who relied for life support on the advances of wages, seeds, implements and credit which he allowed to them. They were tied to his lands and had no means of lessening their subjection. Indeed, until well into the twentieth century it was common for labourers and tenants to be sold with an estate as part of its capital equipment.[98]

---

[93] Kumar, *Land and Caste in South India*, pp. 14–23.
[94] 'Statement of the Rent Roll' in *Land Revenue 1918–19*.
[95] *Ibid.*   [96] *Ibid.*
[97] *Royal Commission on Agriculture in India*, xiv, 269; *Swadesamitran* 11 February 1912, *Hindu Nesan* 12 February 1912. R.N.P.; Kumar, *Land and Caste in South India*, pp. 86–7, 178.
[98] Kumar, *ibid.*, p. 75. *Royal Commission on Agriculture in India*, iii, 314; see also,

There is no evidence to indicate that before the 1930s at the earliest, the Tanjore economic systems underwent any fundamental change.[99] Within his estate, the *mirasidar* was the centre of commodity exchange: he drew off the produce of the soil and distributed food, clothing, shelter and other necessities to his subordinates. He insulated his workers from the external forces of the market. Contemporary observers noted the apparent timelessness of agricultural operations in the districts. Money never became a significant element in the composition of rural wages or rent agreements nor did the price mechanism come to regulate the distribution of foods and services.[100] Subordinate groups had been driven into a position of economic slavery, the rules of which were written now by custom.

Yet if serfs and tenants were held at more or less the same economic level, the prospects of the *mirasidar* himself were more expansive. The development of Pax Britannica greatly raised the value of the produce which he controlled. Many of Tanjore's old marketing connections, which had been broken by the wars of the eighteenth century, were repaired and new links, with Burma and Northern India, were established. During the later nineteenth century, the price of rice rose steadily and the *mirasidar's* purchasing power followed it. He accumulated large stocks of paddy at the harvest, which he had the capital to hull and mill and to transport directly to the railheads and ports.[101] Enormous grain warehouses were a common feature of the Tanjore countryside and, between 1910 and 1927 the number of power-driven mills (built mostly with *mirasidar* investment) leapt from four or five to 215.[102] Tanjore became unquestionably the wealthiest district in the presidency and its *mirasidars* by far the wealthiest economic group.

The type of economic stratification which was appearing in the dry districts was at its apogee in Tanjore, as was the type of social stratification. The *mirasidar* elite ruled its agrarian dependents with a rod of iron and established a great social distance between itself and them. In Anantapur or Coimbatore, with the exception of a few families, status differentials were only beginning to reach the stage at which they made it obvious that the rural-local boss was socially distinct from his poorer tenants, debtors and labourers. The degrees of caste status, like the degrees of clientage, gradually shaded

B. Hjejle, 'Slavery and Agricultural Bondage in the Nineteenth Century' in *Scandinavian Economic History Review*, XV: 1 and 2 (1967).

[99] *Royal Commission on Agriculture in India*, XIV, 269.
[100] *Ibid.; Land Revenue 1911–12*, p. 77.
[101] *Royal Commission on Agriculture in India*, XIV, 268–9.
[102] *Ibid.*, III, 447.

down from him' through his various neighbours to a small group of total dependents who were held outside the pale of decent society. Along the Cauveri, the gap between respectability and untouchability was much wider. *Pariahs* provided a very high (21 per cent)[103] proportion of the labouring population and the lesser Kallar lineages, which also worked the fields, were considered barely clean. At this lower end of the social scale, religion, culture and social custom were very similar to those to be found generally in the dry region: the most important gods were not those of the Hindu pantheon but of the locality and the clan; marriage networks were territorially minute; social relations were conducted within areas of a few square miles.[104]

At the top of the social scale, however, there were considerable numbers of people claiming the highest forms of social status and involved together in a uniform cultural system which the dry zone could not match. This cultural system was not the hybrid, which was to emerge in the dry region, but was emphatically state-level in all its attributes. The much longer-term and higher volume of market transactions had promoted a regional basis to superior economic organisation in Tanjore. When making their initial settlements, the British had not found dominant landholders buried in separate localities: many *mirasidars* held land not in one or a few adjacent villages but in widely dispersed *taluks* and their *mirasi* rights were treated as freely saleable.[105] Equally, much wider systems of centralised government had been established: members of the same state-level families were littered across the entire district and beyond.[106] The high agrarian surplus enabled this greater breadth of organisation to be matched by greater depth. Previous state integrations had not stoppped short of local-level groups but had taken over the resources on which their autonomy had been based. The Brahman population of the Cauveri delta was six or seven times higher than elsewhere in Tamilnad and was much richer.[107] Brahmans formed about one-third of the *mirasidar* elite.[108] Other social groups which were logically

---

[103] *Census of India. 1921. Madras. Volume XIII. Part 2* (Madras, 1922), pp. 4, 21.

[104] E. K. Gough, 'Caste in a Tanjore Village' in Leach (ed.), *Aspects of Caste; M.D.G.* Hemingway, *Trichinopoly* I, 88–9.

[105] Kumar, *Land and Caste in South India*, pp. 15–16.

[106] For example, Smartha Brahman 'service' families possessed long-standing kinship links not only across the district but into North Arcot. See K. S. Ramaswami Sastri, *Vita Sua* (Madras, n.d.) and K. S. Ramaswami Sastri, *Professor Sunderama Ayyar* (Srirangam, n.d.).

[107] *Census of India. 1881. Madras* (Madras, 1883), II, 140.

[108] *Evidence taken before the Reforms Committee (Franchise)* (Calcutta, 1919), II, 119–23.

state-level also maintained a major local presence and power; for example, Shiyali *taluk* was dominated by Thondamandala Vellalas who had migrated from Chingleput to serve previous regional governments.[109] Under this much heavier pressure from above, elite members of the local-level cultures had themselves been drawn out towards the superior state. The Kallar aristocracy of Tanjore had long ceased to resemble lesser, cultivating members of the Kallar caste. The Vandayar family of Pundi and the Papanad family had cut most of their connections with the local-level and were fully immersed in the culture of the state.[110]

Although it continued to maintain its control over dependents through rural-local economic means, the *mirasidar* elite itself was not conditioned by the circumstances of the rural locality. Its patterns of religious worship were broad. It was by no means unusual for there to be ten or more temples or *maths* in a single *taluk*, each drawing a following for its ceremonies from members of the elite spread widely across the countryside. In the 1860s, of the twenty largest religious festivals in the presidency, no fewer than eight took place along the banks of the Cauveri.[111] The culture displayed in this worship was literate and involved veneration of gods of an all-Indian pantheon. Equally, marriage patterns were very wide: Tanjore Brahmans married over circles of one hundred miles or more,[112] and Vellala and Kallar aristocrats across three or four *taluks*.[113] The ritual and customs of the elite were determined less by lineage reference than by recognition and emulation of social models derived from the Hindu scriptures.

A similar type of political structure was thrown up in Malabar by very similar types of pressure. Space prohibits us from investigating it fully here. But we may note that economic control to the point of continued slavery was exercised by a very small group of *jenmis* and *kanomdars*; that social patterns among agrarian dependents more or less retained their local-level characteristics; and that economic and political factors of long duration had produced a high

---

[109] See C. Krishnamurthi Mudaliar, *Life and Activities of K. Chidambaranatha Mudaliar* (Shiyali, 1938).

[110] They were deeply involved in Brahmanic festivals and culture. See, for example, *Hindu* 12 and 14 September 1916.

[111] Letter No. 749 A, Sanitary Commissioner for Madras to Chief Secretary, Government of Madras, dated 11 July 1868. Copy in Cambridge University Library.

[112] Gough, 'Caste in a Tanjore Village' in Leach (ed.), *Aspects of Caste*, pp. 44–5.

[113] For the Kallar Odayars, see *Hindu* 15 June 1888.

degree of integration among the elite whose culture was strongly state-level in orientation.[114]

The Kistna and Godavari deltas. The shape of economic relations in the Kistna and Godavari deltas was in sharp contrast to those in the dry region and in Tanjore and Malabar. No small oligarchy existed to dominate agrarian production and its absence was a crucial factor in the organisation of society. The Kistna and Godavari deltas were effectively the creation of Sir Arthur Cotton in the 1840s and 1850s. Certainly, there had been irrigation works on the rivers for centuries before this, but the area of irrigated land was never more than a few thousand acres. Cotton's *anicut* schemes increased it to over one and a half million acres.[115] By the 1880s, the region had joined Tanjore as a centre of intensive rice cultivation, which sold its produce in international markets. At harvest time, 'the whole country [looked] like a single rice field, the groves around the villages, the roads and avenues and the white sails of the boats gliding along the main canals breaking the uniform sea of waving green crop'.[116]

The economic changes which the sudden arrival of irrigation made to the deltas were considerable. As the size of landholdings indicates, patterns of property ownership in this previously dry, or at best mixed, farming area were similar to those in the dry region as a whole. In 1880, for example, the average *patta* in the wet zone of Godavari district covered about 8 acres of land, and in dry Madras about 8 acres.[117] Equally, prior to the construction of the *anicuts*, marketing arrangements had been fragmented and the volume of trade, reflecting the nature of the subsistence economy, had been low.[118] The expansion of irrigation facilities both altered the significance of landholding size and promoted new systems of marketing. Under dry cultivation, 8 acres of land would pay somewhere between Rs $2\frac{1}{4}$ and Rs 18 p.a. in revenue and its cultivator would be somewhere between poverty and beggary. Under wet cultivation, however, 8 acres would pay between Rs 36 and Rs 70 p.a. and its cultivator would

[114] See Kumar, *Land and Caste in South India*, pp. 70–5; *M.D.G.* C. A. Innes, *Malabar* (Madras, 1908); G.O. 1675 (Home, Misc.) dated 2 December 1919. *T.N.A.* The 'Cauveri' pattern also extended to patches of irrigated cultivation along the Coromandel coast, in Chingleput and South Arcot districts, and to small pockets of tank and river cultivation in several other predominantly dry districts.

[115] A. V. Raman Rao, *Economic Development of Andhra Pradesh (1766–1957)* (Bombay, 1958), pp. 86–90.

[116] Quoted in Spate, *India and Pakistan*, 690.

[117] Calculated from *Land Revenue 1880–1*, pp. 10, 34.

[118] *Selections from the Madras Records. XXII* (Madras, 1870), pp. 62, 264–5; *ibid., XXXII* (Madras, 1872), p. 78.

be a substantial, if not particularly rich, peasant. Moreover, the coming of water had obliterated subsistence farming. The deltas specialised in the production of rice to the exclusion of all other crops. In every village, a majority of the harvest had to be sold away and everything necessary for life except rice imported.[119] This greatly stimulated trade. Cotton's *anicuts* produced an agrarian revolution, be it only in one corner of the province.

In the Godavari district, only 4 per cent of *ryotwari* wet land was held in *pattas* of less than Rs 10 p.a.[120] Over 62 per cent was held in the middle range of *pattas* from Rs 30 to Rs 250 p.a.[121] The deltas had a large number of peasants whose wealth was sufficient for them to be able to provide their own cash and equipment for cultivation, to hoard their crops after harvest and to meet transportation expenses. They were freed from many of the production and marketing restraints so common elsewhere. Many delta peasants carted or sailed their paddy straight to the principal railheads and ports. Those who sold in their villages, to local millowners or export agents, did so from choice rather than necessity. The Royal Commission on Agriculture (1928) noted that the resources of the producers and the multiplicity of outlets available to them put Andhra rice in a sellers' market. There was a more or less uniform regional price structure: prices in the village were based closely on prices in the principal exporting towns, which in turn were related to the prices of rice being imported into the presidency.[122]

The development of this substantial 'middle' peasantry in the Kistna and Godavari deltas profoundly influenced the economic structure of the region. In the dry zone we saw that only small groups from the village made contact with the main towns and that they brought or took away only small quantities of goods. Most commodity exchange took place between circles of villages. In consequence, the dry region had many small bazaars: in 1929, Coimbatore district possessed 144 licensed markets and Salem 112.[123] The major towns, however, grew very slowly. Although Tanjore possessed a much higher volume of trade, its individually powerful *mirasidars* managed produce-collection and commodity-redistribution from their estates. They undermined the economic functions of the towns, which stagnated.[124] In the Andhra deltas, many landlords were eager to

[119] *Royal Commission on Agriculture in India*, XIV, 268–70.
[120] Calculated from 'Statement of the Rent Roll' in *Land Revenue 1900–1*.
[121] *Ibid.*
[122] *Royal Commission on Agriculture in India*, XIV, 268–70.
[123] *RPBC*, pp. 219–20.
[124] *Census of India. 1921. Madras. Volume XIII. Part 2*, pp. 8–12.

enter superior marketing organisations but few were large enough to do so directly from their fields. Towns at the junctions of communications systems became important points for the assemblage of crops and for the dispersal of imports. They served directly a broad clientele from the countryside around them. As a result, marketing patterns became heavily concentrated. In 1929, for example, Guntur district had only 6 licensed markets.[125] The transport towns of deltas grew very rapidly: Rajahmundry, Cocanada, Ellore and Bezwada doubled in size between 1880 and 1920.[126]

To complement the villagers who were being drawn into the towns, urban-based mercantile and moneylending groups were encouraged to move outwards. The rice trade which they were handling was so profitable and rice land so valuable that they were prepared to throw away their scruples about rural finance and to lend directly to almost any cultivator. Komatis, working through family businesses, broadened and deepened their village networks; Marwaris flocked to the deltas and poured cash into agrarian credit.[127] By the 1910s, these traditional *bania* groups were joined by the more sophisticated institutions of co-operative credit societies and joint-stock banks which, also operating from urban centres, made a greater impact on credit facilities in the deltas than anywhere else in the presidency.[128] The centralisation of trade and credit made 'the urban hinterland' the basic unit of economic activity, rather than the rural-locality or *mirasi* estate.

A second crucial development in the area was the rise of a broadly-based cash economy. In Tanjore and in the dry region, the cash nexus was largely confined to relations between the *mirasidar* or rural-local boss and the superior marketing structure. It was involved in few of the transactions between the *mirasidar* or rural-local boss and his own agrarian dependents. One of the basic reasons for this weakness in the cash nexus, and for the continued importance of custom and kind, was that the labour force of the two regions tended to be immobile and tied socially and politically to particular wealthy landholders. Under the commercial agricultural system of the Andhra deltas, however, labour was highly mobile and relatively free. During transplantation and harvesting, rice cultivation required a much larger supply of labour than was locally available. From the 1860s, poor peasants from the upland *taluks* and Vizagapatam began pouring

[125] *RPBC*, pp. 219–20.
[126] *Census of India. 1921. Madras. Volume XIII. Part 2*, pp. 8–12.
[127] *MPBC*, III, 740–3.
[128] See 'Three Investigations into Godavari District' in *MPBC*, v, 85–225.

into the area for these annual operations.[129] They worked as day labourers and returned to their homes at the completion of their tasks. By the early 1900s, they were paid almost entirely in cash.[130] The fluidity of labour and the purchasing power of labourers influenced the economic structure of the region in two ways. They provided a further stimulus to rural–urban linkages for the labourers both needed supplies and had the money to buy them from any source, and they destroyed the rural-locality as a coherent unit of social life, for labourers were constantly on the move and seldom established close ties with any one locale or employer.

The social consequences of economic development marked off the area along the Kistna and Godavari rivers from the rest of the province. Some delta peasants, of course, were much richer than others; but they could not use their riches to develop anything like the same amount of social control as could their wealth-equivalents in the dry zone or in Tanjore. In the first place, there were too many sources of credit in the countryside and the income of the average cultivator was too high for the wealthy peasant to be able to tie up the local credit system. *Banias* and banks provided alternative places of succour and were seen to do business even with the five acre *ryot*. Secondly, the nature of the labour supply prevented the wealthy from establishing long-term dependency relationships with subordinate, working groups who could be used in their private standing armies. Thirdly, and most significantly, there were also too many substantial men: the clients of any one man could easily find a patron just as important only a few fields away. This last point can be seen clearly in the mass of evidence given to the Forest Committee (1913). It was extremely unusual for witnesses from villages in dry Madras to name more than three or four men in their localities who were sufficiently rich and powerful to be used by the general population as arbitrators in disputes. Witnesses from the deltas, however, frequently listed eight or nine; and one man claimed there were no less than fourteen in his own village.[131] With so many rival jurisdictions packed into the same area, the basis of rural factionalism was greatly widened and the prospective client given considerable scope for manoeuvre. Social order in the deltas was very fragile.

As might be expected in this situation, the scale of communications developed by the economy also opened up broad territorial networks of social and cultural connection to a very large section of

---

[129] *Royal Commission on Agriculture in India*, III, 316; *ibid.*, XIV, 268–70.
[130] *Ibid.*, also *Land Revenue 1902–3*, p. 10.
[131] *Report of the Forest Committee. 1913*, II, passim.

the rural population. Endogamous units among the Kammas, the dominant peasant caste of the region, covered wide areas and expanded from the later nineteenth century to the point at which the concept of sub-caste became almost lost.[132] Through regular urban contacts, village families began to imitate the habits of townsmen, giving the deltas the appearance of a common, regional life-style. Bricks and tiles steadily replaced mud and thatch as the usual building materials for respectable village homes;[133] the literacy rate grew faster than anywhere else in the presidency;[134] the delta towns sustained the most active vernacular journalism industry in Madras, which sold its wares extensively in the countryside;[135] substantial landlords began to send their sons to the towns for work and education and, by subletting their fields, often moved there themselves.[136]

The merging of the town and the countryside had important implications for the dichotomy between state- and local-level cultures. As in the dry region, state-level culture had not deeply penetrated the countryside before the middle of the nineteenth century and had remained embedded in the towns. Ancient irrigation works on the rivers had attracted some state-level groups to the area, who also had obtained some power by acting as spiritual and administrative advisors to various native governments. The Kistna and the Godavari rivers did provide more centres sacred to Hindus than would be found in the dry zone. Yet there is little to indicate that state-level culture had made much more of an impact on the peasantry of the countryside. Mid-nineteenth-century observers commented on the continuation of local-level religious forms, while investigations in the 1860s revealed that, although there were many Hindu festivals in the area, none drew a significant regional following.[137] Towards the end of the nineteenth century, however, it was clear that the hiatus between state and local culture was beginning to disappear with the hiatus between town and country. Sudden and spontaneous religious movements sprang up in the rural areas and rushed towards the towns.

[132] See C. M. Elliot, 'Caste and Faction among the Dominant Caste: the Reddis and Kammas of Andhra' in Kothari, *Caste in Indian Politics*.

[133] Raman Rao, *Economic Development of Andhra Pradesh (1766–1957)*, p. 192.

[134] *Census of India. 1931. Madras. Volume XIV, Part 1* (Madras, 1933), p. 283; *ibid.*, Part 2, pp. 276–7.

[135] By 1925, Rajahmundry had at least five newspapers with a combined circulation of 4700 and Masulipatam also maintained five with a circulation of 8000. No other *mofussil* towns possessed anything like this level of activity. Home Political File 261 of 1926. *N.A.I.*

[136] *Land Revenue 1905–6*, p. 72.

[137] Letter No. 749 A, Sanitary Commissioner for Madras to Chief Secretary, Government of Madras, dated 11 July 1868. Copy in Cambridge University Library.

During the *mohurram* of 1884, for example, a small army of peasants gathered at Gudur, a village near Masulipatam, and marched through the countryside picking up support until it reached Masulipatam, where it attacked the main mosque.[138] Conversely, temples dedicated to all-India gods appeared in greater numbers in the villages as Komati merchants, of urban origin, deepened their rural associations.[139] Festivals, which once were patronised only by a select few, became principal meeting places and markets for thousands. Hindu theatrical and dance troupes, which once served only at the urban courts of rich *zamindars*, found enthusiastic audiences in the villages.[140] Hindu theological controversy began to sweep the countryside as Kammas noted, and disapproved, the place which they were assigned in the *varna* scheme and demanded the right to study the Sanskrit scriptures and to remodel their customs.[141]

In terms of the state–local separation which we have examined in the dry region and in Tanjore–Malabar, the society of the Andhra deltas produced a third variant. The entire distinction between the levels increasingly lost its force. The movement towards the towns was not carried forward by an elite in any meaningful sense. The weakness of economic controls had eroded the bases of elite political control: distinctions of rank and status were of relatively little importance in the deltas. The movement was carried forward by 'a mass' of rural society. This meant that when regional interaction began to take place very little of the local cultures was left in the hands of non-participants and was untouched by the development: it was not preserved by agrarian dependent groups. Equally, state-level culture was heavily modified by the movement. State-level groups could not dominate the new process: they did not command the resources of rural power. Nor could they ignore it: they were a crucial part of the urban hinterland as they were not of the rural locality. They had to bend with it.

In consequence, the Andhra deltas brought forth a peculiar cultural composite which consisted of a fusion of state- and local-level elements. The nature of this composite can be seen, for example, in the way that Brahman priests propitiated local-level deities and in the

---

[138] *Madras Police 1884*, p. 7.

[139] Komatis were great patrons of Sanskrit scholarship and of Hindu revivalism. They were particularly attached to the cow-protection movement. Report of the Director Criminal Intelligence, 9 April 1910 in Home Political B June 1910, Nos 17–25. *N.A.I.*; also G.O. 216 (L and M, M) dated 3 February 1914. *T.N.A.*

[140] Such as the Rajahmundry Hindu Theatrical Company. See Sastri (ed.), *Encyclopaedia of the Madras Presidency*, p. 501.

[141] Ranga, *Fight for Freedom*, pp. 7–11.

95

way that peasants became involved in state-level controversies. In the case of the Gudur–Masulipatam march and riot, which we mentioned above, the procession was led by an image of the idol Anjamar, a local-level god but one committed to a fight with an opponent which existed only at the state-level of culture – Islam. It can be seen again in the attempts by members of certain peasant castes to Sanskritise their culture and in the attempts by members of state-level groups to demoticise their culture: to match the Kamma movement 'upwards', some Brahmans sought to return written Telugu from the high literary dialect which it had become to the language of common speech.[142] And it can be seen yet again in the mutual association of Brahmans, Komatis and Kammas in literary societies in the towns and the villages.[143]

Although there was certainly room for internal conflict between its participants, the regional culture of the Andhra deltas did not itself stand between other antagonistic and separate traditions. It could not clash with the state- and local-level cultures because these had lost most of their existence: the Self-Respect Movement, for example, was meaningless in the deltas. Nor did its continuance rely on the maintenance of political control by a small elite. It represented a highly organised, territorially wide and integrated 'popular' culture. Its type was quite unique in South India.

Zamindars, mittadars and jenmis. The foregoing examination of the structure of rural society has concentrated on methods of production, marketing and credit. It has been concerned, therefore, with the landholders, moneylenders, tenants and labourers who composed rural society and were involved in the creation of rural wealth. The patterns of power which it has outlined were those to be found at various levels of localisation in the countryside. In about two-thirds of the presidency there were no formal economic institutions above these levels and between them and the state. In the remaining one-third, however, political circumstances in the late eighteenth century, and political folly in the early nineteenth, had led the British to support the rights of intermediaries between the soil and themselves to a share of the produce of the land. These intermediaries – *zamindars, mittadars* and *jenmis* – were capable of commanding great wealth and, on

---

[142] For example, the Brahman K. Viresalingam, essayist and journalist, did much to create the language of contemporary Telugu letters and, in his lifetime, saw his writings popularly acclaimed.

[143] M. Venkatarangaiya, *The Freedom Struggle in Andhra Pradesh (Andhra)* (Hyderabad, 1968), II, 266–76.

occasion, were taken by the British to be the leaders of society in their domains. Clearly, it is necessary for us to examine their role in the countryside.

In Madras, *zamindars* came in all shapes and sizes and had been produced by different forces; consequently, they were related to their estates in a variety of ways. As P. J. Musgrave has shown for U.P., it would be impossible to provide a single stereotype of their economic position.[144] In this chapter, as our main interest lies in the nature of production and credit, we shall begin our categorisation of the different types of *zamindar* by using as a criterion the ways in which they interfered in the organisation of the economy. A first category would be composed of those who interfered least, that is of those who drew off rents and taxes but did nothing to provide credit or marketing facilities for their tenants, to stimulate the cultivation of particular crops or to reorganise the economy of their estates. In this category, which was certainly the largest, we tend to find most of the greater territorial *zamindars*. Such families as those of the Maharaja of Vizianagram and the Rajas of Ramnad, Pithapuram, Kalahasti, Karvetnagar, Bobbili, Nuzvid and Venkatagiri inherited their place in late-nineteenth-century Madras from ancestors who had been successful warriors. The coming of peace, however, did not see them beat their swords into ploughshares. They continued to maintain huge retinues and a courtly life-style.[145] Their perception of their social role did not lead them to promote agricultural development nor to finance the village economy. In the eighteenth century they had taken loot by the sword; now they did the same, less successfully, by the law. The estates of the larger *zamindars* were usually very backward. Their rents were collected mostly in kind, thereby reducing the importance of a market economy to their tenants;[146] their irrigation works seldom were repaired or extended;[147] their tenants were often indebted to creditors outside their jurisdiction. Certainly, by the twentieth century, a few of these ancient magnates had become more prudent in business affairs and were attempting to increase their resources. But none did so by developing closer relations with the peasant producers of his estate. Bobbili, for example, found it more profitable to use his grain rents as a basis for the flotation of a provincial grain-

---

[144] P. J. Musgrave, 'Landlords and Lords of the Land' in *Modern Asian Studies*, VI: 3 (1972).

[145] See A. Vadivelu, *Ruling Chiefs, Nobles and Zemindars of India* (Madras, 1915); A. Vadivelu, *The Aristocracy of Southern India* (Madras, 1907), 2 vols.

[146] Until the Estates Lands Act of 1908, *zamindars* were not compelled to commute their rent demands from kind to cash.

[147] *Land Revenue 1905–6*, p. 78.

dealing business;[118] Parlakimedi speculated in railways;[149] Venkatagiri in mica mining;[150] and Pithapuram in lending money to other *zamindars*.[151] In their lands, *zamindars* of this kind remained simply rent-receivers. The economy of their villages was controlled effectively by richer tenant or other groups. Indeed, some of these 'subordinate' groups came to exercise a strong influence over the operations of their *zamindar's* own economy. Kalahasti, Ramnad, Sivaganga and Karvetnagar, for example, were deeply indebted to their wealthier tenants and ultimately had to alienate portions of their estates to meet these commitments.[152]

The appearance of social power, which many of the greater *zamindars* possessed, came much more from their ability to spend huge quantities of money and to patronise state-level cultural groups than from their ability to dictate the nature of production in their realms. As much of their expenditure took place in the towns where they lived, it is arguable whether patronage ties gave them any hold over the countryside. Certainly, during famines they very rarely came forward to guarantee their tenants against starvation, or even to remit the revenues which were owed them.[153] Perhaps, only in Ramnad and other estates in the extreme South, which were based on the old lineage territories of Maravar and Kallar warriors, is there much evidence of the *zamindar* playing the role of rural leader – and even here the role was becoming more limited every year.

In the same category of *zamindar* as the 'ancient' magnates, we might also place those contractors and financiers who made fortunes during the early years of Company *raj* and who bought privileged revenue rights. In very many cases, they tried to imitate the life-style of the warrior elite. As R. E. Frykenberg has shown in Guntur district, these parvenus were more interested in status and ceremonial than in economic resources: they did little to finance the rural economy and the bankruptcy rate among them was staggering.[154] A classic case is provided by the Brahman contractor family who bought the Polavaram estate in Godavari in the 1840s and 1850s. The family became great

---

[148] *Report on the Famine in the Madras Presidency during 1896 and 1897* (Madras, 1898), II, 73.

[149] Sastri (ed.), *Encyclopaedia of the Madras Presidency*, pp. 361–2.

[150] Some of the richest mica deposits in India lay within the Venkatagiri *zamindari* in Nellore district.

[151] *Hindu* 7 December 1920.

[152] *Report on the Administration of the Estates under the Court of Wards in the Madras Presidency for Fasli 1317 (1907–8)* (Madras, 1909); *ibid., 1908–9; ibid., 1909–10; Land Revenue 1911–12 to 1913–14.*

[153] *Report on the Famine in the Madras Presidency during 1896 and 1897*, II, 79.

[154] Frykenberg, *Guntur District 1788–1848*, pp. 136–53.

patrons and cultural leaders in Cocanada town but, by 1919, had so misused its funds that its estates had to be liquidated.[155]

Those *zamindars* who became closely involved with the economies of their estates and who undertook supervision of production were almost invariably of two kinds. Either they were small *mittadars*, owning only one or a few villages, or they were bankers who had obtained the position of *zamindar* by providing credit both to the old estate holder and to his tenants. In Salem and Coimbatore districts particularly, there were several ex-*poligar* families who had been brought into the British settlements of 1799–1802 and allowed to keep revenue rights over some villages. By the later nineteenth century, they were operating economic networks in their localities very similar to those of the rural-local boss. The *mittadar* of Kumaranangalam, who was one of the largest landowners in this group, lent money, grain and cattle to his tenants and insinuated his influence into every corner of his petty domain.[156] Of the bankers who moved into land ownership, the Nattukottai Chetties provide the best examples of tight estate control. In their homelands, inside the Ramnad *zamindari*, they were a village-based group. Although they drew an increasingly large proportion of their resources from urban and international commerce, in Ramnad (and nowhere else in the presidency) they financed local agriculture.[157] This gave them a hold over the rural population around them. They also lent money to the Raja of Ramnad and eventually forced him to lease and then sell *zamindari* rights over their land to them.[158] The Nattukottai Chetty *zamindari* of Devakottah thus exercised a remarkably powerful rulership over his tenant subjects. Indeed, his economic oppression was one of the longest-standing scandals in Madras.[159]

Clearly, however, the territory covered by this second category of *zamindar* was very small. In most of the permanently settled areas of the province, the estate holder did not intrude into the processes of production. The provision of facilities for the continuation of economic life rested with others – usually with the wealthier tenant whose local position was thereby enhanced. Few contemporaries noted any fundamental difference between rural economic organisation in *zamindari* and in *ryotwari* areas, save that the *zamindari* peasant was required to pay rather more rent rather less often than his

[155] *Hindu* 7 December 1920.
[156] *Royal Commission on Agriculture in India*, III, 547.
[157] *RPBC*, pp. 185–90.
[158] Sastri (ed.), *Encyclopaedia of the Madras Presidency*, p. 479.
[159] *Land Revenue 1903–4*, pp. 78–9; *Hindu* 6 September 1893.

ryotwari counterpart.[160] While this doubtless contributed to further economic stratification, in that richer tenants were likely to pay even less often than poorer, it cannot be taken to have created a distinguishable *zamindari* tenant society. As elsewhere, the critical level of economic organisation lay in the village or small rural locality. Consequently, inside nearly every *zamindari* there were local structures of power which did not touch the official landowner and which could oppose his leadership. These structures were moulded by the same forces which influenced social organisation in the dry zone, Tanjore and Andhra; and most often they were dominated by the rural-local boss.

Urban Madras. The main stimulus to urbanisation in the Madras of our period was trade in agrarian produce. In the first half of the nineteenth century, the administration had played a large part in attracting people to towns to work in and around the bureaucracy, law courts and schools. Some towns were founded almost wholly in this way. By 1880, however, the basic pattern of administration had been established and not even Madras city, the capital of government, was growing fast.[161] Equally, heavy industry had yet to appear on any scale and there was little demand for urban industrial labour. The greatest urban growth points were in those areas where movements in the rural economy had been greatest – particularly, in the Andhra deltas and, later, in the Tinnevelly–Ramnad cotton belt.[162]

Clearly, it is difficult to write generally of a category which contained so many heterogeneous elements. The towns of Madras had been created at different times, for different purposes and served different present needs. Some had developed around temples, some around the palaces of princes, some around bureaucratic centres and others still at the cross-roads of trade. Each possessed economic and social organisations which were slightly different from every other. Necessarily we must look at the vaguest outlines of economic and social structure, for only in those outlines can we find material suitable to our general ends. In our examination of rural Madras, we saw that the economy required a variety of facilities to be available if it were to keep running. The provision of these facilities was in the hands of a few men who thereby were able to gain a large measure of economic

---

[160] *RPBC*, pp. 7–8; Srinivasa Raghavaiyangar, *Memorandum on the Progress of the Madras Presidency*, p. 76.

[161] Madras city's growth rate was lower than that of the presidency as a whole. *Census of India. 1921. Madras. Volume XIII. Part 2* (Madras, 1922), pp. 8–12.

[162] *Cenus of India. 1931. Madras. Volume XIV* (Madras, 1933), pp. 10–16.

and ultimately political control. Let us first see what the nature of economic organisation tells us of urban Madras.

In every town of any size, commerce and petty industry employed a majority of the population. Both needed enormous resources of credit to keep them moving: whether to pass large amounts of crop from one town to another, to hold supplies for local sale or to invest in carts, *jutkas*, stalls or even coffee-shops, traders and merchants required credit facilities. For most of our period, there were few impersonal organisations – joint-stock banks and the like – capable of meeting these needs. Credit was supplied by individuals. Although money-lending in the towns was a promiscuous activity – anybody with a few spare coppers would lend them, and many people themselves borrowed only to lend again – it is clear that the lines of credit tended to lead back to the same few hands. The difficulty of accumulating large funds and the specialist nature of money transfers over wide distances produced heavy concentrations of credit in very small banking groups. For example, in Rajahmundry, an Andhra trading town of some 20,000 population, there were in 1900 only some 100 men who lent money professionally. Of these, two lent very much more than the rest: they paid Rs 30 a year income tax, while only twelve of the others managed Rs 6 and the remaining 86 none at all.[163] In Ellore, a comparable and expanding Andhra town, one man, 'Mothey Venkataswami practically finances the trade of this place.'[164] Some credit agents operated on a scale to dwarf all others around them. In the late 1920s, for example, although they were withdrawing their funds from India to pursue better opportunities in Burma and Ceylon, the Nattukottai Chetties still had about Rs 11 *crores* invested in 243 Madras branches – an average of Rs 4.5 *lakhs* per branch, most of it in urban moneylending.[165] In Cocanada, at the same time, three Komati families were working with a capital of Rs 41 *lakhs*,[166] and in Madura two Kallidaikurichi Brahmans (members of a caste of indigenous bankers) had a turnover of Rs 20 *lakhs*.[167] In 1911, in the whole of the Madras Presidency, there were only 16,212 men whose activities were principally in moneylending and whose incomes were more than Rs 1000 a year.[168] If we assume that at least half of them

---

[163] I am grateful of Dr John G. Leonard of the University of California for this information.

[164] A. R. Banerji, Assistant Collector, Ellore, to Collector of Godavari, 29 March 1901 in G.O. 1011 (L and M, M) dated 17 July 1901. *T.N.A.*

[165] *RPBC*, pp. 186–9.

[166] *MPBC*, v, 378–80.

[167] *RPBC*, p. 193.

[168] *Income Tax 1911–12*, p. 13.

operated in the countryside (and certainly it was a great deal more), we are left with only about 8000 medium-to-large creditors in an urban population of $3\frac{1}{2}$ millions.

The systems of productive industry — weaving, metal work and other necessary handicrafts — were similarly organised and were carried on by workmen who depended upon a capitalist either for their wages or for the supply of their raw materials and the marketing of their wares. Although there were many small 'one-workshop' capitalists, these in turn usually were dependent on a larger capitalist, who kept them supplied, and thus were members of a larger industrial empire. At Madura, the silk weaving and dyeing industry, which involved the bulk of the 40,000 local Sourashtra population, was, for most of our period, under the direction of four families.[169] In Madras city, the legendary Pitti Thyagaraja Chetty was said to have some 2000 weavers under him.[170] In Kumbakonam, ten Mallaga Chetties controlled most of the famous brass pot industry which had an annual turnover of Rs 40 *lakhs*.[171] Further, of course, a few employers controlled large numbers of labourers in small food-processing, house construction and transportation industries. Mothey Venkataswami of Ellore kept a private army of low-caste 'Turpu' labourers in his cotton, jute and rice mills and presses;[172] in Bezwada, a rich contractor, G. Appalaswami, had legions of quarrymen at his disposal;[173] in Tanjore, the Porayar Nadar family supported 'a vast retinue' of servants and workers.[174] Industry was not organised on principles which could sustain the hardy, independent craftsmen; rather it promoted the growth of systems of wage and debt slavery.

The pattern of stratification in urban society was further emphasised by the ownership of land. Many towns were situated on the estates of *zamindars*. The Maharaja of Vizianagram, for example, owned the large town of Vizianagram lock, stock and barrel. Similarly, in towns like Masulipatam, Cocanada, Salem and Periyakulam, individual *zamindars* had a considerable property stake.[175] Although less obvious, in *ryotwari* areas large-scale landownership was by no means unknown.

[169] *MPBC*, IV, 298.
[170] *Minutes of Evidence taken before the Indian Industrial Commission. 1916–18. Volume III*, p. 56. *P.P.* 1919. Vol. XIX.
[171] *RPBC*, p. 138.
[172] A. R. Banerji, Assistant Collector, Ellore, to Collector of Godavari, 29 March 1901 in G.O. 1011 (L and M, M) dated 17 July 1901. *T.N.A.*
[173] *Hindu* 9 June 1922.
[174] *Hindu* 23 July, 22, 24 and 27 August 1888.
[175] In Masulipatam, the Nuzvid *zamindari* family; in Cocanada, the Raja of Pithapuram; in Salem, the English *zamindar* of Salem; in Periyakulam, the *zamindar* of Doddapanayakanur.

The landholdings of T. S. Sivaswami Odayar of Kumbakonam, for example, were so extensive that they became the centre of a storm on the municipal council which served him with a compulsory purchase order on twenty-five acres.[176] In Madras city, great commercial magnates like P. Thyagaraja Chetty, the 'Gopathi' Beri Chetty family and the Muslim Badsha family eagerly bought up houses and gardens. By 1895, there were seven men in Madras city whose income from property alone was over Rs 10,000 p.a.[177] If property ownership included a market it was even more valuable, for it gave considerable control of local trading patterns. Although, by the 1900s, most urban markets had to operate under municipal licence, most also were privately owned. In Madras city, such leading political figures as Pitti Thyagaraja Chetty, C. V. Cunniah Chetty and the Gogai family, whom we shall be discussing later, were all closely associated with market control.[178]

As might be expected from the analysis of economic organisation, the distribution of wealth in the towns of Madras was at least as uneven as it was in the countryside. The vast majority of the inhabitants of the towns were desperately poor and lived at or below subsistence level. Table 2 shows in 12 major towns the number relative to the population of men whose income in 1895–6 from non-agricultural sources reached Rs 500 p.a.[179] To them must be added the owners of agricultural land inside municipal limits, market gardeners and rentiers who did not pay income tax. Nonetheless, even if the figures of Table 2 are doubled, the number of people whose incomes made them 'comfortable' – Rs 42 per month was only the salary of a middle-level government clerk – was minute. This picture of urban poverty is confirmed by the figures of the municipal franchise. In all the municipalities of Madras in 1900, only 2.2 per cent of the adult male population was able to meet the modest franchise-requirements of paying income tax or municipal taxes of Rs 3-12-0 p.a. or of holding a University degree.[180]

Information on urban wage-levels is much better than that for rural wage-levels, so we are able to proble a little deeper into the

---

[176] *Hindu* 7 and 21 September 1906.

[177] *Income Tax 1895–6.*

[178] See below pp. 200–14.

[179] *Income Tax 1895–6; Census of India. 1891. Madras. Volume XIV* (Madras, 1893), pp. 4–6. The number of assessees in Madras city does not include government servants or persons in receipt of company salaries. It thus excludes most Europeans and is far below the true figure of assessees. However, it does include most Indians (except senior government servants) and so is not an inaccurate guide to native wealth.

[180] G.O.s 1822 and 1823 (L and M, M) dated 10 December 1901. *T.N.A.*

Table 2
Assessed at income of more than Rs 500 p.a.
in 1895–6

Town	No.	Popn. of town in 1891
Madras city	1394	452,518
Kumbakonam	591	54,307
Trichinopoly	518	90,609
Salem	419	67,710
Mangalore	366	40,922
Negapatam	355	59,221
Bellary	325	59,467
Nellore	323	29,336
Tuticorin	322	25,107
Cocanada	320	40,533
Calicut	318	66,078

society which fell below the line of the income tax. In 1900 in Madras city, Binny and Co.'s cotton mill paid unskilled labourers and coolies about Rs 7-8-0 per month.[181] Binnys offered very few non-monetary benefits to their workers, so that this figure reflects quite accurately the money value of a labourer's service. However, Binnys needed a large and constant supply of labour so that their wage rates were higher than those of most employers in the city. Independent estimates of agricultural labourers' wages at this time put them at about Rs 6 p.m. and of the wages of general labourers in the city at between Rs 6 and Rs 7 p.m.[182] These rates would seem little enough, but they were taken in the capital where prices were higher than elsewhere. In the *mofussil* towns labourers earned even less, probably no more than the equivalent of Rs 4 or 5 p.m.[183] Skilled workers, of course, were better paid. But in the 1890s the maximum rate Binnys had to pay for blacksmiths and carpenters, the aristocracy of the working population, was only Rs 20 p.m., and during the trade recession of 1899–1900, they cut the rate to Rs 15 without losing their workforce.[184] The Rs 7 labourer was just able to buy sufficient food to feed his family in a good year but would almost certainly have to live in a straw hovel unless his employer gave him

[181] *Prices and Wages in India* (Calcutta, 1901), pp. 320–2.
[182] *Land Revenue 1902–3*, 'Report on Madras', p. 2.
[183] *Ibid.*, 1908–9, pp. 78–81.
[184] *Prices and Wages in India*, pp. 320–2.

shelter; the Rs 15–20 skilled artisan was more secure but scarcely able to rent or buy anything other than a hut.

Set against this background of urban poverty, the wealth of a few inhabitants of the towns appears colossal. In 1895–6, for example, 284 men in the presidency earned more than Rs 20,000 p.a. from non-agricultural sources.[185] Rs 20,000 was sufficient to keep about 350 labourers through the year. Some urban magnates earned a great deal more than this. The Maharaja of Vizianagram, based in Vizianagram town and Madras city, drew an income of at least Rs 20 *lakhs* p.a.;[186] and more than 10 other *zamindars* who were urban residents drew more than Rs 3 *lakhs* p.a.[187] Nattukottai Chetty families, like that of Raja Sir Annamalai Chetty, enjoyed the profits of banking businesses worth several *crores* of rupees.[188] Trading magnates could amass improbable fortunes, like the Muslim Abdul Hakim of Madras city who left Rs 12 *lakhs* to his children,[189] or M. Satyalingam Naicker of Cocanada who, on his death, left Rs 9 *lakhs* to charity,[190] or A. V. Jagga Rao of Vizagapatam whose income was sufficient for him to build, equip and run a first-grade college in honour of his wife.[191]

The organisation of the urban economy and the distribution of urban wealth guaranteed that a few, hugely rich magnates would exercise a pervasive influence over social and political life. Large-scale and significant creditors were in short supply, and those who did exist could extort many non-economic rewards as the price of their services. In Ellore, Mothey Venkataswami's 'word was law to the Bania community. Most Banias are moneylenders and have a large clientele. They are thus in a position to exercise pressure on their debtors and the result is that they command a strong influence ... even among other classes of the community.'[192] In Sivakasi, Tin-

---

[185] *Income Tax 1895–6.*

[186] In 1910, his income from agricultural rents alone was Rs 14 *lakhs. Land Revenue 1910–11.*   [187] *Land Revenue 1885–6,* p. 30.

[188] By the late 1920s, official estimates put the capital of the Nattukottai Chetties at between Rs 80 and 110 *crores,* Rs 70 *crores* of which was in banking. *RPBC,* pp. 186–9.

[189] Before dividing his estates, Abdul Hakim already had given away more than Rs 4 *lakhs* to charity. *The Asylum Press Almanack and Directory of Southern India. 1925* (Madras, 1925), p. 1269.

[190] Sastri (ed.), *Encyclopaedia of the Madras Presidency,* p. 505.

[191] *Hindu* 23 January 1904.

[192] A. R. Banerji, Assistant Collector, Ellore, to Collector of Godavari, 29 March 1901 in G.O. 1011 (L and M, M) dated 17 July 1901; for similar comments on the influence of rich Komatis in Guntur, see 'Memo. of Chairman, Guntur Municipality' in G.O. 25 (L and M, M) dated 11 January 1893.

nevelly district, local Nadar merchant-moneylenders were sufficiently powerful to force the whole town, including non-Nadars, to pay taxes to their communal charities.[193] In Kumbakonam, the clients of the Poraya Nadars included Brahman *mirasidars*, local traders and property owners, policemen, revenue officials and, it was rumoured, even the Collector.[194]

In a society without welfare facilities of any kind, without a free labour market and without a secure food supply, workers and labourers were very largely under the dominance of their employers. Most artisans were so sunk in debt to their capitalist that they could never escape and so dependent upon him that when, as in famines, he withdrew his support, they starved.[195]

The direct power of urban property ownership was also considerable. In most towns there was competition for the most central shop sites and the most desirable residences, with the result that the owner was in a position of dictatorship. In Vizianagram, the *samasthanam*'s will had such strength that no local political leadership could exist for long in opposition to it. Even a millionaire banker was prepared to break up his caste conference on its orders.[196] In Kumbakonam, the town landowning family of Sivaswami Odayar was prominent for many years and used its resources to take over the affairs of the municipal council: 'T. S. Sivaswami Odayar made it a rule to fill the council with his friends and supporters. . . . The Municipal Staff were his dependents. The contractors were his tenants.'[197]

By controlling tightly the economic resources of the towns, a small number of men forced the general population to turn to them for the most basic economic services. Members of this minute elite, however, were well placed to make their presence felt in several other ways. In addition to the power that followed from the way that they earned their income, there was the power that they derived from the way that they spent it. Many historians have seen how, in pre-British India, the conspicuous expenditure of political and religious leaders brought whole towns into existence, as tradesmen, artisans and merchants gathered to serve their wants. During the nineteenth century, with much state-power lost to Indians, these developments may have been

[193] R. L. Hardgrave, *The Nadars of Tamilnad* (Berkeley and Los Angeles, 1969), p. 99.
[194] *Hindu* 7 March 1888, 10 and 17 June 1896.
[195] See *Minutes of Evidence taken before the Indian Industrial Commission. 1916–18. Volume III*, pp. 330–31. *P.P.* 1919, Vol. XIX; *Report on the Famine in the Madras Presidency during 1896 and 1897* (Madras, 1898), II, 355–76.
[196] In 1910, the Komati merchant P. Ramamurthi broke up a session of his caste conference at Vizianagram when its activities began to run counter to the orders which he had received from the Maharani. *Hindu* 14 June and 8 July 1910.
[197] G.O. 1133 (L and M, M) dated 23 June 1906. *T.N.A.*

less spectacular but they were, nonetheless, of considerable importance. Wealthy Indians provided the main supplement to government spending on public works and welfare. Every town owed most of its facilities – schools, libraries, hospitals, town halls, rest-houses and parks – to the generosity of native patrons. In some activities, the British deliberately stood back; all support for religion and the poor outside famines came from rich Indian townsmen. Sometimes the scale of these patronage endeavours could be truly fabulous. Between 1860 and 1914, for example, the small community of Nattukottai Chetty bankers spent more than Rs 1.82 *crores* on the restoration of the great temples.[198] Two Nattukottais, the brothers S. R. Rm. A. Ramaswami and Annamalai Chetty, were particularly generous in other areas: Ramaswami built a complete water-supply system for the town of Chidambaram,[199] and Annamalai spent Rs 1 *lakh* on the Madura College[200] and Rs 30 *lakhs* on a University.[201] In the seventy years to 1940, the Gujerati Vaishya family of Lodd Govindoss spent Rs 50 *lakhs* on various projects, including the feeding of 35,000 poor every year in Chidambaram.[202] The Pydah Komati banking family funded cow-protection in the Northern Circars to the tune of Rs 2 *lakhs*, built a library and town hall for Cocanada, and backed the Widow Remarriage Movement with Rs 30,000.[203] The Maharaja of Vizianagram founded schools, Sanskrit *patsalas*, colleges and charities all over the South. If few Madras magnates had the wealth to match these efforts, many were capable of operating significantly in a single locality. In Bellary town, for example, the millionaire industralist A. Sabhapati Mudaliar built two hospitals and a school during the 1880s.[204] In Cocanada, K. Basivi Reddi also built a school and founded three *choultries*.[205] In the crudest economic terms, the extension of this patronage linked the magnate to a wider section of the population and made it dependent on him. However, and more importantly, it also validated his role as an authority.

[198] 'Proceedings of the Religious Endowment Conference held at Delhi on the 16th March 1914, Appendix 3, in Home Judicial A July 1914, Nos 265–87. *N.A.I.*

[199] At a cost of Rs 1.3 *lakhs, ibid.* [200] *Hindu* 8 December 1915.

[201] L. P. K. Ramanathan Chettiar, *Annamalai Aracar* (Madras, 1965), pp. 61–74 (Tamil).

[202] See B. V. Nacharayya, *Biography of Zemindar Lodd Govindass Varu* (Madras, 1942); also, Anon., *Biography of Sriman Lodd Govindoss Maharaj. The Hindu Hero* (Madras, 1942).

[203] Sastri (ed.), *Encyclopaedia of the Madras Presidency*, p. 738; K. Viresalingam, *The Autobiography of Rao Bahadur Kandukuri Viresalingam Pantulu* (Madras, 1911). (Telugu).

[204] *Hindu* 24 October 1883.

[205] *Report on the Famine in the Madras Presidency during 1896 and 1897*, I, 47.

Philanthropy, a religious duty, brought virtue and a heightened social status to its practitioner. Patrons who were seen to be beneficent won the support and respect of the men around them. Religious and cultural forms of patronage activity were especially meritworthy; and incalculable sums of money were poured into movements for the reform and revival of various aspects of indigenous civilisation. Hindu merchants and *zamindars* renovated temples, founded Sanskrit Colleges and fed Brahmans; Muslim millionaires refurbished mosques and set up *Madrassas*. Tamilians, like the Raja of Ramnad and the Nattukottai Chetty *zamindar* of Andipatti,[206] and Telugus, like the Nuzvid *zamindars*,[207] sponsored vernacular revivalism. Everywhere, rich urban inhabitants funded local festivals, music circles and literary associations. In South India, wealth could be translated into social status and the maximum of social influence only through patronage endeavours.[208] The wealth which the few urban magnates enjoyed was used to put them at the centre of the social and cultural life of their towns.

It is not surprising that, with so many means at their disposal for cajoling or coercing their neighbours, the greater urban magnates exercised informal powers of government in the towns. Before the completion of the British legal system in the mid-nineteenth century, they often had acted as arbitrators in the disputes of the general populace. When examining Salem in the 1850s, for example, J. W. B. Dykes noted that its inhabitants usually took their cases to 'Chetties' of various kinds.[209] Chetty, however, does not mean headman, as Dykes seemed to think, but is the Tamil word for merchant. Even in the later nineteenth and twentieth centuries, the larger merchant-

---

[206] Patrons of the Madura Tamil Sangham.

[207] Whose court maintained several endowments for Telugu poetry.

[208] This statement ought not to be taken to mean that patrons need only have been interested in the public influence which they developed through patronage activities. There is no reason why they should not have possessed also a personal interest in the objectives which they were supporting. However, our purpose here is political history and patronage activities served a public, political end. Moreover, the existence of this end was well known to the patrons themselves. While intellectual or religious motivation can account for the particular choices which patrons made when offering their support to one movement rather than another, they cannot explain the external style which was part of every act of patronage. There were no anonymous patrons in the South India of our period and every patron was concerned to maximise the public attention which was drawn to his act of patronage. The patron wanted not only to support a cultural movement but *to be seen* to support it − our explanation above is only of why he should want his act to be seen.

[209] J. W. B. Dykes, *Salem: An Indian Collectorate* (London, 1853), pp. 221−4.

financiers continued to provide courts alongside those of the British, particularly to handle trade disputes.[210] The more powerful *zamindars* in their estate capitals also heard cases.[211] During famines or shortages, the urban population looked to their magnates to fend off starvation by organising grain distributions and by expanding employment facilities.[212] When rioting broke out, it was the same handful of principal citizens who came forward to re-establish order. Following the anti-European riots in Cocanada in 1907, for example, the police reported:

There are 3 or 4 very influential men such as K. Basivi Reddy, K. Suryanarayana, late Pydah Ramakrishniah's son, Krishnamurthi, Nalam Padmanabhan [all merchant-moneylenders] and others who are in entire sympathy with the [*swadeshi*] movement. It is said that it is on account of these people that the riots ended so smoothly. But for these merchants people say that the whole lot of Europeans in Cocanada would have been massacred on that day.[213]

The strength of influence exercised by the wealthier urban magnates can be seen most clearly on the occasions when it ran against the power of the British Government. If rich *zamindars* supported violent mobs, as in Masulipatam in 1886,[214] or Komati merchants fomented riots, as in Salem in 1882[215] and Guntur in 1917,[216] there was nothing that the British could do to prevent mayhem. Similarly, if dominant merchant groups refused to co-operate with municipal government, as in Masulipatam in 1891,[217] Guntur in 1892[218] and Vanniyambadi in 1904,[219] it became impossible for the British to find men willing to take over the functions of the municipal council. In some towns, the British were forced to recognise that unless a certain man or group were allowed the powers of rulership, no government could exist. In 1901, for example, the Collector of Godāvari and his

[210] See below pp. 139–40.
[211] For example, see the *durbar* held by the Raja of Ramnad in *Hindu* 15 October 1894.
[212] *Report on the Famine in the Madras Presidency during 1896 and 1897*, I, 47.
[213] 'Confidential Report No. 1₂ R. W. D. Ashe, Collector and District Magistrate, Godavari District, dated 8 July 1908' in Venkatarangaiya (ed.), *The Freedom Struggle in Andhra Pradesh (Andhra)*, III, 255.
[214] G.O. 2555 (Judicial) dated 6 December 1893. *T.N.A.*; see also P & J File 258 of 1894. *I.O.L.*
[215] G.O. 1374 (Judicial) dated 23 May 1883. *T.N.A.*
[216] G.O. 2461 (Judicial) dated 26 November 1917. *T.N.A.*
[217] G.O. 564 (L and M, M) dated 16 April 1891. *T.N.A.*
[218] G.O. 25 (L and M, M) dated 11 January 1893. *T.N.A.*
[219] G.O. 802 (L and M, M) dated 28 April 1904. *T.N.A.*

Assistant Collector became aware of the extent of Mothey Venka-taswami's influence in Ellore. After considering the alternatives to him, however, the Assistant Collector came to the conclusion that it would be more expedient to leave him alone.[220] At least in Ellore, government officials eventually had managed to find witnesses prepared to tell them what was happening in the town. But in very many areas, particular magnates were able to operate networks so powerful that the British were unable to detach from them anybody of significance and could not even contemplate taking action. In Bezwada, between 1916 and 1919, a deputy-collector and a *tahsildar* tried desperately to make a case against G. Appalaswami, the contractor-banker who ran the town, but finally had to give up for want of a single reliable witness.[221] Similarly in Madura, investigations into one of the agents of K. V. Ramachari, a Sourashtra millionaire dye-merchant, came to nothing when the prosecutor had to admit that 'the impeachment could not stand the test of legal proof' although, by any standard other than that of the British law, the agent was guilty of rigging elections and embezzling public funds.[222]

The wealthy urban magnate operated a series of dependency networks which were strictly analogous to those of the rural-local boss. Through his control of economic resources, he was able to provide vital facilities which put him at the centre of local life. To take a single case, Mothey Venkataswami counted among his men the influential Brahman lawyer C. Sitaramayya, who handled his legal affairs and conducted his relations with the institutions of British government; Brahman priests who lived by his patronage; fellow merchant-moneylenders who traded on his capital; government servants whom he bought; local landowners and members of the professions to whom he lent money; the principal Muslim Kazi family of the area, which owed him *lakhs* of rupees and did his bidding on the municipal council; respectable families of all kinds who lived on his property; low-caste Turpu labourers who worked in his factories and mills; and everybody who attended the festivals which he patronised or needed his support for any project.[223] Mothey Venka-taswami had his counterpart in nearly every town; indeed, in the larger towns he usually had several. In Madura, between about 1890

220 Collector of Godavari to Secretary, Local and Municipal Department, 9 January 1902 in G.O. 140 (L and M, M) dated 7 February 1902. *T.N.A.*

221 G.O. 1017 (L and M, M) dated 5 July 1919. *T.N.A.*

222 G.O. 236 (L and M, M) dated 2 February 1916. *T.N.A.*

223 A. R. Banerji, Assistant Collector, Ellore, to Collector of Godavari, 29 March 1901 in G.O. 1011 (L and M, M) dated 17 July 1901. *T.N.A.*

and 1910, there were four rival magnates of great power: K. V. Ramachari, the Sourashtra dye-merchant; Robert Fischer, a European banker, *zamindar* and barrister; a Komati banker-trader;[224] and the resident Nattukottai Chetties. In Kumbakonam, between the mid-1880s and the 1910s, the highest level of urban leadership was split between the Porayar Nadars, T. S. Sivaswami Odayar (who himself was allied to the Nattukottai Chetties)[225] and S. A. Saminatha Iyer, a *mirasidar*, property-owner, lawyer and moneylender. The size of the networks which were at the disposal of men of this kind, and their obvious strength at times of riot or in opposition to the government, suggests that in urban as in rural Madras, structures of power are best seen in terms of patron–client relationships.

If, for the time being, we accept this suggestion, then to judge change in urban society we must look in several directions. Firstly, we must examine the economy and the distribution of wealth to see if any significant alterations, which could upset magnate structures, were taking place in them. The expansion of trade in agricultural produce, which recommenced after the Great Famine, obviously brought increasing wealth to towns which were situated on railways and harbours. Both income-tax and municipal tax payments increased faster than can be accounted for by improvements in collection techniques and, before the Income-Tax and District Municipalities Acts of 1919 and 1920, by changes in the rates.[226] The number of factories grew.[227] Demands for new urban services, such as those based on oil and electricity, created new channels for business activity. The population of most towns increased.[228] Admittedly, outside the Andhra deltas none of these developments was in any way dramatic, and Madras society remained overwhelmingly rural in character. Yet, clearly, the towns were becoming richer. An initial question must be what difference did this make to the structure of urban wealth.

[224] Known colloquially as Sriman Chetty.

[225] He was deeply in debt to them and repaid some of the interest by providing them with political favours. In return, they backed him in the municipal council and temple committee. Collector of Tanjore to Secretary, Local and Municipal Department, 17 March 1903 in G.O. 528 (L and M, M) dated 6 April 1903. *T.N.A.*

[226] Income tax from Rs 27 *lakhs* in 1899–1900 to Rs 75 *lakhs* in 1918–19, *Income Tax 1899–1900* and *ibid., 1918–19*; and municipal tax from Rs 31 *lakhs* in 1900–1 to Rs 94 *lakhs* in 1918–19, G.O. 1822–3 (L and M, M) dated 10 December 1901 and G.O. 550 (L and M, M) dated 20 April 1920. *T.N.A.*

[227] *Census of India. 1921. Madras. Volume XIII. Part I* (Madras, 1922), p. 190.

[228] *Census of India. 1931. Madras. Volume XIV* (Madras, 1933), pp. 10–16.

A complete answer is very difficult to provide, but one point is certain: the distribution of incomes was not becoming more even. Between the mid-1880s and 1912–17, the price of the poorer food-stuffs in most urban markets doubled. The most reliable evidence indicates that wage rates only just kept pace with this increase. In Binnys cotton mill, the wages of coolies rose from about Rs 7.5 per month to about Rs 14.[229] The wages of runners in the post-office – again an employer whose wage rates can be trusted – rose in the same period from a maximum of Rs 16 p.m. to about Rs 30.[230] The presence of inflation in an economy without trades union organisations, however, led to a rapid stratification of the wage structure. In Binnys' mill in 1900, for example, the minimum wage paid to a blacksmith was Rs 0.5625 per diem and the maximum Rs 0.75.[231] By 1917, the minimum had risen to only Rs 0.6875 p.d. but the maximum had shot up to Rs 1.6532.[232] The differentials among Binnys' bricklayers were even greater: from a scale of Rs 0.4219 to Rs 0.500 in 1900 to one of Rs 0.4531 to Rs 2.0156 in 1917.[233] And among postal runners they were growing: from a scale of Rs 10 to Rs 16 p.m. in 1900 to one of Rs 14 to Rs 30 in 1917.[234] The rates suggest that the ties of dependency by which employers held down their work force were increasing in strength. Only those workers whom the employers chose were being protected from the effects of inflation; the rest suffered a steady decrease in their standard of living.

Changes in the distribution of higher incomes present the same sorry picture. The only general sources which we have for higher incomes are the income-tax statistics, which include rural incomes and are not precise. Yet, if they provide us with no more than a general impression of the change, they at least point us in its direction. By 1895–6, the income-tax administration had been operational for a decade and had sorted out most of its original problems. Its administrative categories, with a few specific exceptions, did not alter until 1919. In 1895–6, about 64 per cent of assessees on incomes of above Rs 1000 per annum fell into the middle-income bracket of between Rs 1000 and Rs 2000.[235] In 1918–19, the percentage was 59.[236] It would indeed be difficult on this evidence to find important new groups who were making money and beginning to alter the very hierarchical structure of urban wealth. Of course, the absolute number of people in the Rs 1000 to Rs 2000 bracket had grown, from 16,500 to

[229] *Prices and Wages in India* (Calcutta, 1920), pp. 219–21.
[230] *Ibid.*, pp. 197–200.   [231] *Ibid.*, pp. 219–21.
[232] *Ibid.*   [233] *Ibid.*   [234] *Ibid.*
[235] *Income Tax 1895–6.*   [236] *Income Tax 1918–19.*

30,000,[237] but given the background of inflation, this increase is remarkably small. In 1895–6, there had been 47,500 people in the Rs 500 to Rs 1000 bracket, who, if they were only holding their own, ought to have appeared higher up in 1918–19.[238] If there were a significant change between 1895–6 and 1918–19, it did not come from a rise in the number of middle-income earners who would be likely to form an independent factor in urban political life. Rather it came at the other end of the incomes scale. In 1895–6, only 284 men were classed as earning an income of more than Rs 20,000 per annum; and of these only 50 earned more than Rs 50,000.[239] By 1918–19, however, there were 826 assessees in the Rs 20,000 class and 201 in the Rs 50,000 class.[240] Most of the new wealth which was accruing in the towns was going to support or create greater magnates. The absence of a dynamic middle-level income sector is confirmed also by municipal voting figures. In 1920, the franchise qualification was dropped to bring in all those who paid only one rupee per annum in municipal taxation. But it enfranchised just 5.4 per cent. of the municipal population.[241]

The magnate structure of economic power and influence was not being undermined, at least by economic movements. But how secure were the finance of those who belonged to the magnate stratosphere and how readily did new men rise to join them? No precise answer can be given to this question but there is much to suggest that mobility, although it was taking place, was fairly slow and of a kind unlikely to promote social disturbance. The significance of the total increase in Rs 50,000 plus earners is scaled down when set against a background of inflation and of an urban population of more than three millions. There were not many more very rich men in urban Madras in 1918 than there had been in 1895. Moreover, most of the identifiably powerful urban magnate families of 1895 (and indeed of 1875) were maintaining their positions. The Nattukottai Chetty bankers of the South, the great Komati families of Mothey, Pydah, Nalam and Majeti of the Andhra deltas, the Roche-Victoria Christian family of Tuticorin, the Maracair Muslim community of Negapatam, and the 'Gopathi' and 'Pitti' Beri Chetty families and the 'Badsha' Muslim family of Madras city lived through the period with their influence undiminished. The casualties, such as A. Sabhapati Mudaliar of Bellary, whose *abkari* contracting and cotton-purchasing and manufacturing empire collapsed in 1896, and Raja Sir Savalai

---

[237] *Income Tax 1895–6; ibid., 1918–19.*   [238] *Income Tax 1895–6.*
[239] *Ibid.*   [240] *Income Tax 1918–19.*
[241] G.O. 973 (L.S.G.) dated 30 May 1921. *T.N.A.*

Ramaswami Mudaliar, whose finance and commodity business fell with his creditors, Arbuthnot and Company, were not heavy.

The stability of the magnate elite was not the result of a complete absence of opportunities for 'new' men to get in at the lower levels of the urban economy. Obviously, the expansion of trade must have provided some openings for the razor-sharp entrepreneur. There were also two important economic institutions which lay outside the 'natural' processes of the economy and from which quick fortunes could be made. The first was the government which in addition to an administration was a huge commercial company, operating monopolies in salt, opium and alcohol, and building roads and railways. It could offer a lucrative source of income to anybody it chose, no matter what his financial standing. In Cuddapah, for example, the family of V. G. Vasudeva Pillai made a small fortune in army contracting during the Second Burma War;[242] in Tanjore, the great Porayar Nadar family started its rise with an *abkari* contract in the 1830s;[243] in Bellary, A. Sabhapati Mudaliar also began with a distilling contract.[244] The second institution was the temple. Temples often owned landed property, markets and warehouses in urban Madras and could be important sources of credit. Anybody who could obtain influence with the governors of a temple could dip his hands into a deep till. In Madura in the early twentieth century, K. M. Alladin Rowther was able to lift himself out of the profession of brothel-keeper, petty criminal and extortionist into that of real estate agent by developing a connection with a member of the Sri Minakshi temple committee. He became a successful property speculator.[245]

The significance of these two institutions in creating new pockets of wealth, or rather in placing wealth in new hands, however, was reduced by two factors. In general, it would seem that the number of opportunities for initial gain provided by the government and the temples declined steadily from a peak in the 1820s and 1830s. In the early days of the British *raj*, when the government was reorganising and inventing administrations, the coffers of the *Sirker* were wide open. Not only were the provincial scope and requirements of the government novel in South India but British officials had little knowledge of the indigenous banking and commercial systems. Improbably

---

[242] V. G. Venugopala Pillai to Secretary, Local and Municipal Department, 14 October 1919. In G.O. 182 (L and M, M) dated 2 February 1920. *T.N.A.*

[243] *Hindu* 7 March 1888.

[244] By 1885, he held *abkari* contracts in most of the Ceded Districts. *Abkari 1885–6*, p. 15.

[245] G.O. 1384 (L and M, M) dated 16 August 1917. *T.N.A.*

unimportant groups were able to latch onto government contracts and monopolies, and some men's fortunes were made more because the *raj* deemed them to be financially sound than because they were. As, at this time, the British also had taken over temple management, the disruptive influence of governmental innovation and ignorance created opportunities for speculation in temple properties as well. By the 1880s, however, the administration had stabilised and the myopia of the British had become less serious. Monopolies and contracts tended to be concentrated in the businesses of men of proven worth; and when new schemes were developed, it was these magnates who were given the first choice of them. Thus, by the 1890s, the *abkari* contracts for the entire presidency were held by only six firms;[246] thus also, successful operators, such as the Porayar Nadars and the Nattukottai Chetties, were able to engross several monopolies at the same time. The Porayar Nadars added the salt trade to their extensive liquor empire;[247] while the Nattukottai Chetties who, by 1916, controlled salt supplies to the central eastern seaboard,[248] were able to take up an option on a new distillery.[249] As the larger magnates expanded across several districts and trades, the chances for the 'new' man diminished. Moreover, from the 1860s, the government steadily withdrew from several areas of previous activity and created in them political institutions which were open to local control. As we shall see, this meant that it opened them to direct magnate dominance. It is not surprising that, under the municipal council's rule, the Mothey family had the tolls farm of Ellore;[250] nor that the farm of the Trichinopoly municipal council's celebrated Fort market should be in the pocket of one of the area's richest merchants;[251] nor that, under the regulations for the election of members of temple committees, which came into force in 1863, the dominant temple politicians of Kumbakonam should be T. S. Sivaswami Odayar, S. A. Saminatha Iyer and T. Ponnuswami Nadar of Porayar.[252]

On the rare occasions when a would-be tycoon managed to make an initial breakthrough, he was faced with a further, and in most cases insurmountable, problem − that of credit. Security for loans was as much of a difficulty in the towns as it was in the countryside.

---

[246] *Abkari 1896−7*, p. 15.

[247] *Hindu* 1 August 1894.

[248] *Hindu* (weekly) 27 January 1916.

[249] *Abkari 1918−19*, p. 1.

[250] G.O. 1360 (L and M, M) dated 1 December 1888, *T.N.A.*

[251] G.O. 2089 (L and M, M) dated 16 December 1919. *T.N.A.*

[252] *Hindu* 23 July, 22, 24 and 27 August 1888.

The primary concern of any entrepreneur, once he has brought off a successful deal or gained a position in the market, is to find cheap money for expansion. But in Madras, this operation could take a considerable time and be fraught with danger. On loans to the uncreditworthy, moneylenders insisted on interest rates of between 20 and 40 per cent, and often took their charges from the principal when it was given. To meet large or long-term interest payments, the entrepreneur would have to make quick and fabulous returns. The Madras economy, while buoyant, seldom stretched to these. In order to obtain reasonable rates for credit, the entrepreneur had two courses open to him. He could establish his creditworthiness by proving the financial stability of his businesses over the years. Once this was accomplished he had access to funds from Nattukottai Chetties, Marwaris, Multanis and even the Bank of Madras. However, if he chose this path it is obvious that he would be held down at a low level of commercial activity for decades, if not generations. Moreover, he was likely to find himself going round in circles, for until he could demonstrate his ability to handle big business operations he could not get the cash to start big business operations.

The more common course followed by rising magnates who were successful was to forge marriage connections, which acted as security, with families who were capable of providing credit. This condition naturally reduced the number of potential stars on the commercial horizon, for marriage possibilities in any one generation were limited by factors of sub-caste and of acceptance.

Movements from rags to riches, therefore, were achieved most usually by groups of interrelated families and not by individuals; and this process also took time. The Nadar traders of northern Tinnevelly and Ramnad, for example, moved into the area before 1820 as petty-traders and haulage contractors.[253] By making marriage alliances, some of their leading families were able to provide credit facilities for each other, be it only at first in a small way, and to combine the accumulation of capital with the development of the high degree of liquidity necessary for taking opportunities in various places when they came. However, it was not until the 1870s at the earliest (and not until the 1890s truly) that the Nadars of Kamudi, Sivakasi and Virudhunagar began to show their magnate position by challenging for local political power.[254] Similarly, it took most of the nineteenth century for the Christian Bharatha fishermen of

---

[253] Hardgrave, *The Nadars of Tamilnad* pp. 96–8; *Hindu* 7 March 1888.
[254] Hardgrave, *ibid.*, pp, 105–29.

Tuticorin to produce the great houses of Roche-Victoria and Cruz Fernandez or for the Telaga ex-peasant traders of the Cocanada–Rajahmundry area to produce the families of K. Basivi Reddi and K. Suryanarayanamurthi Naidu.[255]

In the absence of joint-stock banks which were prepared to deal in the commerce of the interior, financial institutions in Madras continued to be based on familial or quasi-familial organisations. The great Nattukottai Chetty banks were essentially family businesses built up over generations by sending out scions to various localities with capital which was steadily increased and passed back to the family home. New inflows into any particular bank owed more to marriages than to deposits from outsiders; as late as 1929, the Chetties were trading with a capital 80 per cent their own.[256] Komati families in Andhra, such as the Pydah, Mothey, Nalam and Majeti, and Tamil Muslim families operated similar organisations.[257] Where a number of families related by caste worked out of a common base, supra-familial ties between them developed in order to improve security and raise credit. The Nattukottai Chetties, whose international empire centred on a block of villages in Ramnad, had carried this furthest and recognised a form of joint-liability in their dealings.[258] In their particular towns, Komatis and Tamil Muslims also were often linked in their operations.[259] The basic unit of activity, however, always remained the family and, within any communal group, individual family businesses continued to rise and fall. Obviously, this factor put a considerable brake on effective upward mobility. Few families could break through into the magnate elite, and those who succeeded took a generation or more to consolidate their position. When movement was this slow, it allowed time for the rising family to be assimilated. Although it increased the possibilities of magnate rivalry, it did not upset the magnate system.

The major economic resources of Madras remained in the hands of a small urban elite, the social composition of which was stable. This conclusion is supported also by an investigation into the mechanics of investment. In his study of 'Tezibazaar' in Northern India, Richard Fox has shown how, over a considerable period, urban

[255] See Sastri (ed.), *Encyclopaedia of the Madras Presidency*, p. 510.
[256] *RPBC*, pp. 186–9.
[257] For the Komatis, see F. J. Richards, 'Cross-Cousin Marriage in South India' in *Man*, 97 (1914); E. Thurston, *Castes and Tribes of Southern India* (Madras, 1909), III, 307–11.
[258] *RPBC*, pp. 186–9.
[259] G.O. 3360 (L.S.G.) dated 8 September 1928. *S.A.H.*

merchant groups used their financial power and new systems of administration to take over power in the town from the local *zamindar*, whose influence was based only on property ownership.[260] Obviously, in an expanding commercial economy, the profits of trade were likely to be greater than those derived from legally controlled rents. In Madras, however, very few towns fit the model of Tezibazaar. Of the larger conurbations, only in Masulipatam was there anything approaching a simple landlord/merchant conflict.[261] Elsewhere, patterns of investment make it extremely difficult to divide economic activities between neatly defined social groups. On the one hand, as we mentioned before, many *zamindars* were diversifying their private economies and becoming involved in urban trade, commerce and manufacture. Rural-boss groups also were coming into the towns and the wealthiest families among them were leaving agents to trade and bank in their own right.[262] On the other hand, mercantile families were moving their surpluses into urban property and into privileged *zamindari* and *inamdari* rent rights. The Mothey and Majeti families of Andhra, the Nattukottai Chetties of Ramnad, the Gopathi and Pitti Beri Chetties and the Muslim Badshas of Madras city all came to own estates and extensive house properties in their respective locales.[263] By 1880, probably by 1850, the distribution of investments had become so wide that most magnates had come to have interests in most aspects of their local economies. As individuals, they sat across property ownership, credit, trade and manufacture, and drew profits and powers from them all. They were able thus to preserve themselves from a decline in any one sector of the economy and maintain their positions more securely. While, undoubtedly, there were status rivalries between 'ancient' and 'modern' merchant-landowners, these ought not to be seen as class rivalries derived from different relationships to the methods of production. There were rivalries no less bitter between one 'new' merchant-landowner and

---

[260] See R. G. Fox, *From Zamindar to Ballot Box* (New York, 1969).

[261] The particular fields of confrontation were the municipal council and various committees which administered public facilities. See, for example, *Hindu*, 11 May 1907.

[262] For example, T. Ramalingam Chetty (q.v.) of Coimbatore whose family cluster originally were Vellala landowners. By the later nineteenth century, the family were running an urban banking business worth Rs 7 *lakhs* and had become known as 'Chetty' trader Vellalas.

[263] See 'Landowners of Madras' in *Asylum Press Almanack and Directory of Madras and Southern India. 1910.* (Madras, 1910).

another;[264] and there were alliances of great strength between ancient *zamindars* and new merchant-landowners.[265] In the South, a better model would be of magnates of promiscuous origin but presently involved in very similar activities, each vying with and temporarily allying with others of the type for prestige, status and power. We shall see this more clearly when investigating the politics of the municipal council but such a system, of course, could only operate in conditions of considerable economic and social stability.

Thus far, our analysis of the foundations of political organisation in the towns has excluded consideration of the role of the educated Indian. This omission may seem strange. In much historiography of modern India, educated groups have been characterised as the most dynamic elements in social and political change. As their activities were largely confined to the towns, their most profound impact came in the sphere of urban life. In recent works, R. K. Ray, Christine Dobbin and C. A. Bayly have shown how lawyers, journalists and ex-public servants came to challenge for social power in Calcutta from the 1850s, Bombay city from the 1850s and Allahabad from the 1900s respectively.[266] The Madras Presidency possessed educated groups which were socially analogous to the *bhadralok* of Bengal, the Chitpavan Brahmans of Bombay and the Kayastha/Urdu Muslim 'service' families of the U.P.: the Brahman and Sat-Sudra families, who invested in education, tended to have served as administrators under previous native regimes, to come from an economic background of small landownership and to be concerned primarily with obtaining stakes in government service and the liberal professions. They were numerous – the educated community of Madras was second in size only to that of Bengal – and, from their salaries, rents and fees, would seem as economically independent of magnate in-

[264] As between the Sourashtra dye-merchant and property-owner K. V. Ramachari and several Balija Naidu landlord-merchants in Madura, G.O. 382 (L and M, M) dated 29 February 1912; G.O. 1203 (L and M, M) dated 1 July 1912. *T.N.A.*

[265] As between the *zamindar* of Doddapanayakanur and several traders in Periyakulam. Collector of Madura to Secretary, Local and Municipal Department, 11 February 1919 in G.O. 374 (L and M, M) dated 6 March 1919; also G.O. 1383 (L and M, M) dated 18 September 1919. *T.N.A.*

[266] R. K. Ray, 'Social Conflict and Political Unrest in Bengal, 1875 to 1925'. Unpublished Ph.d. dissertation, Cambridge University, 1972; C. Dobbin, *Urban Leadership in Western India. Politics and Communities in Bombay City 1840–1885.* (Oxford, 1972); C. A. Bayly, 'The Development of Political Organisation in the Allahabad Locality, 1880 to 1925'. Unpublished D. Phil. dissertation, Oxford University, 1970.

fluence as their counterparts in other provinces. They also were very active in religious revival, social reform, cultural regeneration and nationalist movements.

It is one of the main and recurring arguments of this book, however, that their importance as an independent factor in the politics of Madras was very limited. Outside the capital, and there for only ten years, they lacked the institutional power to dictate political commands to any other than fellow-educated 'service' and professional groups. While it would be possible to tell an interesting tale of their own internal debates and conflicts and of their abortive attempts to wield influence, it would be misleading to term this story 'South Indian politics', for it would have very little to do with the exercise of power. The reasons why the western-educated groups of Madras failed to reach the political positions enjoyed by their colleagues in other provinces lie, of course, in the political structure of the South: while the educated themselves may have been very similar to the educated in Bengal, Bombay and U.P., the political structure in which they had to operate was not. The organisation of political power in South India persistently excluded them from places of importance.

In this chapter, we have been examining the economic instruments of power. Let us first see what position the educated occupied in the systems by which wealth was made and spent. In the magnate-dominated economy, they were simple, if valuable, dependents. Komati merchants hired (and fired) Brahman clerks,[267] Nadar traders used Vellala accountants,[268] *zamindars* took their administrators from the same families as the government. All rich men retained the best *vakils* and bribed the best government servants whom they could find. While, as we have indicated, many of the educated came from petty landowning families, the incomes which they derived from land seldom were sufficient to provide them with an independent basis for existence in the towns – had they done so, there would have been no need for the educated to seek alternative employment. Even in those economic activities where they could be seen to be important, the educated had achieved their local places usually by trading on capital which belonged to others rather than themselves. Although clerks, lawyers and officials often were able to keep their masters ignorant of what they were doing and were capable of projecting their own

---

[267] For example, the father of Konda Venkatappayya, a famous Andhra Brahman politician, was a clerk in a Komati firm. K. Venkatappayya, *Sviya Caritra* (Vijayawada, 1952), I, 6. (Telugu).

[268] Hardgrave, *The Nadars of Tamilnad*, p. 100.

ideas into urban society, their dependency always restricted them in what they could be seen to be doing. If they broke faith with their patrons, they lost their sources of support. Only at the very top of the legal and bureaucratic ladders were lawyers and bureaucrats in a position of sufficient wealth and influence to dictate the terms on which they would serve particular magnates.

From the later nineteenth century, however, the primitive institutions of the magnate economy were joined and pressed by more sophisticated financial organisations. The growth of the economy and the instability of existing credit organisation promoted the need for a more advanced financial institution than the moneylender. Towards the end of our period, several joint-stock banks, co-operative credit societies and insurance companies appeared. The men who controlled them often were socially distinct from the older credit magnates. Their abilities lay in literacy and organisational expertise which enabled them to manipulate masses of small deposits rather than in the personal possession of wealth. They could be seen as a managerial element within the society of the educated. By picking up the threads of credit and commerce, they could develop their own economic and political controls. In 1888, for example, the Sub-Collector of Tuticorin reported of his municipal council:

'The Hindus form a compact party and, through the influence of the Bank Cashier [of the Bank of Madras] over the Chairman, they have complete control of the Council. The Bank Cashier, a clever Brahmin, is, in fact, the ruler of the municipality though the Bank would not allow him to be Chairman. . . . Those who have transactions with the Bank are naturally afraid to oppose him.[269]

Later, the cashier was elected to the district temple committee – a sign of great influence.[270] Other Bank of Madras cashiers, in Guntur and Bezwada, also were prominent municipal politicians.[271] Until 1900 or so, most of the activities of the Bank of Madras were confined to the ports; but gradually it shifted its interests inland and was joined by the Indian Bank, the Nedungadi Bank, the Nadar Bank and the Specie Bank of India. From about the turn of the century, co-operative credit societies and Indian insurance companies also began to appear. A whole new financial apparatus, with different men at its controls, was in the process of formation.

[269] Note signed Divisional Officer, Tuticorin, 29 February 1888 in G.O. 508 (L and M, M) dated 17 May 1888. *T.N.A.*
[270] *Hindu* 9 December 1896.
[271] *Hindu* 29 October 1912 and 12 February 1915.

At the other end of the system which gave social pre-eminence to the magnate, new developments were taking place in the organisations of public action. The expansion of the educated community, the arrival of the printing press and the growing consciousness of national, regional and religious identities under foreign rule, all helped to create a new theatre for local activities. Associations for religious and cultural revival and reform shot up in many towns; newspapers and tract societies poured out propaganda to be read by townsmen; debating societies and protonationalist clubs appeared to try to influence the conduct of local and even provincial bureaucrats. Once again, the men who led these were predominantly western educated professionals and literati, who possessed the organisational and educational skills. As the scope of their activities grew, they could hope to become recognised and supported widely by the populace. They could make public opinion, or at least make it aware of its own existence, start new projects of public welfare and sometimes even alter aspects of the administration and government. Naturally, this meant that they began to encroach on the place of the magnate and to usurp his status and function as the authority in local society.

Both of these developments suggest that means were appearing which the educated could use to break their bondage. It must be seriously doubted, however, whether either was significant in the political organisation of Madras before 1920. To take the emergence of new financial institutions first: neither had this gone very far nor were the older magnates simply spectators of their own decline. The initial explosion of joint-stock credit enterprises produced a plethora of companies which were less fly-by-night than gone-by-early-afternoon.[272] In order to restore stability to the world of joint-stock finance, the government enacted legislation which demanded certain minimal guarantees of security, and the law courts passed a series of decisions which weakened claims to limited liability.[273] The result was to slow down considerably the process of capital formation in joint-stock enterprises. The most dynamic element in the new finance

---

[272] *Land Revenue 1905–6*, p. 67. The South was famous for its *nidhis* – voluntary associations formed by various means to provide short-term loans. *Nidhis* were particularly important in and around major trading towns, such as Coimbatore which possessed 125 working with a capital of Rs 70 *lakhs*. However, they were notoriously unstable and open to abuse. They came nowhere near to replacing the old moneylender in short-term urban finance. *RPBC*, pp. 196–7; *MPBC*, III, 1161, IV, 453, 481–3.

[273] For a review of the working of the Indian Companies Act, 1913, see *Hindu* 6 August 1915. In its first year of operation in Madras, the Act reduced the number of joint-stock companies from 472 to 406.

was the co-operative credit society, but restrictions still prevented this from playing a central part in urban finance before at least the 1930s.[274]

Most of the more successful joint-stock enterprises were undertaken by men who already possessed considerable capital resources and were able to take advantage of Indian company law. The great Komati families of Andhra, for example, began to establish supralocal links in order to develop their trading and industrial activities. The Pydah family of Cocanada, the Mothey of Ellore and the Majeti and Nalam, which could be found in several towns, set up paper mills, rice mills and cotton presses under joint-stock finance.[275] The Indian Bank, the first indigenous joint-stock bank in Madras, was created with money from the Gujerati banker Lodd Govindoss, the Nattukottai Chetty S. R. Rm. A. Ramaswami Chetty of Chidambaram and a member of the Nalam family, who were among its first directors.[276] In the late 1920s, Raja Sir Annamalai Chetty turned his Nattukottai Chetty family bank into a joint-stock concern and demonstrated the power which had remained with the old moneylenders. On its opening day it was the second largest bank in Madras, surpassed only by the state-backed Imperial Bank of India.[277]

In the area of public activity also, the magnate managed to preserve himself. Of course, it was usually with the support of magnate patrons that western-educated publicists financed their various associations, presses and tract societies. In these they were seldom more than the agents of magnate interests. Their endeavours were intended to highlight their patrons at least as much as themselves. This is not to deny the intrinsic importance of the new ideas expressed in reformist, revivalist and nationalist circles, which were the results of change in the educated community. But political history must deal more with the extent of influence and the effect of ideas than with the character of doctrines. In Madras before 1920, there is little evidence to suggest that educated publicists were capable of organising movements which could be supported by large-scale public involvement rather than by a few very rich men. South India lacked the broad cultural homogeneity of Hindustan, which enabled reli-

---

[274] In 1920, urban co-operatives in Madras lent a total sum of only Rs 48.15 *lakhs*. *Annual Report on the Working of Co-operative Credit Societies Act (II of 1912) for the year 1920–1*. (Madras, 1921), p. 25.

[275] See the foundation of the Guntur Cotton, Jute and Paper Mills Company Limited (capital Rs 6 *lakhs*) in *Hindu* 13 September 1904.

[276] *Hindu* 9 March 1908.

[277] *RPBC*, p. 28.

gious revival movements, such as Sanatan Dharm, to draw extensive support from village elite groups. It also lacked a tradition of cultural conflict of the intensity of the Hindu/Muslim confrontation in the U.P., which enabled the organisers of cow-protection to count on the subscriptions of hundreds of petty urban Hindu traders. As C. A. Bayly has shown, the strength of movements such as those of the Sanatan Dharmists and cow-protectionists derived from the wide territorial organisations which they developed.[278] Their leaders were able to concentrate on any locality the weight and power which they had picked up, be it only in dribs and drabs, across the province. The organisers of similar movements in Madras had no opportunity to do this.

The celebrated Widow Remarriage movement which appeared in Rajahmundry in the late 1870s, for example, was made possible only by the hard support (in cash) of the Komati millionaire Pydah Ramakrishniah. When he died, the movement withered.[279] Similarly, the Madura Tamil Sangam, one of the central organs of Tamil revivalism, rested on the patronage of the Raja of Ramnad. When that patronage dried up in 1912, the Sangam almost collapsed and was only saved by the arrival of a blank cheque from the Nattukottai Chetty *zamindar* of Andipatti.[280] Again, in Madras city in the 1880s, the Hindu revivalist and anti-Christian campaign of Siva-sankara Pandiah was backed not by a mass of petty donations but by two merchants and a *zamindar*.[281] In like manner, the development of a female education movement and of an educated nationalist press from the 1870s owed much to the purse of the Maharaja of Vizianagram. When he died in 1895, most of his schools were closed or reduced in size for want of funds,[282] and the great *Hindu* newspaper went bankrupt.[283] Of course, as the twentieth century advanced, a broader base for fundraising activity emerged. But as late as 1922, even the Congress could not sustain itself. Most of its old magnate patrons had gone into the Legislative Councils, and its hopes of raising money without them were nil. The non-co-operation campaign in Tamilnad folded within days of the expenditure of the last of the contributions which it had received from All-India funds.[284]

[278] Bayly, 'The Development of Political Organisation in the Allahabad Locality, 1880 to 1925', ch. 2.
[279] Leonard, 'Kandukuri Viresalingam: A Biography of an Indian Social Reformer, 1848–1919'.
[280] G. O. 51 (Education) dated 20 January 1913. *T.N.A.*
[281] *Hindu* 17 September 1888.   [282] *Hindu* 3 March 1904.
[283] V. K. Narasimhan, *Kasturi Ranga Iyengar* (New Delhi, 1963), p. 6.
[284] C. J. Baker, 'Noncooperation in South India' in Baker and Washbrook (eds.), *South India*.

In Madras, the publicist could not develop wide territorial linkages nor could he find significant caches of wealth, which were outside the control of a few magnates. In consequences, he could never establish an independent authority apart from his magnate patrons. While the developments in education and in communications had an impact on the intellectual life of the traditionally literate elite, they did not provide the foundations of a single political empire. Indeed, in many ways the growth of quasi-political publicist activities in the towns can be seen as emanating as much from the will of the patrons as from that of the publicists themselves. For many centuries before the British arrived, rich townsmen had tried to convert wealth into social status by patronising religion and the arts, and by spending on public welfare. Status expenditure is necessarily a competitive activity and is used to establish positions of superiority and inferiority. Thus, although the direction which this spending took was always, in part, determined by the priests and literati who were the custodians of culture, it was also, in part, determined by the competitive needs of each magnate to demonstrate his position in relation to other magnates. From the later nineteenth century, the increasing wealth of the towns threw up new magnates – be it only slowly and sporadically – and put more resources at the disposal of those already established. This development generated greater magnate competition and hence drove magnates into looking for new and more varied cultural activities with which they could be associated. The changes in education, in the impact of foreign philosophies on the Indian intellect and in the relationship of theology to social organisation, which affected educated Indian society, certainly were instrumental in promoting social reform and religious revivalist movements. But of at least equal importance was the pressure of magnate competition which created much wider social demands and political purposes for the movements.

The problem of communal identities

Our examination of the economic instruments of political control must lead us to stress the significance of the clientage or dependency network in the political organisation of South India. As, perhaps, we might expect to find in any pre-industrial society, in which dire poverty was general and economic opportunities narrow, the mechanisms by which wealth was made and distributed forced large numbers of men to recognise the authority of one or a few leaders. Our analysis must also suggest that the direction followed by the clientage networks of leaders was vertical rather than horizontal to the social order. To take Mothey Venkataswami's empire as typical, we have seen that men in every occupational group from labourer to priest were linked together under him. Similarly, if we make caste and religion the terms of reference, we find that his authority touched men at every level of the caste system, from *pariah* to Brahman, and in every religious category from orthodox Hindu to reformist Hindu to Muslim. In the processes of decision-making through which most South Indians earned their daily bread, the more obvious class and cultural divisions had little relevance as organising principles.

Our emphasis on the patron–client relationship as the basic nexus of politics, however, ought not to be taken to mean that we totally disregard the existence of socially horizontal relationships. While perceptions of class may have been extremely weak, it would be impossible to deny that the behaviour of most South Indians was strongly affected by those elements of religion and culture which underwrote the contemporary system of social values. As the authorities controlling economic life need not always have been the same as those controlling religious and cultural life and as, indeed, the dictates of economic prudence could clash with those of cultural worthiness, there existed conditions in which cultural sentiment became an independent mechanism of control. In order to assess the extent to which our working model of the clientage network requires modification, it is necessary for us to examine in some detail the political implications of cultural institutions and determine the conditions on which their influence undercut that of economic organisation. As the caste system is generally taken, in South India at least, to be the dominant influence on behaviour, we should begin with a consideration of it.

In a recent article, Richard Fox has suggested a useful approach to the apparently insoluble problem of defining satisfactorily what the word 'caste' means. He sees several related but logically distinct categories of caste activity. Firstly, there are the Sanskritic *varnas* of Brahman, Kshatriya, Vaishya and Sudra which cover the whole of India. Secondly, in each region of India there are castes (in the case of the South, castes such as the Vellalas, Reddis, Kammas or Nairs) which occupy positions within the Sanskritic *varnas*: these regional groupings he terms 'sub-regional *varnas*'. Thirdly, within each 'sub-regional *varna*' lie further groupings divided from each other by prohibitions on intermarriage, ritual celebrations and, often, commensality: in the South, these would be represented by sub-castes such as the Chooliya, Karkatha, Thondamandala and Gounder Vellalas. Finally, within each sub-caste there are further divisions mapped out by actual intermarriage and ritual and social intercourse:

these would be represented by particular lineages or family clusters.[285] If we take Fox's model as a guide, we can begin to see at what level and in what ways the caste system must modify our political dependency structures.

It would be difficult to argue that Indian society was (or is) tightly organised into communities along the lines of Sanskritic *varna*. The categories were so vast and the social heterogeneity they masked so great that there were no institutions or organisations to link the various Brahmans or Sudras of India together. Essentially, *varna* represents a notion of social status – a matter of psychological perception – not a concrete political institution. By the same token the sub-regional *varnas* of Southern India were loosely defined status groupings and not organised communities. Within the category Vellala, Chetty or Nair subsisted distinct groupings which could be differentiated from each other by occupation, intermarriage, ritual practice and historical origin. These sub-castes simply recognised each other as possessing roughly the same social status over a series of contiguous territories. Until the twentieth century at the earliest, few sub-regional *varna* groupings possessed any central institutions to regulate the behaviour of their members or to serve the ends of common welfare. If they are to be regarded as political communities, the nature of their union is better understood by the metaphysician than by the political historian.

If we accept sub-regional *varnas* as loose status categories, then it is likely that they would become important principles of political organisation only when the status which they described was in some way attacked. Relative status, when commonly accepted, does not need to be defended and is not a category of political action. During our period, there were several examples of caste-status confrontation in Madras. Under the impetus of Christianity and new educational opportunities, for example, 'untouchable' Shanar toddy-trappers in southern Tinnevelly in the 1860s began to press for a general recognition that their sub-regional *varna* belonged to the Kshatriya Sanskritic *varna*. This not only linked together disparate Shanar groups but forced their neighbours into unity in order to resist their claim.[286] Sudden increases in wealth often produced

---

[285] R. G. Fox, 'Varna Schemes and Ideological Integration in Indian Society' in *Comparative Studies in Society and History*, XI (1969), 27–45; also, R. G. Fox, *Kin, Clan, Raja and Rule* (Berkeley, Los Angeles and London, 1971), ch. 2. It should be noted, however, that our version of Fox's categorisation is foreshortened from his own. Our purpose is political history and we are interested only in the major categories which imply differences in political relationship.

[286] Hardgrave, *The Nadars of Tamilnad*, pp. 43–70.

similar results. In the 1890s, Hindu Shanars-turned-Nadars, who had become rich merchants in the towns of northern Tinnevelly and Ramnad, also aspired to the Kshatriya *varna*.[287] At the same time, rich Komatis in the main towns of the northern Circars began claiming the right to perform Vaishya ceremonies;[288] in the same area, Kammalas (artisans) claimed recognition as Brahmans,[289] and in Madura, wealthy Sourashtra silk-weavers demanded that local society should accord them the privileges of Gujerati Brahmans.[290] Another stimulus to status activity of this kind came from the census which sought to fix caste groups in permanent *varna* categories and naturally cut across some of the aspirations of their members.[291]

In South Indian historiography, much has been made of these developments. Yet, when studied in a general context rather than in isolation, their significance before 1920 is very limited. Neither economic nor educational change nor the census succeeded in creating viable political organisations out of the sub-regional *varnas*. In the first place, the nature of economic development was such that, as we have seen, it promoted less the social groups made rich by new economic processes than those groups which were already well established in control of economic resources. Certainly, this was more true of the countryside than the town, but even so success on the scope and scale of the Nadars was rare. Equally, the major changes in the composition of the educated community were the product not of the nineteenth century but of the late 1920s and 1930s. English education remained the preserve of 'traditionally' literate families and even the non-Brahman movement of 1916 cannot be tied to significant change.[292] Education, even in the vernacular, seldom reached dependent labouring groups.

The character of economic and educational change meant that there was no general pressure on the status categories of the existing social hierarchy. The flexibility of the caste system itself, however, also took much of the steam out of communal politics. The Indian caste system was not a caste system in the technical sense: the ranks of persons, or rather of social groups, inside it were not immutable and fixed by birth. As historians such as Burton Stein and R. Inden have

---

[287] *Ibid.*, pp. 95–129.
[288] *Hindu* 1, 3, 4 January, 1 September, 9 October, 10 and 20 November 1894.
[298] *Hindu* 3 May 1894, 1 June 1897.
[290] *Hindu* 10 March 1920.
[291] S. and L. Rudolph, *The Modernity of Tradition: Political Development in India*, (Chicago, 1967), pp. 49–64.
[292] See below pp. 271–2.

pointed out, there were mechanisms which allowed groups to move up the social scale and down again.[293] Equally, modern anthropologists have seen how, through the practices of hypergamy and social emulation, castes like the Rajput and the Gounder could be open.[294] In British South India, several factors guaranteed that these mechanisms not only continued to exist but were frequently used.

Firstly, as we have seen, marriage networks among the bulk of the population which lived off the countryside were intensive rather than extensive. Reflecting local-level culture, they tended to cover geographically small areas and small numbers of people who intermarried repeatedly.[295] It was thus relatively easy for an endogamous unit to break away from the larger status grouping in which it was set and to claim attachment to another status grouping. As André Beteille saw in Tanjore, 'Since intermarriage with close relatives is frequently practised by many Non-Brahmins, a section of people, by confining marital relations among themselves, can claim to be Vellalas, Ahamudiyans or Padaiyachis.'[296] Secondly, local-level culture provided no centralised communal institutions governing membership of a sub-regional *varna*; thus there were no awkward authorities to challenge the antecedents of groups claiming membership. And thirdly the majority of Southern sub-regional *varnas* were gathered in and around the Sudra Sanskritic *varna*; thus social mobility between them was possible without crossing any very obvious and contentious ritual gap. In Madras, more than anywhere else in India, small groups were able to raise their effective social status without causing disturbance to the prevailing status structure and without mobilising other groups or endogamous units either in the status categories which they were leaving or in those which they were entering.

The social origins of those who were seen to fill the 'dominant' caste of any area were often obscure. In his manual on Coimbatore district, for example, F. A. Nicholson freely admitted his inability to

293 B. Stein, 'Medieval South Indian Hindu Sects' in J. Silverberg (ed.), *Social Mobility in the Caste System in India* (The Hague, 1968), pp. 78–94; R. Inden, 'Social Mobility in Pre-Modern Bengal'. Unpublished paper read at Study Conference on Tradition in Indian Politics and Society. University of London, 1–3 June 1969.

294 Fox, *Kin, Clan, Raja and Rule*, pp. 34–9; Beck, *Peasant Society in Konku*, pp. 257–9.

295 See L. Dumont, *Hierarchy and Marriage Alliance in South Indian Kinship* (London, 1957).

296 A. Beteille, *Caste, Class and Power: Changing Patterns of Stratification in a Tanjore Village* (Berkeley and Los Angeles, 1965), p. 82.

separate 'true' Gounder Vellalas from the hosts of rich peasants who had adopted or were adopting Gounder ceremonies, dress and customs.[297] In the census of 1891, Sir Harold Stuart noted the ability of the Nairs of Malabar to absorb immigrants from Tamil and Canarese areas in a single generation without apparent friction;[298] and the internal structure of the Nairs provides ample evidence of the rise and fall of indigenous social groups within it.[299] Similarly, Thurston recorded a famous Tamil proverb which describes the regular generational flow between the Maravar, Aghumudayar and Vellala castes.[300] In more recent work, S. A. Barnett has suggested the diverse origins of those presently filling the category of Thondamandala Vellala.[301]

In these conditions, in which sub-regional *varnas* were so amorphous, the politics of caste confrontation were rare and circumscribed. We find them only on those exceptional occasions when the normal paths of mobility were blocked, either by difficulties over speed and information,[302] or by the law which administered the word of the Vedas rather than that of custom, or by aspirations which touched Brahman sensibilities. Moreover, where conflicts occurred, there is much to suggest that their claims to be caste – that is, subregional *varna* – confrontations owed more to rhetoric than to fact. Obviously, only those groups within a caste, which had gained money or power to aid their desire for upward mobility, could attempt seriously to improve their status. Unable to escape from their ignoble backgrounds, they were forced to contemplate establishing a new status category for their whole caste. But it is by no means clear that their energy in pamphleteering and polemic made much impact on the less privileged members of their caste, who formed the majority and whose ambitions were limited by lack of power. After sixty years of activity, for example, the Christianised Shanars of southern Tinnevelly had not managed to expand their movement widely even in their own district:

It must not be supposed that the 'Sanror' theory has by any means spread a general infection over the whole community. In villages near the source of

---

[297] Nicholson, *Coimbatore District Manual*, pp. 57–61. Also, Beck, *Peasant Society in Konku*, pp. 257–9.

[298] *Census of India. 1891. Madras. Volume XIII* (Madras, 1893), p. 222.

[299] M.D.G. Innes, *Malabar*, I, 93–103.

[300] Thurston, *Castes and Tribes of Southern India*, I, 7.

[301] S. A. Barnett, 'Development and Change in the Kondaikatti Vellala Community' in *Justice Party Golden Jubilee Souvenir. 1968* (Madras, 1968), pp. 382–3.

[302] Obviously, the prevailing systems of social mobility meant that movement could not be rapid nor could it take place easily if the origins of the mobile group remained obvious to the rest of the society.

its origin it finds often vehement supporters; but one need not go far . . .
to find the story either treated with derision or even not known.[303]

Equally, the movement of the Shanar–Nadar traders of northern
Tinnevelly and Ramnad was unable to establish connections with non-
trading Shanars further south.[304] Or again, although an association of
richer Pallis had been set up in 1888 to claim Kshatriya status and to
change the name of the caste to Vannikula Kshatriya, by 1911 90 per
cent of the 'community' was still returning itself as Palli to the census
reporters.[305]

Before 1920, the sub-regional *varna* level of activity was not an important political category. While challenges to it could certainly lead
to disturbance and to the temporary breaking of cross-communal
clientage networks, they were unusual and generally incapable of
attaining an institutional permanence. Nadars and Maravars, for
example, could be found in political alliances which were mutually
beneficial,[306] and the Vannikula Kshatriya movement never meant
that rich North Arcot Pallis were unable to indulge in faction fights
against each other. We must look below the level of sub-regional
varna, to the sub-castes and endogamous units which composed it,
to find more significant political categories of caste. Once we attempt
this, however, it becomes necessary to take the notion of caste beyond
the concept of status and to relate it to the context of political and
economic life. Familial and quasi-familial organisations played an
important part in the obtaining and distribution of material resources
and power: their internal structure was to a considerable extent determined by the functions which they performed. Thus families and
lineages involved in the control of land would be likely to have different internal structures from those involved in, say, trade or
religion.

Caste in rural Madras. Let us first look at those castes related to the
peasant economy in the countryside. As M. N. Srinivas has seen, rural
society can be roughly parcelled into territorial divisions, each of
which was under the control of a 'dominant caste' – that is, a caste
which controlled most of the land and possessed effective political

[303] *M.D.G.* Pate, *Tinnevelly*, I, 129.
[304] Hardgrave, *Nadars of Tamilnad*, p. 184.
[305] Rudolph, *The Modernity of Tradition*, pp. 49–64; *Census of India. 1911.
Madras. Volume XIII. Part 2* (Madras, 1912), pp. 116–17.
[306] Hardgrave, *Nadars of Tamilnad*, pp. 222–4.

power.[307] Of course, these dominant castes were of the sub-regional *varna*-type; they were merely status groupings not practical organisations. Within each were further subdivisions, each also, usually, of a territorial nature. How powerful were the sub-caste institutions of the various Reddis, Vellalas, Kammas, Nairs, Kallars and other dominant castes? Obviously, there were considerable differences, but in general the answer must be that they were fairly insignificant and were tending to lose progressively what influence they had. By the end of the nineteenth century, very few of those dominant sub-castes involved in agriculture had retained *panchayats* to enforce discipline within their territories. In Trichinopoly district, for example, only three of twenty Vellala sub-castes possessed operational *panchayats*.[308] In the Ceded Districts, Reddis had long since abandoned their use, while in Andhra *panchayats* among the Kammas were virtually unknown. The removal of large-scale warfare from politics made the sub-caste and extended lineage redundant as units of military recruitment. At the local level, the administration no longer recognised or worked through caste institutions but handed revenue collecting, police and judicial powers to particular families. The processes of the economy were working to the advantage of individuals and families, rather than of larger social units, and were increasing social stratification within sub-caste groups.[309] Whatever role local-level caste institutions may have had in 1800 was whittled down in the course of the following century. A classic case of this erosion can be seen in the history of the Kallars of Tanjore and Madura. Originally warriors and cattle-thieves, they used a very strong lineage organisation to carry on their economic and political activities. During the nineteenth century, however, several lineages became settled in agriculture, under the great Periyar irrigation scheme in Madura and in eastern Tanjore. Very rapidly, lineage discipline in the settled areas disappeared and the agrarian Kallars become scarcely distinguishable in organisation from other dominant peasant groups.[310] Only in the extreme South, where they continued to perform criminal and private police functions, did Kallar and related Maravar lineage organisations keep their importance.

[307] M. N. Srinivas, *Caste in Modern India and Other Essays* (Bombay, 1962), pp. 9–11, 89–93.
[308] *M.D.G.* Hemingway, *Trichinopoly*, I, 102; see also, F. R. Hemingway, *Tanjore* (Madras, 1906), I, 84.
[309] In an hypergamous marriage system, this social stratification was likely to lead to the further fission of sub-castes.
[310] Dumont, *Une Sous-Caste de l'Inde du Sud*, pp. 7–9; *M.D.G.* Francis, *Madura*, I, 92–3.

One of the few cases in which a dominant peasant group is said to have preserved its caste institutions into the twentieth century is that of the Gounder Vellalas of Coimbatore and Salem, about whom much has been written. The Gounders are credited with having an elaborate structure for the maintenance of caste discipline, which reached up from the village through several intermediate levels to four *pattagar* leaders who each held a separate territory. In theory, the prescriptive ritual authority of the *pattagars* permeated the Gounder Vellalas and held them together in a tightly organised community.[311] By the nineteenth century, however, practice seems to have been very different.

There is no gainsaying the fact that the *pattagars* possessed great social influence; but there is some question of whether the basis of this influence was material rather than ritual. Most of the *pattagar* families were landowners and credit controllers on a grand scale. They formed a natural centre of authority for their neighbouring lesser cultivators, many of whom were Gounders.[312] They acted as arbitrators in the disputes of some of their caste-fellows and exacted penalties for what they saw as social indiscipline.[313] Yet several other Gounder families, such as the Vellakinar of Coimbatore *taluk* and the *zamindars* of Utukuli, who also were very powerful but who had no prescriptive ritual position, acted in a very similar way and exercised a very similar species of authority. Eventually, the Vellakinar and Utukuli families came to marry into the *pattagar* theocracy, making a social unit coherent in its wealth but disparate in its relationship to clan hierarchy.[314] Moreover, *pattagar* prestige was entirely incapable of withstanding the collapse of its economic fortune; those *pattagar* families who lost their land also rapidly lost their social pre-eminence.[315]

Beneath the *pattagars*, the intermediaries who were supposed to carry their writ into the village seem altogether to have disappeared. In a recent book, Brenda Beck has noted how extremely shadowy becomes the structure and personnel of the middle level of caste organisation once it is brought under the analyst's microscope: few people can be found to fit into the hypothetical system. Apart from the *pattagars*, Beck can define major authorities in the Gounder

---

[311] Nicholson, *Coimbatore District Manual*, pp. 58–9; Beck, *Peasant Society in Konku*, pp. 40–9.
[312] Beck, *ibid.*, p. 43.
[313] *Ibid.*, p. 40.
[314] Baker, *Politics of South India, 1920–1937*, p. 115, fn 114; p. 235, fn 268.
[315] Beck, *Peasant Society in Konku*, p. 42.

hierarchy only at the very local level where, again, ritual role is congruent with economic power.[316] In her case, working in the 1960s, this level is that of the village street and immediate neighbourhood; in ours, working in a period of different economic design, it was larger – the kingdom of the rural-local boss. Above these bosses, however, unless they wished or were forced to call in their *pattagar*, there existed no obvious political organisation of caste.

The duties of maintaining social discipline and control, which once may have fallen to caste *panchayats* and lineage heads, were being taken over by particular families who were *de facto* rural-local bosses. Superior systems of caste organisation were shattered. Of course, this development made very little difference to caste *qua* status in the rural locality. There, bosses still needed to preserve the dignity and ritual position of their dominant caste status and were wont to punish severely lesser members of their caste who had broken the rules of conduct. But no system of power existed to ensure that they themselves were subject to the same discipline, and frequently they flaunted the regulations which they insisted others should obey.[317]

Formal caste institutions among rural dependent groups were much more vigorous. Village priests, musicians and artisans tended to belong to kinship and caste organisations which reached over several rural-localities and were coherently structured.[318] Although much more localised, subordinate labouring groups also used *panchayats* or recognised 'headmen' to preserve social discipline in their village streets or separate hamlets.[319] It ought not to be supposed, however, that the mere existence of these institutions meant that these castes preserved a separate political existence, apart from other groups in the countryside, nor that they formed separate political communities. Certainly, the institutions of priests and artisans acted in part as trade unions, to exact better conditions for their members and to protect the exclusivity and sanctity of their occupations. But they were economically dependent and could seldom push their demands to the point at which dominant castes were seriously inconvenienced. Where, for example, one group of priests refused to

---

[316] *Ibid.*, p. 70.

[317] For example, V. C. Vellingiri Gounder, an important rural-local boss, who ran a purity and temperance campaign among his caste but who, himself, was a notorious drunkard. See Reforms Franchise B March 1921, Nos 34–99. *N.A.I.*

[318] For example, see Kammalans in Thurston, *Castes and Tribes of Southern India*, III, 106–49.

[319] For example, see Kannavars in *M.D.G.* B. S. Baliga, *Madurai* (Madras, 1960), p. 129.

perform heterodox ceremonies for their patrons or one troupe of musicians refused to take part in a novel festival, dominant village groups would be able to dismiss them and bring in others who were more pliable.[320] Communal solidarity, even among these highly specialised and important village servants, did not extend beyond the immediate territorial unit nor go far when faced with starvation.

In the case of labouring groups, it would be possible to argue that caste *panchayats* remained so active because they were used by the rural-local bosses to hold the lower orders in their place. They enforced obedience to customs which clearly marked off their members as inferiors. There was no sign in British South India, as there was in Travancore, that they were being used to upgrade the status of their members or to organise strikes against dominant castes.[321] The subservient position which they exercised can also be seen in the type of disputes in which they had jurisdiction. Quarrels over property or economic rights were much more likely to be taken to a rural-local boss of another caste than to the caste body or headman.[322] The economic leaders of the countryside were very unwilling to let slip from their grasp any matter of consequence to their position.

Caste in urban Madras. The different nature of economic, social and political relations in the towns naturally created some differences in the character of caste relationships between rural and urban inhabitants. The greater complexity of town life and the greater interaction of ritual groups of various origins tended to make communal organisations more solid. Immigrant groups were drawn to those areas of a town in which they had kin connections; wider employment opportunities broke up ritualised master–servant relationships; social competition during festivals and ceremonies was much more intensive; officials often fostered caste organisation by referring disputes to caste headmen or *panchayats* whom they had found or invented. These factors helped to promote the development of politically important communal ties which extended beyond the family and which did not rely on status challenges to make them apparent. Nonetheless, it would be wrong to consider that the whole area of a town and all the social groups within it were subject to these speci-

[320] *Madras Police 1886*, p. 24; Obituary of P. Subrahmanyavadhayajulu in *Hindu* 31 July 1897; *Hindu* 31 August 1896. The flexibility of (even Brahman) service castes before the economic power of a dominant caste has been noted in Beck, *Peasant Society in Konku*, pp. 154–80.

[321] Hardgrave, *Nadars of Tamilnad*, pp. 65–7.

[322] Beck, *Peasant Society in Konku*, pp. 76–7.

fically urban pressures. Most of the conurbations of Madras were no more than collections of villages, interspersed with agricultural land, which had been linked together for administrative convenience. The warehouses, daily bazaars, workshops, government offices and law-courts, which created the urban setting, were but a part of the average town and involved but a proportion of its residents. Only in the fast-growing towns of the Andhra deltas and, later, the southern cotton belt, were these 'urban' elements increasing appreciably. The agricultural landlords, labourers and dependent groups, whom circumstances had placed inside a municipal boundary, conducted their affairs in ways very similar to their counterparts in the countryside proper. The significant urban communal organisations were only those of artisans and skilled workmen, of bureaucrats and members of the educated professions and of traders.

Although by 1880 most of the hereditary caste occupations of artisans had been broken down and invaded by other groups, in particular places particular artisan businesses were organised on communal lines. In the towns of the Ceded Districts, for example, those weavers who were working together either in the same workshop or under the same petty capitalist usually would be bonded by caste as well as by economic ties. They would participate in a ritual life which separated them, in the weaving area of the town, from other weavers. At this low level of neighbourhood activity, there tended to be endemic conflict between caste groups in the same trade. In towns such as Nellore or Cuddapah, which had thriving weaving industries, Hindu Khattri, Muslim and Hindu *pariah* weaving groups were constantly at each others' throats. The petty capitalists, who were of the same community as their workers, encouraged these fights and often led their employees into the attack, for the victor gained not only prestige but a larger share of trade.[323] However, as we saw earlier, the petty capitalist was himself tied to a higher commercial power for his credit, supplies and marketing arrangements. The bonds of caste usually did not extend this far. In the towns of the Ceded Districts, the men who linked producers to markets in the rest of the presidency and Bombay were essentially financiers whose clients included petty capitalists from many communities.[324] They

[323] Deputy Inspector General [of Police], Central Range, to Inspector General, Madras, 14 December 1914 in G.O. 2821 (Judicial) dated 16 December 1914. *T.N.A.*; see also *Madras Police 1912*, p. 18.

[324] Bombay Multanis were particularly prominent in the piece-goods trade of the Ceded Districts; further south, the trade was in the hands of the Nattukottai Chetties.

had little sympathy for disruptive trade wars and could be counted on to interfere in them to re-establish peace. Moreover, even where financiers shared caste ties with petty capitalists, as among the Sourashtras of Madura, other factors kept them from supporting neighbourhood confrontations. They tended to be involved in other areas of commerce and in close relationship with the government, both of which would suffer if they were seen to be inciting communal violence. They too clamped down on neighbourhood conflict and prevented it from spreading.[325] The great outbreaks of rioting and disorder, which occasionally appeared in the Ceded Districts' towns, coincided with famines and trade depressions when the rivalry between petty capitalists became intense and when the flow of re-sources from superior magnates dried up.[326] But in times of normality, communal dissension of this kind was locked away in one corner of the town and had a very limited importance.

Communal linkages between families involved in government service and the liberal professions also were tight. 'Service' families needed considerable resources to educate their children. As education could suffer from economic instability, they often lived together in one neighbourhood and combined to protect themselves. They founded small local schools and, from the 1870s, began to set up *nidhis* and mutual insurance schemes.[327] Technically, there was nothing in this activity which was bounded by caste. Neighbourhood schools, like the Thondamandala High School in Madras city, took pupils from different castes, while mutual insurance companies, like the Mylapore Hindu Permanent Fund, took deposits from anybody. Several other factors, however, guaranteed that caste-community did play a role. The number of social groups in any one area who were interested in service was very limited. Brahmans and a few Sat-Sudra groups predominated. Within the neighbourhood, they would tend to be separated from each other by streets.[328] Moreover, being of a very high status they enjoyed active ritual lives which, at ceremonies and festivals, divided them from each other.

[325] Deputy Inspector General [of Police], Central Range, to Inspector General, Madras, 14 December 1914 in G.O. 2821 (Judicial) dated 16 December 1914. *T.N.A.*

[326] As during the 1918 famine, see 'Judgement of C.C. No. 1, Special Deputy Magistrate, Cuddapah', in G.O. 1538 (Judicial) dated 1 July 1918. *T.N.A.*

[327] Such as the Thondamandala High School, Madras city, see below pp. 203–4, and the Mylapore Hindu Permanent Fund, see Nicholson, *RAB*, II, 221–37.

[328] In Madras city, for example, a large block of Thondamandala Vellalas lived tightly packed in one municipal ward, see below pp. 203–4.

Although more than one caste would be educated at these schools and protected by these benefit societies, very often membership of the school and benefit society rested largely with one community. Further, once a man had gained access to a consequential government office, or had established a successful legal practice, he would tend to use connections of family and friendship to maximise his profits and to cut out rivals. Jobs and cases could be fed back to fatten relations and contacts who would be loyal clients. Moreover, at the low level of neighbourhood activity and among such prestigious ritual groups, friendships commonly were made by participation in ceremonies and cultural associations.

As in the case of artisans and workmen, however, compact local units of caste among 'service' groups were broken by economic ties with outsiders. Lawyers had to find members of other communities to give them cases, clerks and *gumastahs* needed employment with brokers and contractors who seldom were of their caste, and lower government servants had to rely on the co-operation of various local notables. Very rarely were these 'service' groups free to take political action as communities. In Madura in the early 1880s, for example, there was a storm of protest over an aspect of municipal government from the area of the town in which most of the Brahman clerks and lawyers lived. A Ratepayers Association was formed to campaign at the impending elections for the protection of Brahman religious privileges. Yet, when the votes were counted, it became clear that the Brahmans were unable to poll a majority even in the ward in which they formed most of the voters. A merchant-financier, living in another part of the town, was returned as their candidate.[329] It was also in Madura in 1915 and 1917 that K. M. Alladin Rowther, the notorious Muslim criminal, was elected from the same Brahman-dominated constituency.[330] Later, we shall see that the Thondaman-dala Vellala constituency in Madras city was equally open to extraneous influences.

Only among trading caste groups was there sufficient economic independence for a significant communal solidarity to develop in politics. As we saw earlier, the basic financial organisations of Madras were constructed on familial or quasi-familial models. Although no group apart from the Nattukottai Chetties developed institutions capable of linking together caste members from many dispersed localities, particular trading groups in and around particular

[329] *Hindu* 21 April 1884.
[330] G.O. 1384 (L and M, M) dated 16 August 1917. *T.N.A.*

towns did produce local communal organisations which attempted to control business and to provide welfare facilities for their members. R. L. Hardgrave has described the communal institutions to be found among Nadar merchants in their 'six towns' in Ramnad and northern Tinnevelly.[331] In the principal Andhra towns, Komatis were organised on almost identical principles. They levied communal fees, set up their own schools and charities, built their own temples, provided arbitration for business disputes and enforced a fierce social and economic discipline.[332] When, for example, Komati elders ordered a religious *hartal* in Madras city in 1898, not one Komati bazaar seller dared to disobey.[333] Maracair Muslims on the east coast, rising Tiya traders and bankers in northern Malabar and Christian Bharatha merchants in Tuticorin worked to the same pattern.

In his work on Northern Indian bankers, C. A. Bayly has raised critically the question of whether these tight caste connections among mercantile groups were so much the result of caste identity as of the practical necessities of business.[334] The strength of communal rule came not only from recognition and sentiment but from the fact that it protected an essential credit-raising institution. An out-casted member was likely to be bankrupted very quickly. In some ways, Bayly's point may seem irrelevant here: whatever its causes, local mercantile caste groups did work together as communities. In other ways, however, it is crucial, for if we examine the mechanics of credit, these institutions cease to be communal – in the sense of a spontaneous combination of equals – and become features of the rule and discipline of urban economic powers.

In South India, trading capital was concentrated in a few families in each town. As we have seen, these families worked with or through a cross-section of society. However, their willingness to lend and the terms of interest which they demanded were not equal for everybody. They needed greater guarantees of security than the British law could supply and, consequently, they tended to judge the safety of an investment by the 'creditworthiness' of the debtor. 'Creditworthiness' in a debtor could be assessed by his social position, known responsibility and available assets. But it became much less a matter of speculation when the creditor possessed an instrument of direct social control over

[331] Hardgrave, *Nadars of Tamilnad*, pp. 95–129.
[332] G.O. 3360 (L.S.G.) dated 8 September 1928. *S.A.H.*; Thurston, *Castes and Tribes of Southern India*, III, pp. 307–11; *Hindu* 30 May 1896.
[333] *Hindu* 6 January 1898; see also a Komati *hartal* in Salem in *Hindu* 20 June 1894.
[334] Bayly, 'Development of Political Organisation in the Allahabad Locality, 1880 to 1925', ch. 2.

the debtor. It was this instrument which caste institutions formed. Urban financial powers knew that they could lend out a high proportion of their assets to their caste-fellows and use caste discipline to enforce repayment if necessary. In Ellore, Mothey Venkataswami financed local trade through other *banias* most of whom were Komatis;[335] Tamil Muslims gathered at Vanniyambadi provided each other with a pool of capital for business in the hides trade;[336] Nattukottai Chetties lent extensively to each other and took each others' *hundis*.[337] It was very much in the magnate's interest to preserve a tight caste or communal discipline for it secured his own financial stability.

There is much to suggest that caste institutions among mercantile groups functioned largely on the personal authority of the magnates behind them; and that once that authority was withdrawn, they collapsed in confusion. Ritual institutions, and prescriptive positions within them, did not count for much unless the power of resource control was present to lend them support. In Madras city, for example, the family of the Komati headmen were able to discipline the caste only so long as their great wealth and control of the caste temple and its properties clearly marked them out as economic leaders. By the 1890s, the growth of other wealthy Komati merchants in the city and attacks by the courts on the estates of the current headman, C. V. Cunniah Chetty, had weakened the family's position. Caste regulation of marriage was flouted openly and groups of dissident Komatis challenged Cunniah Chetty's authority and right to control the caste temple.[338]

The dependence on magnate leadership can be seen also in the more 'secular' and properly political organisation of caste constituencies. In Guntur town, the leading local banker, trader and factory-owner, Lingamalee V. Subbaya, and his Brahman lawyer V. Bhavarnacharlu, put together a Taxpayers Association which was in reality a Komati caucus. From the 1890s, when it was formed, it brought political unity

[335] A. R. Banerji, Assistant Collector, Ellore, to Collector of Godavari, 29 March 1901 in G.O. 1011 (L and M, M) dated 17 July 1901. *T.N.A.*

[336] They also financed explorations in the Kolar Gold Field, Mysore, and the spice and areca nut trades from Malabar.

[337] *RPBC*, pp. 186–9.

[338] In 1900, the temple and its charities possessed an income of over Rs ½ *lakh* and owned the largest market in the city. *Suryalokamy* 17 March 1901. *R.N.P.* See also *Hindu* 4 May 1894, 2 May 1896, 8 September and 13 December 1904, 27 March 1913.

to the Komatis and would have dominated the town completely had not the Collector interfered with it.[339] However, this Komati solidarity proved very short-lived. Hardly were Lingamelee V. Subbaya's ashes cold, than rampant factionalism destroyed the community's political base.[340] Similarly, in Ellore, where the power of the Mothey family was strong, the Komatis were organised behind it. Mothey Gangaraju, the leader of the family in the 1910s and 1920s, was able to take his local community with him in whatever politics he chose to play. In 1917, for example, he made contacts with the Justice Party; in 1921 he non-co-operated; in 1923, he joined the Legislative Council as an Independent.[341] His contortions produced no difficulties in his home base. But by the depression of the 1930s, the family empire was on the rocks and was losing power through unprofitable *zamindari* investments and an abortive factory project. Increasingly dependent on the government for protection of their land and for loans for their factory, the Motheys were forced into loyalism between 1935 and 1937. Many members of their local caste rebelled against them and, in the 1937 elections, the Ellore Komatis were split down the middle between the Congress and the Justice Party.[342]

A close analysis of the Nadars of Sivakasi and Virudhunagar brings out the same points. In Sivakasi in 1921, hosts of petty Nadar traders raised a rebellion against the foundation of a municipal council. They closed the bazaar and boycotted the council chamber. However, the leading Nadar families of Sivakasi, through the Nadar Mahajana Sangham, had just concluded a deal with the British for a caste Legislative Council seat and were eager to appear loyal. They put pressure on their lesser brethren and forced them to reopen their shops and to return to the council.[343] In Virudhunagar, the wealthier Nadar families reinforced their caste rule with what Nadar petitioners described to the Secretariat as terrorism.[344] As in the case of the Motheys, however, the economic basis of their supremacy was revealed by the havoc caused to their leadership by the depression. From civil disobedience onwards, the Nadar leaders were under

[339] G.O. 1298 (L and M, M) dated 5 August 1892. *T.N.A.*

[340] Venkatappayya, *Sviya Caritra*, I, 155–9.

[341] G. V. Subba Rao, *The Life and Times of Sir K. V. Reddi Naidu* (Rajahmundry, 1957), p. 31; *Hindu* 28 July, 6 and 19 August 1921; Home Public File 953 of 1924 *T.N.A.*

[342] Baker, *Politics of South India 1920–1937*, ch. 3.

[343] G.O. 7 (L.S.G.) dated 3 January 1921. *T.N.A.*

[344] G.O. 2767 (L.S.G.) dated 29 June 1926. *T.N.A.*

constant pressure from members of their own community, and local caste units were torn apart by increasingly rancorous disputes which they no longer had the power to settle.[345]

For political action, these communities were bonded by their common dependence on one or a few families: there were no institutions to hold them together if that dependency were broken. While certainly the ties between the financial magnate and his caste members were stronger than the ties between him and outsiders, both sets of ties were structurally similar. During Mothey *raj* in Ellore, the family's influence reached non-Komatis as well as Komatis; and when that *raj* declined, its influence was ignored as much by Komatis as non-Komatis. In Sivakasi, the Nadar merchant princes raised taxes for communal purposes from non-Nadars as well as Nadars; and in 1921, their order of a return to work was accepted by non-Nadars as well as Nadars. If a magnate so willed, his community would be taken into political alliances which were ritually obnoxious and absurd: the Nadar merchant-princes forged an alliance with the Maravar Raja of Ramnad when both parties found themselves serving the Justice ministry; in Madura, Sourashtra dye-magnates consistently worked behind Brahman lawyers, with whose caste they were supposed to be in dispute.[346] Neither of these alliances caused any noticeable dissatisfaction in the Nadar, Maravar, Sourashtra or Brahman populations. Indeed, in instances in which local trading groups found themselves economically dependent on an outsider, they were prepared to take his word as law even in matters of caste ritual and custom.[347]

Formal caste-institutions of themselves did not create independent political corporations of caste. Once again, we come back to the point at which it seems caste outlined important political constituencies only when questions of status were mooted. As urban settlement patterns were complex, there were more occasions of status rivalry in the towns than in the villages. No large town was under 'one-caste' domination,[348] and many different social groups[349] were active in the same trades and occupations. Magnates, who spent so largely on cultural and religious patronage, could create communal hostility to

---

[345] Hardgrave, *Nadars of Tamilnad*, pp. 184–8.

[346] G.O. 382 (L and M, M) dated 29 February 1912; G.O. 1074 (L and M, M) dated 12 June 1912; G.O. 1843 (L and M, M) dated 24 October 1916. *T.N.A.*

[347] As in the case of the Komati merchant P. Ramamurthi and the Maharani of Vizianagram cited above. See *Hindu* 14 June and 7 July 1910.

[348] Given that caste was not a political institution, by this we mean under the domination of a group of families who shared the same caste status.

[349] That is family groups who were of different caste statuses.

themselves. Rich Muslims who built mosques and *Madrassas*, Hindus who protected the cow, or Tiyas and Nadars who bought a new caste status and founded their own temples and rituals, sometimes were offering overt challenges to existing social hierarchies. In circumstances of economic instability, status competition between local communal groups could become chronic. In the fast-growing towns of the Andhra deltas, for example, rising Komatis demonstrated a ritual and cultural assertiveness which set by the ears resident Muslims and non-Komati Hindu magnates.[350] In fast-declining towns, like Salem, squabbles between family-organised businesses for shares in a diminishing pot produced serious situations of communal polarisation. In Salem, Komatis, Beri Chetties and Tamil Muslims came to blows.[351] Whenever a town economy faced crisis, as during famines, spontaneous communal rioting could break the cross-communal clientage network of the strongest magnate.

A single-minded concentration on these features of conflict, in which linkages of caste (and other perceived cultural statuses) cut through the ties of economic clientage, would give the impression that caste and religious sentiments were the dominant influences on urban political organisation in Madras. Indeed, several previous historians of urban South India have analysed their material entirely in this way and without any regard to the operations of the economy.[352] A broader view, however, puts the proportion of activity explicable by reference to cultural antipathy more firmly in its place. Firstly, categories of cultural antipathy simply were not generally politicised by magnate expenditure on personal status. Only the north-east of the presidency had felt any weight of Muslim oppression so that only there was the overt support of Hinduism or Islam capable of being interpreted as an aggressive political act. Elsewhere, Hindu and Muslim magnates could be found involved in a range of religiously promiscuous practices. In Madras city, for example, the millionaire Calivalla brothers, who were Komatis, supported both Arabic education and Hindu revivalism;[353] in Vanniyambadi, Muslims paid for the upkeep of the Hindu temple;[354] in Negapatam,

---

350 G.O. 2461 (Judicial) dated 26 November 1917. *T.N.A.*
351 G.O. 1374 (Judicial) dated 23 May 1883. *T.N.A.* Salem town declined rapidly in the later nineteenth century following the closing down of its army barracks.
352 See, for examples, Srinivas, *Caste in Modern India*, pp. 1–40; Hardgrave, *Nadars of Tamilnad*, pp. 1–11.
353 *Hindu* 12 March 1918; see also *Hindu* 21 December 1887, 30 March 1888, 23 April 1908, 25 April 1912, 14 April 1920 for other examples of Hindu–Muslim cross-communal patronage.
354 G.O. 2099 (L and M, M) dated 8 November 1912. *T.N.A.*; in 1936, Abdul Hakim bought an elephant for the local Hindu temple, *Hindu* 27 April 1936.

Hindus contributed to the main mosque;[355] in Palni, Hindus and Muslims even worshipped at the same shrine.[356] Similarly, low-caste groups which had reached magnate proportions did not have to attack the culture of the dominant groups which they had just joined. In most cases they bought their way to respectability slowly and without occasioning caste confrontations. Most of the towns of Madras were cosmopolitan and, if he were to achieve one of his primary ends, a magnate had to win the recognition of his status from as many areas of local society as possible. Except in unusual circumstances, most magnate patronage was spent in cross-communal and, particularly, cross-caste activities. This can be seen most obviously in the fact that rich non-Brahmans continued to support Brahman religion and scholarship. But magnate patronage reached down as well as up the religious scale. Annadana Samajams (for feeding the poor), famine-relief kitchens, rest-houses, night schools and *pariah* schools, which were funded by magnates, were aimed specifically at relating low-caste groups to their authority.

Secondly, as we have seen, the conditions of economic instability which promoted communal tension were by no means normal in the South India of our period. There were few fast-rising or fast-declining towns and, after 1878, famine was an infrequent visitor. Moreover, even where economic turbulence did produce communal confrontation, it ought not to be supposed that communal divisions completely subsumed all other types of division, particularly those formed by the rivalry of various magnate clientage networks, nor that they became built into the structure of urban politics. Bezwada, for example, was among the fastest-growing towns in Andhra and its Komati population among the most ritually assertive. Yet, between about 1908 and 1922, the town was run by G. Appalaswami, a low-caste Nagara labourer, who, his social status notwithstanding, employed Brahmans and Vaishya Komatis to work in his interest.[357] Nor need communal divisions last long after they had been politicised for a particular purpose. In Salem, only two years after the 1882 riots which stemmed from Tamil Muslim–Komati rivalry, the municipal council was being operated without internal friction by a Muslim merchant chairman and a Hindu (including Komati) mer-

---

[355] G.O. 789 (L and M, M) dated 20 May 1911. *T.N.A.*

[356] R. K. Das, *The Temples of Tamilnad* (Bombay, 1964), p. 97.

[357] *Hindu* 12 January 1911; *Kistnapatrika* 9 June 1911 and 19 July 1912. *R.N.P.*; G.O. 306 (L and M, M) dated 15 February 1913; G.O. 2028 (L and M, M) dated 10 December 1919. *T.N.A.*; Kaleswara Rao, *Na Jivita Katha–Navya Andhramu*, pp. 291–360 (Telugu).

chant majority.[358] Equally, after any orgy of famine rioting in the Ceded District weaving towns, the reassertion of magnate authority quickly put the lid back on communal disharmonies, leaving little trace of them a few months later.

And thirdly, a concentration on the occasions of communal conflict tends to ignore all those many other occasions when the cultural conditions for conflict were present in a situation but were ignored by the actors. What can be said, for example, of the limitations of political power imposed on an individual by his untouchability when, in Cuddapah in the 1890s, the *pariah* family of V. G. Vasudeva Pillai, which had grown rich on the second Burma War, won elections in constituencies of caste voters to the municipal council;[359] or when, in Madura in 1914, Brahman municipal councillors voted a Christian convert from the Nadar caste to the chairmanship in preference to another Brahman of a different faction;[360] or when, in Kumbakonam in 1888, a high-caste electorate voted an untouchable Nadar to a temple-committee seat.[361] In these three (and many other) cases, supposed caste prejudices were made nonsense of by the political behaviour of the actors. That behaviour, however, appears less absurd when it is set against reference points in the system of economic clientage. The results of the three election situations are perfectly in accordance with the structure of magnate power in the three towns.

In summary, then, while we may recognise the existence of a number of factors which could destroy temporarily the pattern of the clientage network, none was so strong or so long-lasting as to make us alter our categories of political analysis. In particular, the factor of caste sentiment was, for the most part, complementary to the economic order, providing a religious validation of positions attained and supported by economic power. The enormous practical flexibility of the South Indian caste system guaranteed that the circumstances of conflict between the appeal of status-worthiness and that of economic reward would be rare. But even where they occurred, the evidence suggests that caste considerations were at least as often subordinated to the dictates of economic clientage as they were superordinated to it.[362]

---

[358] G.O. 1304 (L and M, M) dated 16 November 1888. *T.N.A.*

[359] V. G. Venugopala Pillai to Secretary, Local and Municipal Department, 14 October 1919 in G.O. 182 (L and M, M) dated 2 February 1920. *T.N.A.*

[360] G.O. 1203 (L and M, M) dated 1 July 1912. *T.N.A.*

[361] *Hindu* 23 July, 22, 24 and 27 August 1888.

[362] This discussion is developed further in my 'The Development of Caste Organisation in South India, 1880 to 1925' in Baker and Washbrook (eds.), *South India*.

4
Local structures of political power

The British, then, were faced by a series of a strong, local political structures which rested upon the organisation of the economy. Based on the provision of a variety of facilities – for the continuation of production, for social welfare and for the patronage of culturally worthy objects – these structures were extremely hierarchic in orientation. They placed in the hands of a few men means to control the behaviour of many. During the nineteenth century, of course, the British could not destroy these structures and, as it were, build for themselves the type of political society which they would like to administer. They were not prepared to commit themselves to providing directly the same facilities as the various rural-local bosses and magnates – and certainly would not have been able to meet such a commitment had they made it. They had to use the local political systems which were waiting for them in 1800 and which, to a considerable extent, developed independently beneath them through to 1947. Yet, although weak and compromised by the locality, the British were not entirely unable to influence the course of local events. The resources and the powers which they could mark into or erase from the social design did enable them to elongate or foreshorten the patterns which they found. From the later nineteenth century, as it was forced into ever greater activity, Fort St George came to use its rubber and its pencil with increasing regularity. In this chapter, our purpose is to examine the social and political consequences of the ground-level enmeshment of the formal administration with local political structures.

Rural Madras

The 'dry' region
In the dry areas of the presidency, there is much evidence to suggest that the impact of British government served to protect and enhance the position of the rural-local boss, and hence to continue the process of social stratification which the economy was promoting. At the turn

of the nineteenth century, as Brian Murton has shown, rural-local society was dominated by elite groups of agrarian decision-makers.[1] However, sitting over and above them, there existed a further warrior elite which had risen with the Vijayanagar empire and had thrived on the wars of the eighteenth century. In varying degrees, according to local circumstance, warrior rulers had pressed down on the resident agrarian population, drawing off revenue and loot, and enforcing political and legal decisions of their own choosing. This check from above formed one of the main restrictions on the power of agrarian decision-makers.[2] Between 1800 and 1850, the British slowly but steadily demilitarised the warrior elite over most of South India. This did not mean that they necessarily destroyed it: some warriors were transmogrified into landlords and others into commercial magnates. However, many were liquidated and the power which their armed force had given them over the countryside was generally eliminated.[3] As Burton Stein has shown, this led to an easing of the pressure on agrarian society and, thereby, removed a check on the rural-local boss.[4]

British rule also weakened another restraint on local power. Wherever previous warrior regimes had sought to exercise a tight control over rural affairs, they had introduced into the countryside new social groups which were tied to their interests and which usually participated in their own species of 'state-level' culture. They supported these groups in the villages with political offices and conducted their relationships with local society through them. The social history of South India is layered with the bones of successive groups of village administrators, each brought in by one conquest and wiped out by the next. In the Northern Circars, for example, Visvabrahmana administrators had been replaced and depressed by Lingayat administrators who themselves had to give way to the Niyyogi Brahmans who were tied to the next wave of conquerors.[5] Similarly, in Salem and Coimbatore, the Vijayanagar invasion had led to replacement of various administrative groups by Sri Vaishnava Brahmans who were the servants of Vijayanagar warriors.[6] The most usual office to suffer

---

[1] Murton, 'Key People in the Countryside'.
[2] Stein, 'Integration of the Agrarian System of South India', pp. 188–96.
[3] Particularly after the recommendations of the Torture Commission (1855) had led to the removal of police powers from *tahsildars*, who often had used them to aid *zamindari* interests. See Frykenberg, *Guntur District 1788–1848*, pp. 48–9.
[4] Stein, 'Integration of the Agrarian System of South India', p. 202.
[5] Frykenberg, *Guntur District 1788–1848*, pp. 12–17.
[6] See C. M. Ramachandra Chettiar, *Konku Natu Varalaru*. (Annamalai, 1954), pp. 339–45 (Tamil).

by these changes was that of *kurnam* (accountant) for it was through the mechanisms of revenue collection and accountancy that the village was most obviously related to superior powers. Behind the office of *kurnam*, however, there lurked the more stable office of headman. Most regimes permitted headmanships to lie with dominant families among the supposedly cultivating peasantry for the headman was expected to keep order and to supply force to back up governmental decisions. These families were usually participants of the 'local-level' culture which was distinct from that of the state. Warrior regimes could not provide coercive force everywhere, all of the time. Government under them, therefore, rested on a nice balance between state demands and sanctions on the one hand and local power and obstruction on the other.

In local terms, the existence of this balance implied several important questions about social and political control. At the risk of over-simplification, we may see these questions as turning on the relative position of the offices of *kurnam* and headman.[7] When the state was strong and the *kurnam*, as its creature, able to bring into the locality force and resources derived from his connection to it, his own local position tended to become dominant. Local society could not deny his influence if government troops answered his call or if senior administrators, who were members of his kin group or caste group, accepted his version of the revenue accounts, and his alone. When this happened, rural society to a large extent passed under his influence and that of the 'state-level' cultural group of which he was a member. The development of this control greatly weakened the power of the resident 'local-level' agrarian decision-making elite. However, if the state became weak or if, for some other reason, the *kurnam* were unable to reach it, then his position declined rapidly. Against the tight economic and social[8] empires of the larger land-

[7] The author recognises that there is some difficulty in reading back beyond 1800 the exact bureaucratic division between headman and *kurnam*, which characterised British rule. As many warrior regimes tended to lease complete village rights to a single man (*pedda ryot, patel, kadim,* etc.), the same permanent duality in the personnel of government was not as noticeable. However, even where state-level groups obtained village leases, they had to rely on peasant leaders to provide them with police control in their villages. Thus there was always some form of state/local division, and village authority rested with at least two different groups who derived their power from two different sources. See, for example, the account of Rudravaram village, Guntur district, in R. E. Frykenberg, 'Village Strength in South India' in Frykenberg (ed.), *Land Control and Social Structure in Indian History,* pp. 231–47.

[8] 'Social' because in central and southern Tamilnad there remained some relationship between land control and clan organisation. See Beck, *Peasant Society in Konku.*

holders, whose interests were voiced through the office of headman, he could offer little resistance. Then, the rural locality passed back under the hegemony of its greatest inhabitants. For several centuries, political power in the countryside ebbed and flowed between an office which relied on the effectiveness of state intrusion and one which relied on state exclusion.

During the course of the nineteenth century, the overall effects of British policy were to alter dramatically the nature of this balance. The British simply did not bring in their baggage train an army of petty administrators whose loyalty to them was unquestioned and who shared their culture. Instead, they had to work their rural administration with the same social material which they found in it. In many areas, this material already possessed channels of interested communication between the state and local levels. Early British rule led to the broadening of these channels and hence to the broadening of *kurnam*-type control in the localities. For example, as R. E. Frykenberg has shown, the close relationship between various Brahman groups in the *huzur* offices and the villages of Guntur district produced conditions in which *kurnam* groups thrived.[9] However, and importantly, these early developments owed nothing to the conscious intentions of the British themselves. They took place largely because the British were distant from and ignorant of Indian political systems. The incumbent Indian administrative groups were thus allowed free rein to use state power as they pleased for their own ends. As the British became more aware of the real situation, however, they reacted violently to it and introduced a wholly new principle into the state–local connection. Instead of trying to bring inside the formal administration the existing web of relationships between the *huzur* offices and villages, and thereby converting a strong network of government which had worked outside their interest into a strong network which could work inside it, they sought to destroy the entire system by which the state could penetrate the locality. Haunted by fears of 'Brahman conspiracy', they pursued with remarkable singlemindedness the eradication of all social ties between state and dominant local administrative groups and the establishment of the headman's office as the centre of rural administration. In achieving these aims, they succeeded firstly in guaranteeing the political autonomy of the locality and, secondly, in laying the foundations of an entirely new species of supra-local political culture.

In 1802, when first settling Madras, the British had made the offices of both headman and *kurnam* hereditary in the families of those who

[9] Frykenberg, *Guntur District 1788–1848*, pp. 93–8.

presently held them.[10] For the next half century, Fort St George practised little administrative engineering, leaving rural government to those who had captured it at or before the conquest. From the 1850s, however, the attack on 'administrative cliquism' and the policy of aid to the village headman began in earnest. Orders were passed to prevent blood and caste relatives from sharing the same government duties and, more seriously, to reduce the powers and prerogatives of the *kurnam*.[11] In the revenue department, where he held his only office, the *kurnam* became simply the man who added up the accounts. The headman had responsibility for collecting the revenue, for issuing the notes of demand and restraint, for the selling of defaulters' lands and for calling in the higher authorities over matters of debate. In view of the real nature of the *ryotwari* system, this made him virtually responsible for apportioning the revenue demand in the village. It would be difficult to overestimate the influence given to the headman by his revenue office. It was generally recognised, for example, that the ludicrously low prices obtained at auctions of revenue defaulters' lands were due to the headman and his subordinates who prevented high bids being made and who often absorbed the land themselves.[12] From 1886, the headman was also responsible for collecting the income-tax.

In the first half of the nineteenth century, headmen had maintained their age-old petty police functions with little help from the state. How effective they were, in relation to the remnant of the warrior elite or to the *subedhar* troops who often acted for district administrators, it is difficult to guess. However, by the middle of the century, most of the warriors had gone and the troops had ceased to back up revenue collection. The headman was left on his own and, by Sir William Robinson's police reforms of 1861, he began to receive government assistance on his own terms. His staff of watchmen, previously paid entirely by an informal contribution from the villagers or by grants of rent-free land, was supplemented by state-paid assistants who were appointed, however, by the headman himself.[13] The provincial police organisation was connected to the village only through the headman and was largely dependent upon him for all its information. The natural result of this policy was that the headman was able to

---

[10] B. B. Misra, *The Administrative History of India 1834–1947* (Bombay, 1970), pp. 458–62.

[11] See Frykenberg, *Guntur District 1788–1848*, pp. 243–4.

[12] *Report of the Indian Famine Commission. Appendix. Volume III. Condition of the Country and People. P.P.* 1881, LXXI, pt 2, 416; *MPBC* III, 679.

[13] *Madras Police 1885*, pp. 1–5.

dominate his locality by force. Many headmen maintained private armies for use against enemies and for pillaging each other's villages. Of Salem, in 1896,

The Superintendant of Police remarks that almost all the violent crime in this district is committed by Koravers who act in very many cases as private Kavalgars in the villages. He considers that in very many cases these men are in the hands of the Village Magistrates [headman], who use them as their servants and, in consequence, protect them, taking care when crimes occur not to mention any of their dependents in their first reports on which the Sessions Court sets so much value. The Village Magistrates, of course, obtain a considerable share of the proceeds of these looting expeditions.[14]

Similar reports came in regularly from all the dry districts.[15] The system of terror at the disposal of the headman was also available for keeping under control his village subjects, whose attitude to him was seen as one 'of mingled fear and trust'.[16] The murder rate – even the revealed murder rate which was but a fraction of the whole – was extremely high. Headmen forced the obedience of their dependents by personal violence, the burning of crops and the ham-stringing of cattle. Few of their neighbours could or dared give evidence against them, for it was difficult to reach the provincial police forces except through the headman himself. Indeed, so closely involved with the external police was the headman that the criminal courts usually took his word as that of the law.[17] This enabled him to prefer all manner of charges against people who displeased him and back up his accusations by swearing in his dependents as witnesses. By the second decade of the twentieth century, when information from the villages was improving, the problem of false prosecutions appeared so serious that the Commissioner of Police began to keep a special set of 'false' crime statistics.[18] But until this time, the headman's prerogatives were completely preserved by governmental ignorance.

In addition to the physical powers of a chief of police, village headmen were also magistrates with their own jails and stocks, who

---

[14] *Madras Police 1896*, p. 35.

[15] *Madras Police 1888*, App. C, pp. xxi–xxii; *Madras Police 1895*, pp. 33, 185; *Madras Police 1912*, p. 10; 'Report on Cuddapah' in *Land Revenue 1904–5*, p. 72.

[16] G.O. 121 (Judicial, Confidential) dated 28 January 1922, quoted in Venkatarangaiya, *Freedom Struggle in Andhra Pradesh*, III, 285.

[17] *Madras Police 1897*, p. 12.

[18] In 1918, the police were called in to investigate 5290 false complaints and were involved in what turned out to be 4160 false prosecutions. *Madras Police 1918*, pp. 18–21.

could try petty criminal cases and execute their own sentences. The British also used them in civil matters as small cause judges against whose decisions no appeal was possible.[19] Headmen tried about two-thirds of the cases in their competence and also were known to arbitrate informally in a great many more important village disputes which went far beyond their legal competence.[20] In spite of the warnings of the Torture Commission (1855), which recommended that the separate powers of government should not be held in the same hands, the headman was responsible for all three functions of government – taxation, arbitration and coercion.[21]

From the later nineteenth century, as British administrative activity increased, the office of the village headman became further inflated. In order to stimulate agrarian improvements, the government began to grant *takavi* loans (cheap credit for long term purposes). Of course, these loans were administered through the regular revenue machinery, that is through the headman. In order to conserve forest resources, new laws were enacted and a new department founded; in the village, their work was carried out by the headman.[22] In order to protect its territory from the worst effects of famine, Fort St George, in common with other provincial governments, elaborated a Famine Code; government grain doles, recovery loans and entry permits to public works were administered on the ground by the headman.[23] In order to extend local roads, sanitation and primary education, Fort St George pushed through local self-government reforms on Lord Ripon's model. The smallest unit of rural local self-government was the village union. By 1920, there were six hundred of these unions, controlling about Rs 3000 per annum each. Headmen were ex-officio members of unions in their territories and usually ran them.[24] In order to expand litigation facilities without increasing

---

[19] *Report on the Administration of Civil Justice in the Presidency of Madras for the year 1885* (Madras, 1886), pp. 16–17; G.O. 2298 (Judicial) dated 10 October 1887. *T.N.A.*

[20] *Report on the Administration of Civil Justice in the Presidency of Madras for the year 1884* (Madras, 1885), p. 23; Nicholson, *RAB*, I, 312.

[21] Concern at this state of affairs was expressed regularly in the native press; for example: 'Apparently, criminal justice, in the view of the Madras Government, is quite safe in the hands of the village headman, who is tax-gatherer, police officer, Criminal and Civil Judge all in one.' *Hindu* 3 May 1915.

[22] See *Report of the Forest Committee. 1913* (Madras, 1913), II, *passim*.

[23] *Appendix to the Report of the Indian Famine Commission, 1898, being Minutes of Evidence, etc., Volume II, Madras Presidency*, pp. 33, 165, 169, *P.P.* 1899, vol. XXXII; *Report on the Famine in the Madras Presidency during 1896 and 1897* (Madras, 1898), II, 203.

[24] G.O. 1337 (L.S.G.) dated 13 July 1921. *T.N.A.*

expenditure, the government steadily raised the competence of the village headman's civil court.[25] In order to cheapen rural credit, Acts in 1904 and 1912 legalised a variety of co-operative credit associations. Although there was nothing in the legislation to command it, those village co-operatives which appeared in the dry districts before 1920 were naturally dominated by the village economic elite which put up most of the capital. And out of this elite, it was most usual for the village officers to run the co-operative as part of their general duties.[26]

British policy, then, concentrated administrative powers in the hands of the headman.[27] It sought to break down the networks of social and cultural connections between members of local and state administrative groups, which it feared it could not control, and replace them with connections of a purely institutional kind between the village and the desks of senior British officials. The policy certainly was of advantage to the headmen and their interests. It enabled them to exercise an official influence untrammelled by the presence in their locality of groups who could use external force. Indeed, it was they themselves who manipulated such external force as was available. But Fort St George soon discovered that its own share of advantage was extremely small. The same spirit of reform which was driving the British to expand their administration and heap powers on the headman also brought with it a demand for responsiveness from the village. In the first half of the nineteenth century, it had not mattered much how village powers behaved, or who they were, so long as a steady revenue flowed and some order was kept. But in the second half, a much more active village collaboration was required. Yet the character of the personnel and the mechanics of collaboration guaranteed that this would not be forthcoming. All orders going into the village and all information coming out of it had to pass

---

[25] In 1881, village headmen heard 47,656 civil cases; in 1910, they heard 96,597 cases; and between 1913 and 1918, with the help of *panchayats*, they heard an annual average of 126,959. *Report on the Administration of Civil Justice in the Presidency of Madras for the year 1881* (Madras, 1882), p. 31; *ibid., 1910*, p. 4; *ibid.,* 1920, p. 3. It ought to be noted, however, that much of this increase may not have been 'new' litigation but could have appeared on the record simply because headmen were being forced to register a higher proportion of the litigation which they handled.

[26] *Report of the Forest Committee. 1913* (Madras, 1913), II, 462; *Royal Commission on Agriculture in India*, III, 549, 647.

[27] '... all influence [in village society] is sought to be exercised through the village headman.' *Madras Police 1885*, p. 4; the headman 'becomes daily of greater importance'. Nicholson, *RAB*, I, 312.

through the hands of the headman's establishment. Consequently, the Secretariat, and even the Collector, were able to know no more and do no more than the establishment would allow. Of course, it might be supposed that the senior authorities had power at least to sack obstreperous headmen and to change the personnel of the village administration. But even this was doubtful. The 1802 Act had established the hereditary rights of headmen in law and any attempt to remove a headman took the government along the extraordinary and exhausting paths of Anglo-Indian property law. In the opinion of J. H. Garstin, a member of the Board of Revenue in 1883, the only reason for which the government could dismiss a headman – short of a successful criminal prosecution – was for being female, and even then, the headmanship would pass to the next senior member of her family.[28]

From the 1870s, a series of governmental enactments began to press on the village administration. Resurveying and resettlement operations gave the Secretariat far more knowledge of the presidency– and of the actual revenue administration of the presidency – than it had possessed before. By 1920, most districts had been resettled twice and some three times, so that the Board of Revenue at least knew how many villages it governed. Following J. H. Garstin's 1883 report on the revenue administration and Curzon's 1902 Police Commission, more revenue inspectors and police deputy inspectors were created to provide closer supervision of village headmen. Village establishments were moved progressively from payment by *inam* or rent-free land to payment from a local land cess and in 1906 to payment as state stipendiaries. New rules demanded that village officers should be literate, and reforms cut both the number of minor posts at the disposal of the headman, which had served to swell his private army, and his power to issue notices in distraint of property. Finally, in 1918, the government introduced a bill to remove the hereditary right of village officials to their posts.

Under this bureaucratic onslaught, it might be supposed that the village authorities were better controlled by the higher administration. Yet, in fact, they survived into the twentieth century with their independence scarcely impaired. The only reformist policy which

---

[28] J. H. Garstin to Secretary, Revenue Department, 3 April 1884 in G.O. 787 (Revenue) dated 24 June 1884. *T.N.A.* Garstin wrote a detailed report on the organisation of the Revenue Department and recommended that much greater powers of interference and control were necessary if senior officials were to curtail village officer independence. J. H. Garstin, *Report on the Revision of Revenue Establishments in the Madras Presidency* (Madras, 1883).

met with any measure of success was one of very minor consequence: the abolition of many minor posts and the curtailment of the right to issue demand and restraint notices at will. This proved an irritant but, of course, did nothing to check the abuse of village officer authority.[29] The attempt to turn the headman and his assistants into state stipendiaries proved of little use while the government could not withhold the stipend for misbehaviour without becoming involved in a series of delaying law suits.[30] It seems likely that its main effect was to put more money at the disposal of the senior village officials than before. Most had managed to manipulate their records so that the amount of rent-free land actually surrendered to government was worth less than the new salaries paid.[31] The new rules, issued in 1894, to make it compulsory for village officers to be literate and to have some competence in their tasks were greatly weakened by a clause which allowed all present officials and their probable heirs who registered within two years to avoid the penalties for failure.[32] This put off for a generation any effect the rules might have had. At best, the reforms and resettlements slightly cheapened the cost of administration and brought to Fort St George's attention more land on which revenue could be paid. But they did not alter the mechanisms by which village officials controlled intra-village payments nor did they even manage to maintain per acre land revenue demand in the face of inflation.

The reasons for Fort St George's failure to mount an effective assault on village officer power are not far to seek. It had, of course, picked up precisely the most difficult people to draw into its central bureaucratic system. The level of active collaboration which it could expect in this political situation varied in direct proportion to the degree to which its collaborators depended for their local positions on the resources which it provided. When that proportion was high, its collaborators would obey its commands explicitly; when it was low, they would obey as few commands as possible. Having set up this

---

[29] For the decline in the number of notes in restraint of property, see 'Prosecutions for Arrears' in *Land Revenue 1907–8* and *1919–20*.

[30] See, for example, 'Report on Cuddapah', p. 21, in *Land Revenue 1875–6*.

[31] For example, in 1870, the village officers of Trichinopoly surrendered 16,304.37 acres of *inam* land and were obliged to pay an assessment of about Rs 10,000 p.a. on it. In return, by 1875, the cesses collected by government and redistributed to them increased from Rs 652 p.a. to Rs 1, 72, 340. 'Report on Trichinopoly', p. 10 in *Land Revenue 1870–1*; 'Report on Trichinopoly', p. 68 in *Land Revenue 1875–6*. See also, Proceedings of the Board of Revenue, No. 1451 (Misc.) dated 18 May 1885. *T.N.A.*

[32] G.O. 361 (Education) dated 24 May 1894. *T.N.A.*

system, Fort St George found that not only was it unable to offer many positive resources but that it was giving what it had to the local men who needed them least.

Most village headmen came from families who possessed large quantities of land and who directed great economic influence in their localities, quite apart from any powers which they received as village officials. They were part, often the major part, of the rural-local boss elite.[33] While, due to the nature of the land revenue statistics, it is impossible to provide overall figures of their riches, that they did possess great wealth was a fact assumed, and seldom challenged, in the political lore of Madras. In a 1920 Legislative Council debate on their stipends, for example, it was stated and never contradicted that village officers did not really need to be paid, for their salaries formed but a small portion of their total incomes.[34] Equally, in considering the probable effects of the Montagu–Chelmsford franchise, Sir Charles Todhunter thought that, given their wealth and local prestige, 'the village officers are likely to have so much influence over the electorate that it would be easy for them to secure a mandate to elected members'.[35] The few cases in which the actual wealth of headmen reached the light of day confirm this impression. In Bellary in 1865, for example, village officers held no less than 635,000 acres of land on privileged *inam* tenure in addition to their ordinary *ryotwari* holdings.[36] As headmen were top of the village service list, it was they who possessed most of these *inams*. In Cuddapah in 1875, the 168 village officers mentioned in a resettlement operation admitted to paying Rs 22,507 p.a. in land revenue between them.[37] In Kistna district, the Kasu family of Reddis, who were the headmen of a village in the upland *taluks*, were said to be so wealthy that they were one of the only two families in their locality who could afford to eat rice.[38]

---

[33] Given the extent to which political power and social status influenced marriage patterns, most of the wealthy families in the dominant peasant caste of any region would possess marital links with the headman's family in their neighbourhood. Looked at in terms of extended kinship organisation the headman's family and the families of other rural-local bosses in the same locality were likely to be synonymous.

[34] Home Judicial, File 931 of 1922. *N.A.I.*

[35] Note signed C. Todhunter dated 11 December 1919 in G.O. 1958 (Revenue) dated 14 August 1920. *T.N.A.*

[36] *M.D.G.* Francis, *Bellary*, I, 175.

[37] 'Report on Cuddapah', p. 10 in *Land Revenue 1875–6*.
C. H. Benson noted how village officers, holding *inams*, also held a large amount of their villages' revenue-paying lands. Benson, *Account of the Kurnool District*, p. 112.

[38] See Kasipathi, *Tryst with Destiny*.

In Rajapalaiyam, Ramnad district, the headman family of A. K. D. Dharma Raja owned great lands, a market and, later, even a cotton factory.[39] In Vellakinar, Coimbatore district, the Vellakinar family, headmen of their village, paid over Rs 2000 p.a. in land revenue.[40]

Compared to the enormous concentration of local political influence already in the hand of the headman, the positive resources offered to him by the British were of small account. Chronic shortages of funds kept the amounts of cash available in *takavi* loans or famine doles so low that, while a useful addition to any patronage chest, they were never sufficient to finance a political empire.[41] The other powers given to the headman also were little more than toppings to his local jar. The provincial police could help him only if a case broke out of his village but did not have the manpower to help him if it stayed inside. The superior law-courts could support his magisterial role only in the case of a major crime or dispute but could not touch the mass of petty litigation which he handled from day-to-day and which was of much greater concern to village society. The revenue department could rescue him from situations of large-scale revolt but could not provide the machinery for getting revenue out of every reluctant payer. It was indeed to avoid becoming involved in these vital but petty affairs that the British employed the headman at all. He had to rely on his locally derived powers as a premier rural boss to give him most of his local authority. In the rare cases (outside the Andhra deltas) where his official standing was not congruent with the realities of local power, almost inevitably he succumbed to the greater weight of the local bosses around him and became their tool. In parts of Tinnevelly, for example, where warrior Maravar lineages continued to dominate rural society by force of arms and so to limit the political influence of agricultural wealth, peasant headmen, who had to rely on the power of their offices alone to give them local control, seldom were more than agents of the warriors.[42]

---

[39] See Venkata Raja, *Brief Life Sketch of P. S. Kumaraswami Raja.*

[40] See biography of V. C. Vellingiri Gounder in Reforms (Franchise) B. March 1921, Nos 34–99. *N.A.I.*

[41] *Takavi* loans, for example, seldom reached even Rs 10 *lakhs* p.a.

[42] *Madras Police 1897*, p. 146; *ibid., 1899*, p. 147. It should be noted that, because of its reliance in *de facto* local power, the headmanship was effectively a floating office, moving to whomever had power, and only nominally an hereditary office. Consequently, our discussion of it should be seen in institutional terms (the headmanship) rather than personal terms (the headman himself). Because of its floating character, a number of *kurnam* families were able to continue to wield local influence even after their own office had been eclipsed in importance. Where, in previous generations, they had used their state connections to build

The lack of positive resources from outside – including that of kinship connection once the British had weakened the *kurnam's* role – and the heavy reliance on local resources of power stressed the features of negative political value in the headman's office. The great advantage to a rural-local boss of being the headman was that he could use his economic influence to full effect without worrying about the interference of external authorities. He could seize lands, murder rivals and hold down his neighbours, while at the same time preventing any British law, order or inquiry from disturbing his control. He could maintain the locality which he dominated in splendid isolation. Given that the headmanship was commonly interpreted by its holders in this light, it is not surprising that the demands of the British for a greater co-operation and responsiveness from their village administrators met with no noticeable success and provoked some resistance. Rural society had come to see the benefit of the British connection in the independence which it gave to local authorities. It was hardly eager to exchange that independence for a highly circumscribed position in a tightly linked bureaucratic chain.

The intractability of the local situation can be seen to account for the extreme caution with which Fort St George pushed through its attempts at village officer reform. Having opted for the headman, it could not afford to alienate him, because it did not have the money to build a new administrative system which would have excluded him and because, if his vast local power were turned against it, its position would have become untenable. Calcutta, although sympathetic to complaints from Madras about village officer indiscipline, could spare very little cash to help alter the situation, and Fort St George itself, save during the interlude of Lord Curzon's viceroyalty, was always bankrupt.[43] Any new administrative system had to cost no more than the old one, which itself was virtually self-financing. Moreover, when provoked from above by administrative reform, the powers of local society could place in the field an army of such size that the foundations of the *raj* were shaken. Not only could they deny the British the means of exercising any rural control but they could create the basis of serious and widespread opposition to the continuation of

up private landholdings, they could become dominant local powers even after those connections had been severed. However, and obviously, their continued significance did not now rest on a specifically *kurnam*-type of influence but only on *de facto* local power obtained from control of land and the economy.

[43] G.O. 369 (Revenue) dated 25 March 1885. *T.N.A.*; P & J File 251 of 1888. *I.O.L.*; *Madras Police 1897*, p. 5.

British government. In the face of strong pressure from the village authorities, Fort St George had to bow its head.

We can see precisely how wary the British were of undermining the foundations of their administration from the cases of Curzon's police commission and the Village Officers' Hereditary Rights Bill of 1918. On the advice of the commission, the Madras government created a new cadre of police deputy inspectors, 2000 strong, which was centrally trained and appointed to act between the village and the existing police establishment.[44] This doubled the cost of police administration and posed a serious threat to village autonomy. As a policy it proved a disaster: open war was declared between village headmen and the police deputy inspectors, and the detection rate for crime grew worse.[45] The anger of the village officers echoed along channels of administrative and political connection – which we shall be examining later – to be heard in Madras city. By 1915, the government was forced to compromise. Although keeping its central school for the deputy inspectors, it switched the control of appointments from its own Secretariat to committees of notables in the localities.[46] As these notables included a great many village officers, it transferred power over the deputy inspectors to the very people whom they were supposed to supervise. Not surprisingly, the hostility between the village and the deputy inspector evaporated. Equally, the 1918 bill to abrogate hereditary rights provoked a province-wide agitation which fed into the already serious propaganda movement of the Home Rule League and the Congress. Village Officer's Associations appeared in every district to press for the withdrawal of the bill.[47] Once again, Fort St George found discretion to be the better part of valour and shelved its proposals.[48] It could not stand up to the rage of its most important collaborators.

Zamindari villages

Although *zamindari* tenants were economically very similar to *ryotwari* landholders, administrative and legal factors made them less politically independent. The *zamindar*, like the government, was a rent collector but, during our period, he possessed far greater

[44] *Madras Police 1919*. Appendix D, p. x.
[45] *Madras Police 1907*, pp. 5–6; *ibid., 1912*, pp. 9, 33; *ibid., 1914*, pp. 72–6; *ibid., 1915*, pp. 17–18.
[46] *Ibid., 1915*, p. 18.
[47] *Hindu* 12 November 1920. *Andhrapatrika* 4 February 1919 and 7 September 1920; *Desabhimani* 8 January 1919; *Gramapulana* 10 September 1921. *R.N.P.*
[48] G.O. 1958 (Revenue) dated 14 August 1920. *T.N.A.*; Home Judicial File 931 of 1922. *N.A.I.*

legal powers than the British allowed themselves. Following an 1870 High Court decision, a *zamindar* was permitted to raise his rents at will whereas the government was tied to a policy of resettlement only every thirty years. The 1908 Estates Lands Act somewhat curtailed the possible despotism of the *zamindar* but also gave him a much clearer title to the lands of his tenants than ever before. *Zamindari* rents were said to be consistently higher than government revenue demands, but information is lacking on exactly how much higher.[49] Moreover, the *zamindar* was not restricted, as was government, in the means he could employ to collect his rents. In parts of Ganjam and the Northern Circars, it was common for an estate to be auctioned off in lots every year to *mastajas*, who paid a fixed sum for the privilege of farming the rent.[50] Similarly, in the south, many estates were leased to tax farmers who rack-rented the tenants.[51] Further, the 1802 Act which gave hereditary rights to village headmen did not apply to *zamindari* areas. Much of the village establishment held office only at the *zamindar's* pleasure and was subject to his will.[52]

Yet we could go too far in emphasising the weakness and subjection of tenants in the *zamindari*. The processes of the economy supported and favoured the development of rural-local elite groups and, for all their powers on paper, the *zamindars* were not entirely kings in their own territories. There was a tendency, particularly under the influence of the Court of Wards, for *zamindars* to undertake direct rent collection from their tenants through bureaucracies. The actual management within these looks remarkably like the management of the *ryotwari* system. The same power derived from control of the records lay with the village authorities, and the same possibilities for collusion and corruption existed in the supra-village bureaucracy. In the Ramnad and Sivaganga estates, 'The zamindars' dishonest subordinates allowed the tenants to have their own way in the village' and *lakhs* of rupees disappeared every year.[53] When the Pithapuram estate in Godavari passed under the Court of Wards in 1892, it was found that the previous managers had allowed Rs 10 *lakhs* of arrears to build up with various tenants.[54] In the Ettiyapuram estate in

[49] *RPBC*, pp. 7–8.
[50] *Land Revenue 1905–6*, p. 67; *ibid.*, *1906–7*, p. 14.
[51] *Land Revenue 1903–4*, pp. 78–9.
[52] *Madras Police 1882*, p. 25.
[53] *Land Revenue 1903–4*, pp. 78–9.
[54] *Report on the Administration of the Estates under the Court of Wards in the Madras Presidency for Fasli 1302 (1892–3)* (Madras, 1894), p. 6.

Tinnevelly, the Court found that Rs 7,16,992 of arrears had been allowed to outstand for so long that action against the defaulters was time-barred.[55] Of course, more than in the *ryotwari* areas, this collusion could have benefited *kurnam*-type groups, whose relationship to higher bureaucratic offices was not restricted by British fears of conspiracy. *Zamindars* were under no pressure to raise the office of headman in their villages or to aim their offer of collaboration at rural-local bosses. Yet, in order to avoid alienating the *de facto* local powers, private administrators had to make some bargains with the bosses. Moreover, the British began to intrude into the interior of *zamindari* estates in order to improve administrative performance. In 1894, an Act was passed to curtail complete *zamindari* control of village establishments and to place certain aspects of their work under the supervision of government departments.[56] This change introduced the principles of headman-*raj* into *zamindaris* and hence promoted the power of the rural-local elite.

Even in those *zamindaris* which steadfastly refused the advice of the Court of Wards to bureaucratise and continued to auction their revenues, changing management techniques began to favour wealthy tenant groups. In order to raise revenue, many *zamindars* auctioned smaller and smaller units of revenue and, particularly in parts of the Northern Circars, it was noticeable that by the end of the nineteenth century many of the buyers were rich *ryot*/village officers, tendering for the revenue of their own villages.[57] A successful bid, of course, would give the purchaser control of the village's revenue in a more direct manner than ever was open to his *ryotwari* colleague and make him even more powerful in relation to his fellow villagers.

Although the tenancy law in Madras favoured the landlord more or less throughout our period, the very fact that a legal system was replacing – or rather, being written round – a series of relationships often previously based on force gave certain advantages to the tenant. Against raids from the *zamindar's* private army, at which many government officials had connived during the first half of the nineteenth century, the villager was often powerless.[58] But with rights, however weak, in a confused legal system and with a guarantee of at least three years' delay in any civil action, the tenant possessed arms

---

[55] *Ibid.*

[56] The Proprietary Estates Village Services Act of 1894.

[57] A. V. Raman Rao, *Economic Development of Andhra Pradesh (1766–1957)*, (Bombay, 1958), p. 193.

[58] Frykenberg, *Guntur District 1788–1848*, pp. 48–9.

with which to defend himself. In 1905, even before the Estates Lands Act, the Collector of Chingleput complained: 'The summary suits in this district are the most troublesome part of Revenue work in this division. Every inch of the ground is fought tooth and nail between both parties and the tenants seem to be able to hold their own against the rapacity of the landlords.'[59] A standard ploy in battles for succession to *zamindaris* or for transfers after bankruptcy was for the losing party to ally with the tenantry in opposing the new regime.[60] The devastating effects this could have indicates that the tenants were far from powerless.[61] Again, the rural-local elite was at least as successful in controlling the sale of defaulting tenants' property under *zamindari* as under *ryotwari* tenure.[62]

Legislative interference at the beginning of the twentieth century more positively helped the tenant to some independence. The Estates Lands Act of 1908 created a framework for the recognition of occupancy tenure and a procedure by which tenants could force their landlord to convert grain into money rents – an important consideration at a time of rising grain prices.[63] Although the powers of the Act were minimal, they allowed the tenant yet a further means of litigation to disrupt the grasping landlord's administration and to freeze his assets for further periods of time. The Madras banker Lodd Govindoss found that his attempts to raise rents in the portion of the Kalahasti *zamindari* which he had bought were met with 8,000 suits from his tenants, which took several years to clear;[64] and the Nuzvid estates in Kistna district, long noted for their turbulence, were pushed towards breakdown as tenants ceased to pay rent for years at a time.[65] Of course, the full advantages of the Act went only to the wealthier section of tenants who had money to play legal dice and who were likely to control village records in order to prove occupancy. The strengthening of their position in relation to the

[59] *Land Revenue 1905–6*, p. 78.

[60] For example, in the Ayakudi *zamindari*, *Land Revenue 1913–14*, p. 12; or in the Biridi *zamindari*, *Land Revenue 1908–9*, p. 14.

[61] For example, the Raja of Karvetnagar achieved so tight an alliance that his tenants succeeded in destroying or distorting all estate records. *Report on the Administration of the Estates under the Count of Wards in the Madras Presidency for Fasli 1317 (1907–8)* (Madras, 1909), p. 10.

[62] In the decade 1907–17, the sale of defaulting tenants' lands realised only 22 per cent of their estimated value. G.O. 1167 (Revenue) dated 14 April 1917. *T.N.A.*

[63] *Land Revenue 1908–9*, p. 14; *ibid.*, *1913–14*, p. 12; *ibid.*, *1916–17*, p. 11.

[64] *Land Revenue 1913–14*, p. 12; *Hindu* 23 November 1913.

[65] *Land Revenue 1910–11*, p. 59; *ibid.*, *1913–14*, p. 12; G.O. 3076 (Revenue) dated 22 October 1913. *T.N.A.*

zamindar both through their protection as village officers and through their hold on the forces of tenurial law, once again stimulated social stratification and increased the distance between them and the smaller *zamindari* tenants.

The growth of rural politics. In the dry areas of Madras, under both *zamindari* and *ryotwari* tenures, much the same social and political processes were taking place. Economic, administrative and legal changes were producing – or rather heightening – the powers of rural-local elite groups. The term 'rural-local' is very imprecise and we have used it thus far only because of the difficulty of defining anything more suitable. Here, however, we may attempt to be less obscure, for the rise to supremacy of the rural locality had a crucial impact on the spatial dimensions of political power in South India. With the demilitarisation of the warriors, the restrictions on the use of government troops, the smashing of local–state social connections among administrators and the combination of powers in the office of headman, coercive force to back up political power was available only from inside the rural locality. In consequence, this locality became virtually the only arena in which important political decisions were made. How large and how wide this arena would be, then, would be determined by the size and width of the instruments of control within it. During most of our period, these instruments were effective only over very short distances. Economic clientage may not have been confined to the physical village but it would seldom extend beyond a circle of adjacent villages which exchanged their products through a common bazaar. Revenue control could be exercised only through the 'revenue' village which was usually no more than one or two hamlets with a population of one thousand or so. Police control could be stretched a little further, to areas of settlement which fell under the practical suzerainty of a headman's terror machine. But these had to be easily accessible from his headquarters. Members of the next layer of government officials above 'the village' might be enlisted to help or to turn a blind eye to a rural-local boss' activities. But their jurisdiction, and their ability to conceal without aid from above, was limited to the revenue *firka* or police circle. Struggles for rural control and pre-eminence, therefore, could take place over localities of no more than a few square miles.

We are provided with an excellent opportunity of looking at one of these struggles by a battle which developed in the Gooty area of Anantapur district between 1904 and the mid-1920s. The two factions concerned were led by two wealthy Reddis from village officer families – Chinnarappa Reddi and Thimma Reddi – and their forays against each other were estimated to have cost about two murders a month and to have filled the local courts with dozens of cases, most of them originating in false charges by one side against the other. Chinnarappa Reddi proved the more successful of the two, for not only was he able to hold his own in gang battles involving hundreds of dependents but also he was able to block the higher authorities. He managed six times to prevent the stationing of punitive police on the area while his faction was winning, and to harass Thimma Reddi with police prosecutions when his own gang was in difficulties. At the height of his power, he was regarded as 'the sole monarch' of forty villages. He took what land he pleased by burning the crops standing on it and sending in his retainers to hold it until the previous owner gave way. His enemies disappeared with a remarkable regularity. He drew a private revenue from his domains and arbitrated in the disputes of his subjects.[66]

Chinnarappa's forty villages were a large territory for the kind of immediate resources he used but they still represented less than a single revenue *firka*. In his use of superior officials he was far more concerned to shut out the influence of the wider world on his little empire than to take his battle with Thimma into a larger arena. His connections with the police and courts enabled him to isolate his locality and do what he pleased in it. British administrative practice had broken whatever greater unities there had been in political activity under native regimes. It left only fragments behind it.

The new demands of British policy, however, guaranteed that these fragments could not remain in isolation. Rural administration had to do more and some way had to be found to make it do more. Clearly, a simpleminded attempt to smash the power of rural-local bosses and turn them into officers of the central bureaucracy would not work. Fort St George found that its new *abkari*, forest and irrigation programmes were going the same way as its attacks on village officer power and producing more opposition than it cared to handle. Between 1913 and 1915, the excise department was faced with a rapid rise in illicit distilling and sales which even its savage prosecutions could do nothing to halt;[67] forest administration was degenerating into open and bloody warfare between forest department subordinates and rural-local bosses;[68] the corruption of irrigation officers became the subject of a major agitation in the delta tracts, and the government's

[66] The case was fully reported in *Hindu* 20, 22, 29 and 30 June and 16 July 1925.
[67] See *Abkari 1913–14* to *1917–18*.
[68] See *Forests 1911–12* to *1916–17*.

new Irrigation Bill of 1915 was greeted with such a storm of abuse that it had to be shelved until after the war.[69] The old methods of direct and despotic rule, with which the British tried to galvanise the presidency, were unable to produce the administrative results they now required.

In consequence, the Madras Government came to apply to a wide range of matters the solution found to the problem of Curzon's police deputy inspectors. Committees of local notables were formed to advise or administer the distribution of water for irrigation, the siting and number of liquor shops, the conservation of forests, the assessment of the income-tax and local self-government. These new institutions had a profound impact on rural political life. They clearly exercised considerable power: excise committees, as in Salem in 1916, could persuade Collectors and other authorities to close down all the *arrack* shops in their vicinity;[70] forest committees could allocate or withhold grazing rights from individuals; irrigation committees could control the flow of water along any channel.

They also changed the physical dimensions of the rural locality and introduced new types of political activity. The rural-local boss could no longer rely on his immediate power network and on his ability to keep external forces away in order to preserve his local position. In order to gain even the same amount of influence, he had to capture administrative machines which could cover many square miles and touch the affairs of a large number of other men of his type. Much faster and more purposefully than the expansion of trade, the extension of the administrative locality brought members of the rural elite into contact with each other and forced them into alliances and battles in arenas which outlined broad areas. To take a concrete example, when the forest department ran jungle conservancy on its own, conflict over forest resources was very restricted in its scope. Rural-local bosses, with the aid of the headman's power, organised the allocation of forest rights in their own interests and within the localities of their dominance. Forest department subordinates were detached from their administrations and brought to coalesce in these arrangements by a mixture of bribery and threat. Any battle for forest rights between bosses could take place only in areas in which they shared immediate interests and wanted the same bundle of leaves.[71] Once forest committees were created, however, the situation

[69] Home Public B November 1916, No. 56. *N.A.I.*; *Hindu* 11, 14 and 23 November 1914.
[70] *Hindu* 14 February, 5 and 18 March 1918; see also *Hindu* 19 and 31 July 1918; *Abkari 1921–2*, p. 9.
[71] *Report of the Forest Committee. 1913* (Madras, 1913), 1, 7.

was changed. An institutional machine had been built which could force the distribution of forest rights over a wide terrain. Rural-local bosses from the entire area of the committee were brought together to fight for the allocations. New linkages and oppositions were formed between men who may never have had political contact before.

The institutions not only widened political activity, they also carried it to new levels. Most of the boards and committees were formed under rules drafted in the Secretariat, which often interfered in their operations and supervised their administration. As, at this time, the Secretariat was itself becoming more open to influence exercised by Indians and by forces below it in the bureaucratic hierarchy, rural-local bosses – becoming now local politicians – were provided with both the means and the incentive to carry their struggles into the upper reaches of provincial government.[72]

Singly, the most important of all the new institutions of government created by Fort St George were the rural boards, which linked together not only rural localities but also the affairs of towns and a host of other, previously separate, interests in religion, education and public welfare. We can best illustrate the nature and the force of political development by examining their history in detail. From the second quarter of the nineteenth century, the Madras Government had been extending local taxation to pay for roads and sanitation. Until 1884, the institution used most for these purposes in the countryside was the Local Fund Board, a loose agglomerate of government servants, local landlords and merchants. Under Ripon's local self-government reforms, a much tighter and more formalised organisational structure was set up. At the bottom of the pyramid, village unions were created to look after the administration of basic amenities in the village; above them sat *taluk* boards which supervised their affairs and possessed direct responsibility for supra-village services such as roads and schools; above the *taluk* board sat the district board which directed the overall policy of development in the district. Under Ripon's scheme, provision was made for a continuing decentralisation of administration and the gradual transfer of power from officials to non-officials by means of elections and the placing of executive posts in the hands of non-officials.[73] Taxation was

---

[72] For example, P. Kesava Pillai, the lawyer of the Chinnarappa Reddi faction in Gooty, Anantapur district, became a Legislative Councillor in 1909 and pounded away at the Madras Government on the issue of the forest laws. He was largely responsible for persuading the government to set up the Forest Committee (1913) and became known in Madras city as 'the Member for Forests and Jails'.

[73] Madras District Boards Act of 1884.

increased steadily throughout the period: in 1880–1, prior to the Ripon reforms, Local Fund Boards handled an average budget of Rs 4 *lakhs* each; by 1893–4 this had reached Rs 5 *lakhs* and by 1909–10, Rs 7 *lakhs*.[74] Administrative powers were also increased to include the supervision of institutions of higher education, of markets, wells and buildings and the implementation of major construction programmes such as railways[75] and jungle clearance. The rural boards of Madras were richer and more influential than their counterparts in other provinces: their powers and patronage were of concern to all local empire builders.

Yet, in spite of their considerable wealth and responsibilities, rural boards made little impact on the structure of Madras politics before the 1910s. The Madras Government, though extremely eager to implement Ripon's ideas on financial decentralisation, was slow to introduce non-officials into positions of executive authority.[76] Rural boards tended to be run by government officers as part of their general duties. A. Subbarayalu Reddiar, who became the first non-official president of the Cuddalore *taluk* board in South Arcot in 1912, complained of previous administrative practice:

As matters have stood, with exception of Dispensaries, Schools and Taluk Board Roads, almost the whole of the outdoor work was managed by the Revenue Divisional Agency. The village sanitation, the maintenance and opening of the village roads, the repair and construction of the drinking water wells, and ponds, the clearance of encroachments, the removal of the prickly pear, etc., were all in the hands of the Revenue Department.[77]

Of the three aspects of administration not managed by the Revenue Department, dispensaries were supervised by the Medical Department, schools by the Education Department and *taluk* roads by the Public Works Department. Although the Madras Government allowed some elections to the district and *taluk* boards, these were dominated by government officials seeking places on the boards of higher juris-

[74] *Report of the Committee on Local Self-Government in Madras. 1882* (Madras, 1883), p. 146; G.O. 2541 (L and M, L) dated 6 December 1894; G.O. 1702 (L and M, L) dated 12 December 1910. *T.N.A.*

[75] Madras district boards were permitted to raise loans on the open market to finance the building of railway branch lines. See, for example, *Hindu* 10 and 17 June 1896.

[76] *Report of the Committee on Local Self-Government in Madras. 1882* (Madras, 1883), p. 4.

[77] A Subbarayalu Reddiar to P. S. Sivaswami Iyer, 12 April 1912. P. S. Sivaswami Iyer Papers. *N.A.I.*

diction. They were virtually intra-department elections.[78] While effective executive authority lay with government officials the boards could not develop as mature political institutions. The character of politics was conditioned by the petty rural locality. 'Bosses' used their private networks to control local affairs and went to particular bureaucrats for a rubber stamp on the deals.[79] There was no need for the district board to become an instrument of district politics when the officials who possessed the power on them could be detached and used to protect the rural locality. The famous Tamil novelist Madhavaiah has faithfully recorded the politics, or lack of them, which went on in the boards at this time:

In these assemblies, I first discovered what a shameful farce local self-government was. Not a few of my fellow members were almost illiterate, and altogether ignorant of the English tongue, in which our deliberations were conducted. They were wealthy and so they were elected. They came more for the travelling allowances they obtained for attending meetings than for the subjects discussed at those meetings, unless they happened to hold a secret brief from any contractor to get an extravagant bill passed.[80]

The institutional importance of the boards dates only from the last decade or so of our period. Under pressure from the Government of India and the Decentralization Commission, which commented on its poor performance in local self-government, the Madras Government was forced to take further measures of financial and administrative decentralisation.[81] The taxation gathered by the rural boards increased much faster than before, and rose by 70 per cent, to a district average of Rs 11 *lakhs*, between 1909–10 and 1919–20.[82] Government officials stepped back to allow non-officials a larger share of the executive: by 1919–20 51 of the 98 *taluk* boards and 11 of the 25 district boards had non-official presidents.[83] Allied departments, particularly the Educa-

---

[78] In 1915, *tahsildars* held six of the elected district board seats in South Arcot, six in Kurnool, five in Salem, five in Kistna, four in Bellary, four in Godavari and others elsewhere. Memorandum 31–41, dated 5 February 1915 in Confidential Proceedings of the Madras Government, 1916, vol. 23. *I.O.L.* In all, officials (excluding village officers) held 102 of the 354 places open to election. *Hindu* 9 February 1915.

[79] See, for example, *Vijayadwhaja* 26 July 1888; *Jananukulam* 17 June 1899. *R.N.P.*

[80] A. Madhavaiah, *Thillai Govindan* (London, 1916), p. 118.

[81] G.O. 616–7 (L and M, L) dated 27 April 1908; G.O. 916 (L and M, L) dated 12 July 1911. *T.N.A.*

[82] G.O. 1337 (L.S.G.) dated 11 July 1921. *T.N.A.*

[83] *Ibid.*

tion Department, were stripped of their powers of intervention.[84]
Quite suddenly, rural-local bosses found themselves provided with
a machine of tremendous power, which they could use to develop
their support and crush their enemies: through control of taxation,
contracts and services in the district they were given the means of
extending their empires.[85] Few were slow to seize them. In South Arcot,
A. Subbarayalu Reddiar became district board president in 1917
and quickly replaced revenue department servants in the board
bureaucracy with local board servants appointed at his discretion
and subject to his whim;[86] he demanded the right to transfer *taluk*
board staff regardless of the wishes of *taluk* board presidents, something no Collector had attempted;[87] he used his powers of nomination
to put friends onto the board and to remove enemies, such as the
Muslim merchant M. Razak Maracair with whom he had a long-
standing feud.[88] In Bellary in 1919, the appointment of H. Latchmana
Rao to the district board presidency brought groans from many local
inhabitants. As soon as he took office he winkled out two *taluk* board
presidents and appointed his own men in their stead. A petitioner
complained: 'All the three are natives of the District with a host of
relations and connections in the District. It is the duty of the
Government to see that the administration does not degenerate into
a Brahmin oligarchy.'[89] The Secretariat itself fully recognised the
implications of a district board presidency: in arguing for the speedy
appointment of more non-officials before the first Montagu–Chelmsford elections, Charles Todhunter wrote: 'Finally, I would observe
that we must not lose sight of the coming elections. An appointment
as President of a local body will undoubtedly be a valuable asset in
these.'[90] Several district board presidents were reported in the press
to be using the patronage of their institutions in their Legislative
Council campaigns[91] and, of the ten who stood for election in 1920,
none failed to be returned.

[84] G.O. 1168 (L and M, L) dated 18 August 1915. *T.N.A.*
[85] 'Landlords with local influence discovered that, as presidents and members of
local boards, they could wield a large amount of influence in their locality and
exercise greater power over their neighbours.' M. Venkatarangaiya, *The
Development of Local Boards in the Madras Presidency* (Bombay, 1939), pp. 66–7.
[86] *Hindu* 5 February 1918.
[87] *Ibid.*; G.O. 1021 (L and M, L) dated 8 August 1918. *T.N.A.*
[88] *Hindu* 12 June 1918, 9 October 1920; G.O. 1010 (L and M, M) dated 29 July
1920. *T.N.A.*
[89] *Hindu* 6 August 1919.
[90] Note signed C. Todhunter dated 17 January 1920 in G.O. 548 (L and M, L)
dated 7 June 1920. *T.N.A.*
[91] *Andhrapatrika* 17 August 1920. *R.N.P.*; *Hindu* 29 November 1920.

In ten short years, rural board politics had been transformed out of all recognition and had altered the nature of rural politics in general. It was not only that new powers had been made available to self-seeking bosses-turned-politicians. Any man with interests to protect or with projects to implement became committed to playing the new games and to obtaining a majority decision in the board, for in isolation he was both vulnerable and impotent. In Rajapalaiyam, Ramnad district, for example, the landlord A. K. D. Dharma Raja's greatest aim in life was to run his little market without interference. For the first few years after its foundation, he had accomplished this end by using his family's position as village headmen to have it expunged from the records. Later, as information about its existence trickled through to higher officials, he had to bribe his *tahsildar* to look after it in the *taluk* board. By the early 1920s, however, he was able to rely no longer on these 'informal' political techniques. The Raja of Ramnad, as soon as he became non-official district board president, began to extend his political power by taking over control of all the markets in the district.[92] Dharma Raja, and the Nattukottai Chetties of Chettinad who also had maintained their rights over local markets by bribing subordinate officials, were forced to seek contacts with and secure election to the district board in order to preserve their positions.[93] Once they were on the board, they forged alliances with other politicians from across the district and formed a faction which opposed every move which the raja made.

Similarly, although for more noble purposes, the Sanskrit scholars and patrons of Kallidaikurichi, Tinnevelly district, found themselves swept into the vortex of district affairs through no action of their own. In 1915, in order to rationalise Sanskrit education in the area, they had approached their local *taluk* board and asked that an endowment be transferred from one school to another. In the past, the *taluk* board had complied with similar requests and, on this occasion, it did so again. However, a faction in the Tinnevelly district board, none of whose members came from Kallidaikurichi, was outraged by the decision and put pressure on the district board executive to have it overruled.[94] For the first time, the educational politicians of Kallidaikurichi had to seek alliances and support at the district level in order to enforce their decisions in the locality.

[92] G.O. 1984 (L.S.G.) dated 7 September 1923. *T.N.A.*
[93] G.O. 783 (L.S.G.) dated 3 May 1922; G.O. 811 (L.S.G.) dated 9 May 1922. *T.N.A.*; *Hindu* 16 March and 31 July 1922.
[94] *Madras Mail* 18 June 1917; G.O. 175 (L and M, L) dated 7 February 1918; *Hindu* 5 November 1918; G.O. 1090 (L and M, L) dated 13 September 1919. *T.N.A.*

The increase in rural board powers and the withdrawal of the bureaucracy from the rural board executive had opened the way for a much larger and more overt system of politics than before. Rural board executives could no longer be guaranteed of majorities by their bureaucratic connections; they had to work for security by managing their patronage and alliances judiciously. Rural politicians could no longer protect or promote their interests by buying individual officials; they had to organise and seek election and exercise pressure on the board majority. Political groupings, formed to work as factions within the institutions, began to link together magnates whose bases were a hundred miles or more apart. In Coimbatore by 1913, for example, a district-wide political combination was clearly visible. Certain Coimbatore town politicians had seized the district board and raised rural taxation. Immediately, political powers in the larger villages and *mofussil* towns put together a protest movement which drew support from all four corners of the district.[95] Similarly, in Godavari by 1919, the pro- and anti-president factions were marshalling their forces in every *taluk*. Similarly again, in Guntur by the early 1920s, those who favoured and those who opposed the rule of P. C. N. Ethirajulu Naidu, the district board president, were organised across four *taluks*.[96] By 1920, the old rivalry between Chinnarappa and Thimma Reddi in Gooty was being channelled into the politics of the new order. P. Kesava Pillai (who worked as a lawyer for Chinnarappa) became district board president and Chinnarappa joined the district board; they used their combined power in the district to have Thimma removed from all local self-government offices.[97]

The expansion of political activity, however, did not stop at the frontier of the district. While local affairs had been handled by semi-autonomous district officials, the Secretariat could expect to have little say in how their decisions were made. But once power was concentrated in institutions which had to report to and were subject to the control of a department in the Secretariat, its interference was both more possible and more telling. The Local and Municipal Department could reverse board decisions, hear appeals against board election results and, most importantly of all, until 1922 it could nominate the vast majority of *taluk* board and all district board presidents. In the next chapters, we shall see more closely how the links between district and provincial levels of politics were developed.

---

[95] *Hindu* 22 and 24 September and 1 and 7 October 1913.
[96] C. J. Baker, 'Political Change in South India, 1919–37', Unpublished fellowship dissertation, Queens' College, Cambridge, 1972, pp. 200–14.
[97] G.O. 180 (L and M, L) dated 27 February 1920. *T.N.A.*

But here we can show some of the effects which interference from above could have on district interests and ambitions. The Coimbatore town banker, T. A. Ramalinga Chetty, was at the centre of the rural protest movement which appeared in 1913. As district board vice-president, he was largely responsible for raising the land cess. He was the object of intense hatred in the Coimbatore countryside and, indeed, was publicly reviled by a cross-section of the rural populace when he deserted the nationalist cause for the non-Brahman movement in 1917.[98] Yet, through his Secretariat connections, he became Coimbatore's first non-official district board president in 1920 and unquestionably its most powerful politician.[99] Similarly, it was essentially through the interference of Madras city that the Kallidaikurichi Sanskrit College affair was drawn into district affairs. The *taluk* board's decision was passed without opposition when it was first put to the district board. But afterwards, under pressure from the nascent Justice Party leadership in the capital, which had excellent Secretariat contacts, a Tinnevelly district board group demanded that the question be reopened.[100]

Although creating the framework for much broader political contacts in the districts and for new connections with the capital, the institution-building of the 1910s and 1920s was designed not to upset the social balance of politics in the localities. The British were intent on harnessing the power of the rural elite; they did not wish to undermine the local roots of that power. The nominations to administrative committees went to men of substance, not to paupers; and the franchise requirements for the rural boards were pitched at a level which excluded $97\frac{1}{2}$ per cent of the rural population.[101]

The real social impact of the administrative reforms was much less on the relationships between rural-local bosses and their dependents than on the relationships between the rural-local bosses themselves. As we noticed when examining the economy, their participation in local-level culture meant that social connections between them were extremely fragmented. Economic development had just begun to forge supra-local linkages. The processes set in motion by the economy

---

[98] K. V. Srinivasa Iyer to P. S. Sivaswami Iyer 18 June 1917. P. S. Sivaswami Iyer Papers. *N.A.I.*

[99] Note signed Panagal dated 16 May 1923 in G.O. 1131 (L.S.G.) dated 17 May 1923. *T.N.A.*

[100] G.O. 175 (L and M, L) dated 7 February 1918; G.O. 1090 (L and M, L) dated 13 September 1919. *T.N.A.*; *Hindu* 5 November 1918.

[101] Calculated from *Evidence taken before the Reforms Committee (Franchise). Madras* (Calcutta, 1919), Appendix 1.

were picked up by the new institutions and carried much farther much faster. Rural-local bosses had to expand the bases of their operations not simply to increase their wealth but to keep their existing political dominance. The traditional fight with sticks and knives between tiny private armies was rapidly being replaced by the less bloody but infinitely larger, strategically considered war of attrition between factions which balanced the interests of dozens of rural-local bosses. By expanding the structure of political contact, these institutional wars also expanded the structure of social contact: rural-local boss families were encouraged to extend their marriage networks in order to make alliances; they saw and came to appreciate the benefits of education; they began to reside together at headquarter towns. Ultimately, these factors would lead on to the development of distinct regional patterns of integration out of the elite members of previously separate local-level cultures.

Importantly, however, as we mentioned earlier, this final stage was barely emergent in 1920. The secondary social and cultural accretions of the movement had as yet almost no separate existence apart from the forces which were bringing about the movement. These forces were partially economically driven but consisted mostly of the political advantages to be gained by participating in the new institutions. Consequently, it is not surprising that the political behaviour of the early regional elite came to be dominated by the necessities of institutional politics. Patterns of district politics tended to be purely factional. They consisted of endless interest-swopping, horse-trading and parlour diplomacy as rural politicians strove to capture points of executive power.[102] There was as yet no sign of wider social or ideological conflict in them.

From the British point of view, of course, this type of development was near-perfect. As the British had built the institutions and had preserved powers to alter, rebuild and interfere with them, they could control the course and character of political expansion. Yet, obviously, their success with the institutions was due mostly to the peculiarities of the social and political structure of the dry region. The isolation of the rural-locality in the nineteenth century and the continued ability of the rural-local boss to hold down subordinate groups in the locality were basic conditions for the growth of administrative, institution-orientated, factional politics. Where these conditions did not apply, however, British administrative reform was less likely to produce such happy results.

[102] See Baker, *Politics of South India, 1920–1937*, ch. 2.

The Cauveri delta and Malabar

In the Cauveri delta and in Malabar, the social and political structure thrown up by the economy was broader than that of the dry region. Whereas changes in the dry economy were only beginning to promote social interaction among the now dominant rural elite, in Tanjore and Malabar a regional landed elite had been in existence for centuries. Naturally, this fact impinged heavily on the operations of the British administrative settlement. The rural locality would never become as autonomous as it was in Anantapur or Coimbatore. The British were less able to break the crucial social tie between the higher offices of district and the lower offices of local government for the neat distinction between *kurnam*-type and headman-type social groups did not exist. Nearly all dominant local groups were literate and participants in the regional, 'state-level' culture. Consequently, external resources were more freely available and more freely used by rural-local bosses and the rural-locality was more closely meshed to the state. Equally, the long-term presence of wide social arenas had led to the development of a large number of political arenas. The trend towards fragmentation, which followed in the wake of the British conquest, by no means touched all of these. Status rivalries at festivals or struggles over accepted religious orthodoxy could produce political splits which, albeit for a few days, ran the length of the districts and tore into rural society. When the British designed new institutional political arenas, therefore, political formations which had been built up before and independently of them were able to mount an invasion of them. In Tanjore and Malabar, district politics were not as sterilely factional and as geared to the simple winning of institutional place as those of the dry region. Occasionally, they contained a hint of real social war.[103]

Nonetheless, we ought not to go too far in pointing to the dissimilarities between the areas. British administration attempted to follow the same pattern as it had done in the dry region and consequently produced many of the same results. It passed village office to members of the *mirasidar*, *jenmi* and *kanomdar* elites, and relied on the

---

[103] For example, when the Porayar Nadars put up a candidate for election to the local temple committee in Kumbakonam, S. A. Saminatha Iyer, the Brahman committee chairman, organised a campaign against them on the issue of their untouchability. The campaign was extremely bitter and violent. Admittedly, it did little good, for the Nadars' wealth was such that, their status notwithstanding, their candidate was elected by a huge majority. Nonetheless, it is indicative of the nature of political constituencies in the Cauveri delta that Saminatha Iyer should have tried this tactic at all. *Hindu* 23 July, 6, 15, 22, 24 and 27 August 1888.

powers given them by their stranglehold on economic production to keep order in the countryside for it. Apart from allowing the continuation of the state–local level social tie, the British provided few positive resources of their own for the continuation of rural government. The possession of rural dominance, therefore, hinged on the means by which economic control could be exercised and, as these means operated only within the confines of the restricted rural locality, rural power itself was largely locally derived. When *mirasidars* and *jenmis* jousted with each other in regional socio-political arenas they were seldom fighting battles which were material to the continued existence of their own local bases. Their mock wars were much more about the status and respect which should be accorded to them by other members of their rural elites and much less about the numbers of dependents whose behaviour in the locality they hoped to control. The battle for local power was still a matter for the locality.

The emergence of the new administrative institutions, therefore, was potentially as traumatic to political life as it was in the dry region. District boards and irrigation committees exercised corporate functions which previously rural-local bosses, using their economic positions and fissures in the formal bureaucratic structure, had exercised in their own right and in isolation. To protect some of the important pillars of their local power, Tanjore and Malabar rural-local bosses also had to plan their alliances to gain administrative power and hence were lured into object-orientated, factional district politics. Many of the status and social issues, which once had split the elite, were buried for mutual benefit in the institutions. Around Kumbakonam in the 1880s and 1890s, for example, elite political divisions had turned sharply on questions of caste propriety. In local politics, confrontations had occurred repeatedly between, on the one side, the high-caste Sat-Sudra Pandarasanidhi of Dharmapuram and the Brahman *mirasidar*-lawyer S. A. Saminatha Iyer and, on the other, the low-caste Odayar T. S. Sivaswami Odayar and the untouchable Porayar Nadar family. Certainly, much more than caste status lay behind the feuding – economic and political considerations were inextricably involved; certainly also the caste issue was perceived more by the faction leaders (the elite) than by their followers – each man's dependency network was of an entirely cross-communal character.[104] Nonetheless, the vocabulary of caste was much in evidence during the skirmishes. However, in 1896 the district board decided to build its own railway line, and completely overturned the relationships of the faction leaders. The value of land sited next to a railway track was so handsomely increased, and the political power to be drawn from it

[104] See above pp. 106, 111, 145.

so greatly raised, that matters of mere status had to take second place to matters of profit and power. S. A. Saminatha Iyer and T. S. Sivaswami Odayar discovered a mutual interest in routing the proposed line through their Mayavaram properties. The Nadars split with the Odayars in order to take the railway down to their holdings in Tranquebar. And the Pandarasanidhi began to put forward a third alternative.[105] District political formations now moved along wholly different channels.

The steady intrusion into supra-local politics of more and more matters which affected the foundations of local power altered the terms of Tanjore and Malabar district politics and made the new administrative institutions central to them. If institutional factional alignments were never the only kind of district political groupings, they soon became the most usual. This, of course, well suited the purposes of the British – as, indeed, had the older administration. Except in the upland *taluks* of Malabar,[106] social order had seldom collapsed in either district during the nineteenth century, for the chosen collaborators were able to perpetuate their dominance over subordinate groups. Later, the administrative reforms harnessed this local power to district and provincial institutions where it could be used to promote development. The British had to be more cautious in Tanjore and Malabar, for the pre-existence of regional elite ties made the danger of an elite revolt against them more likely.[107] But by judiciously manipulating important institutional powers, Fort St George could still control the responses which it received.

The Andhra deltas

The only major area of the presidency in which the British administrative machine created serious problems for itself was the Andhra deltas. As we saw earlier, the development of the Kistna–Godavari *anicuts* had produced a profound economic revolution. The region became characterised by its extensive pattern of rural–urban trade and by the mobility of its labour force. These factors had led to a deep integration of social as well as economic life. In many ways, the rural locality as a meaningful unit of economic and social life had been replaced by the urban hinterland. Moreover, in the countryside at

---

[105] *Hindu* 10 and 17 June 1896.
[106] The Moplah country.
[107] Revenue resettlement policy, in particular, was ultra conservative for incautious demands could bring a united front of opposition. See above, p. 52.

large, there was no small elite capable of holding down the mass of the rural population. This was pre-eminently the region of the middle-peasant and, although some landholders were certainly richer than others, the nature of economic organisation prevented their differences from being turned into ties of clientage and dependency. Every square mile of the deltas contained many independent landholders whose conduct towards each other produced incredibly complex patterns of rivalry.

The formal processes of British administration, however, took no notice of the social changes wrought in the area by economic development. The British tried to govern the Andhra deltas in exactly the same way as they governed elsewhere in Madras – through the unit of the rural locality and with the help of a small rural elite. It is scarcely surprising that government in the region steadily degenerated into chaos. The village police were incapable of maintaining order. The Kistna and Godavari districts had the highest crime rates in the presidency. Most of this crime was not the organised murder and looting expedition of the dry districts, which was the result of clashes between internally stable rural-local kingdoms; it was petty house-breaking and theft on a scale to suggest a serious breakdown in social order.[108] Local courts (formal and informal) were incapable of meeting the litigation needs of the rural populace. The courts of higher jurisdiction in the deltas were choked with a vast number of intricate local disputes, which elsewhere would have stayed in the locality.[109] The district *munsiffs'* courts at Rajahmundry, Ellore, Masulipatam, Amalapur and Guntur were consistently the slowest to complete cases and were considered the most arduous postings in the Madras judicial service.[110] The possibilities of calling in the urban authorities to influence affairs in the countryside also made the village revenue establishment incapable of producing a steady flow of revenue. Appeals against the income-tax, which was village officer assessed in the countryside, were highest in the Kistna and Godavari districts. For many years, the rate of appeals ran at 50–60 per cent of the assessments.[111] As senior revenue officers in the towns had to

[108] See 'Statistics of Crime' in *Madras Police 1878* to *1920*.
[109] *Statistics of Criminal Courts in the Madras Presidency for the year 1915* (Madras, 1916), p. 2. Around Bezwada and Masulipatam 'litigation [was] developing with extraordinary rapidity'. *Report on the Administration of Civil Justice in the Presidency of Madras in 1890* (Madras, 1891), p. 14.
[110] *Ibid., 1900*, p. 5.
[111] *Income Tax 1890–1*, p. 13; *ibid., 1893–4*, p. 78.

hear the appeals, the cost of administering the tax in the deltas was almost equivalent to its gross yield. Similarly, in their ordinary revenue work, village officials ran into constant difficulties. By the time of the civil disobedience movement, their position had become so bad that they were completely unable to collect the revenue in the face of village opposition. In 1930, when the British tried to dismiss officials of defaulting villages, they found that, in a great many cases, the officers had been carried away on a tide which they could not control.[112]

The attempts by the British in the later nineteenth and early twentieth centuries to tighten their rural control and break down obstructions in the village hit the delta village officer, who was already under pressure from below, particularly hard. The improved information given to senior officials by the revenue resettlements, the reduction of village establishments and the removal of the power to issue notices of demand and restraint at will, weakened the few vestiges of authority which remained to distinguish the village officer from his fellows. Many decided that the powers in local society given to them by their office no longer matched the responsibilities they had to undertake. Some quite simply quit their posts;[113] others began to take action against their employers in order to improve their position. Curzon's deputy inspectors met their greatest difficulties in the delta districts.[114] By 1914, even the revenue department was on the point of collapse: the Collector of Kistna reported,

My taluk officers inform me that they find constant recurring difficulties in getting their ordinary revenue duties done by the village servants. Resignations are very common, temporary absence from duty a monthly occurrence, and wholesale strikes by village servants are by no means unusual.[115]

Although weaker than his colleagues in the dry districts, the delta village officer had much better means, through the closeness of rural–urban contacts, of making his grievances felt. Between 1916 and 1920, officer associations petitioned and campaigned for better conditions

---

[112] G.O. 639 (Public) dated 5 June 1931; G.O. 938 (Public) dated 11 September 1931; G.O. 939 (Public) dated 11 September 1931; G.O. 980 (Public) dated 21 September 1931; G.O. 1075 (Public) dated 20 October 1931. *T.N.A.*

[113] Minor village servants found that they could make more money by working as field labourers during the paddy harvest than by remaining in their posts. *Madras Police 1913*, Appendix p. 9.

[114] G.O. 1675 (Judicial) dated 18 August 1913. *T.N.A.*; *Madras Police 1914*, Appendix D, p. 72; *ibid., 1919*, Appendix E, p. 68.

[115] *Madras Police 1913*, Appendix, p. 9.

and more power.[116] During the non-co-operation movement, a large number of village officers resigned their posts and threatened to bring down the whole revenue administration.[117] The Collector of Guntur interviewed some of the more militant headmen and found: 'They maintain warmly that they have not resigned for political reasons, but because Government have not redressed their service grievances put forward by the Village Officers' Association.'[118] Of course, their very weakness made them vulnerable to government pressure, and the strike soon collapsed when they were threatened with dismissal and revenue defaulters with loss of their lands. But social instability remained a serious factor in Andhra rural politics and spilled over once again into the civil disobedience movement.

British administrative design was based on social assumptions which were too static and too local for the Andhra deltas. By the 1880s, the social forces released in the area were beginning to require a much broader based political structure than Fort St George was prepared to allow them. Already anti-administrative (and thereby anti-government) campaigns were taking on the appearance of mass political action. Whereas in the dry region over forest rights, we saw that the point of contact between local powers and the formal government came at the edge of the locality, in the Andhra deltas over water rights it was beginning to come at the edge of a much larger territory. Obstreperous forest subordinates tended to meet their end at the hands of the rural-local boss' army but obstreperous P.W.D. subordinates soon were having to run before payment strikes and press agitations organised across several *taluks*.[119] There were simply too many separate, independent political decision-makers in the countryside and far too many means of communication between them for political activity to be contained in British-made packages.

In default of a workable administrative system provided by Fort St George, the Andhra deltas began to develop their own. The critical economic and social construct of the region had become the urban

---

[116] *Hindu* 12 November 1920; *Andhrapatrika* 4 February 1919 and 7 September 1920, *Desabhimani* 8 January 1919, *Gramapulana* 10 September 1921. *R.N.P.*; *Hindu* 27 January 1919 and 3 February 1920.

[117] See my 'Country Politics: Madras 1880 to 1930' in *Modern Asian Studies* VII: 3 (1973), 517.

[118] 'Guntur/Collector's report on Resignations of Village Officers – 3' in Venkatarangaiya, *Freedom Struggle in Andhra Pradesh*, III, 264.

[119] For example, in the 1890s, a chain of district conferences was set up across the deltas to discuss and co-ordinate action on, particularly, the irrigation issue. *Hindu* 17 April and 5, 6, 11, 12 and 15 June 1896.

hinterland and it was this which progressively became the critical political construct. Urban-based lawyers, journalists and government servants, already linked to middle-level peasants and rural–urban traders through the facilities of litigation, petition and religious expression which they provided in the towns, began to forge more actively political links. It was they who developed the organisation for the anti-P.W.D. campaigns, for the village officer protest movement and for agitations to reduce land revenue demands following resettlements. Increasingly, they went out into the countryside to find grievances which they could represent and problems which their expertise as publicists and organisers could help to solve.[120]

The nature of political expansion in the delta tracts had two important consequences, the first on the relationship between the area and British rule and the second on the social composition of political leadership. Political development was not only taking place independently of British institutions, it was in many ways taking place in opposition to them. The points at which the new political culture displayed itself most clearly were precisely those at which the interests of rural society clashed with those of the British government. The failure of Fort St George to accommodate the 'urban-hinterland' to its administrative technique left that construct outside and antagonistic to the administration. In the short-term, this meant that rural–urban political leaders had very little to gain by association with the British and held their constituencies together mainly by undertaking antigovernmental agitation. In 1907–8 and 1920–2, those leaders who were committed to the Congress cause had no difficulty in taking their followings into the boycott and non-co-operation campaigns. The Andhra deltas were by far the most active regions of the presidency in these movements.[121]

When the British began to expand their administrative institutions in the 1910s, they found that they were able to seize back only part of the initiative which they had lost during the previous thirty years. The powers which they offered in the district boards and other committees were formally the same as those offered elsewhere but they were too few and were coming too late to have the same impact.

---

[120] For example, see the meeting of *ryots* of Ellore *taluk*, which was addressed by S. Bhimasankara Rao, Rajahmundry municipal chairman, in *Hindu* 12 October 1894. See also the pilgrimage of N. Subba Rao through the Godavari villages in *Hindu* 4 October 1894; and *Hindu* 9, 10, 11, 12 and 17 June 1897.

[121] For a detailed account of Extremism and Non-cooperation in the Andhra deltas, see Venkatarangaiya, *Freedom Movement in Andhra Pradesh*, vols. II and III.

Certainly, control of railway building and of the allocation of local taxation, and even of water rights, were not matters which the rural population could ignore. Certainly also, a number of urban hinterland political networks were drawn into the institutions and persuaded to play entirely by their rules. Major battles for control of the district boards and for access to the government in Madras city were not wanting in the Andhra deltas.[122] Yet they did not come to dominate supra-local political activity. In the first place, the new institutions did not absorb to the same extent the political functions which had been exercised by the rural-local boss and which had formed the basis of his power. Control in the countryside, such as it was, was practised more through the power of public opinion and of spontaneous mass action than though the supplying of vital economic resources. The new institutions, of course, barely catered for this type of control which continued to make itself felt most strongly in protest against the government. Secondly, the manner in which the political rural-hinterland had developed meant that it contained a wide variety of linkages which were more social than political in origin. In particular, militant religious and cultural revivalism had helped to draw it together. Again, the new institutions took little account of this factor.

In consequence, they were unable to create or to impose their pattern on supra-local political activity but, instead, were patterned by what was there before them. District board politics in the deltas made free use of ideological and social issues which were unheard of elsewhere. Movements of caste solidarity and reform,[123] cultural conflict between Brahman and non-Brahman,[124] and class conflict between *zamindar* and tenant appeared inside the boards and helped to define the political struggle.[125] Although factional alignment was not absent and, indeed, sometimes lay behind the manipulation of caste, class and cultural symbols, it formed only part of the entire political web. In particular, the appeal of the Congress cause was very strong. From the earliest days of the new institutions, local Congress committees played a major role in electoral and 'chamber' politics and, rather than becoming pawns in a British-controlled game, they

---

[122] See my 'Country Politics: Madras 1880 to 1930', pp. 519–22.

[123] Such as 'the Kamma scare' in Guntur in the early 1920s. See Baker, 'Political Change in South India 1919–1937', pp. 196–213.

[124] M. Venkataratnam Naidu led a campaign to oust the Godavari district board president, D. Seshagiri Rao, because he was a Brahman. The campaign failed but it is interesting that it was ever started. *Hindu* 7 May 1920.

[125] Kaleswara Rao, *Na Jivita Katha—Navya Andhramu*, pp. 434–60.

used their institutional positions to attack the British themselves. In 1915 and 1916, for example, the Guntur *taluk* board could be found voting government moneys to nationalist funds.[126] During the Home Rule League agitation, several local boards passed resolutions in support of League objectives, refused to co-operate with the senior administration and crippled local government by resigning *en masse*.[127] By the early 1920s, the vote-pulling capacity of the Congress had become so great that some local elections were practically decided in the Congress district office – whoever received the Congress ticket was guaranteed of victory at the polls.[128]

The consequences of these developments on the social composition of the political world are not difficult to envisage when set against the background of the rest of the presidency. In the Andhra deltas, economic freedom allowed factors of independent moral conviction and political persuasion a much greater role in determining questions of authority and obedience. It was not, of course, that considerations of authority and morality did not matter in the dry zone or in Tanjore–Malabar. But it was simply that the extreme economic and political weight of the dominant local powers of those areas pressed rural society into accepting their authority more or less automatically: narrow economic and political opportunities and the prevalence of local-level culture gave most countrymen no experience of an alternative authority. In the Andhra deltas, large numbers of people were in a position to know and to choose between several sources of authority and several courses of action. This fact threw into sharp relief the activities of the publicist whose skills in communication gave him access to public opinion, for the influencing of public opinion was an essential prerequisite to the organisation of groups for political conflict. In the deltas, effective political authority passed increasingly to educated publicists who were domiciled in the towns and whose equivalents elsewhere in the province had no rural positions of any note. By using the economic connections of the urban hinterland and the cultural connections developed by the vernacular press, urban publicists built significant regional followings. A. Kaleswara Rao, for example, a Brahman lawyer from Bezwada town, and Konda Venkatappayya, a Brahman lawyer from Guntur town, stood at the head of political networks which stretched through the countryside of

---

[126] G.O. 211 (L and M, L) dated 15 February 1919. *T.N.A.*
[127] G.O. 873 (Public) dated 18 November 1921. *T.N.A.*
[128] See Rajahmundry municipal and *taluk* board elections in *Hindu* 10 May 1921, 4 September 1922, 14, 19, 20 April 1923.

their districts and which were composed of middle-peasant (among other) groups. Venkatappayya showed the breadth of his contacts in the non-co-operation rent strike,[129] and Kaleswara Rao not only in agitational but also in electoral politics – in the early 1920s, he broke the dominant faction on the Kistna district board.[130] The complexities of political life in the deltas, with the thousands of independent minds to be found there, put a high premium on organisational talent. The expert publicists of the towns moved smoothly into positions of rural leadership.

Temples

Within the complex of institutions which acted as the brokers of political power in South India lay the major area temples. From the later nineteenth century, administrative change was altering the political character of these as quickly and in the same ways as it was altering the other institutions of politics. The particulars of administration, however, were rather different and so require special consideration.

In point of culture, of course, the major area temples pertained only to state-level social groups; their relationship to local-level cultures was at best indirect. But their influence on the limited sector to which they catered was very considerable. The cultural world in which Hindu social groups lived was defined by religious status, and the control of ritual ceremonies, which temple powers enjoyed, made the temples arbiters of social mobility and authorities on matters of social behaviour. A strong relationship to temple power was essential if a social group were to preserve its existing place in society or to improve its general standing. Rising Nattukottai Chetty and Nadar merchants, for example, bid heavily for the temple offices which would help them to achieve their much-desired increase in social status.[131]

Beyond ritual and beyond state-level groups, however, the temples also possessed economic power which made them relevant to everybody. In 1879, the capital of the temples was estimated officially at $8\frac{1}{2}$ *crores* of *pagodas*, which yielded an annual income of 50 *lakhs* of

---

[129] Venkatappayya, *Sviya Caritra*, I, 226–301; Venkatarangaiya, *Freedom Struggle in Andhra Pradesh*, II, pp. 250–308.

[130] Kaleswara Rao, *Na Jivita Katha – Navya Andhramu*, pp. 434–60.

[131] Nattukottai Chetty and Nadar ritual assertiveness occasionally led to bitter political fights with the social groups who held the temples which they were storming. See *Hindu* 9 February 1922; Hardgrave, *Nadars of Tamilnad*, pp. 108–14.

pagodas.[132] But these figures excluded the capital value and income of land which was held on tenures other than *inam* and whose worth may have been as high as half as much again. The enormous amount of wealth held by the temples may be appreciated readily when set against the entire education budget of the presidency at this time, which reached only Rs 30 *lakhs* or $8\frac{1}{2}$ *lakhs* of *pagodas* a year.[133] Besides possessing land, major temples drew pilgrims from across the whole of India, whose purchasing power supported entire local economies; they controlled legal monopolies over the sale of many sacred commodities; they organised huge markets and fairs to coincide with their principal festivals.[134] They represented important sources of wealth and political power in themselves.

Before the arrival of the British, all native governments had exercised a close supervision of temple activities. Indeed, it was through religious institutions that Chola and Vijayanagar warriors had extended the arms of the state into the locality.[135] In the first half of the nineteenth century, the East India Company – through its maid-of-all-work, the Board of Revenue – had continued to scrutinise temple affairs, although not in the same systematic fashion: unlike its predecessors, it did not use religious ideology and the manipulation of religious resources in its methods of rule. However, under pressure from the Government of India, which sought to bring its Southern presidency into line with its general policy of religious neutrality, even this light measure of control was steadily relinquished. By Act XX of 1863, the Madras Government withdrew completely from the administration of the Hindu religion and handed over its rights more or less to whomever it could. Where *zamindars* could prove an hereditary interest in a temple, they were made its chief executives; where, particularly in *maths*, a head priest could be found (or invented), he was given virtual private property rights in the entire endowment; where no intermediaries were available, elected committees were formed to carry on the administration. At a single stroke of the pen, the British had cut all connection with the institutions of religion. Try as it might – and it was to write eleven Bills over the next sixty years – the Government of Madras could not persuade its overlord,

[132] Home Public A October 1879, Nos 149–62. *N.A.I.* A Madras *pagoda* was worth Rs $3\frac{1}{2}$.

[133] *Report on the Administration of the Madras Presidency during the year 1880–1* (Madras, 1882), p. lxxv.

[134] For example, during the Chittrai festival at Madura, one of the greatest cattle fairs in the province took place. As many as 200,000 cattle could change hands.

[135] See, for example, Spencer, 'Religious Networks and Royal Influence', 42–56; Spencer, 'Royal Initiative under Rajaraja I'.

the Government of India, to reverse its decision. The Government of India, packed with men whose experience of Hinduism came from Northern India and who possessed a quaking fear of fanatical priests, did not understand the nature or the significance of the temples of Madras, and, in the manner of lofty superiors, refused to be told.[136] Act XX was just another of the many issues which divided the many governments of Madras.

Although the vast majority of the 75,000 religious institutions covered by Act XX were small and possessed only a few acres, some were of enormous wealth, and their trustees and servants men of great influence. The *pandarasanidhi* of the non-Brahman *math* at Thiruvadathorai in Tanjore, for example, controlled 3,000 acres in his home district, 25,000 in Tinnevelly, 1,000 in Madura and lesser amounts in several other districts. He also possessed rights of appointment of priests and trustees to fifteen other temples each with its own considerable endowments.[137] The Dharmapuram Pandarasanidhi, also from Tanjore, owned 2,500 acres in the district and appointed to twenty-seven temples.[138] At Madura, the Sri Minakshi temple committee possessed lands which yielded Rs 2 *lakhs* per annum.[139] The leading pilgrimage centres at Srirangam, Rameswaram, Kumbakonam, Tirupati and Kalahasti had incomes sufficient to embarrass the richest *zamindar*. The power and influence of the major temples of Madras were such that no politician could afford to ignore them.

The greatest problem with Act XX was, quite simply, that the legal provisions which were supposed to guarantee the administration of public endowments in the interests of the public were totally inadequate. Certainly, there were procedures for taking trustees and *pandarasanidhis* to court; but the Act gave the court no power to force the accused to produce his records, with the result that accusations were impossible to substantiate. Further, of course, litigation was expensive and the only brake on it was money. A defending trustee could pay his lawyers from temple funds; a public spirited citizen had to meet the costs himself.[140] For all practical purposes temple trustees were outside the law.

Appointments to temple committees and *pandarasanidhi*-ships

---

[136] See note signed A. P. Macdonnell dated 20 July 1894 in Home Judicial Deposit January 1912, No. 10. See also Home Public A October 1879, Nos 149–62; Home Public A September 1894, Nos 312–18; Home Public A June 1903, Nos 363–4; Home Judicial A July 1914, Nos 265–85. *N.A.I.*

[137] *M.D.G.* Hemingway, *Tanjore*, I, 234.

[138] *Ibid.*, p. 232.

[139] *Hindu* 18 July 1929.

[140] Home Judicial A July 1914, Nos 265–85. *N.A.I.*

were for life and, once in office, there was little to prevent a man using the endowments as he pleased. Leases on land and markets, employment in the temple service and money were all at his disposal, and few men resisted the temptation to use them as political tools. The first Mahant of Tirupati temple was accused of putting Rs 92,402 to his own purposes, excluding private legal fees; the second of misappropriating Rs 2,28,000; the fourth of Rs 1,30,000; the fifth of Rs 6,26,000. The third Mahant, Bhagvan Dass, was known to have misplaced Rs 2,27,000 and, while serving a prison sentence for theft and embezzlement, was accused of diverting a further Rs 14,00,000.[141] And all this was in addition to the perfectly legitimate practices open to the Mahants in the administration of their vast properties.

The Kumbakonam temple committee was notorious:

The local Temple Committee has been labouring for the past many months to nominate a few reliable trustees to some of the temples in the town and elsewhere, but has been able to do little so far. The state of temple management cannot be worse. There are many temples each with an income of many thousands of rupees, managed by a single trustee. Each member of the committee has his favourite and has amassed a number of temples under particular individuals. Even committee members are direct managers of temples; for instance one Mahalinga Chetty, a committee member, directly manages Sri Kimpeshivara temple ... the fine estates attached to the temples are fattening the vultures of the land.[142]

The Tinnevelly Shaivite committee, the Madura district committee and the Negapatam committee were no better.[143] In 1927, the first Report of the Endowments board reviewed sixty-four years of Act XX:

Proper accounts of receipts and expenditure of temples were seldom maintained, surplus moneys were not always properly invested, and temple lands were in some cases leased out in favour of relations and friends of trustees and in some cases alienated on inadequate grounds or for personal ends.[144]

From the highest in the land to the lowest, all sought financial succour from religion. Whether by the legitimate means by which the early Congress begged money from such as the Sankarachariar of Kumbakonam, the Pandarasanidhi of Dharmapuram and the Tham-

---

[141] Home Public A September 1894, Nos 312–28. *N.A.I.*; *Hindu* 21 November 1910. By the late 1920s, the income of Tirupati was estimated at Rs 50 *lakhs* p.a.

[142] *Hindu* 30 May 1896.

[143] *Hindu* 12 December 1896, 22 and 27 September 1910; *Hindu* 15 May 1896; G.O. 1074 (L and M, M) dated 12 June 1912. *T.N.A*

[144] G.O. 1337 (L.S.G.) dated 9 April 1927. *T.N.A.*

biram of Tirupanandal[145] or by which V. S. Srinivasa Sastri gained the endowment of a Sanskrit chair at his National College,[146] or by the more dubious methods which the brothel-keeper K. Alladin Rowther used to speculate in temple property in collaboration with the Madura committee member C. Sambasiva Mudaliar, all recognised the importance of the religious potentates of the South.[147]

Except in the case of hereditary trustees such as *zamindars*, the passport to entry into the world of temple politics was stamped by election. The heads of *maths* and the Mahant of Tirupati were elected by their disciples and, as may be expected, the politics surrounding such elections can be described only by the epithet Byzantine. As *pandarasanidhis* and *mahants* held office for life, one of the most obvious methods of advancing a political cause was by murder: a Tirupati Mahant,[148] and *pandarasanidhis* at Dharmapuram and Sivarankoil were killed by opposing faction during our period,[149] while no fewer than three Pandarasanidhis of Thiruvadathorai died under dubious circumstances.[150] The members of temple committees also held office for life but, as there were several places on the committees, assassination was a less necessary political tool. The temple committee electorate varied from district to district and was tied to a high land revenue or income-tax payment. Temple elections themselves, which were initiated by the 1863 Act, provide the earliest example of the form of politics which the British were to introduce in many other fields. As elsewhere, they were also dominated by men of considerable economic power, who possessed many levers by which to mobilise followers. A classic of its kind was the Kumbakonam election of 1888, won by the *abkari* contractor T. Ponnuswami Nadar. He used his influence with local officials to obtain the help of the local police and revenue departments in canvassing, and with local aristocrats, like V. Appaswami Vandayár of Pundi, who could supply him with their dependents. He had contacts already inside the temple committee, who put some of its resources at his disposal, and other voters who were not tied to him and his friends by pre-existing links of

---

145 *Report on the Proceedings of the Third Indian National Congress held at Madras on the 27th, 28th, 29th and 30th December 1887* (London, 1888), Appendix 1.
146 V. S. Srinivasa Sastri to G. K. Gokhale, 8 March 1908. V. S. Srinivasa Sastri Papers. *N.A.I.*
147 G.O. 1384 (L and M, M) dated 16 August 1917. *T.N.A.*
148 *Madras Police 1900*, p. 5.
149 *Madras Police 1882*, p. 71; *Hindu* 4 March 1925, 5 July 1931.
150 *Hindu* 7 May 1920, 9 February and 30 September 1922 and 8 August 1935; see also, V. Kandaswami Pillai, *Tiruvavadathurai Kurisanam* (Madras, 1921) (Tamil).

patronage and welfare were bought for silver rupees at the polling booth.[151] A whole cross-section of society worked together in his interest, held together by a variety of strands which led to him personally.

The material character of much temple power meant that the committees which managed the temples and acted as the guardians of state-level culture often took on a remarkable appearance. In areas of predominantly local-level culture, many of their members could barely be described as being religious participants of them. In districts like Coimbatore or Anantapur, rural-bosses from the Gounder and Reddi castes often won seats. In areas of complex communal interaction, Christians and Muslims could gain access to their influence.[152] Even in regions where state-level culture was strong, the social order which regulated temple power could be the reverse of that which was supposed to be regulated by it. At Kumbakonam, for example, in the heartland of the Tamil Brahman, the committee was dominated for many years by V. Appaswami Vandayar and T. S. Sivaswami Odayar who came from different branches of the low Kallar caste and T. Ponnuswami Nadar who was an untouchable Shanar. The three, however, were among the wealthiest and largest landowners in the district. In 1915, the Raja of Ramnad took over the committee.[153] He was a Maravar, of the same equivocal status as a Kallar.

In battles between magnates for local power, temples could be perfectly secular weapons. Raja Rajeswara of Ramnad, for example, sought to reassert his authority over the Nattukottai Chetties, who had leased large parts of his estate from his father, by resuming the temples in the leased portions.[154] Similarly, V. Appaswami Vandayar and T. Ponnuswami Nadar further extended their power by backing the Thambiram of Thirupanandal in his bid to win independence from the Thiruvadathorai Pandarasanidhi, who was their enemy.[155] Temples and temple property were often vital elements in the composition of a local hegemony.

Until about 1908, however, temple politics did not extend their significance beyond the area of the committee. The resources used to control committees and win elections were those readily available only around the temple and within the electorate – they were locally

[151] Hindu 23 July, 22, 24 and 27 August 1888.
[152] Such as K. M. Alladin Rowther of Madura whom we have seen. For the attempt of a group of low-caste weavers to obtain a seat on a temple committee, see Hindu 10 June 1915.
[153] Hindu 8 February and 24 March 1915.
[154] G.O. 4139 (L.S.G.) dated 25 September 1926. T.N.A.; Hindu 8 and 9 April 1921.
[155] Hindu 30 October 1894.

derived. Connections with the higher bureaucracy and the law mattered very little when the temples were virtually beyond the control of the government and the law. The only effective right the government maintained was that of allowing District Judges to appoint committee members if vacancies were not filled within a specified time. Given that almost every committee was faction-riven and that factions which were likely to lose would do everything in their power to prevent an election, this right was exercised on a number of occasions. But the most usual form of appointment was by the ordeal of the polling booth where the personal influence of the magnate or rural-local boss was supreme. Moreover, as elections were held only at long intervals, and as they were the only times when local powers could fight for temple control, temple political conflict was as infrequent as it was socially prescribed.

In 1908, changes in the Code of Civil Procedure suddenly opened out temple politics in the same way that administrative decentralisation was to open out district board politics. It became feasible to take temple committees and trustees to court for malpractices, to have them removed, to contest election results and to alter the political balances inside institutions. Temple politicians could no longer rely on their life-franchises of office and on the irregularity of elections to preserve their positions for them; they had to manage their alliances and their distribution of patronage judiciously to prevent strong enemy factions from ousting them. Battle between them was joined on a much broader front and there were no longer any respites between engagement. In Madura, the Sri Minakshi temple committee immediately fell apart as two contending factions sought to gain complete sovereignty over each other.[156] The cases which they began to bring against each other were to be more than twenty years in the courts. In Mayavaram *taluk*, Tanjore district, the immensely rich *mirasidar* T. Somasundram Mudaliar took on the Pandarasanidhi of Dharmapuram *math*, supposedly the spiritual leader of his caste, for control of two local temples.[157] In Kumbakonam, defeated electoral candidates crippled the temple committee by lodging petitions against their victorious opponents, which took months to clear.[158] Everywhere, the struggle grew more vigorous, and politicians attacked each other not only at the polling booths but in the temple offices and during religious ceremonies themselves.

As with the case of the district boards, however, these developments

---

[156] G.O. 1074 (L and M, M) dated 12 June 1912. *T.N.A.*; *South Indian Mail* 21 August 1911.
[157] *Hindu* 23 August 1910 and 12 October 1915.
[158] *Hindu* 8 February and 24 March 1915.

did more than draw local politicians into wider district arenas. They also linked the local arenas to the presidency capital. In Madras city, a group of leading Indian lawyers and administrators formed themselves into a Dharmarakshana Sabha to use the new legal provisions to purge the temples of sin. Over the next few years, their association launched cases at most of the major temples in the South, including Rameswaram, Srirangam, Madura, Tirupati and Kalahasti, and won the right to dictate the appointment of various committee members, trustees and temple managers.[159] As we shall see later, its inordinate success was due in no small part to the enormous influence which its organisers had over the career prospects of the judges who heard its cases.[160] However noble may have been their intention, decisions taken in the Dharmarakshana Sabha could have a dramatic impact on the balance of local power. In a few years, actions taken by the Sabha had affected deleteriously the interests of such great powers as the Raja of Kalahasti, the Zamorin of Calicut, the Mahant of Tirupati and the Pandarasanidhi of Madura. Of course, connection to the Sabha became an important positive resource in local factional battles. At Mayavaram, T. Somasundram Mudaliar called on its aid to help him defeat the Pandarasanidhi of Dharmapuram.[161] In Madura, one of the factions on the Sri Minakshi committee sought to bring prosecutions against the other in its name.[162] Yet again, institutional changes were forging a new set of political connections and altering the nature of political life.

The administration of the towns

The types of administrative change which the British implemented in the towns of South India followed similar patterns to those in the countryside and patterned politics in very similar ways. They require separate consideration, however, for two reasons. Firstly, the greater political role which status and cultural activities possessed in the towns could have been affected profoundly by the changes. As historians of other Indian regions have noted, educated publicists often used the new institutions to establish political dominance in their own

[159] *Kerala Patrika* 9 November 1912. *R.N.P.*; *Hindu* 20 November 1915 and 10 June 1918; K. Raghavayya to P. S. Sivaswami Iyer, 26 October 1916. P. S. Sivaswami Iyer Papers. *N.A.I.*; *The Fourth Year's Report on the Working of the Dharma Rakshana Sabha* (Madras, 1911).

[160] G.O. 175 (L and M, L) dated 7 February 1918. *T.N.A.*

[161] *Hindu* 12 October 1915.

[162] G.O. 1074 (L and M, M) dated 12 June 1912. *T.N.A.*

right.[163] And secondly, the cross-communal networks of urban economic powers were under greater pressure from outbreaks of communal hostility than were those of rural powers. Again, urban administrative change elsewhere has been connected with the politics of communal conflict.[164]

Specifically urban administrative systems began to develop in British Madras only from the middle of the nineteenth century. Previously, government had been continued by informal association between agents of the bureaucracy and the principal inhabitants, some of whom were granted formal revenue and judicial offices, much as in the countryside. From the 1860s, as Fort St George was pressed by the Government of India both for more money and for the greater development of its resources, urban administrations became more specialised. Municipal councils were formed in a few of the larger conurbations to raise their own taxes and regulate their own programme of conservancy and sanitary improvement.[165] These councils were chaired by the local Collector and filled with other government officials. But they also contained several nominated non-officials who did most of the work. Although they possessed some corporate powers, the councils tended to conduct much government through the medium of individual councillors. The men nominated by the Collector each represented certain wards in the town and were personally responsible for executing council decisions within them.[166] Many were further nominated as Honorary Magistrates to try breaches of council rules and transgressions against the bye-laws. They thus possessed considerable influence as individuals within the urban political structure. House-fronts which encroached on public property could be torn down at their whim, shops closed as a danger to health and men fined for petty offences. Reviewing his municipal administration in 1874, the Governor of Madras saw that: 'The Government of a Municipality is in fact an oligarchy dependent upon a superior power'.[167]

It would be difficult to characterise all the people whom 'the

---

[163] C. A. Bayly, 'Local Control in Indian Towns: The Case of Allahabad' in *Modern Asian Studies*, v:4 (1971).

[164] F. C. R. Robinson, 'Municipal Government and Muslim Separatism in the United Provinces 1883–1916' in *Modern Asian Studies*, vii:3 (1973).

[165] *Report of the Committee on Local Self-Government in Madras, 1882* (Madras, 1883), pp. 9–12.

[166] J. G. Leonard, 'Urban Government under the Raj: a Case Study of Municipal Administration in Nineteenth-Century South India' in *Modern Asian Studies*, vii:2 (1973), 230, 233–6.

[167] *Report of the Committee on Local Self-Government in Madras. 1882*, p. 9.

superior power' nominated to the councils across this twenty-year period. The power of nomination lay with the Collector and he could appoint whomsoever he liked. It seems probable, however, that the bulk of nominations went to the most prominent local citizens – which means, more or less, the leading urban magnates. It would make little sense for the Collector to ignore the men on whom he relied to restore the peace during times of trouble, to provide arbitration in social disputes, to come to his assistance during famines and to provide religious, educational and other facilities, when looking for agents to undertake the responsibilities of urban government. All councils were liberally sprinkled with wealthy merchants and landlords whose own networks of influence and control were thereby expanded. In Rajahmundry throughout the 1870s, for example, four of the five most important councillors were merchants;[168] in Negapatam, Muslim Maraciar and Hindu Pillaima merchants were prominent;[169] in Tuticorin, European and Christian Bharatha businessmen;[170] in Kumbakonam, the council was virtually led by a rich *mirasidar*, S. A. Saminatha Iyer, who acted as a lawyer and political agent for many other *mirasidars*.[171]

The arenas in which these powers were allowed to operate remained small and informal. Authority centred much more on the ward councillor than on the council, and his influence was essentially personal. The District Municipalities Act of 1884, however, which followed Lord Ripon's initiatives in local self-government, radically changed the face of urban politics. The powers of taxation and administrative interference vested in the councils were further and greatly increased. More importantly, the organisation of council authority became much more institutionalised. Under the Act, the council as a body controlled – within limits – the nature and level of taxation and of urban administration. The council chairman was vested with full executive powers. He was responsible for carrying out the orders of his council and for hearing, or appointing committees to hear, appeals against council resolutions. In addition, he appointed most of the municipal staff, which stretched from sweepers to senior accountants and clerks, drew up the budget and conducted all correspondence between the council and its supervisors.[172] The focal point of municipal politics switched from a few

[168] Leonard, 'Urban Government under the Raj, p. 235.
[169] *Report of the Committee on Local Self-Government in Madras. 1882*, p. 20.
[170] G.O. 508 (L and M, M) dated 17 May 1888; G.O. 1016 (L and M, M) dated 13 September 1888. *T.N.A.*
[171] *Hindu* 26 June 1888; G.O. 1077 (L and M, M) dated 26 September 1888. *T.N.A.*
[172] *Madras District Municipalities Act of 1884. T.N.A.*

individuals to the council itself, and although it was quite usual for some aspects of administration to be conducted by ward, ward councillors were under the authority of the council as a whole. These clauses in themselves would have been bound to create some political changes but the 1884 Act went further. It envisaged the gradual replacement of all government officials in the councils by elected non-officials and provided for the transfer of the crucial office of chairman to Indian hands. The old informal relationship between British officials and local magnates was to be broken by the creation of democratic governmental institutions from which government officers were excluded.

Although Ripon's municipal legislation was designed to take effect very quickly, most of the provincial governments found ways of prolonging the implementation of its more novel ideas. In Madras, for example, the extension of electorates, the withdrawal of the bureaucracy and the transfer of executive authority to native non-official chairmen was nearly as slow and sporadic in the municipalities as it was in the rural boards. It was not until 1912–13 that the majority of municipal councillors were elected and, until 1920, a considerable proportion of non-official chairmen were government nominees.[173] Between 1885 and 1920 almost no two municipal councils were constituted exactly alike. We are thrown back on general explanations and 'ideal' types if we are to make any sense of Madras history.

Until recently, it had been widely accepted that municipal government in British India was hollow and that most councils were so tightly controlled by the superior agencies of government that they had no room for independent action.[174] However, John Leonard has challenged this assumption and demonstrated the great importance of municipalities to the inhabitants under them.[175] The tightness of superior control has often been overestimated. As local officials were withdrawn from the administration, their knowledge of council affairs naturally decreased and there is much to suggest that, even when they were present in municipal politics, the pressure of other work prevented them from taking a very active part. Although the Secretariat possessed enormous powers of interference, it tended to use them as individual crises arose rather than to conduct permanent and detailed administration, which would have been very difficult from its distant perch. Indeed, as the whole purpose of decentral-

---

[173] K. K. Pillai, *History of Local Self-Government in the Madras Presidency 1850–1919* (Bombay, 1953), p. 66.

[174] For example, H. Tinker, *The Foundations of Local Self-Government in India, Pakistan and Burma* (London, 1954), pp. 51–60.

[175] Leonard, 'Urban Government under the Raj', pp. 227–51.

isation was to relieve government of supposed responsibilities, a policy which centred on regular interference would have been self-defeating. The councils certainly appeared very attractive political arenas to the urban population: voting turn-outs were extremely high[176] and municipal budgets, though not large when compared to the private incomes of some municipal inhabitants, could provide a living for many employees.[177] More importantly, the council possessed executive powers which interfered materially in the lives of its subjects. Local inhabitants would find their burial grounds closed,[178] their trading activities restricted,[179] their houses pulled down,[180] their taxes raised,[181] their property compulsorily purchased,[182] and their places of worship desecrated.[183] They could find roads driven through their front gardens,[184] markets in which they had invested heavily prevented from working,[185] and occupations they had long practised outlawed.[186] Alternatively, they could be sold cheap land and given building permission,[187] receive valuable contracts,[188] and have their taxes slashed to nothing.[189] All depended on the action of the council majority. The general effect of the Ripon reforms was to lead to the slow but

---

[176] Between 1900 and 1920, 60 to 70 per cent of all enfranchised voters went to the polls every year. In 1914–15, the proportion reached 73.6 per cent. See *Annual Reports on the Working of the District Municipalities Act* (Madras, 1900–20).

[177] In 1920–1, there were 73 municipalities in Madras, which had total budgets of Rs 93,14,610 or an average of Rs 1.27 *lakhs* each. Although there were fewer municipalities in Madras than in any other major Indian Province, the average municipal budget was higher than in Bombay, Bengal and Punjab. *Memorandum on the Working of Representative Institutions in Local Self-Government* (Calcutta, 1928), pp. 76–9.

[178] Madras city, *Hindu* 11 June 1894.

[179] Bellary, G.O. 2120 (L and M, M) dated 19 December 1908. *T.N.A.*

[180] Erode, G.O. 1250 (L and M, M) dated 19 July 1916. *T.N.A.*

[181] Bellary, G.O. 2000 (L and M, M) dated 7 December 1892. *T.N.A.*

[182] Kumbakonam, *Hindu* 21 September 1906.

[183] Conjeeveram, *Hindu* 11 October 1893.

[184] Madura, G.O. 411 (L and M, M) dated 20 March 1900. *T.N.A.*

[185] Madras city, *Hindu* 5 March 1907.

[186] Such as butchery, G.O. 1101 (L.S.G.) dated 30 April 1924. *T.N.A.*

[187] Rajahmundry, G.O. 387 (L and M, M) dated 1 March 1912. *T.N.A.*; *Desamata* 31 May 1911. *R.N.P.*

[188] Madura, *Hindu* 5 May 1896, 9 April 1907.

[189] In Ellore, Mothey Venkataswami, although the richest inhabitant, never paid any taxes. G.O. 1011 (L and M, M) dated 17 July 1901. One of the main concerns of merchants everywhere was to gain control of councils in order to lower the rates of taxation, particularly on themselves – as in Guntur, G.O. 25 (L and M, M) dated 11 January 1893; in Vanniyambadi, G.O. 802 (L and M, M) dated 28 April 1904; in Masulipatam, G.O. 564 (L and M, M) dated 16 April 1891. *T.N.A.*

steady concentration of urban power in one institution and to make control of the council, for the first time, vital to all urban politics. The relevance of the new municipality to the educated publicist, trying but usually failing to establish for himself an influence based on persuasion rather than the manipulation of hard sanctions, is not difficult to see. If he could persuade enough voters, on one day, to support his candidature and to put him onto the council, he had at his disposal patronage and administrative influence with which to consolidate his position and develop a personal political empire apart from his patrons. Western-educated publicists, if they could generate enough support at the elections, could at last manipulate levers of social control. From the 1880s, the towns of Madras witnessed the growth of organisations designed to gather together grievances and to put organisers into the municipal council. Ratepayers and Taxpayers Associations shot up, and, in the larger towns, constituency associations appeared. Popular cultural and religious movements began to supply the fuel for agitation and the organisation for caucuses in municipal politics. Publicists stood at the head of all these. But did their political tactics work?

At the first election in any newly enfranchised town, certainly, there was much chaos at the hustings and many of the patterns of previous government seem to have broken down. Publicists usually were quite successful.[190] Further, the bringing together of the many and previously discreet channels of political influence in one council chamber had created the opportunity for the emergence of the 'broker' politician who worked between interest groups without himself having to be clearly tied to any. He could use his middleman position to become central to the working of the council. In Rajahmundry, for example, the Brahman lawyer N. Jaladurgaprasadarayadu dominated the council in the 1890s: having used agitation and private legal connection to get the chairmanship, he judiciously manipulated patronage and influence for a decade.[191] Equally, in Bellary at the same time, the Brahman lawyer K. Venkoba Rao became chair-

---

[190] As at the first elections in Salem town, where the young Brahman lawyers W. Viraswami Iyer and C. Vijayaraghavachari, both of whom came from outside, were able to use the local Komati–Muslim confrontation of 1882 to become accredited spokesmen of the Hindus and to win election. In the opinion of the Collector, 'they were persons of no weight in the town'. *Report of the Committee on Local Self-Government in Madras. 1882*, p. 22. Also, 'Rajahmundry experienced several years of political instability following the Ripon reforms.' Leonard, 'Urban Government under the Raj, p. 238.

[191] Leonard, *ibid.*, pp. 238–9.

man and built for himself a basis of support by redistributing taxation and rewards.[192]

Yet the development of 'new' politicians from the 'new' style of urban politics was not nearly as clear as it might at first seem. The older leadership groups had always employed lawyers and literati to work for them. By simple extension, they continued to employ, and to control, them in the municipal institutions. In Ellore under Mothey *raj*, for example,

Pure Bania members will always be few and it is vakils and other intelligent persons they try to enlist who can expound the law to them and show to them the way in which their machinations can best be forwarded consistently with the law or the law evaded if possible.[193]

A simple change in personnel would not necessarily tell us much about who controlled municipal politics: western-educated professionals were not necessarily their own masters. In general, however, there does not even seem to have been a radical long-term change in personnel. By the early 1900s, the municipal administrations of towns as diverse as Cocanada, Vanniyambadi, Madura and Tinnevelly were filled with merchants and landlords cut on the old magnate die.[194] Although there were some western publicists, they were usually tools to be used by others.

Viewed from another angle, the survival of the magnates is less surprising. The municipal franchise was pitched at a high level and relatively few people possessed the vote. The electorate remained sufficiently small to be influenced on a personal basis by direct ties of debt, tenantry and patronage.[195] Popular appeals, based on outrage or sympathy, could not find a wide enough audience. In Ellore, the economic power of the Mothey family still gave it control of the council. Similarly, in Cocanada in the 1880s, the Pydah Komati family commanded its debtors to vote at its will and controlled the chair-

---

[192] G.O. 2000 (L and M, M) dated 7 December 1892. *T.N.A.*

[193] A. R. Banerji, Assistant Collector, Ellore, to Collector of Godavari, 29 March 1901 in G.O. 1011 (L and M, M) dated 17 July 1901. *T.N.A.*

[194] In Cocanada in 1894, all the elected seats were held by merchants, *Hindu* 29 October 1894; for the mercantile preponderance in Vanniyambadi, see G.O. 802 (L and M, M) dated 28 April 1904; for Madura, G.O. 463 (L and M, M) dated 18 March 1896, G.O. 2135 (L and M, M) dated 11 October 1905; for Tinnevelly, G.O. 1848 (L and M, M) dated 4 October 1912. *T.N.A.*

[195] It was extremely rare for there to be even 200 voters in any one ward of a municipality, G.O. 2207 (L and M, M) dated 13 December 1911. See also, note by Chairman of Mayavaram in G.O. 2512 (L and M, M) dated 17 December 1907. *T.N.A.*

manship;[196] and we have seen the power of the bank cashier at Tuticorin and of the rich Nadars of Sivakasi. Most municipalities for most of the time remained dominated by the local resources – whether debt, employment, landownership, patronage or terror, or all five – of a few magnates. At Vizianagram, the Maharaja's nominees swept every election;[197] at Salem, the *zamindar*'s lawyer was chairman continuously between 1901 and 1914;[198] at Bezwada, the contractor G. Appalaswami controlled three-quarters of the elected seats for fifteen years and all municipal executives had to come to terms with him.[199] In general, the older style of urban leadership was able to survive the onslaught of democratic institutions remarkably easily and to use the new sources of conciliar power to extend its influence.

In sheer economic terms, the municipalities did not handle enough money to rival the economic networks of wealthy landowners and merchants. Only in areas where there were no very rich men, or where they were many and heavily divided, or where great concentrations of population depended on non-magnate sources for their income – as in the few towns in which the offices of the administration, law and education were the largest employers – could the municipality become a vital economic centre and men whose primacy was not based on financial control grasp it for themselves. Otherwise, access to municipal power was choked by magnate influence.

As may be guessed from the failure of the publicists, the politics of communal sentiment also promised much but delivered very little in the municipalities of Madras. Certainly, there were occasional outbreaks of communal violence at the polls. Equally, there were some caste constituencies, particularly among merchant communities. But no interpretation of municipal politics could make caste or community central. To take the example of the Muslims: how would it be possible to explain the fact that in 1909 at Vanniyambadi, the Muslim trading capital in the South, Muslims possessed 321 votes out of a total of 469 (68.44 per cent), yet held only two of the six elected seats and were given two more by nomination (to make 33.3 per cent of representation)?[200] Nobody could doubt that Muslim interests were

---

[196] G.O. 1411 (L and M, M) dated 11 December 1888. *T.N.A.*

[197] *Hindu* 22 January 1902; *Andhra Advocate* 18 October 1916. *R.N.P.*

[198] E. S. Ramaswami Iyer, see G.O. 1616 (L and M, M) dated 5 November 1901. *T.N.A.*

[199] *Hindu* 12 January 1911; *Kistnapatrika* 9 June 1911 and 19 July 1912. *R.N.P.*; G.O. 306 (L and M, M) dated 15 February 1913; G.O. 2028 (L and M, M) dated 10 December 1919. *T.N.A.*

[200] G.O. 1400 (L and M, M) dated 25 August 1909. *T.N.A.*

dominant in the town, but the Muslims worked through others. On the other hand, in Madura Muslims had only 78 of 2326 votes but they held two of the twelve elected seats.[201] Here, they worked in front of Hindus; and by 1917 one of their number, K. M. Alladin Rowther, was to be returned for the ward containing the leading Hindu merchants and lawyers.[202] While trade rivalries between Hindu and Muslim merchants and weavers might occasionally break down cross-communal alliances, much the more usual form of communal municipal politics was that to be found in Negapatam, Vanniyambadi and Trichinopoly where Hindu and Muslim prospective candidates patronised each other's temples and mosques.[203] Similarly, as we saw earlier, even the barrier of untouchability need not be relevant to municipal politics: in Cuddapah, Kumbakonam and Madura untouchable families could and did play a leading part in municipal life.[204]

Although municipal institutions may have done little to alter the social base from which urban leaders came, it would be wrong to underestimate their purely political importance. They brought together the principal informal leaders of urban society, placed them next to each other in a single arena and left them to fight it out for pre-eminence. Whereas previously, the informality of urban government had kept the magnates apart, now they were necessarily drawn into conflict. Factional divisions between them were deepened as each sought to capture the council. Not only was status in question, but also the considerable powers of council office which gave a man a hold over the whole rather than part of the town. Whatever the influence of Mothey Venkataswami or T. S. Sivaswami Odayar before the coming of the 1884 Act, after it there was scarcely a man in their respective towns who was not somehow connected to them through the council administration. In large towns, where several magnates contested power, the victor could use his control to harass unmercifully the enterprises of his enemies in ways previously unknown.

The growing bitterness and greater depth of factional warfare can be seen in the manner in which new styles of politics were used to conduct old rivalries in the new arenas – styles which owed much to the energies of dependent publicists. In Bellary, for example, the local rivalry between the *abkari* contractor and industrialist, A. Sabhapati Mudaliar, and the railway contractor, M. Ramanjulu Naidu, boiled

---

[201] *Ibid.*
[202] G.O. 1384 (L and M, M) dated 16 August 1917. *T.N.A.*
[203] G.O. 798 (L and M, M) dated 20 May 1911; G.O. 2099 (L and M, M) dated 8 November 1912; G.O. 1347 (L and M, M) dated 9 August 1917. *T.N.A.*
[204] See above p. 145.

up into class conflict when Ramanjulu Naidu backed a lawyer-led faction of petty bazaarmen, which organised a *hartal* and finally threw Sabhapati Mudaliar out of the council office.[205] Similarly, in Bezwada, the Brahman lawyer A. Kaleswara Rao brought the image of Gandhi to a purely municipal battle and used the tactics of non-co-operation to give his Komati backers the council.[206] Similarly in Kumbakonam, serious 'popular' municipal agitations broke out when T. S. Sivaswami Odayar's family found·itself out of power.[207] Political activity became much more overt and the role of the publicist much more prominent. But usually he was working for one group of urban notables against another. Municipal politics served largely to promote magnate rivalries and to broaden the means by which the magnate controlled the behaviour of his dependents.

As in the case of the district boards also, the reform of municipal administrations built a series of new connections between Fort St George and the locality. The Local Self-Government Department in the Secretariat supervised administration and the construction of councils and heard appeals against election results. As the extension of electorates and electoral offices was so uneven, it also possessed large powers of nomination. Prior to 1884, and, of course, still in those many municipalities from which local officials were slow to withdraw, powers of supervision and nomination had been exercised virtually autonomously by the official on the spot; as we have seen, one of the principal dangers to central government was always the independence of the lower bureaucracy. By assuming supervisory powers itself, however, the Secretariat strengthened its own hand and had a much better chance of influencing local affairs. Naturally, this development produced a new dimension in local politics. By gaining the support of the Secretariat, a local politician could tilt political balances in his favour. As early as 1895, for example N. Subba Rao petitioned the department about Rajahmundry municipality. Although a Legislative Councillor of considerable standing, Subba Rao had been squeezed out of local politics by an enemy faction. He asked that the ratio of elected to nominated seats be altered in favour of the nominated, thereby weakening his opponent's electoral strength.[208] As a

[205] *Hindu* 8 March 1893; G.O. 2000 (L and M, M) dated 7 December 1892; G.O. 972 (L and M, M) dated 4 June 1892; G.O. 1625 (L and M, M) dated 27 November 1893. *T.N.A.*

[206] Kaleswara Rao, *Na Jivita Katha – Navya Andhramu*, pp. 291–360 (Telugu).

[207] G.O. 300 (Public) dated 14 May 1921. *T.N.A.*

[208] G.O. 1029 (L and M, M) dated 27 June 1895; G.O. 5 (L and M, M) dated 7 January 1896. *T.N.A.*

Legislative Councillor, it was natural that his influence at the centre should prevail and his petition was granted. The Secretariat, particularly after about 1910, received more and more such requests, with some of which, at least, it complied.

Equally, the disfavour of the Secretariat could have a shattering impact on an urban situation. In Kumbakonam, for example, the empire of T. S. Sivaswami Odayar withstood all local challenges for fifteen years. Sivaswami Odayar's greatest enemy was the Brahman lawyer and landlord N. Krishnaswami Iyengar who worked in front of a coalition of interests suffering at Sivaswami Odayar's hands.[209] But by 1906 Krishnaswami Iyengar could show little for his endeavours. In that year, however, Sivaswami Odayar's conduct became too outrageous and the Secretariat removed him and nominated Krishnaswami Iyengar in his place. The new chairman rapidly dismantled the contract and favour machine of his predecessor, redistributed the patronage and won security in the council. He launched an offensive against his rival's landed base and stood for election to the local temple committee which had been in Sivaswami Odayar's pocket.[210] From Ganjam to Malabar, the eyes of previously autonomous politicians had to turn increasingly to Fort St George.

Madras city

The affairs of one particular town demand a more detailed examination both because they again demonstrate the political importance of administrative change and because specific events which took place within the council chamber were of vital importance in the wider political world. Madras city was the centre of the British *raj* in South India. It had grown up around the East India Company's Fort St George which had been founded in 1612. It contained the Governor's Residence, the Legislative Council, the Secretariat, the High Court and the University – in sum, the heart of the administration – and the head offices of many British commercial agency houses which carried on business in the province. It was the presidency's leading port and, from the 1890s, possessed the largest industrial complex in the South. Although it drew the bulk of its native population from its immediate environs, it contained conspicuous minorities from a variety of sources: the governmental and educational institutions attracted men from every district in the presidency, while

---

[209] Collector of Tanjore to Secretary, Local and Minicipal Department, 17 March 1903 in G.O. 528 (L and M, M) dated 6 April 1903. *T.N.A.*

[210] *Hindu* 7 and 21 September 1906, 8 February and 24 March 1915.

Armenians, Gujeratis and Persian Muslims jostled with more locally based Beri Chetties, Komatis, Vellalas, Brahmans and Kammavars in its commerce.[211]

The Madras Municipal Corporation was the oldest in India, having received its first charter from James II. For two centuries, its members were nominated by government, its budget remained minute and, as an institution, it stagnated. Under the general pressure of reform in the later nineteenth century, however, it began to swell in importance. In 1878, elections were introduced for the first time, and half of the 30 members were elected on an extremely high franchise.[212] By the Madras Corporation Act of 1884, the number of elected commissioners rose to 24 out of 36 and the franchise was lowered to include about 4000 people or 1 per cent of the total population.[213] By a further Act of 1904, elected representation was reduced to 20 of 36 members,[214] but amendments to the franchise laws, and the price rise which reduced the effectiveness of restrictions based on taxation, steadily increased the number of voters to about 11,000 or $2\frac{1}{2}$ per cent of the population by the time of the First World War.[215] Much more dramatic was the increase in the income and expenditure and the use of the administrative powers of the Corporation. Between 1880 and 1918, the budget rose from Rs 7.5 *lakhs* per annum to a staggering Rs 34.8 *lakhs*,[216] and the Corporation became involved in building new markets, laying out a completely new drainage scheme, licensing and constructing electric tramways, altering the water-supply and, of course, building an enormous palace for itself. The constitution of the Corporation was somewhat different to that of the district municipalities. The executive head was a president, nominated by government and a member of the I.C.S. throughout our period. He was supported by two executive vice-presidents, also officials, but elected by the commissioners. To help them in their deliberations, there was a Standing Committee, elected out of the commissioners every year. Naturally, this body monopolised policy-making and presented the other commissioners with a series of *faits accomplis* which were seldom challenged.

[211] In 1921, the city had about 450,000 inhabitants. Of these, 10,000 came from the Malayali-speaking west and 14,000 from the Northern Circars. *Census of India. 1921. Madras. Volume XIII. Part 2* (Madras, 1922), pp. 85–94, 118–23.
[212] *Administration Report of the Madras Municipality for 1879*, pp. 1, 34–6.
[213] *Ibid., 1884–5*, p. 1.
[214] *Ibid., 1904–5*, p. 3.
[215] *Ibid., 1915–16*, p. 1.
[216] *Ibid., 1880* and *1918–19*.

The commissioners themselves were drawn from a variety of backgrounds and represented the many interests of the capital city. Most prominent, of course, were native merchants and the *dubashes* of European agency houses who wielded great financial power in the town. Pitti Thyagaraja Chetty was typical of these – moneylender, capitalist weaver, hide and skin merchant and joint-stock banker.[217] The Corporation also contained men whose social position was dependent on the ownership of land, such as the 'Gogai' Kammavar family, hereditary *shrotriemdars* of Chintadripet which was in the heart of the city.[218] As we mentioned before, however, no real distinction can be made between landed and mercantile wealth in urban politics: many of the merchants and *dubashes* were extensive property owners[219] while the 'Gogai' family supplied the city with one of its most successful *dubashes* and moneylenders, B. Chitti Babu Naidu, who was a Corporation member continuously from 1905 to the late 1920s. Through their extensive patronage of a wide range of social activities, as well as through the influence their economic empires gave them, these financial magnates dominated local affairs in Madras.[220] They were seldom opposed during elections and were only seriously pressed when faced with rivals of the same character as themselves.

Alongside these individuals existed a number of political organisations less personally based. In a few parts of the city, there were definable caste constituencies which operated as caucuses at election time. At Royapuram, for example, the Kurukula Vanisha community lived tightly clustered around St Peter's, their church. In spite of economic differentiation among them, their social isolation as Christians and continual conflicts with the local Catholic Bishop over the patronage and endowments of their church helped to keep them

[217] Other 'city fathers' of this type, who filled the Corporation seats between 1878 and 1920, were Raja Sir Savalai Ramaswami Mudaliar, *dubash* to Arbuthnot and Co. and the greatest public patron of his day; Gopathi Mahadeva Chetty and his son, Narayanaswami, who were moneylenders and merchants; P. Somasundram Chetty, related to the Gopathi and also moneylender and merchant; the Calivalla brothers, Cunnan and Ramanjulu Chetty, who were Komati merchants and proprietors of Messrs King and Co.; and Chathubhujar Doss Govindoss and Lodd Govindoss who were Gujerati Vaishya bankers.

[218] See obituary of G. Vurthia Naidu in *Hindu* 27 June 1910.

[219] Such as Pitti Thyagaraja Chetty, the Gopathi family and Raja Sir Savalai Ramaswami Mudaliar.

[220] To give an idea of the range of these, Raja Sir Savalai Ramaswami Mudaliar contributed to hospitals, university hostels, horse troughs, statues, Annadana Samajam, Tamil and Sanskrit revivalism and local religious societies.

unified.[221] They returned their lawyer–headman, R. N. Arogiyaswami Mudaliar, to the Corporation at every election between the early 1880s and his death in 1902. Another obvious caste representative was C. V. Cunniah Chetty, headman of the Komatis, who won a seat in the 1890s and early 1900s.

As we saw when discussing the urban political structure, however, there is considerable ambiguity in the roles played by many of these caste leaders. Both R. N. Arogiyaswami Mudaliar and C. V. Cunniah Chetty controlled communal institutions of great wealth, which gave a sharp edge to their authority. Cunniah Chetty, besides large family properties, managed the Kanyaki Paremaswari temple of the Komatis, which owned the largest bazaar in the city.[222] This asset gave him influence over not only the Komatis but a large section of the mercantile population in general. Moreover, within his constituency, the existence of these great institutional funds provoked factional splits. From the 1890s a ginger-group of Komatis, led by the lawyer Salla Guruswami Chetty and backed by some rich merchants, began to form caste associations in order to undermine Cunniah Chetty's authority.[223] On the latter's death in 1912, they attempted to oust his son from the *dharmakartha*-ship of the temple and to gain control of it and its properties for themselves.[224] The economic power of the temple meant that this cleavage was of significance not only within the community but also in wider city affairs. S. Guruswami Chetty leaned towards one faction in the Corporation, which, after about 1910, was associated with High Court lawyers such as C. P. Ramaswami Iyer and which, as we shall see, presented a real threat to the interests of a number of financial magnates. Cunniah Chetty was allied to these very magnates who had helped to obtain for him his Corporation seat in 1888.[225] Caste ties overlapped so heavily with other ties and support from outsiders was so vital in winning the support of even caste voters, that the concept of the caste constituency ceases to be self-explanatory. The influence of cross-communally organised power was often essential in providing the appearance of a solid caste constituency.

We can see this problem very clearly in the classic Black Town election of 1910. A group of Thondamandala Vellala families, working

[221] *Hindu* 28 June 1907.
[222] *Hindu* 27 March 1913.
[223] *Hindu* 13 December 1904.
[224] *Hindu* 27 March 1913.
[225] *Hindu* 22 June 1888.

extensively in lower government service and in the professions, dominated one of the Black Town wards by possessing about two-thirds of the votes in it. For many years, they returned to the Corporation one of their caste leaders, P. M. Sivagnana Mudaliar, who was trustee of their temple and president of their high school. On the Corporation, Sivagnana Mudaliar was allied to P. Thyagaraja Chetty. In 1910, Dr T. M. Nair, one of Thyagaraja Chetty's greatest enemies, persuaded Dr M. C. Nanjundan Rao to stand against Sivagnana Mudaliar in the Thondamandala ward. Nanjundan Rao, of course, was not a Thondamandala but, as a member of the Gaekwar of Baroda's family, he was extremely wealthy, with financial ties in various parts of the city, and, as a leading spokesman of the educated professionals, he had influence with senior officials. When he brought these extraneous connections to bear on the Thondamandala ward, he all but destroyed Sivagnana Mudaliar's caste base. After a bitter election, in which Sivagnana Mudaliar had mobilised his allies Thyagaraja Chetty and K. C. Desikachari to put their influence behind him and had run the most openly corrupt campaign that the city had yet seen, the caste leader scrambled home by only a handful of votes.[226]

In addition to those elected, the government nominated members of interest groups which could not find electoral support and professionals and government servants who would help push through unpopular measures – particularly of increased taxation. Among the former nominees were European businessmen and Muslims, most of whom were financial magnates in their own right and some of whom did, in fact, win elections when it became necessary.[227] The latter consisted of a mixture of old and tried faithfuls who were nearing, or past, retirement after long careers, and active government servants who could link wider government policies to the Corporation.

Politics within the Corporation, at least until about 1910, are extremely difficult to describe. There were no parties in the sense of a government and an opposition but rather a series of interest groups gathered around the bureaucracy. The main concern of the commis-

[226] G.O. 261 (L and M, M) dated 15 February 1911. *T.N.A.*; *Hindu* 26, 29 and 31 December 1910.

[227] In spite of the overwhelmingly Hindu electorate, Europeans and Muslims who were personally powerful could win elections if they tried. Eardley Norton, a barrister, held an elected seat from 1885 to 1893 and several members of the Muslim mercantile elite also were returned. See, for example, *Hindu* 25 July 1885.

sioners was the effective distribution of taxation, services and contracts between themselves and their constituents; the Corporation was not a body which had powers to initiate policy of a controversial or ideological nature, and the character of the commissioners suggests that had it possessed them it would not have used them. Divisions were essentially factional and tied to specific issues such as the awarding of a particular contract to a particular man, or the construction of a sewer in one part of the city rather than another. The personnel of the factions, naturally, changed with the issue, although handfuls of confederates might form small cliques which voted together. In spite of the outwardly democratic appearance of the Corporation, it was heavily weighted with bureaucrats who, in collaboration with the Standing Committee, conducted its executive affairs. As elsewhere in the Madras bureaucracy, this led to 'private' government between officials and various local powers, regardless of rules and laws. For example, although it was specifically prohibited for commissioners to have business dealings with the Corporation, throughout our period European business houses acted as contractors and loan brokers to the Corporation while their directors sat as commissioners.[228] Again, although it was prohibited for contractors to hold materials, carriage and labour contracts at the same time, in 1890 Etiyalwar Naidu, who was rumoured to be the *sowcar* of the president, Colonel Moore, held all three.[229] Commissioners used their position to place relatives and friends in Corporation jobs and to manipulate taxation to their best advantage.

Although civilian Corporation presidents came and departed, during the later nineteenth century one vice-president, the revenue officer Pulicat Ramaswami Chetty, went on forever. He held his post from 1869 until his retirement in 1896 and continued to exert a strong influence over local affairs through a variety of honorary offices until his death in 1912. Corporation taxation during his long reign was known to be a scandal as the effective rates depended less on the amount of property held than on his favour. The nearest Ramaswami Chetty's empire came to collapse was in the mid-1890s when he refused to lower the assessment on some houses owned by the commissioner G. Varadappa Naidu, who was an enemy of some of Ramaswami's friends. Varadappa Naidu attempted to give the state of the taxation register a public airing but was quickly put down by

---

[228] See reports of Legislative Council debates on this malpractice in *Hindu* 11 February and 11 and 13 March 1919.

[229] *Hindu* 7 and 8 March and 24 April 1890.

other commissioners who had their own interests at stake.[230] Rama-swami Chetty, although a government servant, was very much a local man. His Beri Chetty community was prominent in the commerce of the city and he represented a family network of interest within it. His sons and in-laws could be found in most of the important European companies, in the legal profession and even in the Madras customs house.[231] Ramaswami Chetty used the Corporation as though it was a family business — gaining part of the Electric Tramways contract for one son,[232] avoiding taxation on his properties[233] and employing large numbers of relatives and caste-fellows in his department.[234]

In so far as the endless shifting of faction on the Corporation developed any coherent shapes, it did so as interested parties approached particular bureaucrats. Ramaswami Chetty, for example, was close to his caste-fellow Pitti Thyagaraja Chetty and to R. N. Arogiyaswami Mudaliar, who advocated his appointment as president during Colonel Moore's absence in England in 1896 and his retention in office beyond retiring age.[235] Ramaswami Chetty's other connections included the merchant-princes P. Somasundram and G. Mahadeva Chetty, who also were his caste-fellows: in 1892 they petitioned against a revision of the house-tax register but, from obvious knowledge 'were prepared to admit that a good number of houses might have escaped taxation, and that some houses might have been assessed at a very low figure.'[236] The Health Officer, Jesudesan Pillai, at this time had his party too — headed by the great lawyer and publicist P. Ananda Charlu — and Colonel Moore, the head of the executive, was not without connections among the commissioners. In return for support and protection in the Corporation chamber, the official arranged jobs and contracts to the satisfaction of his clients. In the decade or so after Ramaswami Chetty's retirement, and under succeeding presidents, little changed as officials and their friends con-

---

[230] *Hindu* 19 December 1896; G.O. 823 (L·and M, M) dated 13 May 1896; G.O. 913 (L and M, M) dated 1 June 1896. *T.N.A.*

[231] *A Brief Life Sketch of M. R. Ry. P. Subramanyam* (Madras, n.d.), pp. 1–2.

[232] *Ibid.*, pp. 4–5.

[233] *Hindu* 20 October 1896.

[234] He admitted employing six of his relatives and fifteen other caste connections in his office. G.O. 913 (L and M, M) dated 1 June 1896. *T.N.A.*

[235] *Hindu* 9 June 1892 and 16 June 1896; G.O. 823 (L and M, M) dated 13 May 1896; G.O. 1104 (L and M, M) dated 3 July 1896. *T.N.A.*

[236] The revision had been forced on the reluctant Ramaswami by a Government Order. G.O. 1274 (L and M, M) dated 1 August 1892. *T.N.A.*

tinued to run the Corporation between themselves. In 1902, the *Hindu* commented bitterly: 'The few honest and really useful men are utterly powerless against the self-constituted Whips who manage all business beforehand.'[237]

Until the 1910s, local political organisation in Madras was similar to that which we would expect to find in any district municipality before the Ripon local self-government Acts: effective decision-making lay with semi-autonomous bureaucrats who worked closely with and relied on the informal power of local economic magnates. Madras city, however, was also the administrative capital of the presidency and it possessed a profusion of western-educated literati. Equally, it was a major economic centre with relatively more opportunities than in other towns for 'new' magnates to arise or to come in from outside. These two factors gave the public life of Madras city much greater activity than elsewhere. From the 1860s, religious and cultural revival associations, social reform *sabhas* and proto-nationalist political clubs appeared in great numbers as western-educated publicists attempted to create constituencies for themselves and as magnates struggled against each other for status and public esteem. Given the relatively large number of literates in the city and of people who could be reached through or become involved in street propaganda, Madras city was the one town in the presidency where we could expect the publicist to be able to establish himself as an independent power. By the 1880s, such archetypal publicists as A. C. Parthasarathi Naidu, newspaper editor, social reform advocate, organiser of a string of religious revival *sabhas* and occasional *swami*, as T. Venkatasubba Iyer, lawyer and religious teacher, and as S. Guruswami Chetty, caste reformer, religious devotee and Congressman, were making their presence felt in several arenas of city government and were members of the Corporation.

However, if success on the Corporation is used as an acid test, it is clear that even in Madras city the publicist had to have a magnate patron, for he could not hope to build on the substance of popular opinion. In 1904, for example, A. C. Parthasarathi Naidu had the temerity to advocate an increase in municipal taxation in order to improve social services, and was severely beaten at the polls.[238] A few years later, T. Venkatasubba Iyer attacked the richest contractor in the city, A. Subramania Iyer. He was beaten by 217 votes to 3 in a

---

[237] *Hindu* 17 January 1902.
[238] *Hindu* 3 September 1907.

constituency in which, two years before, he had won comfortably.[239] S. Guruswami Chetty lost all hope of a seat when S. Venkatachellam Chetty, a fellow Komati and rich merchant, stood against him.[240] In spite of the advantages for public politics, which the capital possessed, no publicist succeeded in challenging magnate power at the hustings.

But the hustings were not the only place from which influence over the Corporation could be exercised. The Corporation was more heavily bureaucratic than any district municipality and Madras city was the centre of the bureaucracy. Publicists – lawyers and journalists by profession – were drawn from the same state-level social groups (often from the same families) as the Indian bureaucrats who moved in the higher echelons of government around the Secretariat, the High Court and the University. Many of them had obvious connections of sympathy and interest with men who enjoyed senior positions of power in the administration. It was possible, in theory at least, for them to capture the Corporation by influencing the decisions of the superiors of the Corporation bureaucracy. This would give them a hold over the distribution of Corporation patronage and make them indispensable to both magnates and Corporation bureaucrats alike.

Before about 1910, however, the extreme localisation of political authority in Madras, which we have seen everywhere, served to keep the affairs of the Corporation and those of the Secretariat apart. There was little machinery through which senior administrators could interfere in the local politics of the city. Moreover, there were as yet few Indians in the positions from which interference was possible, and European civilians, who were suspicious of the very movements and campaigns which gave publicists prominence, were not as useful. The Corporation bureaucracy, as characterised by P. Ramaswami Chetty, was typical of lower officialdom anywhere in the *mofussil*. It was orientated entirely towards local concerns, being appointed in the locality and operated through lucrative connections with local magnates. Without direct power to discipline and reward, all that the publicists could expect of their Secretariat, High Court and University contacts were offers to Corporation bureaucrats of career help and prestige. These meant nothing to a man like Ramaswami Chetty, who wanted only to stay where he was in his locality. During the 1880s

---

[239] A. Subramania Iyer, who worked with various European companies, held Corporation contracts worth Rs 10 *lakhs* in the 1910s. *Hindu* 6 December 1910; *Hindu* 6 January 1911 and 24 February 1914.

[240] *Hindu* 5 November 1919.

and 1890s, even publicists belonging to the two most powerful families in the higher administration were unable to carve a place for themselves in the Corporation.[241] We can see their problems clearly in the way that another leading publicist, P. Ananda Charlu, was broken on the rack of Corporation intrigue.

P. Ananda Charlu was a prominent city *vakil* who sat for the Triplicane constituency throughout the 1880s. He organised local petitions, channelling the grievances of Hindu merchants against European missionaries and Muslims,[242] and was instrumental in the organisation of the Madras Mahajana Sabha and, later, the Madras branch of the Indian National Congress. He was seldom out of the press or off the public platform, and numbered among his clients, both legal and more obviously political, many of the wealthiest merchants of the city, various *zamindars* and the sole *dharmakartha* of the Triplicane temple. In all these activities, however, his role was that of representative. But once inside the Corporation, he could hope to develop an influence with the administration which would make him more. He became closely linked with the Health Officer, M. Jesudesan Pillai, who was the second Corporation vice-president and ran a parallel rival network to that of P. Ramaswami Chetty. By protecting Jesudesan Pillai from attacks in the Corporation chamber and by supporting his administration, Ananda Charlu could reasonably expect to influence the character of Jesudesan's government. In 1891, however, an epidemic which swept the city was traced to the Health Officer's maladministration: his subordinates were shown to be patronage appointments who had no qualification for their jobs and the contractors he employed had seldom completed their tasks. In the ensuing uproar, Ramaswami Chetty moved in for the kill and his men, P. Thyagaraja Chetty and R. N. Arogiyaswami Mudaliar, savaged the performance of the health department. Ananda Charlu reacted by removing the relevant papers and sitting on them for more

---

[241] In the next chapter, we shall be discussing the Vembakkam family and 'C. P. Ramaswami Iyer's community', who dominated the world of the western-educated. They represented the most powerful of Indian bureaucratic interests. However, in 1885 the lawyer Vembakkam Krishnamachari upset his magnate supporters by espousing the cause of increased taxation, and was beaten repeatedly at the polls although he had been sitting on the Corporation for the five previous years. *Hindu* 25 and 27 May, 1 and 3 June and 25 and 27 July 1885; at about the same time, C. V. Sundara Sastri, who was C. P. Ramaswami Iyer's father-in-law and a prominent *vakil*, suffered a similar fate. Although he had once been a member of the powerful Standing Committee, he was beaten in no fewer than seven consecutive elections. *Hindu* 4 and 6 June 1888.

[242] *Hindu* 27 August 1884, 17 and 18 May 1889.

than a year.[243] But in spite of his excellent connections with members of senior government departments and the University, he could do nothing to ease the pressure on Jesudesan Pillai. For two years, the Ramaswami Chetty faction pounded away,[244] and the affair reached a crisis in 1893 when Ananda Charlu stood for the Corporation seat in the new Legislative Council. With Thyagaraja Chetty leading the opposition to him, the Corporation was deadlocked for five meetings. Finally, it agreed to elect P. Rungiah Naidu, a close friend and Congress ally of Ananda Charlu, but a man not involved in the scandal.[245] Ananda Charlu withdrew from city politics and, through the influence of his high-placed friends, was elected to the Imperial Legislative Council – the equivalent of being kicked upstairs. The Thyagaraja–Ramaswami Chetty combination of local magnate and bureaucrat had resisted the challenge of the man supported from above.

Fifteen years after Ananda Charlu's eclipse, a series of important changes altered the structure of Corporation politics. Although before 1920 there was no reconstruction of the constitution, institutional pressures made the Corporation much more central to the general affairs of the city, and so changed the relationships between it and the city populace and the senior offices of government. The Corporation began to undertake new and large-scale public works programmes, financed by public loans and government grants. Its administrative competence was increased so that it touched new areas of city life. It was given a role in the administration of several independently constituted charitable trusts; for example, it nominated members to the board of Pachayappa's charities which spent more that Rs 1 *lakh* a year on education and religion.[246] Obviously, these developments began to create new political interest groups which needed representation on the Corporation. Publicists naturally came forward to provide this representation. Moreover, publicists and politicians whose ambitions lay beyond the locality and in the higher councils of government also were made to look again at the Corporation. After the Morley–Minto reforms, the Legislative Council became a crucial arena of provincial politics, in which the government sought to test the opinions of the province on a wide range of matters. The Corporation was the smallest and most manageable electorate to

---

[243] *Hindu* 1, 22 and 25 August, 28 November and 5 December 1893.
[244] They succeeded in voting Ananda Charlu off the Standing Committee in 1893. *Hindu* 28 November and 19 December 1893.
[245] *Hindu* 10 May 1893.
[246] M. Tiruvenkataswami (ed.), *Pachaiyappa's College, Madras. Centenary Commemoration Book. 1842–1942* (Madras, 1942), p. 85.

this Council. Further, several touring commissions came to Madras in the early 1910s to solicit information on the state of the public services, on the scope of decentralisation, on the development of industry and on many other matters. Politicians who wished to exercise a provincial influence had to give evidence before these, yet the Madras Government denied access to them to representatives of informal associations such as the Congress and the Mahajana Sabha. By becoming a Corporation commissioner, however, a politician was well placed to have his case heard, for the Corporation, as a body, frequently was invited to provide witnesses.

From about 1910, then, western-educated publicists became increasingly eager to enter the Corporation. And changes in the attitude of the Secretariat to the Corporation enabled them to play a fuller part in its affairs. To match the growing power of the Corporation, the government began to insist on a much higher standard of efficiency, which it sought to obtain by raising the standard of the Corporation bureaucracy. In 1908, T. Raghavayya was appointed to the revenue office and broke the succession of Ramaswami Chetty-like executives. Raghavayya had no local interests and his ambitions stretched outside the Corporation. He had joined service as a centrally-appointed deputy collector under the new recruitment policy, and he was to become a Collector, a Departmental Secretary and a knight. He was a bureaucrat whose personal and career contacts lay not with the commercial barons of the city but with Secretariat officials, High Court Judges and University Senators. His first actions in the Corporation were to tighten up on the collection of the property tax, thereby adding Rs 80,000 a year to the treasury, and to reorganise his staff to prevent bribery and the employment of dependents of the commissioners.[247] He was thoroughly disliked by many of the old commissioners, particularly Pitti Thyagaraja Chetty who tried to cut his salary and to replace him with a less highly ranked officer.[248] Raghavayya was followed into office by T. Vijayaraghavachari and Mahommed Bazlulla who were of the same stamp as himself. Publicists who were well connected to the senior Indian bureaucrats and educationists who were the colleagues and masters of Raghavayya, Vijayaraghavachari and Bazlulla, now came into their own. They could influence Corporation policy and the distribution of patronage in ways not available to the local magnate.

To see best what this meant, we can contrast the career of T. M. Nair, a publicist without 'pull' in the right quarters, with those of

[247] G.O. 838 (L and M, M) dated 24 May 1908; G.O. 1362 (L and M, M) dated 21 August 1909. *T.N.A.*; *Hindu* 17 November 1909.
[248] *Hindu* 22 October 1913.

C. P. Ramaswami Iyer and G. A. Natesan, publicists who had it in abundant quantities. T. M. Nair had created a great reputation for himself in Triplicane, a communally heterogeneous and volatile area of the city.[249] He led a series of agitations against Corporation policies, attacked the corruption of many of the old commissioners and declared war on Thyagaraja Chetty whom he denounced for various tax, property and contract manipulations.[250] He was unquestionably the most powerful stump orator in the city and, between 1904 and 1913, was returned regularly to the Corporation. If ever there were a politician on the Corporation who had a 'popular' base, it was T. M. Nair. But he had few contacts with men in the higher institutions of government. His hatred of the Hindu religion and all things Indian made him repulsive to other leading members of the professions and bureaucracy, many of whom were deeply interested in the revival of Hinduism. In 1910, when he stood for the Imperial Legislative Council, he was heavily defeated and blamed his fate on 'the wire-pullers', particularly V. Krishnaswami Iyer, a member of the Governor's Executive Council, who had kept him out.[251] In 1913, by attacking the free supply of water to the Sri Parthasarathi temple, Nair managed the remarkable feat of irritating both P. Thyagaraja Chetty and the ex-High Court Judge Sir S. Subramania Iyer to such an extent that, though opposites in all their political and ideological stances, they joined together to defeat him in a Corporation election.[252] Thereafter, Nair's presence in the Corporation was due to nomination by his few British friends. Like the dependent publicists of the 1880s, he could be chopped down without difficulty.

Very different, however, was the impact on the Corporation made by the arrival of C. P. Ramaswami Iyer and G. A. Natesan. C. P. Ramaswami Iyer, one of the leading *vakils* of his day, was connected, by relationship and intimate friendship, to many of the highest government servants in the presidency and possessed sufficient wealth to be an independent patron in his own right; while G. A. Natesan, a rich publisher, was one of V. Krishnaswami Iyer's right-hand men. Their attack on the old bases of Corporation power struck home where Nair's had proved ineffective. Natesan denounced a list of commissioners, including Thyagaraja Chetty, P. M. Sivagnana Mudaliar and about a dozen others, for filling Corporation offices

---

[249] Triplicane contained Muslims, around the old palace of the Nawab of Arcot, devout Hindus, around the Triplicane temple, and young students, around the University.

[250] *Hindu* 3 November 1909, 27 February and 19 March 1913, 10 December 1910.

[251] *Hindu* 5 January 1910.

[252] *Hindu* 22, 23 and 24 April 1912, 15 September 1913.

with their relatives.[253] Thyagaraja Chetty found himself arraigned in battle against them as they sought to alter the pattern of contract distribution: he defended against their attacks men who failed to complete contract work, subordinate staff caught in bribery and the Electric Tramway Company, in which he was substantially interested and whose track rent C. P. Ramaswami Iyer wished to raise.[254] All this was to no avail. He was equally impotent to prevent a revision of the house-tax register and, by 1919, could not even persuade the Corporation to build, at public expense, a road to the houses of some of his friends.[255] The takeover in the Corporation can be seen in the contrast between the Standing Committee in 1910 and in 1915. In 1910, the elected members were P. Thyagaraja Chetty, his allies P. M. Sivagnana Mudaliar and K. C. Desikachari, the dependent publicist A. C. Parthasarthi Naidu and T. M. Nair; in 1915 they were C. P. Ramaswami Iyer, G. A. Natesan, the Brahman Congressman K. N. Ayah Iyer and the Muslim publicist Yakab Hasan.[256] Thyagaraja Chetty and his allies, who had run the Corporation for a quarter of a century, were under severe pressure. J. C. Molony, President of the Corporation between 1914 and 1920, has recorded their reaction to the change:

Pitti Theagaraya Chetty was the Father of the Madras Corporation, the Nestor among his Fellow Councillors. At the time I became President he led a bloc known as 'the northern Councillors': his and their chief function in life was the criticism of the Corporation executive and opposition to all innovation.[257]

G. A. Natesan and C. P. Ramaswami Iyer had, quite simply, captured the Corporation bureaucracy, which was a very different beast from that of the 1880s. In spite of the play they made with previous Corporation corruption, their rule was scarcely different, except that they were the arbiters of it. C. P. Ramaswami Iyer diverted public advertisements into the Congress and Home Rule press, in which he was deeply interested, and he was accused of stacking the Corporation bureaucracy with his own appointees.[258] In 1920, G. A. Natesan

253 *Hindu* 24 April 1912.
254 *Hindu* 2 April 1910, 20 January 1915, 24 March 1915, 22 September 1916.
255 *Hindu* 17 April 1918 and 22 September 1919.
256 *Administration Report of the Madras Municipality for the year 1910–11*; *ibid., 1915–16.*
257 J. C. Molony, *A Book of South India* (London, 1926), p. 154.
258 G.O. 175 (L and M, M) dated 7 February 1918; A. C. Parthasarathi Naidu to A. Cardew, 16 September 1916 in G.O. 414 (Home, Misc.) dated 26 April 1917. *T.N.A.*

happily admitted touring his constituency with the acting Revenue Officer who was his protege, making revisions of the property tax while he was canvassing votes and using a revised register which had not been made available to other candidates. Applications for house-tax revision were sent to him rather than the revenue department.[259] This control of the bureaucracy gave Natesan and Ramaswami Iyer power to act as the brokers between the Corporation and outside interests.

From 1916, Thyagaraja Chetty was to raise the anti-Brahman cry against his enemies and to take his case into provincial politics where, of course, it now belonged. His anti-Brahmanism, however, was more political than racial: he himself was associated with Brahmans, such as K. C. Desikachari (an in-law of Kasturi Ranga Iyengar, the editor of the *Hindu* and an opponent of the C. P. Ramaswami Iyer clique), while C. P. Ramaswami Iyer distributed Corporation favours to such solid non-Brahmans as the Calivalla brothers, who were Komati millionaires, and Lodd Govindoss, the Gujerati banker. Ramaswami Iyer and Natesan needed magnate supporters but, unlike the earlier breed of publicist, they had enough currency to choose whom they wanted. Thyagaraja Chetty was losing a battle which had been started not by communal aggression but by institutional change.

In the Corporation, the nature of this change led to something of a transformation in the kind of men who were politically powerful. This was because the penetration of the locality by the centre of government was more direct than in the *mofussil*. The continued bureaucratic hold on the Corporation meant that changes in the structure of the bureaucracy itself made an immediate impact on the personnel of local politics; in the *mofussil*, bureaucratic centralisation was mediated by the growth of non-official office and elected power. However, the general process of change, which was both broadening the bases of local competition and tying the politics of the locality to those of the centre, was similar to that which we have seen in the temples, the district municipalities and the rural boards. What was taking place in Madras was the gradual emergence of a structure of provincial politics, in which political power in each district and town was influenced for the first time by events and personalities at the capital. Local politicians now had to take account of the shape of politics in the higher administrative institutions at the 'centre'.

[259] *Hindu* 24 March 1920.

5

The emergence of provincial politics

The growing presence of the capital in the political affairs of the *mofussil* may be seen as the major factor of political change in the period which we are examining. Thus far, however, we have viewed this development in detail only from the position of the *mofussil*; we have seen how local politicians were brought into contact with the administrative and political institutions of Madras city and how they came to need, fear and use this connection. The emergent centre of the new political system itself has not come under our gaze except as a distant and vague mass of energy which outsiders could tap. Yet the material form which this energy took was very much to condition what the outsiders were able to do with it. The manner in which the power of the capital was organised determined both the lines along which it could be approached and the types of approach which were most likely to engage it. As the separate political institutions of the locality came together largely through the capital, these lines and types of approach influenced not only relations between the local politician and the capital but also relations between one local politician and another. They were the links in the provincial political system. Clearly, our next task must be to examine the political organisations and interests which were developing within and around Fort St George at this time.

In the context of the British Empire, of course, Fort St George was a very inferior outpost, responsible to at least three, and sometimes four, layers of superior authority; it was a mere office-boy in the Grand Imperial Company. In the context of the Madras Presidency, however, it looked more like an all-powerful despot. London and Calcutta exercised only a loose discipline over its activities and very seldom directly interfered beneath it. Moreover, before 1920 there were no popular political institutions in the presidency and Fort St George's will remained unchecked from below. What was promulgated by the Governor of Madras was the law of the land and although this law might be ignored, no other authority existed to issue rival promulgations. For most practical purposes, the Governor was an absolute ruler.

As might be expected in this situation, the politics which were played around the Governor, throughout the nineteenth century and beyond, were very similar in kind to those being played around the Indian princes who occupied analogous positions. The Governor's immediate councillors intrigued for his ear (or more correctly his seal) and, having obtained it, drew favours and patronage from him, which they carried away to their offices to distribute as they pleased. In these offices, they were joined by clients of their own, who in turn intrigued for a share of the favours and patronage and carried off whatever they received. And so the process went on, right down to the rock-bed of the rural-local boss' or urban magnate's control, where it stopped. The higher political system of the Madras Presidency can best be described by the epithet 'court' and characterised as a series of interlocking patron–client relationships through which resources and executive and judicial decisions were passed. In the very early nineteenth century, those at the top of the patronage ladder, dealing directly with the Governor, had included a variety of Indian 'country powers' – warlords, commercial magnates and semi-autonomous chiefs. From the 1830s, however, the Governor's inner circle came to consist largely of civil servants. For the rest of the century these civil servants were to be entirely European. Moreover, their own immediate clients tended increasingly to be Indian civil servants rather than Indian local powers. As civil administration spread across South India, it pushed indigenous political leaders further and further away from the centre of provincial authority until contact between locality and centre was mediated, if it were mediated at all, by many layers of bureaucracy. It was this development, of course, which had led to the fragmentation and localisation of indigenous political activity in Madras.

Given the relatively small number of people who orbited the Governor, the quantity of resources and power in their hands was considerable. The Arbuthnot family, for example, was able to fund one of the largest mercantile houses in India out of the private contracts and services which it received while providing four generations of Madras civil servants.[1] In the 1880s, as we have seen, other I.C.S. officers were able to supplement their already large salaries with earnings in gold and plantation speculations made under the protection of their own government. Equally, Indians who reached the higher grades of government appointment could expect to build large fortunes both from their pay and from any perquisites which

[1] For hints at the extent of the family's influence, see A. J. Arbuthnot, *Memories of Rugby and India* (London, 1910).

might come their way; Sir T. Muthuswami Iyer, the first Indian High Court judge, for example, started life as a penniless orphan but left an estate worth nearly Rs 4 *lakhs*.[2] Nonetheless, when set against the amount of wealth and power left to groups in the locality, the resources at the disposal of men in the higher political system were relatively meagre. The Governor and his minions were dividing only the quantity of cash which could be extracted safely from rural-local bosses and urban magnates after the Government of India had taken its share, and were commanding only those limited competences and jurisdictions which local powers could be forced to recognise. In effect, they were distributing among themselves the scraps of the political system.

Among these scraps, probably the juiciest morsels were appointments to a variety of government jobs. By far the greatest amount of Fort St George's internal expenditure – the cash-flow which it put back into Madras – was directed towards the payment of its bureaucrats. By the standards of the day, the salaries of posts at *huzur sheristidar* level and above were attractive even when possible perquisites are not added. Posts below the *huzur sheristidar* level at least offered subsistence and the hope of better things to come. Technically, all posts in the government service were filled by the Governor and his senior administrative staff; appointments down to the level of deputy collector being at the discretion of the Secretariat and appointments below at the discretion of the Collector. Before the early 1900s, however, no systematic effort was made to build a machine which would distribute the considerable patronage represented by government employment in a way which was efficient and impersonal. In consequence, the patron–client relationship, which lay at the heart of the entire higher governmental structure, was most noticeable in the organisation of service appointments. Senior British civilians casually offered plum jobs to their friends and to any Indian in whom they became interested. The spirit of the appointments' system was well caught by K. S. Ramaswami Sastri in his autobiography when he noted that: 'I could have gone out as a D[istrict] M[unsiff] in 1905. Mr Justice Davis would have given me the post for the mere asking as he liked me very much.'[3] A recent biographer of V. V. Giri also has captured it accurately: 'Justice Ayling was earlier District Judge of Ganjam and knew Giri's father well. As a gesture to the family, he straightaway offered to appoint Giri a munsiff.'[4]

[2] *Hindu* 7 February 1907.
[3] Ramaswami Sastri, *Vita Sua*, pp. 36–7.
[4] G. S. Bhargava, *V. V. Giri* (Bombay, 1969), p. 22.

Farther out from provincial and district headquarters, as we have seen, Indian officials themselves took over the functions of appointment distribution, making the *huzur sheristidar's* office the centre of favour for the *mofussil* bureaucracy.

The centralisation of appointments and control in the bureaucracy, which we discussed in Chapter 2, gradually pulled an increasing amount of service patronage towards the capital and laid before members of the Secretariat a much greater array of places than they could have hoped to fill before. This development in the bureaucracy proper soon came to be matched by a parallel movement in the ancillary institutions of government. From the 1860s, the High Court in Madras city became the focal point of the expanding litigation of the presidency. Every year it heard more and more original cases, while in its appeals capacity it responded to the general growth in the use of the courts and dealt with a mass of cases referred to it from subordinate judges.[5] Lawyers serving before the High Court stood at the top of their profession. Their incomes were incomparably higher than those of pleaders and *vakils* who worked in the *mofussil* courts: as late as 1920, it was almost unheard of for a district court lawyer to earn even Rs 1,000 per month but, as early as the 1880s, some Madras High Court *vakils* were pocketing Rs 10,000 per month. Moreover, by handling the affairs of the great and the powerful from all over the presidency, leading High Court lawyers built up provincial practices and influence which enabled them to affect the retention of *vakils* in subordinate court cases. The increase in litigation across our period also led to an increase in the number of vacancies for judicial servants and thus to an increase in the patronage of the Judicial Department and the High Court which appointed all sub-judges and district *munsiffs*.

Similarly, the expansion of western education concentrated new powers in the capital. The growth of the bureaucracy and the law was accompanied by a demand for higher standards of education among government servants and lawyers. This demand produced a spate of college building and gave the Education Department in the Secretariat and the University more aggressive supervisory roles. The Education Department exercised a considerable patronage in the schools and colleges of the South, appointing masters, controlling the management of educational foundations and influencing access to educational institutions. From 1877, when it first began to affiliate colleges

[5] See *Report(s) on the Administration of Civil Justice in the Madras Presidency* (Madras, 1880 to 1920, annual).

outside Madras city to teach for its degrees, the importance of the University also grew daily. Anybody wishing to found a school or college or to undergo higher education required recognition by it.[6] The University, though nominally representing all-presidency interests, was dominated by Madras city residents who composed the majority of active Senators and who, by Statute, were alone allowed to sit on its executive (the Syndicate). The tight control of patronage enjoyed by city residents indicates their great influence. It was notorious that the professors in the two main colleges of the capital packed the examination and text book committees, that students from city colleges did better in examinations than outsiders and that endowments and foundations made in the *mofussil* had a habit of being transferred to Madras.[7] Moreover, when the Government of India in 1912 gave the Madras University a gift of Rs 4 *lakhs* and a recurring annual grant of Rs 65,000, not one anna was spent outside city boundaries.[8] Naturally, this led to a great deal of animosity between *mofussil* educational interests and the city colleges.

The gains of the centre, therefore, were very much the losses of the districts. The independent realms of the *huzur sheristidar*, the subordinate court pleader and the small town schoolteacher steadily shrank in size before the advance of the capital. The career structure of the services and education was in the process of being shifted from a local to a provincial base. Not surprisingly, therefore, it was the service families, who made their livings in the bureaucracy and the learned professions, who felt first the pull of the capital. From the 1870s, ever larger numbers of boys flocked to the schools and colleges of the capital from homes all over the presidency; by 1914, there were over 3000 students in Madras city.[9] They left behind them deserted and decaying schoolhouses which previously had flourished by providing for the needs of petty local clerks and pleaders. Between 1882 and 1910, for example Presidency College in Madras city increased its size from 241 students to 532, while Kumbakonam College, once 'the Cambridge of South India', declined from 267 to 123.[10] Some of the leading families among western-educated Indians, who dominated the government service and professions of their

---

[6] *Madras Universities Commission* (Simla, 1902), II (Madras), 4.

[7] Evidence of J. Cork in *ibid.*, pp. 51–2; *Hindu* 8 March 1916; G.O. 593–4, (Education) dated 15 October 1888. *T.N.A.*

[8] *Hindu* 15 and 26 October 1912, 6 and 8 March 1916.

[9] A. Besant to P. S. Sivaswami Iyer, 12 January 1914. P. S. Sivaswami Iyer Papers. *N.A.I.*

[10] *Hindu* 22 January 1915.

districts, moved to establish their presence and credentials at the emerging centre of provincial affairs. In 1880, C. Sankara Nair, the fourth generation of his family to serve the British, came up from Malabar and apprenticed himself to a city barrister;[11] in 1884, S. Subramania Iyer – the associate of Collector Crole in Madura – moved his practice to the capital;[12] a year later C. Pattabhirama Iyer, the leading light of the Tanjore bar, also found chambers near the High Court.[13] About the same time, several young men of good family – V. Krishnaswami Iyer and P. S. Sivaswami Iyer from Tanjore, T. V. Seshagiri Iyer from Trichinopoly and L. A. Govindaraghava Iyer from North Arcot – bore witness to the changing times by preferring to stay in Madras city, after qualifying from the Law College, rather than returning to their home districts where their family connections would have guaranteed them a secure living.

The aspiration for career success, therefore, was instrumental in drawing the prominent western-educated 'service' families of the *mofussil* towards the capital. In some cases, it was joined also by the aspiration to change the bases of social organisation in Madras. The rise of the power of the central institutions of government presented any man interested in promoting social reform with the new weapon of legislation. The impact of western ideas obviously had made its deepest impression on that segment of society which had been exposed most to western education and, among the members of families who were building connections with the capital at this time, were several intellectuals dedicated to reform. In the mid-1880s, for example, C. Sankara Nair became involved in an attempt to alter the marriage system of his caste.[14] Equally, a few years later, V. Bashyam Iyengar, one of the principal lawyers in the city, began to press the government to change the laws governing inheritance among Hindus.[15] The personal social needs of some of the western educated of South India, then, also formed a cause of the movement towards Fort St George.

It would be a mistake, however, and one all too commonly made, to view the political activity developing around the core of the capital as being the concern of the western educated alone. Certainly, it was they who led this activity; certainly also career prospects and social reform pertained to them alone. Yet, of the total political system of the province, service careers and social reform constituted a minute

---

[11] K. P. S. Menon, *C. Sankaran Nair* (New Delhi, 1967), pp. 13–16.
[12] Raja Rama Rao, *Sir Subramania Aiyer*, p. 48.
[13] C. P. Ramaswami Aiyar, *Biographical Vistas* (Bombay, 1968), p. 208.
[14] Menon, *C. Sankaran Nair*, p. 27.
[15] Home Judicial A May 1902, No. 88. *N.A.I.*

fraction. As we have stressed repeatedly, in political function the western educated cannot be seen as autonomous agents. In the localities and districts their chief purpose was to represent the interests of urban magnates and rural-local bosses. They accomplished this end both by mediating between the local power and the institutions of government and by leading religious and cultural movements which expressed the local power's personal status. The shift of locale among the western educated, from the district to the capital, did nothing, initially at least, to alter this fundamental relationship. Indeed, the shift had taken place only because the locale of governmental institutional power had changed – a fact reflected in the centralisation of service careers. At the capital, the leading western-educated men continued, as before, to place before the government and the city populace a range of interests which they derived from the local powers who paid their fees and funded their projects. Leading *vakils*, such as S. Subramania Iyer, V. Bashyam Iyengar and C. Sankara Nair, spent most of their time pleading before the courts on behalf of *zamindars* based as far north as Ganjam and south as Malabar and of merchant princes from the Northern Circars down to Ramnad. In the University, they, and other Senators, protected the schools and colleges founded by the wealthy and sought University help for many cultural movements which had started in the purses of the great. In the Board of Revenue and Secretariat, senior Indian officials pushed forward to their superiors files concerning closely the interests of major local figures. Through the press and on the public platform, they drew attention to the grievances of *zamindars*, merchants and *mirasidars*, and organised religious and cultural activities which, though no doubt conditioned by their new social perceptions, were financed and made important by the magnates who gained prestige from them. Certainly, the lines through which the western educated now worked for their patrons were much longer than before, stretching from the locality to Madras city, but the interests which the lines joined had not altered. The western educated could not function politically as an isolated group; they were an intermediary segment. Their success in public life depended as much on the confidence they inspired among rich Indians as on their ability to manipulate career structures and the still weak legislative power. Indeed, without clients to support them they could not advance their careers nor persuade government that they were sufficiently important to be given legislative power.

Once we begin to view the political system of Madras in this broad perspective, a number of the more significant political events of the

1880s and the 1890s start to take on a new meaning. In particular, the often-seen emergence of agitational politics and the institutions of the nationalist movement can be set more firmly in the political context in which they arose. Fort St George's drive to administer more carefully the resources of its presidency was subjecting local powers to unprecedented pressures. Between 1878 and 1886, bills were put before the Legislative Council to alter the institutions of religion, the organisation of *zamindari* estates, the allocation of forest rights, the maintenance of irrigation works, the structure of local self-government, and the nature of the income-tax. Very few men of local substance were not touched by these issues. Moreover, very few failed to realise that the new potency of the central institutions of government could be used to aid more positively their own interests – especially by providing funds and support for their religious and cultural objectives. Local powers, then, came to need desperately an influence on the way that affairs were conducted at Fort St George. They instructed their various lawyers, bureaucrats and publicists, who had gathered at the capital, to make representations of their views.

Importantly, however, there were few means by which these representations could gain a hearing. In spite of their increased power, the central institutions of Fort St George remained very narrowly based. The Legislative Council consisted of a small, government-appointed and self-perpetuating clique.[16] The principal executive officers of government were entirely European and were being pulled, by Government of India demands for improved performance, away from such contacts with Indian opinion as they might once have had. The High Court bench, with one exception, also was European. The University, which related to an increasing number of Indian cultural interests, was dominated by a Syndicate consisting largely of missionaries who were inimical to Indian culture. Although the western-educated representatives of local native power were congregating around Fort St George, they were not allowed entry to its halls. Not surprisingly, then, they began to put their cases from the street. In 1882, the Madras Native Association, defunct since the 1860s,[17] was

---

[16] Of native members, for example, Raja G. N. Gajapati Rao, a conservative *zamindar* from Vizagapatam, was nominated for nine terms; T. Rama Rao, an effete city lawyer, also was recalled for several two year terms.

[17] The M.N.A. was originally founded to protest against the increasing influence of missionaries and to petition Parliament on the 1853 Charter Act. It died shortly after the 1861 Legislative Council Act, when two of its founders and leading members became Legislative Councillors. R. Sunthralingam, *Politics and Nationalist Awakening in South India, 1852–1891* (Arizona, 1974), pp. 45–57.

resurrected by Madras city lawyers, publicists and a variety of government servants, and used to press government for greater measures of representation in local self-government.[18] The sharp reaction of Fort St George to the sight of its Indian bureaucrats playing their real political role, as the spokesmen of local powers against the administration, quickly killed this association. The next year a new society, the Madras Mahajana Sabha, was founded by the same city lawyers and publicists (but not the bureaucrats) and met with immediate success.[19] It led campaigns over temple reform, *zamindari* legislation, the income-tax, the increase in excise duties and land revenue resettlement policies.[20] The Mahajana Sabha built up a considerable provincial following and pilloried the government on every possible occasion, ridiculing its inefficiency and demanding elective representation.

These protest movements were not only negative attacks on current practice. By the early 1880s, it was obvious that the British, in Calcutta and London, were beginning to appreciate the dangers of an over-zealous bureaucracy losing touch with popular opinion. They were considering major changes in the constitution of government. Commissions on the Public Services and Education toured Madras, Lord Ripon began to tinker with the mechanisms of local self-government and the Secretary of State with those of the Legislative Council.[21] As the impetus for change was coming from supra-provincial centres, so politicians in each province saw the need to band together to work in all-India associations. The Indian National Congress in Madras was organised and run by exactly the same people who had founded the Mahajana Sabha, and it carried their demands before the Viceroy and the House of Commons.

The main reforms for which the Congress campaigned at all-India level were in the areas of the Legislative Council, the University and the bureaucracy which, it claimed, should be opened to more Indian talent.[22] This concentration, particularly on the University and bureaucracy, has tended to be seen as a further indication of the real, personal ambitions of Congress leaders for more and better jobs. So, in part, it may have been. But to dwell on this aspect too exclusively is to miss the fact that, in a bureaucratic state, changes in the composi-

---

[18] Government servants were especially active. See *Proceedings of the Madras Native Association on the Resolution of the Government of India on Local Self-Government* (Madras, 1883).

[19] See *The Madras Mahajana Sabha Annual Report for 1885–6* (Madras, 1886).

[20] *Ibid.*

[21] Seal, *Emergence of Indian Nationalism*, pp. 131–93.

[22] *Ibid.*, pp. 245–97.

tion of the bureaucracy can amount to changes in political representation. The local contacts of the more prominent Congressmen would certainly have gained had their representatives obtained places in the central decision-making machines. Moreover, of course, it was inevitable that the Congress should have emphasised these constitutional issues almost exclusively when it was talking to the Government of India and the House of Commons, for it was only in these issues that those bodies had any interest or competence. The Viceroy was hardly likely to bow his plumed head to listen to appeals against the assessment of a field or the cost of drainpipes. In Madras, however, Congress agitation was concerned extensively with just such a range of petty matters: Congress leaders could expect some response from Fort St George on them and knew that it was in these small things that the greatest interests of their constituents lay.[23]

The breadth and depth of involvement in the agitations of the 1880s, as well as the intricate relationship between western-educated publicists and lawyers and their magnate supporters, were laid out fully for us to see in the organisation of the 1887 session of the Congress held at Madras. The work of co-ordinating activities with publicist leaderships in other provinces, of preparing speeches and propaganda and of drafting resolutions to be discussed at the session was, of course, the responsibility of only a tiny group of the western educated at Madras city – P. Ananda Charlu, S. Subramania Iyer, G. Subramania Iyer, Salem Ramaswami Mudaliar, M. Viraraghavachari and a few others. The money, which made the session possible, and the demonstration of political power, which made it important, however, came from other quarters. The greater part of the costs of the Congress was met by the Indian mercantile elite of the capital. Raja Sir Savalai Ramaswami Mudaliar, P. Somasundram Chetty, G. Mahadeva Chetty and T. Namberumal Chetty gave handsome donations to the reception committee.[24] They also recruited cash and support from the areas of the city in which their influence was strongest. They organised collection committees in their suburbs and held meetings which elected delegates to the Congress session.[25] P. Somasundram Chetty even turned one of his businesses, the

---

[23] *Zamindari* rights, land revenue, local self-government and the income-tax, among other local topics, filled a major part of the discussions of the first Congress held at Madras. See *Report of the Third Indian National Congress held at Madras on the 27th, 28th, 29th and 30th December 1887* (London, 1888).

[24] *Ibid.*, Appendix 1.

[25] *Hindu* 12, 14, 16, 19 and 21 December 1887; *Madras Mail* 19, 20, 21 and 24 December 1887.

Metal Trading Company, into a Congress electorate.[26] The support which the mercantile elite of Madras city provided for the Congress reflected its close association with western-educated leaders, such as P. Ananda Charlu, in local politics over the previous decade. Ananda Charlu had led several agitations on its behalf against Corporation decisions[27] and against the proselytising activities of Christian missions,[28] and he was currently involved in articulating its grievances over the income-tax and local self-government acts through the Mahajana Sabha,[29] and in putting forward its cultural demands in the University Senate and from the public platform.[30]

Behind the city merchants came a number of the wealthiest *zamindars* in the province. The Maharaja of Vizianagram, who sat on the speakers' platform, had many links with the prominent professionals of the capital. He left his more important litigation in their hands and was joined to them in several cultural and proto-political pursuits—his patronage lay at the back of the female education movement and the *Hindu* newspaper.[31] The Raja of Venkatagiri, who sent his *diwan* to the session, also was a financier of city journalism as well as a great litigant and investor in the capital. Other leading landowners who offered support to the Congress, either in person or through agents, included the Raja of Sivaganga, the *zamindar* of Chellapalle and V. A. Vandayar of Pundi.[32]

The forces of organised religion also moved at the back of the session. The Sankarachariar of Kumbakonam sent a representative with a large donation and the Pandarasanidhi of Dharmapuram, constituted his disciples into a Congress electorate.[33] Again, both religious leaders had direct ties into the professional elite of the city, members of which were promoting the causes of Tamil and Sanskrit revivalism.

A fourth clearly identifiable interest at the session was that of the greater *mofussil* commercial powers. The major Komati families of the Northern Circars and Nattukottai families of Ramnad attended in person and helped to recruit followers by holding public meetings in their towns.[34] The millionaire industrialist A. Sabhapati Mudaliar

---

[26] *Report of the Third Indian National Congress*, Appendix I.
[27] *Hindu* 17 August 1884.   [28] *Hindu* 7 May 1888, 17 and 18 May 1889.
[29] *The Madras Mahajana Sabha Annual Report for 1885–6* (Madras, 1886).
[30] *Hindu* 7 May 1888, 17 and 18 May 1889.
[31] *Hindu* 3 March 1904; V. K. Narasimhan, *Kasturi Ranga Iyengar*, p. 6.
[32] *Report of the Third Indian National Congress*, Appendix I; *Hindu* 11 January 1888.   [33] *Ibid.*
[34] *Hindu* 12, 16, 19 and 21 December 1887; *Madras Mail* 19, 20, 21 and 24 December 1887.

of Bellary, who had close contacts with the city through his litiga-
tional and social reform activities, even placed his commercial network at the disposal of the Congress leaders.[35] Across the towns of the
Ceded Districts, where he held *abkari* contracts and bought raw
cotton, his agents were ordered to set up public meetings and collect
funds.[36]

Of course, the Congress campaign of the later 1880s not only
outlined an arena in which pre-existing linkages between magnates
and western-educated publicists could be displayed; it represented a
new level of institutional political activity and so was capable of
creating new linkages *ex nihilo*. Congress headquarters in Madras
city sent out touring lecturers to spread propaganda in the *mofussil*;[37]
it devoted a great deal of energy to vernacular pamphleteering in order
to cross the English language barrier which kept most Madrasis
ignorant of higher politics;[38] it built a powerful institutional structure
in which activity was co-ordinated between the capital and thirty-six
mofussil committees.[39] Few local political powers, who were feeling
the weight of Fort St George's new rule, were left in any doubt that
they should come to Madras city to seek redress. In consequence, the
1887 session was attended by a mass of petty urban magnates and
rural-local bosses who were making their presence felt on the provincial stage for the first time – Lingayat merchants from the towns
of the Ceded Districts, Reddi 'Sirdars' from Anantapur and Bellary,
Vellala landowners from Tinnevelly and Trichinopoly and strong
local despots such as T. S. Sivaswami Odayar of Kumbakonam.[40]

The organisation of the 1887 Congress at Madras provides us with
a political map of the presidency in which were drawn both the
boundaries of local political constituencies and the threads which
connected those constituencies to the capital. The Congress represented most of the important political elements of the province
massed against growing governmental interference. As virtually
every indigenous political power, regardless of shape or hue, felt
the prodding of government, so virtually every major political interest

---

[35] *Madras Times* 1 September 1885.
[36] *Hindu* 16 December 1887.
[37] For example, see the itinerary of lecture tours for Easter 1890 in *Madras Times*
4 April 1890.
[38] For example, the famous *Tamil Catechism* was published in 1887, and the
Swadesamitran, a Tamil weekly founded by leading Congressmen, first appeared
in 1882.
[39] 'Annual Report of the Madras Standing Congress Committee for 1889' in Home
Public B April 1890, No. 154. *N.A.I.*
[40] *Report of the Third Indian National Congress*, Appendix 1.

backed Congress demands. At this period, Congress in Madras faced little opposition from anti-nationalist (so-called) communal groups.[41] Most of the leading South Indian Muslims gave active support to the session; some 67 Muslims attended, including the prominent Madras city Persian family of Badsha, and the Maracair Muslims of Nega-patam who were the official Congress agents for eastern Tanjore.[42] The Eurasians, under W. S. Gantz's leadership, also were Congress activists.[43] Even the European business community of the capital, in spite of the recent problems of the Ilbert Bill, praised the objectives of the Congress.[44] It too was under the lash of Fort St George's new driving policy and it too wanted more representation in government. The communal divisions, which later emerged to tear apart provincial and national politics, were as irrelevant to the Congress of the late 1880s as they were to most aspects of local politics all the time.

The unanimity of opinion demonstrated at the Madras Congress session of 1887 was impressive. Importantly, however, the forces which brought this opinion together derived largely from pragmatic responses to particular conditions in the political environment. While leading Congress publicists and intellectuals may well have regarded the session as a triumph for their own national values and as a sign of the awakening of South India to a new consciousness of national political and cultural identity, in fact, as subsequent events were to prove, most of the participants were interested only in a series of very specific and very limited objectives. They sought the establishment of a political system which could convey the grievances, which were being fostered by governmental intrusion, more quickly to the centre and which could harness the new power of the capital to their own growing local needs. Once these objectives had been obtained and a new political framework built, for them the immediate ends of the Congress campaign would have finished and the Congress would have to continue, if it were to continue, as a very different type of political institution. Whatever its leading apologists might have thought, after a decade of ceaseless activity the Congress campaign

[41] There were a few anti-Congress protests from Madras Muslims but an analysis of them reveals that the protesters were, almost uniformly, relatives or close contacts of the Nawab of Arcot. This means that they were government placemen who might have been prodded by the British into activity. See Sunthralingam, *Politics and Nationalist Awakening in South India, 1852–1891*, pp. 264–8.

[42] *Report of the Third Indian National Congress*, Appendix 1; *Hindu* 21 December 1887.

[43] *Hindu* 29 April 1887.

[44] *Madras Mail* 30 December 1887.

had indeed realised most of its primary aims and, by the last years of the nineteenth century, was in the process of changing itself almost out of existence.

During the late 1880s and early 1890s, the British responded to pressures from the Congress, and to their innate fear that by extending the scope of government they would raise political opposition to their rule, by granting many of the requested reforms. On the University Senate, five seats were opened to election by the graduates; in 1892, the Legislative Council was enlarged and six elected seats were created; in the bureaucracy, the 1890s witnessed the introduction of the first Indian Collector, Solicitor- and Advocate-General and the opening of several senior posts in the Secretariat departments to non-I.C.S. officers.

Although these changes may appear to be very limited, they clearly widened the possibility of contact between 'government' and 'society'. In the University, the elected Senators formed a caucus which regularly challenged the official leadership of European and missionary educationists.[45] It was now practicable for opposition to Syndicate policy to be mounted inside the Senate rather than on the street. Moreover, after Curzon's University Act of 1904, this caucus was able to make headway in taking over the decision-making process for itself. Curzon's Act reduced the number of Senatorships granted for civic duties – to Europeans and Indians who were likely to be susceptible to pressure from senior officials[46] – and increased the proportion given to professional educationists. In Madras, by this time, most professional educationists were Indians. The elected Senators, usually men of considerable reputation and power in the law and public life, possessed many cultural, career and familial connections with the educationist Indian Senators and so were able to influence the Senate. Indeed, in 1904 the Senate, for the first time, refused to elect a missionary to the Legislative Council and chose instead one of the elected Senators, P. S. Sivaswami Iyer. The growing power of the Indian political group in the University was seen in the 1912 and 1913 Senate debates on the role of the vernaculars in higher education. The Senate, under the effective leadership of G. A. Natesan, overturned the Syndicate's resolution and forced the Syndics to run to the Director of Public

---

[45] For a glimpse of this caucus in action during a Senate election, see *Hindu* 15 and 19 October 1904.

[46] Before 1904, many 'city fathers' and businessmen received invitations to join the Senate. In 1902, there were 200 members of the Senate. *Indian Universities Commission* (Simla, 1902), II (Madras), 46. The Universities Act of 1904 cut the maximum number to 100.

Instruction for the protection of a Government Order.[47] In 1916, Natesan obtained a High Court order to make the Syndicate obey the Senate, its titular master.[48] In order to keep the University running, the Syndicate often had to stamp decisions made in the Senate where Indian opinion could play its part.

Similarly, in the Legislative Council, the apparently small changes made by the 1892 Act mask a greater alteration in political significance. The Council, of course, was still dominated by British officials who could push through what measures they pleased and prevent the passing of any resolution or Bill emanating from the non-official members. But legislation was never very central to government in Madras so that this fact was not critical. The non-official members, however, were able to draw the attention of senior bureaucrats to a wide variety of administrative malpractices and political grievances and to obtain some satisfaction in them. In the first months of the new Council, for example, K. Kalyanasundram Iyer managed to put an end to the extraordinarily arbitrary procedure by which the Board of Revenue heard appeals.[49] His elected fellow-Councillors pressed a mass of questions on senior officials – about matters ranging from irrigation taxes to the payment of office clerks.[50] Although official answers to these questions may not appear satisfactory, an examination of government files reveals that they did stimulate officials to reopen discussion of procedures and cases and, occasionally, to undertake reform.[51] Legislative Councillors received deputations from local powers and, as can be seen simply from the lists of questions which they put to the government, acted as the mouthpiece of local grievance inside the Council chamber.

Moreover, the Council proved very useful to non-official members as a means of obtaining places in the machinery of government and hence in the process by which political decisions were made. Senior British officials used the Council to test the ability of a much broader spectrum of Indian professional talent than before. Among those who moved from the benches of the elected non-officials to those of the government servants during the next two decades were C. Jumbulingam

[47] *Hindu* 10 and 15 March, 1 May 1913.
[48] *Hindu* 28 October 1916.
[49] *Hindu* 14 November 1893.
[50] For example, N. Subba Rao on the P.W.D. in Andhra, *Hindu* 4 October 1894; C. Sankara Nair on the *Abkari* Department, *Kerala Patrika* 29 October and 5 November 1892. *R.N.P.*
[51] As over the Tanjore revenue resettlement, G.O. 2472–3 (Revenue) dated 26 June 1894. *T.N.A.*

Mudaliar, K. Srinivasa Rao, V. C. Desikachari, P. S. Sivaswami Iyer, V. Krishnaswami Iyer, L. A. Govindaraghava Iyer, T. V. Seshagiri Iyer and S. Srinivasa Iyengar. In 1909, the *Hindu* noted

the fairly large numbers of elected Members who have been the successful applicants for judicial office under the Government. Besides those who have already secured judicial office, we are informed on unimpeachable authority that among the four Members of the Legislative Council recently elected by the Municipalities and District Boards, there are applications pending for such appointments from two of them before the Local Government.[52]

The reforms in the University, the Legislative Council and the bureaucracy suggest a central reason for the decline of agitational politics in the 1890s. It was now possible for political representation to take place inside the constitution. Although, with one exception,[53] only western-educated lawyers ever were elected to the Legislative Council, they represented in the Council chamber the same broad splay of magnate interests which they had represented outside. As the Madras Government argued, when questioned by the Government of India on the narrow social base of its Councillors:

Taking first the case of the raiyatwari tenure, the circumstances of this Presidency are such that there is a most intimate connection between the professional classes and the richer Government ryots. . . . Thus it occurs that though all five native members nominated on the selection of the recommending bodies are lawyers, no better representatives could possibly be found for the interests of the Government ryots. . . . Coming in the second place to the zamindari interest, a close study of the legislative proceedings for some years past has convinced this Government that the one seat assigned to this class is far from being a measure of the influence which this class exercises in the Council. With them too the legal members are associated either in interest or in sympathy. . . . From these and other causes it has resulted that in the several discussions on legislative measures affecting the real or supposed rights and privileges of zemindars, the positions claimed by the latter have constantly been defended by legal members with ability that would certainly not be equalled by the zemindars themselves.[54]

The Government of Madras could have gone further and have pointed to the connection between bankers and lawyers, typified by the opposition led by some Councillors to an Encumbered Estates Act, which undermined the interests of such men as Lodd Govindoss who special-

---

[52] *Hindu* 17 November 1909.
[53] A. Sabhapati Mudaliar, who was on the Council between 1893 and 1895.
[54] Letter No. 7 (Legislative), Government of Madras to Government of India dated 31 January 1899 in Home Public A July 1899, Nos 16–21. *N.A.I.*

ised in lending money to *zamindars*;[55] between merchants and lawyers, typified by council opposition to the income-tax and to regulations in restraint of trade;[56] and even between rural-local bosses and lawyers, typified by C. Vijayaraghavachari who was the legal representative of several wealthy Gounders and Kallars in Salem, P. Kesava Pillai who worked for Thimma Reddi in Anantapur and B. V. Narasimha Iyer who helped to organise a caucus of Gounder landlords in Coimbatore.[57]

By the mid-1890s, large-scale political agitation had lost its most important functions and was no longer necessary to connect public opinion to the centre of government. Representations made through the new constitutional channels had replaced it. With minor alterations for Lord Morley's reforms of 1909, the constitution of the 1890s continued to meet the political needs of Madras until 1916 and, consequently, to dominate the political rhetoric of the South. Moreover, after the bout of reforms in the 1890s, the British ceased to show further interest in altering the mechanisms of government so that continued appeals for major constitutional reform were futile. Agitation not only became unnecessary but also, given that government was no longer sympathetic, unrespectable.

The Madras Congress and the Mahajana Sabha, the formal institutions of Congress agitation, rapidly lost their *raison d'être* and declined in importance. The elaborate structure of Congress organisation collapsed while, between 1886 and 1900, the Mahajana Sabha lost two-thirds of its membership.[58] Congressmen from other provinces began to mock the scarcely disguised lethargy which came to characterise subsequent Congress sessions in Madras. The Lahore *Tribune* asked in 1894: 'By the way, is it true that many Madras notabilities who have up to very recently been steeped to the ears in the Congress, now show signs that they wish to be left alone?'[59] By 1904, the Governor, Lord Ampthill, could afford to ridicule the remnants of an organisation which had outlived its usefulness: 'The Congress as it is worked at present is nothing more than an annual picnic or "tamasha" . . . which has its counterpart in a minor organisation at home which celebrates

---

[55] See *Hindu* 18 February 1902.
[56] For example, N. Subba Rao, a Legislative Councillor, presided at the foundation of the Vizianagram Merchants Association, *Hindu* 13 September 1893.
[57] The rural-local boss interest was represented clearly in protests over the forest laws, over police reform and over the resettlement of the land revenue. See *Hindu* 1, 2 and 17 April 1915.
[58] M.M.S. membership declined from 607 in 1885 to 267 by 1900. *Madras Mahajana Sabha Annual Report for 1885–6* (Madras, 1886) and *ibid., 1899 and 1900* (Madras, 1901).
[59] Quoted in *Hindu* 1 August 1894. See also editorial in *Hindu* 1 December 1891.

an annual "beano" under the name of a Working Man's Political or Athletic Association.'[60]

Constitutional politics 1895 to 1916

The political framework which emerged out of the agitations of the 1880s represented the replication in constitutional form of the linkages which had developed between leading western-educated publicists and professionals at the capital and local magnate powers. The same interests, motives and activities which previously had been fused together in street agitations were now fused together in the Legislative Council, University and High Court. This development, of course, meant that the British had recognised as legitimate the types of political organisations which had been built up during the agitations. The British had brought them inside their governmental institutions and were proposing to govern with them rather than against them. The move towards constitutionality proved disastrous for agitational politics and for the nationalist movement: most of the channels which had been used to communicate hostility towards the system of government were now used to communicate only grievances within an accepted system of government. All local magnates and western-educated publicists who worked within the constitution were strengthening and supporting the *status quo*. It is, perhaps, because of this switch from 'nationalism' to 'collaboration' that the years between 1895 and 1916 have tended to be written off as politically sterile – as years of moderation when very little happened. Such a view, however, would be based on the assumption that it was only through agitation that Indian political organisation expanded and Indian political opinion came to be voiced. All that we have seen thus far, however, indicates that this view is untenable. Agitation and collaboration were tactics used by members of an indigenous political system which existed as a logically independent entity beneath the British and which, like all political systems, was concerned to distribute power. While the pressure of agitation may have helped to develop the system, there is no reason why the practices of collaboration, particularly the new kinds of collaboration taking place from the 1890s, should not have altered it as well. Indeed, as by definition more real power was available to the system when it was working with the government than when it was working against it, it would be more logical to argue that more change was wrought during periods of

[60] Lord Ampthill to Broderick, 7 January 1904. Ampthill Papers. *I.O.L.*

quiescence than during periods of protest. This was certainly the case in Madras. If, between 1895 and 1916, scarcely a single anti-British dog barked on the streets, nonetheless several of the most critical relationships of South Indian political life underwent a dramatic change.

As we have seen, the institutions of the bureaucracy, the law and education played more than one important role in the politics of the presidency. On the one hand, they represented the medium through which a distant government gave orders to magnate-dominated local society and through which that society sent its complaints and aspirations back again. On the other hand, to members of the western-educated community, these same institutions represented career structures which, in their own right, were capable of providing income and status. To use medical terminology, they were both membranes, passing influence from one part of the body politic to another, and organs, capable of generating influence of their own. Until the mid-1890s, however, any ambiguities which might have been created by this duality of role were obscured by the fact that both roles were functioning towards the same end. The educated and their patrons wanted precisely the same reforms, for the broadening of the constitution meant both improved representation and more control over careers in the services. In order to obtain reform also, the educated and their patrons had to work together and exchange their mutual talents – publicity and bureaucratic skills on the one side and wealth and social power on the other. During the 1880s, neither could operate successfully without the other.

The reforms of the 1890s, however, began to alter this symbiosis of circumstance. Improved systems of representation and Indianisation of the services brought a few western-educated men much closer to the centre of government. This made it easier for them to put the cases of the magnates to Fort St George. But is also gave the fortunate few an increasing personal influence over the internal operations of the bureaucracy, law and education. A spanner to grip the career structure of the professions was placed in their hands. Immediately, this development saw the western-educated community, once so united in the face which it showed to the British, tear itself apart in an internal fight for jobs and place. Later, as central governmental power grew and their grip tightened further, the few found themselves in control of the only effective system of representation in the province. They were able to use this control to break their previous dependence on the magnates. During the 1910s, they turned the power of the centre of government into an autonomous political base on which they could stand apart from, and in opposition to, many of their old patrons.

As we noted above, the University Senate and the senior posts in the bureaucracy enjoyed a patronage which was unsystematised and subject to little outside opinion. Colleges were affiliated or disaffiliated from the University by simple Syndicate recommendation and most posts in the government were appointed at the discretion of a superior. This lack of responsibility had led to the emergence of one of the most naked systems of government by favour in the whole of India. Importantly, however, up to the 1890s, the greater share of control over the favours of the central government was in the hands of Europeans who were distant from the indigenous political system. Certainly many Indians gained from the patronage of civilians. Indeed, the whole of the first generation of provincial politicians in Madras city were clients of Europeans, who had been brought to the capital by European favour. Muthuswami Iyer, for example, became, on the intercession of D. Carmichael, the Chief Secretary, the first native High Court Judge in the presidency.[61] S. Subramania Iyer, as we have seen, enjoyed the support of C. S. Crole; C. Pattabhirama Iyer came up to the city in the wake of Mr Justice Parker, who had been his sessions judge at Tanjore, and got a Judgeship for himself;[62] C. Sankara Nair was made a district *munsiff* before he had ever argued a case, when the barrister to whom he had been apprenticed was made a High Court Judge.[63] Yet, in their own right, these Indians were fairly far down the provincial patronage ladder: they received patronage from Europeans but had little themselves to pass on to their own clients and no control over what the Europeans did. Moreover, of course, the amount of patronage available to the centre was limited by the strength of the localities at this time. The reforms of the 1890s, however, began to place certain Indians in much closer contact with the centre precisely at the moment when the centre was breaking into the localities. As the reforms made no attempt to solve the problems of rule by personal discretion, they gave a handful of chosen Indians the means of developing networks of patronage and appointment which covered the entire province and held career success in the bureaucracy, the law and education in thraldom. The centralisation of government in Madras began to mean not the suppression of the

[61] *Hindu* 23 November 1883.
[62] Ramaswami Aiyar, *Biographical Vistas*, p. 208.
[63] C. Sankaran Nair, *The Autobiography of Sir C. Sankaran Nair* (Madras, 1966), p. 8.

principles by which the old *huzur sheristidar* had organised his district bureaucracy but their elevation to the organisation of the presidency. The simplest way of judging the scale on which the new patronage masters were able to operate is by looking at the extent to which they were able to help their families. C. Sankara Nair, for example, used his contacts with the European barrister/Judge to whom he had been apprenticed to build up a lucrative city practice. His clients included the wealthiest Malabar *jenmis* and the independent Raja of Puddukottai. He was able to pass on cases from these clients to his own nominees. In the climate of reform, he became a Legislative Councillor, University Senator, High Court Judge and member of the Viceroy's Executive Council. While his influence was at its height, members of his immediate family circle found that their fortunes were easily made. One cousin, apprenticed to Sankara Nair, picked up a judgeship in the High Court of Puddukottai and a valuable job in the Madras Law College;[64] another was made a professor at Presidency College, Madras, while still in his twenties;[65] two more were apprenticed in Madras and sent out to the *mofussil* bars of Madura and Ramnad where, with the aid of High Court and local self-government patronage from the capital, they soon became celebrities;[66] a family friend, with very small means, was offered a chair at the Law College.[67]

Yet as family connections went, Sankara Nair's were somewhat small and isolated. Much more impressive were those of the Vembakkam family and the complex of families which we shall refer to as 'C. P. Ramaswami Iyer's community'. The Vembakkam Sri Vaishnava Brahman family from Chingleput had been in the capital for a long time when it first begins to interest us: it included a Madras city police chief in the 1820s, leading city lawyers for three generations, the first Indian to be nominated to the Legislative Council in 1861 and two *diwans* of Native States (at that time the highest appointments for Indians in the gift of the British government).[68] It possessed an enormous presence in the local bureaucracy of the capital and its surrounding district and, by the early 1890s, was holding family conferences at which fifty or more administrators met to discuss

---

[64] G.O. 518 (Education) dated 10 September 1909. *T.N.A.*
[65] Sastri, *Encyclopaedia of the Madras Presidency*, p. 617.
[66] *Who's Who in Madras. 1938* (Cochin, 1938), p. 77.
[67] G.O. 518 (Education) dated 10 September 1909. *T.N.A.* This was Dr S. Swaminathan.
[68] V. C. Gopalaratnam, *A Century Completed. (The Madras High Court 1862–1962)* (Madras, n.d.), pp. 270–2; also, G. Parameswaran Pillai, *Representative Men of Southern India* (Madras, 1896).

domestic problems related to government service.[69] In the 1890s, its undoubted leader was V. Bashyam Iyengar, who was also the accredited leader of the native bar. The opening out of the higher posts of government in Madras witnessed its growth into a provincial rather than a local administrative power. By the early 1920s, it had produced another generation of legal giants, three High Court Judges,[70] two Attorney-Generals,[71] the first Home Minister under the Montagu–Chelmsford Reforms[72] and countless minor judges, departmental under-secretaries and government servants.[73]

C. P. Ramaswami Iyer's community of North Arcot Smartha Brahmans consisted of the fusion of the family of C. V. Runganatha Sastri, a Small Cause Court Judge, with that of Ramaswami Iyer's father, C. Pattabhirama Iyer, which had its own service complex in Tanjore. C. Pattabhirama Iyer followed his in-law into a Small Cause Court Judgeship but his son, and the whole of the next generation, were to do even better. Runganatha Sastri's son, Sundara Sastri, and adopted son, P. Ananda Charlu, established rich legal practices and Sundara Sastri's sons, Kumaraswami and Visvanatha, became High Court Judges.[74] C. P. Ramaswami Iyer inherited the Sundara Sastri–Ananda Charlu practice via his brother-in-law Kumaraswami Sastri, turned down the offer of a High Court Judgeship while still in his thirties and followed a member of the Vembakkam family into the Home Ministership in 1921.[75] Various other kin-connections picked up district *munsiff*ships, sub-judgeships and district judgeships in the period.[76] In fact the exploitation of patronage by this 'community' became so outrageous that it caused stirs in the press and in the services generally. The elevation of C. P. Ramaswami Iyer's cousin, the city *vakil* A. S. Balasubramania Iyer, to a sub-judgeship over the heads of men who had been waiting for years for promotion, produced

---

[69] *Hindu* 6 and 27 March 1894.
[70] V. Bashyam Iyengar, V. V. Srinivasa Iyengar and C. Thiruvenkatachari (by marriage).
[71] V. Bashyam Iyengar and S. Srinivasa Iyengar (by marriage).
[72] K. Srinivasa Iyengar (by marriage).
[73] Such as V. Krishnamachari and V. C. Desikachari who became Judges of the Small Cause Court.
[74] C. V. Visvanatha Sastri, *Biographies of a Grandfather and His Grandson* (Madras, 1939), passim.
[75] 'C.P. on himself' in *C.P. by his Contemporaries* (Madras, 1959); also A. Prakash, *Sir C.P.* (Madras, 1939), pp. 1–20.
[76] See Ramaswami Sastri, *Vita Sua* and Ramaswami Sastri, *Professor Sunderama Ayyar*.

a flood of petitions and threatened resignations in the Judicial Department.[77] The appointment of C. V. Kumaraswami Sastri to the High Court in 1913 saw the *Hindu* whip itself up into a frenzy of abuse at what it saw to be the patent corruption of government.[78]

Of course, family connection was not the only channel along which the victorious few of the 1890s distributed their patronage; we have used it here merely to demonstrate the kind of influence they now exercised. They operated a system of appointment by personal discretion which could be used to help friends and business and cultural contacts as much as relatives. For example, V. Krishnaswami Iyer, lawyer, University Senator, Legislative Councillor, High Court Judge, Executive Councillor and the most important man in the capital between about 1900 and his death in 1911, was a close associate in the University of the non-Brahman J. M. Velu Pillai,[79] whose son, Masilamani Pillai, became intimately connected to Krishnaswami Iyer's circle in Madras and received a valuable High Court job.[80] Similarly, cultural interests brought together Sir S. Subramania Iyer and another non-Brahman, J. M. Nallaswami Pillai who was a great apostle of Saiva Siddhanta, the Tamil non-Brahman religious tradition. Nallaswami was brought to college in the capital by Subramania Iyer, apprenticed to him, sent to Subramania Iyer's cousin in Madura to work as a junior and accommodated with a district *munsiff*ship while still with little legal experience.[81] The new men of consequence in Madras city may have been especially fond of their relatives but their personal contacts were much wider than family alone. Indeed, S. Subramania Iyer, on being elevated to the High Court bench, had left his huge legal practice not to a relative but to the brilliant V. Krishnaswami Iyer, who was only a friend.[82]

An idea of the scope and importance of this patronage system is provided by the correspondence of P. S. Sivaswami Iyer, lawyer, University Senator, Legislative Councillor, Advocate-General and

[77] *Hindu* 6 July 1910.
[78] *Hindu* 28 August 1913.
[79] *Hindu* 15 and 19 October 1904.
[80] He became a Recorder in the High Court. See 'C.P. on himself' in *C.P. by his Contemporaries*, p. 18. In 1894, V. Krishnaswami Iyer had especially requested Masilamani Pillai's appointment to the Congress executive committee. 'Proceedings of the General Purposes Committee of the 1894 Congress, 26 November 1894' in Register of Letters, Cards, etc., received from 2nd March 1894. Madras Mahajana Sabha Papers. *N.M.M.L.*
[81] K. M. Balasubramaniam, *The Life of J. M. Nallaswami Pillai* (Tiruchirapalle, 1965), pp. 10–11.
[82] *The Hon'ble V. Krishnaswami Iyer. A Sketch* (Trichinopoly, 1911), pp. 6–8.

Executive Councillor. Most of the letters which he received between 1904 and 1918, the period of his greatest influence, were requests from other western-educated Indians for favours and help with their careers. Whether the requirement was a job, a scholarship for a son, a lucrative University examinership, interference in the management of a college or school or preferment for promotion, Sivaswami Iyer was clearly regarded as one of the principal individuals to approach. Judging by the replies, he was not slow to use his position to aid those whom he favoured.[83] The elaboration of this patronage system created a network of interested contacts which stretched across the province. The centre of the network, however, lay in the houses of a handful of men in Madras city. The aspirant for office or place had to come to terms with these few 'boss-alls and bang-alls' if he wished to have any success in the professions of the western educated.[84]

Between the 1890s and 1916, the struggle for control of the nodes of this patronage system was central to the development of provincial politics. Naturally, some members of the western-educated community were better able than others to make connections at the right places; and those who failed were likely to try as hard as they could to

[83] For example: N. R. Panchapagesan to Sivaswami Iyer 29 August 1912, which warns the receiver not to place the son of sub-judge D. Vengopa Rao in the Registration Department; P. R. Narayanaswami Iyer to Sivaswami Iyer 9 August 1912, which asks for the gift of a lectureship in the Madras Law College; T. S. Balakrishna Iyer to Sivaswami Iyer 10 August 1912, which asks for a job for the writer's son; T. Ananda Rao to Sivaswami Iyer 3 July 1913, which asks for a deputy-collectorship for the writer's grandson; W. B. Patwarden to Sivaswami Iyer 28 January 1909, which asks for a University Examinership; P. P. Pillai to Sivaswami Iyer 8 March 1913, which asks for jobs for the writer's son and son-in-law; R. Srinivasa Iyer to Sivaswami Iyer 30 March 1913, which asks for a place in the Salt Department for the writer's son; M. Thiruvenkatachari to Sivaswami Iyer 22 March 1908, which asks for a government place for the writer's nephew; A. S. Vaidya to Sivaswami Iyer 17 March 1908, which recommends a third party for Chief Examinership in Tamil; R. Ramachandra Rao to Sivaswami Iyer 18 March 1914, which asks for a post for the writer's cousin; T. Varadarajulu Naidu to Sivaswami Iyer 23 August 1914, which asks for a post for the writer's son. P. S. Sivaswami Iyer Papers. *N.A.I.* There are dozens more like this. The character of the men listed above indicates that they did not importune Sivaswami Iyer out of ignorance of the way that the system worked: Ananda Rao, R. Ramachandra Rao and T. Varadarajulu Naidu were themselves government servants, P. P. Pillai and T. S. Balakrishna Iyer were prominent lawyers and *mofussil* publicists. Among Sivaswami Iyer's most regular favour-seekers were his two brothers, who were sub-judges.

[84] Dr T. M. Nair, who detested the system, once described it as operating on 'the principle of the best-backed'. *Hindu* (weekly) 9 March 1916.

shift those who had succeeded. Moreover, the peculiar, almost conspiratorial, nature of political life in Madras city led to the formation of specialised political groupings designed to extract and distribute the patronage. One of the most celebrated of these groupings was popularly known as 'the Mylapore clique' after the suburb in which most of its prominent members lived. It was composed, across our period, of a succession of lawyers and administrators who were on close personal terms, who met regularly in each others' houses, put forward the same demands in Congress, the press and on the streets and aided each other in seeking office. Each generation in Mylapore picked its successor and brought it up through its favour. In the late 1880s, we could take its leaders to be V. Bashyam Iyengar, S. Subramania Iyer and R. Ragunatha Rao;[85] by the turn of the century their apostolic successor V. Krishnaswami Iyer was in command; following his death, his old school friend P. S. Sivaswami Iyer and close legal and University associates G. A. Natesan and L. A. Govindaraghava Iyer achieved prominence and were joined, at the time of the First World War, by C. P. Ramaswami Iyer.[86] Behind this leadership group came a bewildering collection of lawyers, teachers, bureaucrats and journalists tied together by personal contact and the hope of rewards. The organisation of the clique was loose: personal and career rivalries could split it at a moment's notice and disappointed courtiers could move quickly into opposition to it. In general, however, it may be said to have represented at any given time those who were most successful at the delicate game of capturing government favour.

Permanently in opposition to the Mylapore clique, and attracting to their flag at various times many old but disappointed Mylaporeans, were a group known to contemporaries as the 'Egmore' clique. They were even less homogeneous than, and, indeed, existed only as a counterweight to, Mylapore. At the centre of the clique sat C. Sankara Nair whose own personal system of influence was, of course, of exactly the same type as that operated by the leaders of Mylapore. The reasons for his disaffection were several: there was professional rivalry

---

[85] R. Ragunatha Rao, a Maratha Brahman from Tanjore district, was a career civil servant who became deputy-collector of Madras city and *diwan* of Baroda. T. Madhava Rao, a *diwan* of Mysore, was his cousin; T. Ananda Rao, also a *diwan* of Mysore, and R. Ramachandra Rao, a Collector and, later, a Secretary of the Education Department, were his nephews.

[86] The informal yet impenetrable character of the Mylapore clique can be seen in the description which Sivaswami Iyer gave of Mylapore at his arrival in the city. See K. A. Nilakanta Sastri (ed.), *A Great Liberal. Speeches and Writings of Sir P. S. Sivaswami Aiyar* (Bombay, 1965), p. 254.

between himself and the men of Mylapore; his own connections in the European bureaucracy had been different from those of Mylapore; as a Malayali he was culturally isolated in a Tamil city during a period when cultural contacts often led to political contacts. In collaboration with him were men who had failed to make much headway with the Mylapore bosses and whose alternative connections were weak. Most prominent among them was Kasturi Ranga Iyengar whose brother (a senior government servant in the 1880s and 1890s) had quarrelled with the Mylaporeans and, during the militant Congress agitation, had been ridiculed by them as a British puppet.[87] Kasturi Ranga Iyengar, who had qualified as a *vakil* in 1884, had been unable to build a legal practice in the city and had spent nearly a decade in the *mofussil*. He returned to the city in 1894 but, once again, found himself starved of valuable cases, which fell into the pockets of the Mylaporeans, and was forced to give up the law for journalism.[88] He was understandably resentful of the men who held back his career. A third Egmore leader was T. Rangachari, from the same village in Tanjore as Kasturi Ranga Iyengar. Although regarded as one of the most able lawyers of his generation, he could secure relatively few of the plums of civil litigation and concentrated his attention on the much less lucrative criminal bar.[89] Kasturi Ranga Iyengar and T. Rangachari certainly had contacts, familial and otherwise, with the central mechanisms of government, the law and education, and picked up Mylaporeans who were spun off by factional conflict, but their influence and importance were less pervasive.

Examples of the rivalry between Egmore and Mylapore litter the history of Madras politics. Even in the 1880s, when personal feuds were more usually subordinated to common ends, C. Sankara Nair had clashed with V. Bashyam Iyengar and S. Subramania Iyer in a most acrimonious debate in the Madras Vakils' Association over the place of barristers in the appeals court.[90] This had led to a long and bitter correspondence in the press. The 1894 Congress was

---

[87] *Ibid.*, p. 113.

[88] Narasimhan, *Kasturi Ranga Iyengar*, pp. 23–4; V. K. Narasimhan, *Kasturi Srinivasan* (Bombay, 1969), p. 7. A typical example of what it meant to be 'out' in city politics can be seen in the fact that although Kasturi Ranga Iyengar several times stood for election to the Senate, he was always beaten by a Mylaporean.

[89] T. Rangachari rarely appears on the list of *vakils* retained in major High Court civil cases. In 1924, at the height of his career, he was earning only Rs 40,000 p.a., compared to the Rs 2,40,000 of the leader of the Madras bar, K. Srinivasa Iyengar. See Home Public File 953 of 1924. *N.A.I.*

[90] Menon, *C. Sankaran Nair*, p. 18.

nearly wrecked by faction. There was a fight between Kasturi Ranga Iyengar and the Mylaporeans P. R. Sundara Iyer and V. C. Desikachari over the printing and distribution of tickets; T. Rangachari and P. R. Sundara Iyer quarrelled over the membership of the subjects' committee; after the Congress session, S. Subramania Iyer resigned from the executive committee, accusing some of its members of malpractice; the general purposes committee refused to meet T. Rangachari's claims for expenses; and the *Hindu* newspaper, which was already near to the Egmore clique, was accused of presenting a false bill.[91] The internecine strife continued unabated in the succeeding years. When it was rumoured that Sankara Nair was to be made an Executive Councillor, petitions of protest arrived at the Judicial Department from Mylapore.[92] In 1905, Sankara Nair, Kasturi Ranga Iyengar and T. Rangachari joined forces to buy the *Hindu*, which had reached bankruptcy, and used it to denounce the antics of Mylapore in general and V. Krishnaswami Iyer in particular.[93]

The reforms of the 1890s, then, had created openings which various members of the western-educated community in Madras city were trying to fill. Their struggles for place were creating factional divisions. Both Egmore and Mylapore, however, can be defined in simple and conservative terms: they were trying to replace each other at the centre of a system the rules of which they both accepted. Yet outside them, and still within the world of the western educated, there existed forces much less coherent and much more dangerous. In Madras city and every *mofussil* locality, the prizes in education, the law and government service were passing to the men who were 'well connected' to the patronage brokers. Not surprisingly, there were a great many men who were not connected to any of the dominant personalities of the new politics and who began to suffer. Soon, they started a very vocal denunciation of the whole system. They leant more towards Egmore than Mylapore but must be seen as distinct from it. Whereas, in Sankara Nair, Egmore had a man deep inside patronage politics and, in Kasturi Ranga Iyengar and T. Rangachari,

[91] 'Proceedings of the Executive Committee of the 1894 Congress', 25 September and 10 November 1894, 12 January, 7 and 30 March 1895; 'Proceedings of the General Purposes Committee of the 1894 Congress', 4 September 1894 in Register of Letters, Cards, etc., received since 2nd March 1894. Madras Mahajana Sabha Papers. *N.M.M.L.*

[92] Letter of K. Ramamurthi in *Hindu* 12 January 1918.

[93] See V. S. Srinivasa Sastri to V. Krishnaswami Iyer, 27 July 1911. V. S. Srinivasa Sastri Papers. *N.A.I.*

men around its fringes and with certain kin and social connections inside it, this collection of the frustrated had no contacts with it at all. They were much more prepared to wreck the entire game if they could not get Mylapore out.

Among the militant discontented was T. M. Nair, the Madras city doctor whom we discussed when examining the Madras Corporation. He spent much of his time denouncing 'the wire-pullers' who kept him out of Legislative Council politics and who, ultimately, took from him even his Corporation seat. Yet most of the opponents of the dominion of Madras city leaders came from outside the capital. Often they were the local enemies of men associated with Mylapore. Publicist and professional life in the Northern Circar districts of Godavari and Kistna, for example, was in the hands of a group of lawyer-educationists gathered around Nyapathi Subba Rao, a Rajahmundry lawyer, and including Puranam Venkatappayya, the leader of the Kistna bar; K. Viresalingam, a celebrated social reformer; K. Perrazu, a Cocanada lawyer; and M. Ramachandra Rao, another Rajahmundry lawyer. This clique was closely tied through personal connections to Mylapore[94] whose influence it used to hold and extend its local political position. It enjoyed a large share of the legal patronage which came from Madras city, moved on easy terms with a local officialdom which increasingly was coming under Mylapore's control of careers, and was in receipt of many favours in local education from the University. Moreover, it monopolised all Legislative Council elections in Andhra. Its opponents in the Circars found themselves harassed repeatedly by its ability to bring force from the capital to bear on the local situation. For more than twenty years, the main rival of N. Subba Rao and K. Viresalingam in Rajahmundry affairs was Y. L. Narasimhan, a Sristikarnam lawyer and political entrepreneur from Ganjam who had settled in the district. Until the mid-1890s, however, Narasimhan had been able to hold his own against them in a competition for publicist leadership, for his resources of local magnate support were at least as great as theirs.[95] Following the reforms at Fort St George, however, he was progressively outmanoeuvred. His reputation was rocked by a series of abortive

[94] N. Subba Rao and M. Ramachandra Rao were Madras city educated and classmates of the leaders of Mylapore; P. Venkatappayya's brother, Nagabhushanam, was a city resident and long-time secretary of the Madras Mahajana Sabha; K. Viresalingam had contacts with the Madras Social Reform Association, in which certain Mylaporeans were interested, and had spent some time teaching in the capital.

[95] I am grateful to Dr John Leonard of the University of California for this information.

but expensive prosecutions brought against him by the Judicial Department;[96] his place in the municipal council was threatened by constitutional changes in the council, which Subba Rao had suggested to the Local and Municipal Department;[97] his little empire of private schools was challenged by the University's scarcely disguised preference for K. Viresalingam's educational projects.[98] Narasimhan's closest local associates also felt Mylapore's pressure. T. Prakasam of Rajahmundry, for example, who owed his education to Narasimhan's patronage, had a lucrative hold which he possessed over a district *munsiff* broken by a Judicial Department investigation,[99] and his 1903–4 regime as chairman of the municipality pestered by investigations of his conduct by the Local and Municipal Department.[100]

In Kistna, P. Venkatappayya came to enjoy a massive hold over local educational institutions, the bar and the municipality and to extirpate virtually all opposition to his dictatorship of public affairs. Naturally, this position would not be accepted for long by other educated publicists in the leading district town and, by the turn of the century, resentment against him was deeply felt in a group of young western-educated professionals led from Masulipatam by the doctor B. Pattabhisitaramayya, the lawyer Konda Venkatappayya and the journalist Mutnuri Krishna Rao.[101] Narasimhan and Prakasam in Rajahmundry and Pattabhisitaramayya and Krishna Rao in Masulipatam were, logically, only committed to a battle with the Subba Rao–Venkatappayya clique for place in the locality. However, because of the latter's use of power derived from the provincial level, it was not long before the fight was carried to the provincial level. In addition to attacking the clique in elections to municipalities and school boards and at local public meetings, Prakasam and Krishna Rao helped to found newspapers which made their message much more general. Particularly through *Kistnapatrika* (established 1904), they denounced

[96] *Hindu* 17 December 1904.
[97] G.O. 1029 (L and M, M) dated 27 June 1895; G.O. 5 (L and M, M) dated 7 January 1896. *T.N.A.*
[98] For example, Viresalingam spent many years on the University's Telugu Textbook Committee and was able to prescribe many of his own works as set texts. For an account of Mylapore's attempts to interfere in the Cocanada College, see 'Extract from the Memoirs of Dr B. Pattabhisitaramayya' in *Brahmarishi Dr Sir Raghupathi Venkata Ratnam Naidu Birth Centenary Souvenir. Mahanavarmi, 1962* (n.p., n.d.).
[99] Collector of Godavari to Secretary, Local and Municipal Department, 30 October 1903 in G.O. 40 (L and M, M) dated 8 January 1904. *T.N.A.*
[100] *Ibid.*
[101] *Hindu* 8 and 11 May 1907.

the present form of British government, which permitted Mylapore so much influence, and the current moderate tenor of Congress politics, which so suited Mylapore's collaborationist role.

Similar developments could be seen in a number of other areas. N. K. Ramaswami Iyer, for example, was a Tamil Brahman lawyer in Chittoor district who, between 1900 and 1904, was involved in a battle with the family of the great Mylaporean L. A. Govindaraghava Iyer for local pre-eminence.[102] In 1904, he took his struggle to the provincial level by demanding, at the Provincial Congress Conference, that the Congress constitution be altered to weaken the hold Madras city – i.e., Mylapore – had on it.[103] Naturally, he was unsuccessful. In 1905, he moved to Tanjore where he found that local dominance belonged to R. Raghunatha Rao, the doyen of Mylapore in the 1880s, who was in semi-retirement but still preserved his Mylapore connections. As in Chittoor, and as with the T. Prakasam–M. Krishna Rao groups in Andhra, he began to form associations and publish newspapers which attacked the present construction of the government and of the Congress.[104] In Salem C. Vijayaraghavachari formed the kernel of opposition to Mylapore. In spite of great notoriety occasioned by his prosecution of the Secretary of State in 1883,[105] by his victory in three consecutive Legislative Council elections and by his oratorical skills, he had never forged connections with Mylapore or the centre of government and, by the early 1900s, had nothing to show for his eminence. Indeed, in local politics he was eclipsed by T. Subramania Iyer, the close friend of Sir P. S. Sivaswami Iyer, who attracted much central patronage;[106] while, in provincial politics, he received no office or decorations. He was an uncompromising critic of government, Congress and Mylapore.

The reforms of the 1890s had wrought deep divisions in the more or less united front which the western-educated community had presented to the British in the 1880s. The transfer of a limited power

[102] *Hindu* 29 February 1908.
[103] *Report of the 12th Madras Provinical Conference held at Ranipet in May 1904* (Madras, 1904), pp. 103–7.
[104] *Hindu* 17 November 1905, 20 April 1907.
[105] This prosecution followed his acquittal in a case arising out of the Salem riots of 1882. He won Rs 100 damages and became a celebrity overnight. *Hindu* 6 May 1884.
[106] T. Subramania Iyer was one of Sivaswami Iyer's most persistent correspondents. He was Salem public prosecutor and municipal chairman for several years and, during Sivaswami Iyer's term as Executive Councillor, was nominated president of the Salem *taluk* board.

to certain members of the professions had spread tensions across the whole of the province. These tensions lay at the heart of the Congress troubles of 1906–8. Lord Morley, the Liberal Secretary of State, undertook to grant constitutional reforms and the Moderate Congress leadership, understandably, wished to impress him with its loyalty, responsibility and solidarity. V. Krishnaswami Iyer led the Madras Congress and was closely allied in All-India politics to Gokhale in Bombay and Surendrenath Bannerjee in Bengal. It was natural that the enemies of Mylapore in Madras should use Mylapore's need for moderation as a stick with which to beat it and its system. They gravitated towards the opponents of Gokhale and Bannerjee in Bombay and Bengal – particularly B. G. Tilak and B. C. Pal. The confrontation between these fusions of Moderate and of Extremist elements and the debacle of the Surat Congress session in 1907 are well-known and need little further elucidation.[107] The Tilak–Pal 'party' attempted to give the Congress a radical, populist and anti-British stance and to demand an impossible amount of reform just when the Gokhale–Krishnaswami Iyer–Bannerjee leadership required such postures and programmes least.

In Madras city, much of the Extremist disturbance was due to the work of G. Subramania Iyer, one of the oldest enemies of Mylapore. G. Subramania Iyer had been a prominent nationalist agitator in the 1870s and 1880s, a founder of the *Hindu* newspaper, of the Madras Mahajana Sabha and of the Congress. But he had quarrelled with his colleagues over social reform and had virtually outcasted himself by allowing his widowed daughter to remarry. As a result he had been excluded from the inner sanctum of Mylapore, he had failed to be made a Congress president – which his work for the early Congress deserved – and he had been unable to enter the tight world of Legislative Council and bureaucratic politics.[108] Through the 1890s and early 1900s, he remained a penurious publicist while his previous associates became powerful politicians. In 1907, he aimed his polemic against Mylapore and drew a following from young and poor members of the intelligentsia, students, mill workers, *jutka-wallahs* and other similarly frustrated social elements.[109] In the

---

[107] See Johnson, *Provincial Politics and Indian Nationalism.*

[108] S.A. Govindarajan, *G. Subramania Iyer* (New Delhi, 1969), pp. 37, 48–54. Between the mid-1890s and mid-1900s, Subramania Iyer several times failed to win election to the Legislative Council and Senate.

[109] Home Political B October 1907, Nos 80–7; Home Political B December 1907, Nos 2–9; Home Political B January 1908, Nos 19–26; Home Political B May 1908, Nos 36–43. *N.A.I.*

manner of every other Indian agitator of our period, he sought also to tie religious revivalism to his cause.[110] His support was noisy and volatile but lacked influence in society. It was used by the Egmore leaders T. Rangachari and Kasturi Ranga Iyengar to challenge Mylapore in the Madras Mahajana Sabha, which formed the Congress executive. Election meetings were packed with it and several debating sessions broken up by its fury.[111] But it proved a very unsatisfactory following in the type of politics played by Egmore: it was too wild to be controlled and so disreputable that it alienated important opinion. T. Rangachari, Kasturi Ranga Iyengar and, ultimately, even G. Subramania Iyer found it necessary to jettison their popular support when it became violent and threatened to bring down the police on their heads.[112] Further, of course student and worker mobs proved useless against Krishnaswami Iyer's patronage power and influence.[113]

In the *mofussil*, the Extremist leaders attracted much the same kind of following. In Tanjore, N. K. Ramaswami Iyer mixed his religious polemic with appeals to impoverished literati and students.[114] In Tuticorin, V. O. Chidambaram Pillai's work seemed more substantial, for he used a base of pre-existing racial and economic tension. But many of those involved in his main enterprise, the Swadeshi Steam Navigation Company, proved to be politically moderate and his Extremist activities led to his dismissal from the project. His personal following was drawn from students, workmen and those susceptible to religious invective.[115] In Salem, C. Vijayaraghavachari was relatively quiet until late in 1908, but he still posed sufficient a threat for Krishnaswami Iyer to have him removed from the A.I.C.C. in 1907.[116] In Andhra, the T. Prakasam–M. Krishna Rao leadership was very active. It brought B. C. Pal from Bengal for a lecture tour in 1907 and campaigned vigorously.[117] Attempts were made by it to

---

[110] Home Political B December 1907, Nos 2–9. *N.A.I.*

[111] *Ibid.; Hindu* 7 December 1907, 13 and 27 December 1908.

[112] Home Political B December 1907, Nos 2–9. *N.A.I.; Hindu* 13 January 1908.

[113] Even in the Madras Mahajana Sabha, it could not command sufficient votes to oust the Krishnaswami Iyer faction. 'Proceedings of a Meeting of Members', 28 October 1907, 7 August 1908 and 20 November 1908. Madras Mahajana Sabha Papers. *N.M.M.L.*

[114] *Hindu* 20 April 1907.

[115] *Swadesamitran* 1 and 18 July 1906. *R.N.P.; Hindu* 17 March, 2 April and 9 June 1908; P & J File 993 of 1908. *I.O.L.* For a detailed discussion of the Tuticorin episode, see my 'Political Change in the Madras Presidency 1880–1921', Unpublished Fellowship dissertation, Trinity College, Cambridge, 1971.

[116] *Hindu* 25 July 1907.   [117] *Hindu* 2, 3, 4 and 8 May 1907.

found a national college and to set up permanent political institutions.[118] Once more, appeals to students and workmen and to popular religious sensibilities formed the fundament of its local agitations, but it had more success than elsewhere. The close rural—urban connections in deltaic Andhra enabled it to channel the disturbances into the countryside. Further, many of the Extremist leaders were able to find financial support from groups of urban Komatis who had often backed them personally in local religious and municipal politics.[119] Andhra Extremists were able to build a considerable movement, the volatility of which may be seen in the Cocanada riot.[120]

In spite of their ability to find support in a few localities, however, the Madras Extremists did not seriously challenge the position of Mylapore. Although mobs and popular polemic could embarrass the Madras city leaders, and undermine their claims that their Congress represented the opinion of India, they were the wrong weapons in this war. The institutions which could make provincial leaders responsible to popular opinion did not exist. In consequence, the the Madras Extremists had little general success in rousing to their cause large numbers even among the western educated. The enormous patronage control exerted by Mylapore gave it great authority over the educational, legal and administrative sections of society and very few men who were seriously interested in these were prepared to flaunt it openly.[121] Through his hold on the central Congress machinery, Krishnaswami Iyer was able to exclude the Extremists from participation in the Congress and thus deny them a vehicle for the expression of their frustrations. Under the 1908 Allahabad Convention, the Mahajana Sabha was replaced as the Congress executive by a Provincial Congress Committee nominated by Krishnaswami Iyer himself; access to the 1908 Madras Congress session

---

[118] *Hindu* 16 May 1907.

[119] See Venkatarangaiya, *Freedom Struggle in Andhra Pradesh*, II, 177–311.

[120] *Ibid.*, pp. 207–10.

[121] The leading lawyers in most of the *mofussil* bars rushed to Krishnaswami Iyer's aid in opposing the Extremists. B. N. Sarma of Vizagapatam, N. Subba Rao of Rajahmundry, T. T. Viraraghvachari of Chittoor, P. Kesava Pillai of Anantapur, P. Siva Rao of Bellary, A. Subramania Iyer of Madura, A. Sundara Sastri of Tinnevelly and T. S. Balakrishna Iyer of Coimbatore all offered their support to the Moderate cause. For views of the Moderate — Extremist confrontation, which concentrate on the personalities rather than the policies and on which this account is based, see V. S. Srinivasa Sastri's letters to G. K. Gokhale and V. Krishnaswami Iyer between 1907 and 1909 in V. S. Srinivasa Sastri Papers. *N.A.I.*

was made difficult and the attendance was small;[122] the district and *mofussil* machinery of Congress was run down to prevent dissident locals from capturing it.[123] By 1909, it was very obvious that Mylapore had weathered the storm without damage and had destroyed the organisations of those opposed to it. In order to remain in public affairs, Kasturi Ranga Iyengar and T. Rangachari had to enter Krishnaswami Iyer's Madras P.C.C., where they were powerless.

Of course, the Extremist–Moderate split was not fought in the press and from the public platform on the basis of 'ins' against 'outs', which we have suggested was its reality. Great issues were raised and ideological principles held almost to the death. Yet it would be very difficult, looking not at the specific events of 1906–8, but at the careers of the men who were involved in them, to argue that the issues entered the world of politics of their own volition rather than as factors facilitating actions taken on other grounds. Mylapore, at various times in our period, stood for a number of conflicting principles over the presence and the role of the British in Madras. In the 1880s, it demonstrated a strong and trenchant criticism of the British bureaucracy. Between the 1890s and 1916, it was an avid defender of the glories of *raj* and put down an agitational movement similar to the one which it had organised a few years before. In 1916, it was to go over to savage criticism once more and to threaten civil disobedience against the British. Mylapore was playing a strategic game in order to widen its grasp of government power and it required different tactics at different times. Naturally, its enemies were forced into considering their tactics appropriate for each stage. C. Vijayaraghavachari, for example, is best remembered for the extreme stands he took at various times against the mendicant and Anglophile postures of Mylapore. Yet he was also capable of allying with those British elements which felt their position threatened by the expansion of Indian power. In Legislative Council elections, he voted for European missionaries and businessmen in preference to Mylapore candidates[124], and, when defeated in a 1916 Imperial Legislative

---

[122] V. Krishnaswami Iyer to G. K. Gokhale, 5 October 1907. V. S. Srinivasa Sastri Papers. *N.A.I.; Report of the Proceedings of the Twenty-Fourth Indian National Congress held at Madras on the 28th, 29th and 30th December 1908* (Madras, 1909); Home Political B January 1909, No. 108. *N.A.I.*

[123] See K. R. Guruswami Iyer to V. Krishnaswami Iyer, 2 October 1908; C. Y. Chintamani to V. Krishnaswami Iyer, 3 October 1908; T. T. Viraraghavachari to V. Krishnaswami Iyer, 11 November 1908. V. Krishnaswami Iyer Papers. *N.A.I.*

[124] Letter of T. V. Gopalaswami Mudaliar in *Hindu* 15 August 1916.

Council election, he received only European votes.[125] T. M. Nair, on the other hand, is best remembered for his pro-British sentiments which manifested themselves in his dress, his denunciations of Hindu tradition, his alliances on the Corporation with Europeans and, ultimately, his part in founding the loyalist Justice Party in 1916. Yet during the Extremist–Moderate split he made common cause with C. Vijayaraghavachari and N. K. Ramaswami Iyer in attacking the Moderates, even though this involved him in a movement which was attempting to destroy the basis of the British connection.[126]

The responses of the professional opponents of Mylapore were dictated to a considerable extent by Mylapore's own position at any given time and by the availability of the resources of political protest. To attack Mylapore for its Anglophobia, particularly during periods when it was involved in agitation, opened out access to missionary, Indian Christian and British resident support which was disturbed by the growth of Mylapore's influence. To attack it for its Anglophilia, during periods when it was co-operating with government, provided access to areas of society in which dissatisfaction with the government in general was felt. *Jutkawallahs*, subject to constant police harassment, factory hands, in the difficult state of assimilation into an urban proletariat, and students, without material worries, could be drawn into violent demonstration without much difficulty or particular cause. Equally, popular religious revivalism, with its emphasis on parades, preaching and polemic, provided a bank which could be looted whenever anti-government agitation was necessary. The British, however careful they might be to avoid disturbing the religious sensibilities of their subjects, were not Hindus and could be characterised as enemies of Hinduism.[127] In the continuing struggle with

---

[125] C. Vijayaraghavachari to P. Kesava Pillai, 15 July 1916. P. Kesava Pillai Papers. *N.M.M.L.*

[126] V. S. Srinivasa Sastri to G. K. Gokhale, 2 March 1909. V. S. Srinivasa Sastri Papers. *N.A.I.*

[127] However, it is necessary to note that there was no logical connection between religious revivalism and Extremism, nor, indeed, between Christianity and political opposition to Mylapore. The men of Mylapore were deeply interested in and great patrons of Hindu and Indian cultural revivalism. Most of them were associated with Mrs Besant, whose Theosophical federation was certainly the most powerful revivalist organisation in the South. Between 1906 and 1908, she was at one with Mylapore in opposing the programme of the Extremists. The link between political agitation and religious revivalism was simply that, in the localities, revivalist associations possessed organised followings of a semi-fanatical nature. By associating political symbols with those of religion, political agitators could tap these pools of support for any purpose they chose – as Mrs Besant

Mylapore, its enemies had had to recruit their following where they could find it.

The manner in which personal oppositions were continuous, and only the issues changed, was well brought out by the developments which followed the defeat of the Extremists. Following Krishnaswami Iyer's victory in 1908, the main arena of popular political controversy – the Congress – was denied to his opponents. No longer could they launch attacks on the Mylapore system from inside a provincial political organisation. They began to turn, therefore, to a number of peripheral areas of social activity which they politicised and brought into the fray. It was more than coincidence that the first signs of the Andhra movement began to appear in 1909, the year after the Allahabad Convention, and that its leaders were the rump of the Andhra Extremists, T. Prakasam, M. Krishna Rao, B. Pattabhisitaramayya, Konda Venkatappayya and the Tamilian N. K. Ramaswami Iyer.[128] The Andhra movement, more specifically the movement for a separate Andhra province, grew out of the Telugu vernacular revival which had been developing with considerable energy in the towns of the Andhra deltas from the 1870s. But the fact that it took on a political aspect at this time was due less to any logic in the process of its development than to its seizure by Mylapore's opponents. The creation of an Andhra province would break the connections between Mylapore and the Circar towns, which the Andhra Extremists found so debilitating. In the Circars, the main enemies of the movement were Mylapore's placemen in the area – the N. Subba Rao–M. Ramachandra Rao group.[129] They were involved in vernacular revivalism at least as much, if not more, than the Andhra movement leaders but had no

herself was to show when she became a politician in 1916. Similarly, by the later nineteenth century, not all Christians and missionaries were opposed to the advance of Indians, even of Mylapore Hindus. P. S. Sivaswami Iyer, for example, enjoyed the friendship of Father Bertram, a Jesuit headmaster, while several Indian Christians, such as M. S. Devadoss the High Court Judge, were on the fringes of the Mylapore network. Tension between missionaries and Christians and the Mylapore clique, when it occurred, was not so much the result of the conflict of ideologies as of practical political interests. The group of Protestant missionaries who had run the University naturally resented losing their influence to anybody; since it was Mylapore who took their position from them it was Mylapore they disliked.

[128] See K. Venkatappayya, *The Andhra Movement* (n.p., n.d.); also, *The First Andhra Conference held at Bapatla in 1913* (Bezwada, n.d.).

[129] Evidence of N. Subba Rao in *Royal Commission on the Public Services in India*, Appendix, II, 296. *P.P.* 1914, XXI; *Hindu* 14 May 1915.

desire to destroy their existing and lucrative political contacts. In the same way, it was N. K. Ramaswami Iyer again, this time in conservative Tanjore, who organised and politicised the sentiments of orthodox Brahmans against social reform.[130] His *Varnashramadharma* movement was aimed specifically at the mildly reformist views of most of the leading men of Mylapore.

Of course, the fact that these cultural and religious movements were politicised in response to factional struggles implies that, once the factional alignments or tactics changed, they could be depoliticised. This clearly happened to the Andhra movement. Between 1910 and 1917, the campaign for an Andhra province grew steadily more vehement and deepened its following. It was never in a position to challenge Mylapore where it mattered – in the councils of government – but it created an impression of popular power and increased the reputations of its leaders. By 1917, however, Mylapore itself had gone over to anti-British agitation and was prepared to compromise with its old enemies. Pattabhisitaramayya, Prakasam, Konda Venkatappayya and M. Krishna Rao were brought back into provincial politics and organised the Home Rule agitation in Andhra.[131] More than this, Mylapore (under the influence of Mrs Besant) allowed them their own provincial Congress committee, which gave them an independent base in the presidency.[132] By 1919, the old Andhra Extremist leadership had been rehabilitated and was now allied to and able to use the Mylapore system of influence. Konda Venkatappayya, for example, became the first man not directly associated with N. Subba Rao to win a Legislative Council election in the Andhra deltas.[133]

The rise of the Prakasam–Venkatappayya faction naturally changed its political complexion. It was no longer in the wilderness but was at the heart of provincial affairs. The creation of a separate Andhra province now would not only sever its excellent connections with Madras city but reduce the scope of its influence. The Andhra

---

[130] To accomplish this, Ramaswami Iyer was converted overnight from a position of publicly stated agnosticism to one of militant Hinduism. Ramaswami Sastri, *Professor Sunderama Ayyar*, pp. 80–6; *Hindu* 4 May 1910, 15 July and 7 September 1916.

[131] Konda Venkatappayya and Pattabhisitaramayya were on Mrs Besant's payroll. 'Statement of Affairs of the Home Rule League, 10 January 1919'. *T.S.A.*

[132] This was run from Guntur town, the headquarters of the Andhra leaders. See K. Venkatappayya to C. P. Ramaswami Iyer, 17 July 1918 in A.I.C.C. Papers. File 2, Part 3, of 1918. *N.M.M.L.*

[133] More correctly, Venkatappayya now was on the Subba Rao – Mylapore network.

agitation was quickly strangled and its organisations used to campaign for a united Indian nation. So suddenly did this *volte-face* take place that many of the younger, student Andhra activists could not understand what was happening:

The heat of the agitation which we set up eight years ago has been extinguished, if not almost extinct. [sic.] I am quite sure that a few more years agitation would get us not only an Andhra Province and an Andhra University but all we desire to have. But we must wake up our leaders before it is too late."[134]

However, with their leaders determined to sleep, and the organisations denied to them, the activists could do nothing. Although Telugu vernacular revivalism continued to grow in importance, the Andhra political movement shrunk to insignificance during the 1920s.

The provincial political controversy which developed out of the reforms of the 1890s had two characteristics. Firstly, whatever the avowed aims and public statements of its participants, their behaviour makes it clear that their ends were to capture or destroy the central points of influence in the bureaucratic–legal–educational machine. Consequently, the formation of parties or groupings among them was factionally determined and the political methods each adopted were conditioned largely by the likelihood of factional success. The Andhra Extremists were prepared to switch into a cultural movement, and to switch out of it again when it became inconvenient. Similarly, in Madras city in 1907 and 1908, T. Rangachari and Kasturi Ranga Iyengar organised and politicised the sentiments of 'the mob' only to abandon them later and to accept nomination to Krishnaswami Iyer's P.C.C. Similarly, again, we might note the conduct of C. Vijayaraghavachari who, in 1907, ran with the All India Extremists, then offered to accept the Allahabad Convention when he believed Krishnaswami Iyer was about to offer him a P.C.C. seat, and only rejected the Convention when he found that Krishnaswami Iyer would not have him.[135] Or again, T. M. Nair, who ditched his European friends for the Extremists in 1909, then went back to them in the Justice Party in 1916. The movements and causes which these politicians so rapidly espoused and divorced were important only as aids to their wider political ambitions. And, indeed, it was only by becoming an aid to advancement that these social or cultural

[134] *Hindu* 1 March 1920.
[135] C. Vijayaraghavachari to P. Kesava Pillai, 7 October 1908. P. Kesava Pillai Papers. *N.M.M.L.*

movements achieved provincial political importance. Once the
Andhra leaders had dropped the Andhra movement, it ceased to carry
any political weight, and once T. Rangachari and Kasturi Ranga
Iyengar had thrown over 'the mob' in Madras city, it too lost its
existence as a political force. The faction-fighting and the battles for
political place at the capital, therefore, were not incidental to the
political system. They were its essence, for it was only by being
drawn into the struggle between participants that broader social and
cultural considerations entered provincial politics.

The second characteristic of the controversy, however, was that
it concerned only the western educated. After magnate interests
had moved from agitational to constitutional methods of representation in the 1890s, they ceased to take part directly in provincial
political organisations. Except in one or two special areas,[136] neither
the Moderate–Extremist confrontation nor, before 1914, the Andhra
movement elicited much response from them. The battle in the
presidency for provincial political control went on over their heads.
The reasons for their non-participation are not difficult to see. Of the
two political functions which the institutions of the bureaucracy, law
and education served, only one had been rendered politically contentious by the reforms of the 1890s. Centralisation and Indianisation
clearly had altered the politics of career in the professions: they had
changed the answer to the vital question of who dictated career
success. In consequence, they had made the provincial politics of the
careers central to most western-educated men. However, the reforms
did not necessarily disturb the other function which the institutions
served – that of linking the capital to structures of local power.
Disturbance to this function would come only if the influence of the
capital were capable of biting into and significantly damaging the
bases of local power and if members of the Indian collaborationist elite
were capable of controlling the influence. Before the 1910s, neither
of these possibilities was real.

In spite of its movement towards greater interference in local
society, Fort St George still did not possess an administrative machine
which could carry its executive decisions deep into the locality. It had
to proceed by means of broad legislative fiat. This meant that it enacted policies which altered the legal framework around such resources
as forests, irrigation rights and rents but did not shift significantly
the level in the framework from which the crucial executive decisions
were to be made. As we have seen from the failure of direct village

---

[136] Namely, Tuticorin and the Andhra delta towns.

officer and other reforms, the Secretariat simply did not have the practical competence to use its own discretion in the execution of policies nor to interfere in the workings of the locality from day-to-day. For services in bending the new laws to fit local circumstance, the local magnate still had to look to the semi-autonomous and malleable local official. The magnate came to Fort St George only to talk about the desirability of a particular policy not about how it should be run on the ground in his own case. Moreover, in these talks it was extremely rare for one magnate, or even one type of magnate, to find himself having to denounce or fight against another. In part, this lack of faction was due to the very process of representation itself: in government tribunals, most of the grievances which were expressed were naturally grievances against government. In part also, it was because Fort St George's drive for efficiency had as yet done no more than sting the magnates in a few sensitive places. They were howling in irritation rather than desperate pain. The government offensive had by no means succeeded in redistributing local power nor even in shaping the circumstances in which a redistribution could take place. In consequence, the relevance of the central government to the struggle for local power was still marginal.

It was these factors which helped to keep the local magnate out of the provincial political battle. The British were willing to concede to Indians a measure of control over the executive institutions but decisions made in these were not, as yet, critical to the locality. However, they were extremely hesitant to allow their subjects a share in the making of legislative policy which, in any case, tended to be directed from London and Calcutta. In consequence, the new Indian constitutional collaborators remained as far outside the actual elaboration of policy as they had ever been. Their continued debilities meant that they still did not hold a power base in government, which they could use at their discretion to harm magnate interests in general or, more importantly, to raise up one magnate against another. As a result, the individual aims and views of particular western-educated men were irrelevant to local magnates who were not faced with having to choose between particular representatives *before* they had been drawn into the Legislative Council or senior bureaucracy. Whoever was elected or co-opted to the centre could be hired *post facto* to put forward the well-known and general grievances of magnate society — about the erosion of *zamindari* political and economic power, taxation and administrative interference. He would be only too pleased to make these representations, which gave him an income and demonstrated to the British his connections with the real rulers of Madras. If he turned down a case, the cost to him was much greater than that to his spurned supporters. And it was a rare day indeed when one of his colleagues could not be persuaded to take the brief in his stead.

The provincial political struggle, therefore, was not about the nature of the interests which were to be represented to the British; it was about who was to earn the money and achieve the prestige which came from carrying out the representation. Most of the greater local magnates could happily sit back, allow the battle to rage and pick the eventual winners. As it happened, Mylapore's stranglehold on the institutions of the law, education and bureaucracy guaranteed its continuing success, and so the magnates, with few exceptions, fell in behind it. However, had Egmore managed to displace it or any had other group seized the centre over its head, it is difficult to see any reason why the magnates should not have worked as easily with the new provincial leadership as they had done with the old.

From the early 1910s, however, this gentle state of affairs began to alter dramatically. The bolts in the government machine were tightened quickly, shifting the balance between local and central power towards the centre and giving Mylapore a new significance. We have seen how important the new institutions of local self-government became at this time, as they drew into themselves many of the functions of government previously exercised autonomously by rural-local bosses and urban magnates. We have seen also how connection to the Secretariat was becoming a valuable prize to the factions who were fighting for control of local boards and municipal councils. This connection was expressed through the decisions of the Local and Municipal Department in Fort St George, which itself was under the supervision of a member of the Governor's Executive Council. In 1909, Lord Morley, continuing the policy of Indianisation which had been started in the 1880s, commanded the Madras Government to appoint a native to its Executive Council. Among the portfolios handed to him was that of the Local and Municipal Department. At first, the Governor was wary of capitulating further to Mylapore and tried desperately to find others who could take the office.[137] But in 1911, the mantle of authority fell on the shoulders of V. Krishnaswami Iyer. He was followed into office by his schoolfriend P. S. Sivaswami Iyer (1911–16) and by the career civil servant P. Rajagopalachari (1916–20) who, although not a member of the inner

[137] He gave it to the Maharaja of Bobbili who, of course, had neither the skill nor the contacts to run it and who resigned after three months.

coterie of Mylapore, was greatly influenced in political matters by the true Mylaporeans C. P. Ramaswami Iyer and R. Ramachandra Rao.[138] Mylapore's advance in other fields was equally marked. Just as Fort St George found itself possessed of the cash and power to begin to use education as a tool of social engineering, so the Secretaryship of the Education Department fell to the Mylaporean R. Ramachandra Rao. From 1915, this Maratha Brahman was put in charge of the execution of policies designed to weaken the Brahman presence in education and government service.[139] Not surprisingly perhaps, the policies met with but limited success. Mylapore was seizing the executive institutions of the centre at the precise point when, for the first time, those institutions began to bear down on the locality.

At this time also, affairs in the institutions of religion were turning towards executive decisions made at the centre and made by Mylapore. Since the 1880s, Mylapore had been calling, almost annually, for some kind of legislation to replace the absurd Act XX of 1863 which kept both the centre of government and itself out of the temples and charitable trusts of the South. But the Government of India's ban on religious legislation prohibited such moves and guaranteed the continued reign of anarchy in these crucial political institutions. A few charitable trusts, however, were under the authority of the Board of Revenue rather than of the law and, as Mylapore's grip on governmental powers grew, it began to show an interest in them. In 1905, for example, Krishnaswami Iyer led an attack on the management of the great Pachayappa's religious and educational charities. He sought to replace the system of co-option through which various Madras city magnates, such as Pitti Thyagaraja Chetty, maintained control of the charity with a system in which trustees were elected by past graduates of Pachayappa's College – western-educated men who were obviously susceptible to Mylapore's influence. Through the intercession of P. S. Sivaswami Iyer, then Legislative Councillor and University Senator, he received partial clearance for his scheme from the Board of Revenue. Henceforth, two members of Pachayappa's board were to be appointed by the University.[140] Not surprisingly, among the first University nominations to the board were C. P. Ramaswami Iyer and L. A. Govindaraghava Iyer.[141] In 1908,

---

[138] 'C.P. on himself' in *C.P. by his Contemporaries*, pp. 17, 20.

[139] See G.O. 1123 (Home, Misc.) dated 23 October 1917. *T.N.A.*

[140] *Hindu* 1, 2 and 15 November 1907; Secretary, Board of Revenue, to P. S. Sivaswami Iyer, 29 October 1907. P. S. Sivaswami Iyer Papers. *N.A.I.*

[141] Tiruvenkataswami, *Pachaiyappa's College, Madras*, p. 85.

reforms to the Civil Procedure Code cleared the way for Mylapore to attack the temples more openly and, through the Dharmarakashana Sabha, of which Sir S. Subramania Iyer was president, we saw that it had considerable success.

Moreover, the Morley–Minto constitutional reforms enlarged both the size and the scope of the Legislative Council. Increased central taxation deepened the involvement of economic magnates in provincial politics and provided department heads with larger budgets which were used to develop areas of political support for the British in Madras society.[142] The Council began to interfere more widely still in the lives of its subjects: Co-operative Credit and Companies' Acts began to change the shape of Indian finance and commerce; the decentralisation of various aspects of the administration – particularly over matters of irrigation, forest conservancy and police organisation – was discussed and agreed among official and non-official Legislative Councillors; radical reforms in the structure of local self-government, the first mooted since those in the old Legislative Council of 1884, were debated and passed; some of the more fundamental factors of the economy, such as labour supply, emigration and working conditions, came under government scrutiny for the first time. Many more of the crucial interests of the presidency's leading local powers were thus touched by the Council's activities and came to need much more vigorous representation than before. To obtain this representation, however, magnates had to deal with Mylapore as an equal, for Mylapore's domination of conciliar representation was by now almost complete. It was virtually impossible for an Indian not connected to Mylapore to develop, in the large general constituencies, an electoral organisation which was capable of putting him in the Legislative Council. The vast patronage swayed by the Mylapore lords materially helped or hindered all candidates' chances of election. Moreover, by using its official powers, Mylapore was able to fill the seats occupied by government nominees with its own men.[143] More important even than these developments, however, was the fact that the leading members of Mylapore had managed

---

[142] Between 1910 and 1919, the Madras Government's income rose from Rs 16.6 *crores* to Rs 25.1 *crores* and its expenditure in the province from Rs 6.4 *crores* to Rs 9.8 *crores*. *Report on the Administration of the Madras Presidency for the year 1910–1* (Madras, 1911), pp. 68–9; *ibid.*, *1919–20*, pp. 78–9.

[143] M. Thiruvenkatachari to P. S. Sivaswami Iyer, 12 May 1912. P. S. Sivaswami Iyer Papers. *N.A.I.*; V. S. Srinivasa Sastri to G. K. Gokhale, 2 February 1912. V. S. Srinivasa Sastri Papers. *N.A.I.*

to scale the heights of Fort St George and enter the policy-making process itself. As Executive Councillors, Advocates-General and full departmental secretaries, they played a vital part in the drafting of the legislation which was restructuring political society. The individual opinion of the successful constitutional collaborator now was of crucial significance to local magnate society for, with Mylapore's triumph, the western-educated community of the capital ceased to consist of a series of readily interchangeable representatives.

Between 1910 and 1920, Mylapore reached its apogee. It monopolised the only political connections between the locality and the centre and used its command of central power to intervene, often with devastating effect, in previously autonomous arenas of local politics. The whole political balance of the presidency was upset. The decision of a P. S. Sivaswami Iyer, a V. Krishnaswami Iyer or a C. P. Ramaswami Iyer could throw a man, whose family might have governed his territory for generations, out of the institutions of local self-government, the temples, the informal offices of government and the advisory committees to which government was passing so many aspects of its administration. It could leave him bare and unprotected in the Legislative Council when his interests were being discussed and arrest him for sedition if he complained. Equally it could give him patronage, office and support and increase his local power.

Of course, Mylapore's position, like that it had inherited from the British, was not totally despotic. It was more powerful than ever before but its power was not unlimited. Like the British government, of which it was part, it needed collaboration in the localities from men who were informally powerful and needed to use the various magnate networks to support its *raj*. Where it put a nonentity into office, he faced either the united opposition of the local magnates, which rendered his position untenable, or he became attached to one or other local power and worked on its behalf. Mylapore's importance lay not in its ability to rewrite local situations as on a blank card but to pick and choose between magnates and to help some to rise above others. Its new portfolios meant that its interests as a patronage broker passed into society at large. P. S. Sivaswami Iyer, for example, aided the local political causes of such men as the Raja of Kollengode in Malabar,[144] the Raja of Kurupam in Vizagapatam[145] and the great Nattukottai Chetty banker Raja Sir S. R. Rm. A. Annamalai

---

[144] V. P. Madhava Raja to P. S. Sivaswami Iyer, 27 July 1919. P. S. Sivaswami Iyer Papers. *N.A.I.*

[145] Kurupam to P. S. Sivaswami Iyer, 3 August 1915. P. S. Sivaswami Iyer Papers. *N.A.I.*

Chetty.[146] The Dharmarakshana Sabha enjoyed the support of many magnates around the temples in which it interfered; indeed, it was usually invited by them to interfere. Its most vigorous advocates included the Raja of Ramnad, whom it helped at Rameswaram temple; the Komati merchant millionaire T. Sitharama Chetty, whose interests in Srirangam temple it forwarded; innumerable Nattukottai Chetties, who picked up temple board seats at its nomination; T. Somasundram Mudaliar, the richest *mirasidar* in Tanjore, whom it supported in litigation against the Pandarasanidhi of Dharmapuram,[147] and the Calivalla brothers, Cunnan and Ramanjulu Chetty, who were millionaires in Madras city.[148] C. P. Ramaswami Iyer, in his desperate fights with P. Thyagaraja Chetty in the Madras Corporation and Pachayappa's charities, was backed by men like the Gujerati banker Lodd Govindoss and the Calivalla brothers, who received many civic decorations and public acclamations from educated society, honorary appointments from government and a share of power in Pachayappa's charities and the Corporation, in return for their support.[149]

Yet, obviously, wherever Mylapore aided a magnate, it also harmed his opponents who were hit by its irresistible force. These opponents soon came to realise that, as they could not contain Mylapore's influence in their localities, they were faced with only two alternative courses of action: either they could seek to make connections of their own to a source of central power which rivalled that of Mylapore or they could alter the narrow institutional connections

---

[146] S. R. Rm. A. Annamalai Chetty to P. S. Sivaswami Iyer, 11 June 1920. P. S. Sivaswami Iyer Papers. *N.A.I.* Other men who profited in local self-government from Sivaswami Iyer's connection were T. Subramania Iyer of Salem, G.O. 513 (L and M, L) dated 14 March 1914; A. Rangaswami Iyer in Madura, P. S. Sivaswami Iyer to Secretary, Local and Municipal Department, 12 May 1912 in G.O. 1074 (L and M, M) dated 12 June 1912; A. Subbarayalu Reddiar in South Arcot, A. Subbarayalu Reddiar to P. S. Sivaswami Iyer, 12 April 1912. P. S. Sivaswami Iyer Papers. *N.A.I.*; and T. T. Viraraghavachari of Chittoor, P. Ramarayaningar to P. S. Sivaswami Iyer, 29 June 1912. P. S. Sivaswami Iyer Papers. *N.A.I.*

[147] *Hindu* 12 October 1915.

[148] *Fourth Year's Report of the Working of the Dharma Rakshana Sabha* (Madras, 1911); *Hindu* 18 October 1915.

[149] For example, C. Cunnan Chetty became a member of the Pachayappa's charities board shortly after the implementation of Krishnaswami Iyer's reforms. In 1918, he resigned with the C. P. Ramaswami Iyer faction following a dispute with P. Thyagaraja Chetty over the distribution of patronage. *Hindu*, 6, 10 and 11 April, 6 and 20 June 1918. See also, A. Subramaniam to P. S. Sivaswami Iyer, 12 December 1916. P. S. Sivaswami Iyer Papers. *N.A.I.*

between centre and locality which gave Mylapore its dominance. Whichever path they followed – and there was no reason why they could not follow both at the same time – they too were lured into participating in the provincial political arena. Mylapore's rise had immeasurably deepened involvement in the provincial political battle for now the interests of most of the important men in Madras, whether they were with Mylapore or against it, were tied to events at the capital. Factionalism around the offices of the centre of government came to extend beyond the small western-educated community which for so long had been the only section of society vitally concerned there. Merchants and landlords, with their huge personal retinues, were dragged into new forms of politics.

6

The vocabulary of communal politics

One result of the growth of the power of Fort St George, therefore, was the elongation of factional linkages. Political connections
now stretched up from the town and village to men who were placed in
the political institutions of the capital. Importantly, however, this
development did not deeply disturb the previous categories of political
existence. Local politicians, although using and abusing central influence, still derived the largest part of their power from the manipulation of local resources. Central politicians, although distributing
a patronage to all sections of society, still derived this patronage from
the manipulation of the offices of Fort St George. Centre and locality
now were linked as never before, but each continued to maintain
its own identity and its own separate personnel. In this sense, although
the political system of Madras had been expanded in scale, it had not
undergone any qualitative change. Parallel to the process of elongation, however, there emerged another and rather different process.
Not only was power at the centre drawn from different sources to
power in the locality and not only was it held by different people but
also it was organised on wholly different principles. As the influence
of the centre rose, so these principles began to impress themselves
on local society and to change the categories in which the activities of
local society had been grouped. The norms of political conduct to be
found at the capital began to become also the norms of local conduct.

Earlier, we discussed the place of caste relationships in the structure of local political society. We saw that localities could be torn apart
by caste confrontations. Class and religious rivalries also were
capable of polarising the elements of local politics: in towns as diverse
as Bellary,[1] Madura[2] and Trichinopoly,[3] for example, deteriorating
trade conditions and municipal maladministration could produce
organisations and strikes among various kinds of merchants and artisans; in areas as distinct and different as Nellore,[4] Salem[5] and Mala-

[1] G.O. 2120 (L and M, M) dated 19 December 1908. *T.N.A.*
[2] Raja Rama Rao, *Sir Subramania Aiyer, K.C.I.E. D.L.*, pp. 12–13.
[3] *Vettikodayan* 23 October 1886. *R.N.P.*; Home Municipalities A June 1888, Nos 28–37. *N.A.I.*   [4] *Hindu* 18 October 1893.
[5] G.O. 353 (Judicial) dated 10 February 1883. *T.N.A.*

bar,[6] economic imbalances and insensitive official policies could provoke Hindu–Muslim rioting. However, as we tried to demonstrate in the case of caste, it would not be possible to argue that, because incidents of 'communal' division took place, the political societies of these areas were structurally divided into 'communities'. Their members certainly possessed class, caste and religious interests, which they would politicise and protect when challenged. But the basic stability of the economy and the inability of the government to penetrate deep into the locality guaranteed that active defence rarely was necessary. The direction in which patronage, economic welfare and authority (in the form of the arbitration of disputes) flowed in everyday life indicates the continuing importance of the cross-communal rural-boss and magnate network: the lines of the political structure were drawn vertically to the social order.

In the last decades of the nineteenth century, however, political organisation in the province began to emphasise increasingly the type of socially horizontal connections represented by caste, class and religion. Caste associations grew in great profusion, organisations of landlords, *zamindars*, traders, factory workers and many other 'classes' were formed, and Christian and Muslim separatist movements appeared on the political stage. South Indian society seemed to be moving towards new principles of political organisation and a new structure of political relationships. Clearly, the causes of this development are complex. They must include such factors as the building of railways, which broadened the linkages of trade and social intercourse, and the growth of the press, which created wider arenas of social perception.[7] The autonomy of the locality was under challenge and, with it, the narrow base of local resource distribution which had kept the patron–client tie so tight. New directions for the flow of resources through society were being established – directions which could follow the lines of 'community' much more closely than before. However, communal activity was beginning to take place on such a grand scale that it is difficult to allow changes of this type alone to have been critical to its emergence. The factors listed above concern alterations promoted by the improvement of communications and affected only groups whose interests involved them in broad territorial connection. They were thus limited to

---

[6] Rebellion and disturbance were endemic among the Moplahs of upland Malabar. See R. H. Hitchcock, *A History of the Malabar Rebellion* (Madras, 1925).

[7] For a such fuller discussion of these points and of the whole matter of the growth of communal politics, see my 'The Development of Caste Organisation in South India, 1880 to 1930' in Baker and Washbrook (eds.), *South India*.

mercantile and administrative groups of overt 'state-level' culture and to those elite groups of 'local-level' culture, which were being drawn into the new regional cultures.

For the vast majority of society, however, still locked in very localised structures of production, trade, administration and authority and in accepted situations of status, changes in the press and the railways made little difference to practical political ambitions and opportunities. Wherever we have examined a town or a rural locality we have found that the immediate resources of the magnate gave him dominance; and, even with the advance of the central administration, contact between a local political unit and the centre of government was carried out through the magnate.[8] It is puzzling, therefore, to find that virtually every caste which could be identified in Madras, wide ranges of businessmen, landlords and workers, Christians, Hindus and Muslims should all be politicising their previously largely apolitical interests and forming associations at or about the same time. Besides local and specific reasons why particular groups should seek socially horizontal alliances, there must have been also general causes in the political system which made it necessary for a much larger section of society to do so.

An initial factor which can help us to understand the emergence of communal politics can be identified in the way that politics at the provincial level, around Fort St George, were coming to be conducted from the 1870s. As we have noted, most of Fort St George's early policies of interference were legislative in character and very general in application. They sought to restructure certain relationships which greater subjects had with the state and with other groups around them. Mercantile profits were taxed for the first time; the economy and politics of the *zamindari* estate were made subject to a better-defined rule of law; the allocation of forests was taken over by the state; in debates on social reform, Hindu, Muslim and specific caste practices were scrutinised.[9] The contentious issues which arose at the provincial level between government and society, therefore, were likely to revolve only around broad categories of economic and social interest: they would concern the interests of 'the merchants', 'the *zamindars*', 'the tenants', 'the cattlebreeders', 'the Hindus' or 'the Nairs'. Importantly, they would not concern individuals: before

[8] That is through the magnate-dominated institutions of local self-government, religion and administration.

[9] Although the Government of India severely restricted Fort St George's ability to legislate on social matters, some issues of social reform were debated in the Legislative Council and a few minor pieces of permissive legislation passed.

the 1910s, the central government was not competent to deal directly with the multi-faceted empires of magnates at the local level. In consequence, provincial politics developed its own peculiar vocabulary in which only interests were ever discussed and, indeed, only those particular interests which had been disturbed by government action. Individual publicists/lawyers/Legislative Councillors may well have been contacted and briefed by individual local magnates but the realities of the representative system were such that the representatives had to submerge the identities of their clients in that of one or other of their interests.

Of course, the extent to which these interests possessed a tangible existence as interest groups was slight. At the local level, they manifested themselves in political action only at rare and infrequent intervals. But even at the provincial level, the occasions when particular magnates came together to sit on a caste, class or religious platform were but moments in their separate kaleidoscopic movements from issue to issue. All magnates had many interests, and their associates in the defence of one could well be their enemies in the defence of another. How would the Velama caste stand when controversies of the day split landlord and tenant?[10] How would merchants stand when laws were proposed which divided Hindu and Muslim? How would Muslims stand when a commission threatened the relationship between factory owners and employees?[11] The politics of interest groups implied the continual fragmentation of interest organisations as the government switched its attack to different economic, social and religious targets.

Amazingly, however, many of the interests which government had defined did begin to solidify into permanent political associations. By the early twentieth century a number of lobbies, among, for example, Madras landholders,[12] South Indian merchants,[13] Nairs[14] and Muslims,[15] had been formed and standing committees had been

---

[10] Included in the category of Velama, which was developed both by the census and the Velama caste association, were the Rajas of Venkatagiri, Kalahasti, Pithapuram, Bobbili and Nuzvid as well as thousands of impoverished peasants.

[11] For example, Muslims provided both the capitalists and most of the labour force in the tanning and cigar-making industries.

[12] Founded 1890, under the impetus of government's *zamindari* legislation.

[13] The Southern Indian Chamber of Commerce, founded 1910 under the impetus of Lord Morley's search for a mercantile 'interest' in the Indian provinces.

[14] The Nair Samajam, founded 1905 under the influence of changes in the way in which the Education Department distributed patronage.

[15] Several minor Muslim associations appeared in the late 1870s and early 1880s under the influence of the Balkan War, constitutional reform, government

set up to keep government constantly aware of the needs of the specific interest. In spite of continuous internecine strife and regular changes of personnel, as various magnates moved in and out of them, these associations developed a concrete political existence. In the process of becoming concrete, however, they transformed into a 'community' the interest which they had been set up to defend. Once a lobby of, say, landlords or Nairs had been turned into a standing association, it ceased to describe a group of men brought and held together in politics only by a common threat (or reward) which an external force was offering them; it described a group which occupied a particular place in the socio-economic or cultural structures of the province. The act of being made permanent shifted the discipline in which the association worked from the historical, in which it explained why it had come together, to the sociological, in which it described the social facts which underlay its unity. The association had to make this shift in order to account for its own permanence, once the issue which had created it had disappeared. By making the shift, however, it began to argue for a whole new theory of Madras politics: its rhetoric was based on the existence of a congruence between categories of political action and categories of common socio-economic or cultural position. That those categories rarely were congruent, and that most members of the association behaved as though they rarely were, were matters which had to be ignored if the association were to remain in business. By the early 1900s, the desire that communal associations should remain in business was felt keenly by at least one significant section of the political world.

Most communal associations owed their birth less to the needs of the magnates, whose views they were supposed to represent, than to the needs of the publicists who represented them. Publicists and Councillors, who carried on the dialogue with government, gained great advantages from the development of communal associations. Given their personally weak political positions, they could only achieve importance, and obtain the funds and support necessary to carrying out their own projects, by acting as the representatives of those who were powerful. But the rise and fall of topics of controversy, and the consequent emergence and disappearance of interest groups, meant that they could not rely on forming lasting attachments to magnate power. Only the men of Mylapore had any guarantee of a

prompting and the rise of the Congress. However, these associations had a spasmodic life and the first solid Muslim association was the Madras branch of the Muslim League which was created to hold dialogue with Lord Morley.

continuing stream of causes; lesser mortals were more at risk. However, the possession of a communal association lent a publicist a firm political base and often money for an income and newspaper. He could work the designated community as a general constituency, constantly propagandising within it even when government was inactive and laying before its members a limitless range of new activities which they might be persuaded to pursue. It is no surprise that most of the class, caste and religious associations which were established at the capital at this time were founded and organised by educated publicists whose own connections to the particular community they were representing were often tangential.[16]

Moreover, there was no reason why a publicist had to wait for the government to begin talking or for a magnate to come to him. By the early twentieth century, Fort St George's proclivities for action were well known and the vocabulary of interest politics had become deeply engrained in the provincial level. It was perfectly possible for publicists to conceive and develop among the magnates areas of communal interest which as yet government had made no move to define. Thus, from 1900 onwards, a plethora of associations appeared, each representing a different community and each trying to build for its creator a political constituency which he could work. Some of the new constituencies were indeed strange for, once the publicity process had got underway, almost every social title or label demarcated a potential constituency, whether it had ever possessed previously a political content or not. In Madras city in 1910, for example, A. C. Parthasarathi Naidu attempted to establish an association of the 'Naidus'. However, Naidu was an honorific applied loosely to a variety of historically and socially separate Telugu castes and it was by no means clear who precisely the Naidus were, let alone what interests they could be said to hold in common. To solve this problem, and to register his association for legal and tax purposes, Parthasarathi Naidu was forced to use the definition of Naidu supplied by the Christian missionary, Dr Browne, in his Anglo-Telugu dictionary.[17]

[16] For example, the Madras Landholders' Association, which represented the greater territorial magnates, was put and held together by Paul Peter Pillai, a Christian lawyer-publicist; by 1917, the association's very active secretary was G. Varadarachari, a teacher. The success of the Madras Muslim League was the work of Yakab Hasan, an Aligarh-educated, Urdu-speaking Muslim who had very little in common with the Tamil-speaking Muslim mercantile elite of the South who formed most of his proclaimed constituents. See *Non-Brahman* 29 April 1917. R.N.P.

[17] *Hindu* 10 June 1910.

The highly creative role of the publicist also can be seen in the bitter controversies which beset most of the more respectable communal associations after they had been established. Often, several rival publicists found themselves in contention for the leadership of a particular community and produced extremely complicated patterns of division within it. By 1917, for example, there were no fewer than five mutually antagonistic associations among the Kammalas (artisans) of the presidency, each claiming the sole right to speak for the caste constituency.[18]

The increasingly independent position of the publicist, as a manufacturer of publicity, began slowly to alter the nature of the patron–client nexus. Certainly, in their early days, caste, class and religious publicists were looking only for ways of attracting the attention and patronage of magnates. But the terms on which they demanded and sometimes obtained this attention began to invert their previously dependent relationship. Once a magnate admitted his membership of a caste or class political community, his conduct would become influenced by the opinions of his caste- and class-fellows. Their views would decide for him the acceptability of a course of action in any given circumstances. As the publicist, through his press and broadcasting activities, had done so much to awaken or create the community, he exercised a large measure of influence over what the views of that community were. He moulded the community's opinion.[19] Hence, he came to possess a position of power over his patrons. By the early 1900s, educated publicists were dedicated to the development of communal politics not only for reasons of employment but also for reasons of power.[20]

[18] See *Addresses Presented in India to His Excellency the Viceroy and the Right Honorable the Secretary of State for India. P.P.* 1918, vol. XVIII.

[19] Particularly over matters of social reform. Many western-educated caste leaders were eager to 'modernise' the rituals of their caste communities and so to create new values in caste behaviour. See, for example, *Hindu* 14 June and 8 July 1910 on the Komati caste conference.

[20] This phraseology may make the process followed by the publicist sound very Machiavellian: he was concerned to create a power base for himself and did not care particularly what issue gave him the base. The phraseology, however, is imposed by the perspective which we have taken: we are interested in the formation of power bases and, from this view, it is immaterial whether the publicist believed in his issue (as some undoubtedly did) or merely used it cynically (as also some undoubtedly did). Perhaps what makes the South Indian communal publicist seem so self-interested is his failure to create his constituencies. The publicist–constituent relationship (which is general to all western democratic polities) is meant to represent a two-way process in which both parties inform and work for each other. But as, before the 1930s at the earliest, most communal publicists

In several previous interpretations of the appearance of communal politics, attention has been concentrated on the forces of
'modernity' acting on supposedly pre-existing identities, particularly
those of caste. It has been argued that economic, social, educative and
political changes, in the later nineteenth and twentieth centuries,
were responsible for creating a new perception of an old identity
and, thus, a new type of caste organisation out of an old one.[21] As
Richard Fox has shown, however, this argument is unsatisfactory
for, apart from the caste label, the points of contact between the
functions of 'old' and 'new' castes were very few indeed.[22] Yet Fox's
own explanation of the phenomenon of the caste association also is
unconvincing. If caste associations represented no more than some
residual 'husk of sentiment' of traditional caste organisation, why did
so many men invest so much time and effort in developing them?
However, if we move away from any attempt to link the caste association to caste but rather look laterally and seek to set it in the context
of the other political institutions of similar type (class and religious
associations) which were growing with it, an explanation becomes
more obvious. Once the founders of caste associations are recognised
not as 'new' Nadars or 'new' Pallis but as men of the western-educated
professions performing an important role in the political system of the
early 1900s, the mystery of the associations rapidly disappears.

Public debate with government was defining political groupings
in a new way; the press and public platform helped to disseminate
these definitions; and professional publicists, whose occupation it was
to mediate between government and society, developed a very strong
interest in the business of dissemination. Changes in language and the
means of communication were altering the political style of the
presidency. That it was these broader changes, rather than anything
to do with the functions of caste *per se*, which produced the caste
association can be seen in the fact that many of the publicists who
organised constituencies of caste were, at precisely the same time,
organising constituencies of class and religion out of different groups
in society. A. C. Parthasarathi Naidu, for example was not only a
Naidu but also a leader of Hindu religious revivalism, a protector

never won the active support of many members of their communities (or at least
never held that support for long), the traffic was very one-way. What the publicist
gained is obvious; but what his constituents got out of the relationship is more
obscure.

[21] See, for example, S. and L. Rudolph, *The Modernity of Tradition.*

[22] R. G. Fox, 'The Avatars of Indian Research' in *Comparative Studies in Society and
History.* XII: 1 (1970).

of mercantile interests, an advocate of Telugu cultural revival and a spokesman of the united Indian nation.[23] As a publicist, he represented several different communities and built up several different constituencies. Other caste organisers, such as Salla Guruswami Chetty of the Komatis, C. R. Reddi of the Reddis and N. G. Ranga of the Kammas were equally multi-faceted: Guruswami Chetty also promoted the interests of revivalist Hindus, of aspiring Indian nationals and of the mercantile community; C. R. Reddi of Andhras, non-Brahmans and the educated; and N. G. Ranga of non-Brahmans and peasants.

Yet, important as were these changes in the vocabulary of politics and in the way that publicists were coming to act, they did not, of themselves, alter greatly the realities of political life and behaviour. The sums of money which communal associations were able to elicit from magnate pockets were always small, and targets for educational trusts (naturally the publicists' most obvious personal interest) and political funds were very rarely met.[24] Magnate patrons would offer and withdraw their support from each type of communal association, depending on which particular community seemed to matter more at which particular time, and even good and loyal patrons were unlikely to devote many of their resources to causes which were peripheral to their continued existence as magnates. Lacking material resources, the publicist was unable to stir the sea of communal opinion which would give him his full political independence and had to remain little more than a paid hack. He was making an impression on only one small area of provincial politics and none at all on the local political level.

Most of the work of constructing a communal political system was completed by Fort St George which not only talked in communal categories but came increasingly to administer and act in them. A perpetual theme of British policy in India was to identify and contact allies in Indian society. While so much of the effective decision-making remained at the lowest level of government, officials on the ground were able to seek out support in local society and to construct their alliances on a face-to-face basis. As we have seen, they tended to associate themselves with the principal local magnates of their area and to use their networks for government. By so doing, they strengthened the cross-communal web of magnate influence. Oc-

---

[23] See, for example, *Hindu* 22 November 1890.

[24] For example, the Kamma conference failed to develop a popular base for fund raising and depended entirely on the occasional contributions of two *zamindars*. *Hindu* 2 August 1915; the Reddi Sangham's financial support was equally limited, see Files 6 and 24 of 1926–7 in C. R. Reddi Papers. *N.M.M.L.*

casionally, however, individual officials, through mistake or ideological parallax, sought to tailor their policies to fit what they saw to be organised political communities of caste, class or religion. Collector Macleane in Salem, with his pro-Muslim policies, was a classic example.[25] These eccentricities clearly were capable of inducing actual communal divisions but, except in the rare cases where they were coherent with the local distribution of resources, the divisions were unlikely to outlast the individuals who had created them.

A consistent direction of communal policies in the presidency could come only from Fort St George which, during most of the nineteenth century, was in a poor position to implement any policies at all. From its very inception, however, the *idées fixes* of many of its members about the nature of Indian society had guaranteed that some features of a communal political system had been encouraged to develop.[26] In their arbitration of Hindu and Islamic social disputes, for example, British law courts had been ordered to defer to the authority of priests and scriptures, rather than of custom, when making their judgments.[27] Naturally, priests and scriptures took a much harder line on the importance of caste and religious divisions than had the more pragmatically orientated rule of local custom. Equally the courts of Fort St George appointed *kazis*, caste headmen and *panchayats* to arbitrate on their behalf in petty cases between members of the same *jati* or faith. These appointments gave legal identities to local sectarian groups, which often might not have possessed them before, and reinforced the power of sectarian authorities, which often had been weak or non-existent before. When Fort St George first published its censuses, after 1881, its need for clear statistical categories led it to outrage caste groups whose *varna* classifications were not consistent with their local status positions. This outrage could manifest itself in the organisation of communal associations which undertook political activities.[28] Moreover, when, through pieces of legislation like the Marriage Act of 1885, Fort St George imposed a statutory unity on the socially diverse Nair caste, it could succeed in drawing much more clearly than before an identifiable communal boundary around the Nairs.

The overall effects of these early policies have been seen by some

---

[25] There were several others, such as Collector Logan of Malabar who had a partiality for Tiyas. *Hindu* 9 and 27 March 1887.

[26] See B. S. Cohn, 'The Census, Social Structure and Objectification in South Asia'. Paper read at Second European Conference on Modern South Asia. Copenhagen.

[27] S. and L. Rudolph, *The Modernity of Tradition*, pp. 251–93.

[28] *Ibid.*, pp. 49–64.

commentators as solidifying caste divisions and, indeed, as promoting competition between caste and religious communities. Undoubtedly, their influence was towards those ends. Yet before 1900, their impact on the fundamental cross-communal structures of political life was very limited. The British law courts handled only a minute fraction of popular disputes; *kazis* and caste headmen could maintain their jurisdictions only when they could persuade disputants to accept their judgments and not seek arbitration from more powerful outsiders; anti-census activity was limited in scale and, of course, sporadic; the Nair Marriage Act was merely permissive and, although it caused controversy while in the Legislative Council, was scarcely utilised by Nairs until the later 1920s.

It was the growth of the power of the capital, particularly from the second decade of the twentieth century, and the consequent penetration of the locality by the political forms of the centre which really set off the chain of reactions which produced modern communal politics. Once its growing administrative competence had elevated it to a provincial political position, Fort St George had to begin planning a strategy to hold its place in the province. Its new powers meant that it was capable of raising provincially organised forces against itself; consequently, it needed to seek out and attach itself to provincially organised forces of loyalty. Yet what would these forces look like and how would they be organised? The highly complex webs of local magnate power could scarcely be seen from the distant Secretariat building and, between 1895 and 1916, the local magnate himself was making no move to participate directly in provincial politics. In Fort St George, the British, although not Mylapore, would have faced countless practical problems in contemplating a strategy based on a series of person-to-person deals with some of their greater local subjects. Moreover, there is little evidence to suggest that they ever did contemplate it. Their intellectual training, whether in the contemporary European social sciences or in Orientalism, taught them to view Indian society as a series of interlocking caste, class or religious blocks.[29] Each block represented a solid, internally organised political community, and politics consisted of achieving balances between the blocks. Even where British senior officials showed themselves more sensitive to the nuances of local reality, they were often befuddled by what they saw. Earlier in their careers, many senior officials had been present during local religious and status confrontations. Some of them preferred to see in these occasional antagonisms

[29] See Cohn, 'The Census, Social Structure and Objectification in South Asia'.

271

the lines which demarcated the political structures of the locality. Whatever the causes, as the provincial centre grew in stature, so an increasing number of its British members began to conceive their task as that of playing off one community, be it of caste, class or religion, against another and of finding the favour of one provincial interest group to match any anger that they might have occasioned in another. To the Madras I.C.S., provincial politics came to mean communal politics.

During the early years of the twentieth century, communal categories crept into a wide variety of administration. Between 1901 and 1918, for example, the number of 'backward castes' listed in the Education Department's Grant-in-Aid Code grew from 42 to a staggering 138 and included, paradoxically, some of the leading landowning and trading castes in the presidency.[30] For the first time, a provincial policy of recruiting government servants by caste was elaborated and implemented by Government Order in 1912.[31] Considerations of community began to affect the Government's choice of University Senators and the Senate's choice of Text Book and Examination Committee members.[32] Even the Famine Code, which had been developing from the 1870s, came to recognise that relief should be distributed as much by caste as by need.[33]

The most important field of communal administration, however, was that related to places in political institutions. Initially, Fort St George was strongly opposed to the Government of India's policies on the introduction of communal safeguards and electorates into the institutions of local self-government and the Legislative Council. In 1882, 1899, 1908 and 1911, it denounced communal representation as unnecessary and creative of a social divisiveness which did not then exist in South India.[34] Given the fact that, in so many other areas of administration, the Madras Government already possessed communal categories, it is difficult to understand the violence of its

---

[30] *Grant-in-Aid Code of the Madras Education Department for 1901–2; ibid., for 1918–19. T.N.A.*

[31] G.O. 1561 (Public) dated 19 December 1912. *T.N.A.*

[32] G.O. 187 (Education) dated 29 February 1912; G.O. 22 (Public) dated 21 January 1918. *T.N.A.*

[33] *Report on the Famine in the Madras Presidency during 1896 and 1897* (Madras, 1898), II, 26–8.

[34] *Report of the Committee on Local Self-Government in Madras. 1882* (Madras, 1883), p. 43; Letter No. 7 (Legislative), Government of Madras to Government of India dated 31 January 1899 in Home Public A July 1899, Nos 16–21. *N.A.I.*; Home Public A October 1908, Nos 116–46. *N.A.I.*; G.O. 616–17 (L and M, L) dated 27 April 1908. *T.N.A.*; G.O. 916 (L and M, L) dated 12 July 1911. *T.N.A.*

opposition to the Government of India's proposals – except, perhaps, that they were the Government of India's proposals and that, by objecting to the details, Fort St George hoped to avoid having to implement any policy of constitutional devolution at all. Be that as it may, the Madras Government was forced by the fiat of Calcutta to nominate representatives of 'the landlords' and 'the Muslims' to its early Legislative Councils and to create communal electorates for these categories under the Morley–Minto reforms. In the wake of the reforms, however, Fort St George changed its attitude dramatically and of its own volition began to support communal interests. It freely nominated caste and class representatives to the Legislative Council,[35] insisted to Edwin Montagu that the non-Brahmans of its province should be protected by separate electorates,[36] and introduced communal machinery into the municipalities and district boards.[37]

The conversion of the Madras Government to policies of active communal discrimination was the prime factor in the development of communal politics. It laid a cement of patronage and possible favour around particular connections of interest, which before may have been of no more than occasional political importance. By extending its 'provincial' notions of community to the locality, through places on local boards, grants to schools and employment opportunities, it began to shape local organisations of resource distribution to the provincial model. Men obtained positions of power and social advantage not because they were wealthy or related to men of wealth but because they were Muslims, tenants or Kammalas. The criterion of community had never been so exclusively important in the past. Inevitably, this meant that magnates began to lose some of their economic and arbitrational functions. Potential dependents, seeking security or help, were presented with an increasingly viable alternative to submission to the magnate.

The extent to which this alternative was being taken up before 1920, however, ought not to be overestimated. The expansion of the magnate structure to reach Mylapore was having the effect of 'localising' the conduct of provincial politics faster than certain British civilians could 'provincialise' the locality. Debates at Fort St George were beginning to turn on the character of particular individuals with greater speed than local debates were turning on the character

[35] A representative of the Nattukottai Chetties was nominated in 1910 and of the *panchamas* in 1917.

[36] See below pp. 294–6.

[37] By reserving seats for members of the depressed castes and minority religious interests.

of interests. Indeed, even the British recognised this. Their political system was being built on two contradictory principles of representation – the indirect system of Mylapore and the magnate, and the direct system of community. When the two principles clashed, they always deferred to the indirect, whether of the secretive Mylapore variety or of the general constituencies in the Montagu–Chelmsford Councils, which outnumbered the communal constituencies. Their subjects concurred in this deference.

The case of the non-Brahmans

Space prohibits us from investigating the effect of the two general factors – the rise of the publicist and government policy – on the many caste, class and religious political movements of these years. By the examination of one, the non-Brahman movement which can be seen first at the provincial level from about 1912, it is hoped, however, to illustrate significant features of them all. To our interpretation the political division of society into Brahman and non-Brahman makes no obvious sense. Certainly there were status and some cultural differences between the two but status and cultural divisions are not necessarily political divisions, and the occasions, before 1912, when they had become so were very few in number. This lack of antagonism is not surprising when it is remembered that Brahmans supplied status legitimacy to most of the groups of state-level culture but had little contact, and were ignored, by the vast majority of local-level cultural groups;[38] nor when it is recalled that even in their contacts with most other state-level groups, Brahman priests were usually poor dependents who either did what they were told or starved.[39] As most contemporaries remarked, the non-Brahman or, more properly, anti-Brahman movement from 1912 was a new political development and not the continuation by other means of a supposed two thousand year politico-cultural feud.

Moreover, in the political domain itself, it would be extremely difficult before 1912 to separate out a specific Brahman power from a specific non-Brahman power. Brahmans, in their many guises, could be found in almost every position in the networks of the local magnates, most of whom were non-Brahmans. However strongly Brahmans may have wished to operate together (and their constant familial, sub-caste, regional and sectarian feuding makes it clear that they hardly wished to at all), the structure of resource distribution was

[38] See Back, *Peasant Society in Konku.*
[39] See, for example, the account of a dispute between Brahman priests and their Komati patrons in Masulipatam in *Hindu* 31 July 1907.

such that, except in a few localities of Tanjore and Malabar, nowhere could they form a viable, exclusive magnate network of their own. Across the presidency, they performed various tasks for various magnates, were closely related in political action to large numbers of non-Brahmans and in no way existed inside a functioning, political 'Brahman' unit.

The problems of explaining the rise of the non-Brahman movement, therefore, are very great. Not only is it necessary to account for the timing of the phenomenon but also it is necessary to give meaning to the notion of the political Brahman which, before the movement began, would have been incomprehensible to most contemporaries. Let us first examine critically one or two of the arguments which have been put forward before to explain the politics of non-Brahmanism. In a recent book, E. F. Irschick has sought to relate the emergence of the movement to the growth of literacy among higher non-Brahman castes. This, he argues, led to a growing resentment at the monopoly of government office and public life enjoyed by Brahmans.[40] In our terminology, it represented not so much an attack on Brahman political power as pressure on those occupations and positions in magnate networks (particularly those concerned with service) which Brahmans filled in large numbers. The pressure was derived from changes in the composition of the educated community. However, a careful examination of educational development and its significance indicates that this view is difficult to substantiate. The spread of English education among non-Brahman groups was not great and there is no evidence that, before 1920, it had produced a shift in the social pattern of learning. In first- and second-grade colleges, the proportion of Brahman to non-Brahman students was 3.5:1 in 1890 and 3.5:1 in 1918.[41] Obviously, between the two dates, the absolute numbers of students had increased, although, given the changing circumstances, not by very much.[42] In 1890, when most appointments to the government service had been made in the locality, there was much less need than in 1918 for college qualifications. Service aspir-

---

[40] Irschick, *Politics and Social Conflict in South India*, p. 17.

[41] English education, rather than vernacular education, was essential to gaining access to the professions and public life. Consequently, only changes in English education are relevant to Irschick's main argument. *Report on Public Instruction in the Madras Presidency for 1890–1* (Madras, 1891), Subsidiary Tables, pp. 1–2; *ibid., for 1918–19.* (Madras, 1919), II, 2–3. Brahmans represented 67 per cent of university graduates in 1890 and 67 per cent in 1918. G.O. 22 (Public) dated 21 January 1918. *T.N.A.*

[42] From 2863 in 1890 to 6818 in 1918. *Report on Public Instruction in the Madras Presidency for 1890–1*, Subsidiary Tables, pp. 1–2; *ibid., for 1918–19*, II, 2–3.

ants orbited the office of the *huzur sheristidar* who did not run competitive examinations. With the new role of the central government,
higher standards of education came to be demanded and all aspirants
had to go to school. This development alone would surely account
for most of the rise of 150 per cent in the number of first- and
second-grade students: it is not necessary to imagine the involvement of new social groups in higher education. Moreover, government
appointments in the higher grades and court litigation were expanding
fast enough to meet the minimal job ambitions of most of the educated.
There was no serious problem of graduate unemployment, such as was
emerging in Bengal.[43] Perhaps the clearest indication that the pressure
of new non-Brahman groups on the services and professions was
mythical, however, is provided by the behaviour of the Justice Party
(the non-Brahman communal party) and the government themselves.
The Justice Party never argued for the creation of 'fair' competition to allow qualified non-Brahmans the chance to break up a
Brahman monopoly. It demanded a dropping of educational standards
and the building of closed social categories of recruitment to be filled
by non-Brahmans whether they were qualified and competent or
not.[44] It wanted government to promote the growth of an educated
non-Brahman community not simply to recognise the existence of one
which had grown already. Further, in spite of agreeing to these
closed categories, Fort St George in fact found itself having to recruit
ever more Brahmans, for suitable non-Brahmans did not come forward to take the proffered jobs.[45] Indeed, the vast majority of district
Collectors told Fort St George that they could not find many non-
Brahmans who were interested in government employment.[46]

Equally, although the spread of vernacular literacy among higher
non-Brahman castes was prodigious, it cannot be argued that this,
of itself, led to a challenge to the Brahman.[47] Some reason must be
shown why vernacular literacy should produce anti-Brahmanism and
some evidence must be found that the new channels of communication, opened up by increased literacy, were important in propagating

[43] Between 1900 and 1920, the number of gazetted posts and of non-gazetted posts
worth more than Rs 100 p.m. increased by about 80 per cent. The number of non-
gazetted posts worth between Rs 35 and Rs 100 p.m. increased by 160 per cent.
Indian Statutory Commission (H.M.S.O., 1930), vi, Appendix A, pp. 607–13.

[44] See *Justice* 1 March and 5 April 1917. *R.N.P.*

[45] Brahmans held a higher proportion of government appointments worth more than
Rs 100 p.m. in 1927, after six years of Justice Party government, than they had
done in 1900. *Indian Statutory Commission*, vi, Appendix A, pp. 607–13.

[46] G.O. 1157 (Public) dated 3 August 1915; G.O. 1123 (Home, Misc.) dated 23
October 1917; G.O. 986 (Revenue) dated 30 April 1920. *T.N.A.*

[47] *Census of India. 1921. Madras. Volume XIII. Part 2* (Madras, 1922), p. 128.

anti-Brahmanism. On this latter point, such evidence as there is available negates the argument. The vernacular newspapers of the militant anti-Brahman Justice Party were uniform failures.[48] The most successful vernacular newspapers were those which supported the more extreme activities of the Congress and were run by or in association with Brahmans.[49]

A second explanation tentatively offered by Irschick is that the Brahman/non-Brahman polarisation was produced by religious and cultural revivalism, particularly among the Tamilians, which led to attacks on the Brahmans as Aryan invaders, whose Sanskritic culture and Vedantic religion had destroyed the Tamil and Saiva Siddhanta basis of Southern civilisation.[50] Once more, as a causal explanation, this does not stand up to scrutiny. In the late nineteenth and early twentieth century, the cause of vernacular revivalism was aided at least as much by Brahmans as by non-Brahmans. The patronage networks which made the revival possible consisted often of the very same men whether the cause was the regeneration of Tamil or the study of Sanskrit, the development of the philosophy of Advaita or of Saiva Siddhanta.[51] The Mylapore group in the University Senate were the strongest advocates of enhancing the status of vernacular studies;[52] they also founded the Madras Sanskrit College.[53] Indeed a direct connection between cultural and political change begins to look most extraordinary when we realise that T. M. Nair, who abhorred Indian civilisation, was a leader of the non-Brahman movement;[54] that many Justice Party leaders could barely speak or write their

[48] The *Dravidan* and *Andhraprakasikha* failed to establish themselves as dailies and, by 1919, were only weekly publications. *Hindu* 9 August 1917; A. C. Parthasarathi Naidu to A. Campbell 23 April 1919 in G.O. 932 (Home, Misc.) dated 24 May 1919. *T.N.A.*

[49] Particularly, *Desabhaktan, Swadesamitran* and *Andhrapatrika*.

[50] Irschick, *Politics and Social Conflict in South India*, pp. 275–308.

[51] For example, J. M. Nallaswami Pillai was a scholar both of Sanskrit and of Tamil. Balasubramaniam, *The Life of J. M. Nallaswami Pillai*, pp. 10, 64–72; V. Krishnaswami Iyer patronised Sanskrit and Tamil Poetry. P. Mahadevan, *Subramania Bharati, Poet and Patriot* (Madras, 1957), pp. 48–9 and A. S. Balasubramania Iyer to V. Krishnaswami Iyer, 5 December 1906. V. Krishnaswami Iyer Papers. *N.A.I.*; the Nattukottai Chetties, the Raja of Ramnad, the Nuzvid *zamindars* and the major Komati families of Andhra patronised both vernacular and Sanskrit revivalism.

[52] *Hindu* 10 and 15 March 1913; P. S. Sivaswami Iyer to M. Ramaswami Iyer, 29 March 1904. P. S. Sivaswami Iyer Papers. *N.A.I.*

[53] A. S. Balasubramania Iyer to V. Krishnaswami Iyer, 5 December 1906. V. Krishnaswami Iyer Papers. *N.A.I.*

[54] He and C. R. Reddi, another Justice Party publicist, were opponents in the Senate of the expansion of vernacular education. *Hindu* 10 and 15 March and 1 May 1913.

vernacular; and that the party relied very little on the vernacular for propaganda.

Equally, it would be impossible to connect the non-Brahman movement of 1912 to the anti-religious Tamil Self-Respect movement of the later 1920s, as has been attempted by Robert Hardgrave.[55] The Self-Respect movement rested on the support of those elements of local-level culture which were slowly being drawn into the new regional level cultures. However, in the 1910s, these elements were scarcely out of their localities and barely conscious of their future identity. If they related to provincial politics at all, it was more as members of transactional magnate networks than as bearers of a new ideology. Men who later were involved with Self-Respect could be found on both sides of this Brahman/non-Brahman controversy. Indeed, the leader of Self-Respect, E. V. Ramaswami Naicker, was a staunch Congressman whose political contacts were largely with Brahmans.[56] Such cultural debate as there was between 1912 and 1920 was among groups of emphatic state-level culture and did not touch groups of a different orientation. When, from the 1920s, the Self-Respect movement began to emerge, it attacked all groups of state-level culture, Brahman and non-Brahman alike, and thus made enemies of the high-caste leaders of the non-Brahman movement of the earlier period.[57] In social composition, practical aims and doctrine, the non-Brahman and Self-Respect movements were as different as chalk and cheese. The only connection is that they were both anti-elite movements, although not even against the same elite.

The relationship of the non-Brahman political movement to the Sat-Sudra vernacular and religious revival, which was present at this time, was, in fact, very similar to the relationship between Hindu revivalism and the Congress in its agitational periods and between Telugu revivalism and the demand for a separate Andhra province. Cultural movements, logically independent of politics, were dragged into political life because they provided a pre-existing organisation which was valuable in raising manpower. T. V. Kalyanasundram Mudaliar, a student of Saiva Siddhanta and virtually the creator of modern Tamil journalism, was prominent in many Madras city revivalist associations and was on close terms with many Brahmans. He has recorded how, from 1915, non-Brahman agitators began to invade his *sabhas* to preach cultural revolution against the Brahman

---

[55] See R. L. Hardgrave, *The Dravidan Movement* (Bombay, 1965).
[56] See C. J. Baker, 'Noncooperation in South India' in Baker and Washbrook (eds.), *South India.*
[57] See Baker, *Politics in South India 1920 to 1937*, ch. 3.

in the hope of stirring support to their political cause.[58] His own reaction, which was disgust and resignation from the associations, was mirrored in the attitude of many other revivalist leaders, who had been and remained friends with many similarly interested Brahmans.[59]

Both the explanations from educational change and cultural revival presuppose that the non-Brahman movement reflected deep-seated changes in the organisation of society. Non-Brahmans, whether through the influence of new educational opportunities or through the influence of new cultural perceptions, were coming to throw off the Brahman yoke. Yet what is most noticeable about Madras, even through the years of rabid anti-Brahman propaganda, is the continuing social stability. The *jajmani* system, by which deference was shown to Brahmans, was not broken in any significant way: rich non-Brahmans continued to rebuild temples, to found Sanskrit colleges and to support and feed Brahmans. The Justice Party, when looking for votes rather than trying to raise noisy agitations, was fully aware of this. In 1920, its leaders undertook a prolonged tour of the presidency and desperately tried to disassociate their movement from any attack on the spiritual prerogatives of the Brahman. They argued that their challenge was solely towards the secular, political position which Brahmans had attained.[60] Yet, once the Brahman's spiritual role has been stripped from him, how can he remain a Brahman in any meaningful sense? What the Justice Party really objected to was the political position of certain individuals who happened to be Brahmans. Of course, the men they objected to were the men of Mylapore.

Let us try to reconstruct the non-Brahman movement in the light of our general inquiry into the growth of communal politics. The leaders of the movement, that is to say the people who created it, require a careful analysis, for in their ambitions must lie its causes. In nearly every case, the principal propagandists and apologists of the campaign were men drawn from families with generations of involvement in the government service and the professions behind them. Typical examples are provided by Koka Appa Rao Naidu and Tikkani Balijarao Naidu, who came from Andhra families with service records dating

---

[58] T. V. Kalyanasundram Mudaliar, *Valkkai Kurippugal* (Madras, 1969), pp. 596–9 (Tamil).

[59] Neither S. S. Bharati nor Swami Vedachelam, two of the leaders of Tamil revivalism, would have anything to do with the political non-Brahman movement until after 1920, when it had become the government.

[60] See report of P. Thyagaraja Chetty's speech at Salem in *Hindu* 11 June 1920; also *Hindu* 13 May 1920.

back to at least the 1860s,[61] Arcot Ramaswami Mudaliar, whose family had a massive presence in the Chingleput bureaucracy,[62] and B. Muniswami Naidu, whose family had administered the estate of the Raja of Karvetnagar for centuries.[63] There is no sign that these men represented any new social force in Madras; they had been produced as much by the early service policy of the British as had their Brahman service family equivalents. Before about 1912, there is no sign either that they saw themselves as a corporate group of non-Brahmans. They were drawn from several regional caste groups, operated as 'castes' only through kin and personal contacts and worked in local and provincial political structures with Brahmans.[64] What factors not only brought them together but also brought them together as non-Brahmans?

The answer to the first question is, of course, the centralisation of control over the professions at Madras city. All members of the western-educated community now were placed in the same career structure and single lines of division between them could split the presidency. That these lines might come to mark a Brahman/non-Brahman division is suggested by a common grievance which all educated non-Brahmans shared against Brahmans. Their accredited social position was disproportionately low for, although they were performing the same secular roles as Brahmans, they were seldom accorded the same ritual and social prestige. Niggling complaints against

---

[61] The 'Koka' and 'Tikkani' Audi–Velama families intermarried and also served the Hyderabad state. *Hindu* 26 March 1920. See *History of the Services of Gazetted and Other Officers in the Civil Department in the Madras Presidency, Corrected to 1st July 1885* (Madras, 1885); also, Sastri (ed.), *Encyclopaedia of the Madras Presidency*, p. 525.

[62] So massive that when Ramaswami Mudaliar stood for election to the Legislative Council in a Chingleput constituency, the Chingelput D.C.C. petitioned government to remove his relatives from the district bureaucracy. *Hindu* 3 July 1920.

[63] Kotta Bhaviah Chowdary, *A Brief History of the Kammas* (Sangamjagarlamudi, 1955), p. 90. Of other prominent non-Brahman leaders, T. M. Nair's family had a long history of service in Malabar, N. Gopala Menon, *A Short Sketch of the Life of Dr T. M. Nair* (London, 1920); K. V. Reddi Naidu's family had served the East India Company in the eighteenth century and spent most of the nineteenth century in the Kistna police department, Subba Rao, *Life and Times of Sir K. V. Reddi Naidu*.

[64] For example, B. Muniswami Naidu and A. Ramaswami Mudaliar had been apprenticed to Brahman *vakils*; K. V. Reddi Naidu and T. Ethiraja Mudaliar were prominent Congressmen until about 1915; P. Sivagnana Mudaliar and V. Tirumalai Pillai (both lawyers) worked on the Madras Corporation in the faction containing the Brahman K. C. Desikachari; L. K. Tulsiram, a Sourahstra lawyer from Madura, worked on his municipal council in the faction of K. V. Ramachari, a Sourashtra dye-merchant, who also used several Brahman lawyers.

Brahman arrogance, which no doubt could have been heard in separate localities before, began to creep into the provincial press.[65] The importance of this union of complaint, however, ought not to be overemphasised. It is not necessary to like someone in order to work with him, and most of the people who were making the complaints in fact were working with Brahmans and were tied to the same magnate networks as Brahmans. Antipathetic sentiment of itself could not make the non-Brahman movement unless it were provided with a new political structure in which to operate.

The first part of this structure was erected by the rise of the publicist. Most of the family groups of educated non-Brahmans were socially isolated from the non-educated masses of their particular caste communities. Their kin organisations, used for the distribution of service patronage rather than for land control or local power, were of a different shape.[66] Their culture was state-level whereas that of most of their caste was local-level. In many cases, their ritual practices bordered on the heterodox.[67] In each of their castes, they formed a microscopic minority which had severed most of its points of contact with the rest of its caste community. During the last years of the nineteenth century, however, as the new vocabulary of provincial politics, in which broad notions of caste played so large a part, began to emerge, these educated non-Brahman families were given a strong incentive to reverse their courses. Caste, at least the idea of caste as a status interest group, was a viable political constituency which every publicist-politician could profit from working and, indeed, which only the most successful could afford to ignore. In attempting to translate the highly complex and ambiguous perceptions of caste which most of the indigenous population possessed into the neat categories of the provincial political system, the non-Brahman publicist was inevitably drawn into conflict with the Brahman's spiritual prerogatives.

If the caste system can be characterised at all, it can be only as

<hr>

[65] See particularly, S.K.N., *Non-Brahmin Letters* (Madras, 1915).

[66] Educated service families within a caste tended to seek out and marry each other rather than developing alliances with illiterate but wealthy families. This meant that their own marriage networks tended to be much broader than those of the rest of their 'peasant' caste communities. See, for example, the Koka–Tikkani alliance in *Hindu* 26 March 1920.

[67] For example, C. Sankara Nair's advocacy of Nair marriage reform and other social reforms made him extremely unpopular among West Coast Nairs. I am grateful to Dr Susan Lewandowski of Amherst College for this information. Also, the Koka and Tikkani families, and several other educated Audi–Velama families in Andhra, were Brahmo Samajists.

a system of social hierarchy validated by the tenets of the Hindu religion as interpreted by Brahmans. And although Aryan Hinduism may not have plunged very deeply below the state-level in most of South India, it certainly affected, in one way or another, many of the rich men (the local magnates) in Madras. Magnate wealth and splendour were often expressed through expenditure on objects of orthodox Hindu piety, and magnate-driven upward social mobility movements often took the form of attempts to raise an accredited *varna* position. The social models which magnates tended to emulate were, if not actually Brahmanic, at least placed within a Brahman-dominated hierarchy.

Clearly, however, the non-Brahman professional publicist who was trying to build an independent position for himself as a caste leader would have to break this dependence on the good graces of an external social group. He could not lead his caste, as the autonomous political community fighting against other autonomous political communities which it was supposed to be, while its more prominent members were deferring to the authority of outsiders. He had to be anti-Brahman, or at least anti-Vedic, if he were to make the constituency his own. Consequently, from the turn of the century, western-educated Nairs, Kammas, Telagas and Audi-Velamas could be seen organising within their castes campaigns to eradicate the use of Brahman priests and of Vedic practices.[68]

The extent to which this element of politico-cultural antagonism was a primary cause of the events of 1912 to 1920, however, is highly debatable. The number of caste publicists who were affected by it was always very small. Most were too socially conservative to employ a tactic which committed them to advanced social reform; they preferred to concentrate on obtaining material rewards for their caste and to leave unanswered the questions of what this caste actually represented and why it was there. Others were rapidly disconcerted by the hostility which the vast majority of orthodox magnates expressed towards reform, and dropped the anti-Brahmanic elements of propaganda before the magnates dropped them. In consequence, by no means all the publicists who were working the caste issue among non-Brahman groups rallied to the anti-Brahman flag. Indeed, in 1916, when Madras political society divided into pro- and anti-Brahman camps, most found themselves on the pro-Brahman side.[69]

[68] See Ranga, *Fight for Freedom*, pp. 27–8.

[69] For orthodox resistance to caste reform in the case of the Komatis, see *Hindu* 14 June and 7 July 1910; also, Darsi Chenchayya, *Nenu Na Desamu* (Vijayawada, 1952) (Telugu).

Moreover, the leadership of the greater anti-Brahman movement did not consist of men who had a long history of reformist activity within their own specific caste communities. Neither P. Thyagaraja Chetty nor A. Ramaswami Mudaliar nor B. Muniswami Naidu had shown much interest in caste politics before the rise of the movement, and Thyagaraja Chetty was better known as a staunch defender of Brahman spiritual prerogatives. Thus, while recognising the importance of caste-reformist ideology to a few supporters of the non-Brahman cause, it would not be possible to explain the rise of that movement by reference to caste reform alone, or even in the main.

The second and more important prop of the new political structure was direct government policy. Logically and historically, the non-Brahman movement began with government action. During the nineteenth century, the British were keenly aware of the dangers of allowing their administration to pass under the control of local family networks and, in 1851, the Board of Revenue passed orders prohibiting the employment of members of the same family in the same office. This measure seems straightforward and sensible but British notions of kin, caste and rule were not as clear as those of modern anthropologists and the order, in fact, confused family with caste to the extent of not permitting members of the same caste to serve in the same office.[70] Of course, the order was ignored but its spirit was occasionally revived by Collectors who, feeling themselves to be the victims of caste conspiracies, suddenly sacked members of one caste group and set out to recruit members of another. As Brahmans were by far the most literate of ritual communities, they naturally filled most of the government posts, and an attack on any district's dominant office clique was likely to be followed by the appearance of notices in the district gazette offering places to men who were not Brahmans.[71]

This did not matter much while it was the result of only Collectorate activity and although, as early as 1886, Fort St George's attention was drawn to the social composition of its services, it remained unmoved.[72] But centralisation of the bureaucracy rapidly altered the significance of communal calculations. Office conspiracies now could control not only a district but the entire province and British civilians were determined to prevent the formation of the caste cliques which they thought managed such conspiracies. In

[70] Board of Revenue, Standing Order 128(2).
[71] For examples, see *Hindu* 11 May 1909; *Desabhimani* 16 February 1907; *Sadhvy* 1 June 1910; *Kistnapatrika* 26 February 1916. *R.N.P.*
[72] G.O. 386–7 (Education) dated 27 July 1887. *T.N.A.*

1903, for example, Lord Ampthill, and everybody else in Madras, knew that the obvious successor to Sir Bashyam Iyengar on the High Court bench was V. Krishnaswami Iyer. But he gave the post to C. Sankara Nair because 'he is not a Brahmin'[73] and Krishnaswami Iyer, like the three previous native High Court Judges, was. The rise to prominence of Mylapore greatly increased the desire of many civilians to support people who were not Brahmans. Although they recognised Mylapore's usefulness, they were wary of allowing it too much power, for collaborators who have become indispensable are worse than enemies. As the Mylapore leaders were all Brahmans, and as the senior civilians do not seem to have concerned themselves with anything but superficial appearances, they naturally thought that Mylapore could be weakened by introducing non-Brahmans into key posts. Perhaps the greatest proponent of this argument was Sir Alexander Cardew, whose evidence to the Public Services Commission was loaded with vitriol against Brahman literati,[74] and who was very active in providing non-Brahman service families with a private channel to government.[75] In 1912, under his influence, the Secretariat produced its first positive directive on using the Brahman/non-Brahman division as a criterion for making appointments.[76] By 1918, it had gone on to insist on the keeping of separate lists of Brahman and non-Brahman candidates and had ordered its officers to appoint the latter first.[77] The Secretariat had created an interest in being non-Brahman, which cut across the existing structure of patronage.

The responsiveness of the educated community to the recruitment and promotion policies of its major employer was, not surprisingly, very considerable. As early as 1886, when Fort St George had first shown an interest in the communal composition of the provincial services, non-Brahman demands for special privileges had reached the press.[78] Fort St George's decision not to act, however, killed this campaign which, in any case, came too early in the process of administrative centralisation to have stirred a provincial following. The rebirth of government interest in the communal problem in the

[73] Lord Ampthill to Lord George Hamilton, 8 April 1903. Ampthill Papers. *I.O.L.*
[74] Evidence of A. G. Cardew in *Royal Commission on the Public Services in India.* Appendix II, 104–16. *P.P.* 1914, vol. XXI.
[75] G.O. 1616 (Home, Misc.) dated 6 August 1917. *T.N.A.*
[76] G.O. 1561 (Public) dated 19 December 1912. *T.N.A.*
[77] G.O. 19 (Home, Misc.) dated 6 January 1920; G.O. 986 (Revenue) dated 30 April 1920. *T.N.A.*
[78] Anon., *The Ways and Means for the Amelioration of the Non-Brahman Races.*

1910s provoked a much fiercer reaction. In 1912, the same year as the first communal Government Order, a Dravidian Association was set up in the city by a group of non-Brahman government servants and lawyers.[79] Over the next four years it repeatedly petitioned the government to treat non-Brahmans as a special category and to provide reserved posts and scholarships for them.[80] From 1916, when Mylapore went *en masse* into the Home Rule League, spokesmen of the non-Brahman cause were nominated to the Legislative Council and proffered favours by the British to denounce the Home Rule League as a Brahman conspiracy.[81] Non-Brahmanism became for a time synonymous with anti-nationalism – a fact which surely indicates its origins as a product of government policy.

While every non-Brahman had an interest in the non-Brahman category, however, a great many also had contacts and connections with Brahmans, which they wished to preserve and enlarge. The non-Brahman movement, even among 'service' groups, was divided in a thousand ways. The most militant communalists, naturally, were those whose political contacts were weak. Typical of them were men like T. Ethiraja Mudaliar[82] and V. Tirumalai Pillai,[83] city lawyers who had been begging for office for years but never getting it, and T. M. Nair, who was repeatedly beaten in elections. In fact, T. M. Nair's career amply illustrates just how new and opportunistic this non-Brahman combination was. Not only had he, in 1909, been closely associated with Brahmans in the Extremist attack on Mylapore but in 1912, before the communal issue had any general currency, the evidence he had given to the Public Services Commission had been used by the Brahman press to illustrate that Sir Alexander Cardew's evidence on the Brahman hegemony did not mean that non-Brahmans were communally prejudiced: T. M. Nair had not mentioned the Brahman problem once.[84] Those non-Brahmans who were well placed with Brahman agencies and in the old network politics were distinctly cool to the movement when it turned from a simple patronage request into a crusade to destroy Brahman influence. P. Kesava Pillai, for example, an Anantapur lawyer who had served the

[79] *Justice Party Golden Souvenir*, p. 257.
[80] Its most celebrated petition was *The Non-Brahman Manifesto*, see *Hindu* 20 December 1916.
[81] See below pp. 294–6.
[82] 'Ethiraja Mudaliar is a prominent Madras lawyer but where are his Judgeships?' *Non-Brahman* 17 December 1916. *R.N.P.*
[83] V. Tirumalai Pillai to P. S. Sivaswami Iyer, 10 May 1912. P. S. Sivaswami Iyer Papers. *N.A.I.*
[84] *Hindu* 5 April 1913.

Moderate Congress in 1908 and was a Legislative Councillor, came out as a leading opponent of T. M. Nair-style non-Brahmanism and preached co-operation with the Brahman.[85] Further, when the movement was used by the British to promote loyalty and to oppose Home Rule League demands for constitutional reform, non-Brahmans who were powerful in the administration and who stood to gain by reform, rapidly dropped off the communal bandwagon. C. Sankara Nair bitterly attacked the mendicancy of the movement which once he had supported, and his evidence given to Parliament in 1919 is practically indistinguishable in sentiment from that of C. P. Ramaswami Iyer.[86]

Of course, the non-Brahman movement soon expanded beyond the narrow world of the western educated. A great many local magnates were pressed into offering it their support. As we shall see later, however, few of them were to join because of an ideological commitment to the caste cause; rather they came to it because it formed a factional alternative to Mylapore at the centre. But in its earliest phases the movement belonged only to the western educated and was in kind precisely like the Extremist and Andhra movements – a campaign by professionals and publicists who were 'out' to put themselves 'in'. Its origins need not be sought deeply in the cultural history of South India; they lie much more in the very novel types of government and politics which developed under the British in the early years of the present century.

Our analysis of the emergence of the non-Brahman movement reveals three important points which are relevant to all the communal movements of the period. Firstly, the language of the movement was closely related to the language of government. In 1908, for example, when the Morley–Minto reforms were being considered, many of the men who were to attack Brahmans eight years later showed no interest in the offer of communal electorates which was made to them by Fort St George.[87] Morley himself was not thinking in caste terms, and Mylapore's non-Brahman opponents were much more eager to castigate Mylaporeans for being lawyers – the category closest to Morley's mind – than for being Brahmans.[88] The question of Brahmanism was not considered – or reconsidered –

[85] *Hindu* 22 December 1916.
[86] See evidence of C. S. Nair in *Joint Select Committee on the Government of India Bill*, II, 551. *P.P.* 1919, vol. IV; evidence of C. P. Ramaswami Iyer in *Evidence taken before the Reforms Committee (Franchise)*. Madras (Calcutta, 1919), II, 596.
[87] Home Public A October 1908, Nos 116–46. *N.A.I.*
[88] *Hindu* 22 January 1908.

until after 1912.[89] Secondly, these movements, whatever their pretensions, did not need to have, and many did not have, a political existence prior to the creation of the publicist and administrative categories which they filled. It is idle for the student of politics, although not perhaps of ideas, to search through the history and meaning of 'non-Brahmanism' to discover when in the past or at what level of abstraction in 'traditional' thought a notion of the non-Brahman similar to that propagated by the leaders of the non-Brahman movement can be found. The movement emerged when the very novel political processes of early twentieth-century Madras gave it life. What is interesting to political history is not the ideational antecedents of the movement but the contemporary processes. And thirdly, throughout our period and beyond, the old socially vertical systems of political connection continued to control a vast system of rewards. Men moved in and out of 'communal' politics with a remarkable speed as the opportunities for rewards shifted around. Simply because a politician appeared as a non-Brahman, a Nadar or a landlord, it ought not to be supposed that all of his political contacts lay within those communities. If he were an important man, he was also vitally related to a cross-communal network. It is not possible to explain the manifestly variable degrees to which different men subscribed to the same communal identity nor the changing tactics which they were prepared to employ in support of this identity without referring to their other networks of political interest.

---

[89] So close was the connection between governmental ideas and notions of the non-Brahman community, that much of the evidence which non-Brahmans used to portray Brahman oppression had come out of the mouths of civilians first. Thus, for example, *The Non-Brahman Manifesto* quoted Cardew's evidence to the Public Services Commission as proof of Brahman wickedness. When the civilians argued the non-Brahman case before Parliamentary committees, they then proceeded to cite the non-Brahmans' quotations of their own opinions as evidence of indigenous consciousness of the non-Brahman problem. The pattern of governmental initiative and subjects' response had become so complete that a closed circle of argument, quite apart from outside reality, had been formed.

7

The Home Rule League, Justice Party and Congress

The previous chapters have brought us to some understanding of the processes of political change in Southern India between the 1870s and 1916. Those processes were all moving in the same direction. They were linking together the political institutions and political interests of a previously segmented political system. By 1917 the linkages were complete and, although provincial and local systems had by no means merged entirely into each other and although further changes in their relationship would take place, they were now inextricably connected. In the Introduction, we set ourselves a main task: to explain the major political events of 1917–20. Already, we have set the stage for them and have suggested reasons for their occurrence and for their massive significance. Particular lines of conflict were being drawn by the way that the political system was evolving, and the confrontations of 1917–20 represented the first large-scale conflict in the newly integrated system. It remains for us to go through the events of these years to make our suggestions concrete. We must show how the Home Rule League, non-Brahman movement and Congress, as they developed at this time, were the products of their new institutional environment and how, indeed, their development is inexplicable without reference to the processes of political change which we have been examining.

By the end of the second year of the First World War, Mylapore had abandoned its policy of constitutional co-operation with the British and had adopted an agitational posture similar to that of the 1880s. The conditions of the period were perfect for it to press its imperial overlords into a further devolution of power. The war had forced Britain to make increased demands on India for men and money, and many Indian politicians realised that this gave them a chance to confront London with their own demands for political reform. As early as 1915, the India Office itself had recognised that some vague and unspecified changes would have to follow the war and, over the next few years, many powerful Indian interests made sure that it was not allowed to forget its prognosis.

The Home Rule League, the organisation which focused the agitation between 1916 and 1918, was the child of that most remarkable Irishwoman, Mrs Annie Besant. Her decision to enter Congress politics, after many years in opposition to Nationalist aspirations, would be more easily explained by the psychoanalyst than the historian, for it was undoubtedly taken more to bring her increased public attention than to aid the cause of Indian self-government.[1] Of more interest to us is the general effect of her move into the national arena. In her pre-political days, she had been extremely close to many of the leading men of Mylapore and had been involved with them in a host of cultural, religious and educational projects.[2] Indeed, so readily was she identified with Mylapore that she and they shared most of the same enemies – particularly Kasturi Ranga Iyengar, C. Vijayaraghavachari and T. M. Nair.[3] As she advanced into agitational politics, Mylapore provided her with the reputations and abilities of its most celebrated members. Sir S. Subramania Iyer was president of her League, C. P. Ramaswami Iyer her legal adviser, and G. A. Natesan and L. A. Govindaraghava Iyer among her most loyal and vocal supporters.

Mrs Besant's activities, by 1916 when they first achieved any real significance, performed a vital service to Mylapore. So complete had been Krishnaswami Iyer's destruction of the agitational Congress that the organisation had practically ceased to exist outside the Provincial Congress Committee.[4] Although Mylapore, as we have seen, possessed innumerable personal contacts across the presidency, these were unorganised and diffuse. It would have taken considerable

[1] For Mrs Besant's early opposition to Indian nationalism see *Hindu* 8 August 1910; C. Vijayaraghavachari to P. Kesava Pillai, 22 February 1907. P. Kesava Pillai Papers. *N.M.M.L.*; 'A History Sheet of Mrs Besant' in Home Political A March 1918, No. 247 and K.W. *N.A.I.*

[2] Sir S. Subramania Iyer and Justice T. Sadasiva Iyer were said to 'worship her almost as a mother'. P. Kesava Pillai to A. C. Parthasarathi Naidu, 5 October 1917. P. Kesava Pillai Papers. *N.M.M.L.* V. Krishnaswami Iyer, V. S. Srinivasa Sastri and P. S. Sivaswami Iyer were involved with her in the Benares Hindu College. V. S. Srinivasa Sastri to G. K. Gokhale, 6 February and 24 March 1908. V. S. Srinivasa Sastri Papers. *N.A.I.*

[3] Between 1912 and 1914, Mrs Besant sued both the *Hindu* and T. M. Nair for libel. C. P. Ramaswami Aiyar, *Biographical Vistas* (Bombay, 1968), p. 249; T. M. Nair, *The Evolution of Mrs Besant* (Madras, 1918); C. Vijayaraghavachari to P. Kesava Pillai, 22 February 1907. P. Kesava Pillai Papers. *N.M.M.L.*

[4] Following the 1914 session of the Indian National Congress, held in Madras, the Madras P.C.C. ordered an investigation of district machinery. It found 'considerable indifference' everywhere. Of the 22 recognised D.C.C.s, only eight bothered to reply to the P.C.C.'s circular. *Report of the Madras Provincial Congress Committee for the year ending 31st December 1915* (Madras, 1916).

time to redevelop the Congress for agitational purposes. Mrs Besant's great virtue lay in her ability to provide her campaign with ready-made machinery. As the president of the Theosophical Society, she controlled an organisation with several thousand members, which linked the presidency capital to every large *mofussil* town. When she converted this to political purposes, she was able to inaugurate her movement with prepared support and a sophisticated structure of command in as many as thirty-four separate localities.[5] As a newspaper baron of considerable size, she had to hand the means of communicating her message across the presidency.[6] As the creator of a student welfare organisation in Madras city, she possessed close ties with a large body of highly volatile material which could be used to heat any political agitation.[7] Finally, as the head of several educational trusts, she disposed of a large patronage which enabled her to command an even wider following.[8] Mrs Besant provided Mylapore, which was seeking to demonstrate to the British both its anger and its power, with resources to make its arguments felt much more quickly and keenly than would otherwise have been possible.

Yet Mrs Besant's Home Rule League also served the purposes of many of Mylapore's enemies, both of the Egmore and more extreme varieties. Krishnaswami Iyer and the Allahabad Convention had driven them from the Congress and kept them out of provincial consideration since 1908. They had been forced to adopt such hopeless anti-Mylapore ploys as the Andhra movement and the Varnashrama-dharma Association. The Home Rule League campaign, which was looking for agitational support of any character, presented them with an opportunity of returning to central political organisations

[5] *Organisation of the Home Rule League. Passed at the first meeting of the Council, 8th October 1916* (Madras, n.d.); *Hindu* 4 September 1916; *The Theosophist* November 1916; 'History Sheet of Mrs Besant' in Home Political A, March 1918, No. 247 and K. W. *N.A.I.*

[6] In 1914, as part of her initial move into politics, Mrs Besant had bought the daily *Madras Standard* and converted it into *New India*. This, together with her weekly *Commonweal* and her religious journals, made her the most formidable press baron in Madras.

[7] In 1914 Mrs Besant had founded the Young Men's Indian Association to appeal to the 3,000 student population of Madras city. 'Draft Copy of Prospectus and Rules of the Young Men's Indian Association' in A. Besant to P. S. Sivaswami Iyer, 12 January 1914, P. S. Sivaswami Iyer Papers. *N.A.I.* In 1916 and 1917, this association acted as a centre for the dissemination of Home Rule propaganda in the city. Home Political 'Deposit' September 1916, Nos 1–7. *N.A.I.* Home Political 'Deposit' January 1917, No. 42 and November 1917, Nos 6–7. *N.A.I.; Hindu* (weekly) 11 May 1917.

[8] 'History Sheet of Mrs Besant' in Home Political A March 1918, No. 247 and K.W. *N.A.I.*

and of making their presence known once again in Congress circles. Of course, they did not like the association of Mrs Besant and Mylapore with the movement. Kasturi Ranga Iyengar's new ally, S. Satyamurthi, savaged the League leadership publicly,[9] and C. Vijayaraghavachari's Salem protege, C. Rajagopalachari, attempted to weaken the hold of the Madras city politicians on its machinery.[10] But entry provided them all with advantages which they could not ignore. With less than perfect faith, they threw in their lot with Mrs Besant. By the autumn of 1916, the Home Rule League had accomplished the seemingly impossible: it had united the warring factions of the old Congress under a single leadership and it had projected Mrs Besant to a position of national importance.

To many British civilians, perched precariously in the higher regions of the Secretariat, the emergence of the Home Rule League and Mylapore's openly treasonable conduct marked a serious danger, both to the empire and to themselves. From about 1911, Mylapore's growing power had created resentment in the I.C.S., and several officials had spared no pains to oppose any further devolution of power to it.[11] It was from this time that the essays at communalism in the services and the attempt to nominate direct communal representatives to political institutions had begun. The events of 1916 convinced even the more liberal civilians that a policy of finding Indian replacements for Mylapore was an urgent priority. When the Madras Government tried to take steps to deal with what it saw to be the rising tide of sedition, it found itself shackled by the agents of Mylapore, who were now part of it. S. Srinivasa Iyengar, the Attorney-General, used his influence to prevent prosecutions for sedition;[12] the High Court Judges T. Sadasiva Iyer and T. V. Seshagiri Iyer repealed sentences given by lower courts for sedition;[13] by various administrative manipulations, large sums of government money found their way to the Home Rule League press to pay for advertisements;[14] in Madras city, C. P. Ramaswami Iyer appeared to have taken over

---

[9] Home Political 'Deposit' March 1916, No. 50. *N.A.I.; Hindu* 6 September 1916.

[10] *Hindu* 19 September 1916.

[11] For an example of the growing hostility between Mylapore and the I.C.S., see the reply of the Madras Government to the Secretary of State's suggestion that more Senate seats should be opened to election by the graduates. Letter No. 305 (Home, Education) Government of Madras to Government of India, dated 5 March 1917 in Education A May 1917, Nos 1–17. *N.A.I.*

[12] Note signed S. S. Iyengar dated 7 April 1919 in G.O. 653 (L and M, M) dated 25 April 1919. *T.N.A.*

[13] Home Political 'Deposit' November 1917, No. 7. *N.A.I.*

[14] Note signed A. Cardew dated 1 March 1918 in G.O. 340 (Home, Misc.) dated 4 April 1918. *T.N.A.*

the Corporation and to be using its patronage of appointments and contracts to further the nationalist cause;[15] in the University, G. A. Natesan finally succeeded in bowing the largely European Syndicate to his authority in the Senate.[16] For many British civilians, the enemy seemed to be already within the gates.

Moreover, precisely because the Mylapore connection represented not merely the interests of a few western-educated men but also those of many magnates immediately powerful in society, the Home Rule campaign confronted the government with opposition which was both socially deep and diverse. The British could not jest at the movement as a ritual performed by a handful of 'Babus' and a mad Irishwoman while such huge landed proprietors as the Kumara Maharaja of Vizianagram, the Raja of Ramnad, the *zamorin* of Calicut and the *zamindar* of Munagala, and such enormous financial powers as the Gujerati banker Lodd Govindoss, the Muslim Badsha family and the Calivalla brothers could be seen involved in the agitation.[17] As the League's propaganda developed, senior civilians were given a further cause for concern by the way in which significant economic interests, disturbed either by the war or by the advance of administrative efficiency, were also drawn towards it. In 1916,

[15] A. C. Parthasarathi Naidu to A. Cardew, 16 September 1916 in G.O. 414 (Home, Misc.) dated 26 April 1917; G.O. 175 (L and M, L) dated 7 February 1918. *T.N.A.*

[16] *Hindu* 28 October 1916.

[17] Most of these involvements were the result of personal connection either in cultural and religious patronage movements, or in the courts and councils or in the distribution of Secretariat and Dharmarakshana Sabha rewards. The Kumara Maharaja of Vizianagram and the Raja of Ramnad sought to give the Madras Landholders' Association a strong Home Rule flavour when Montagu visited Madras in December 1917. *Desamata* 17 November 1917; *Swadesamitran* 14 December 1917; *Dravidapatrika* 23 January 1918. *R.N.P.* The *zamorin* of Calicut was drawn into Home Rule politics by his relatives, particularly the lawyer K. P. Raman Menon, who were local organisers. *Justice* 15 May 1917. *R.N.P.* Munagala was a personal patron of the old Andhra Extremists. The Calivalla brothers and Lodd Govindoss we saw before. In 1918, C. Cunnan Chetty sided with C. P. Ramaswami Iyer in a factional struggle with P. Thyagaraja Chetty on the Pachayappa's trust board. *Hindu* 6, 10, 11 April, 21 May, 6 and 20 June 1918. Lodd Govindoss was a founding vice-president of the Home Rule League-oriented Madras Presidency Association. *Madras Mail* 17 September 1917. The Badsha family we saw in the 1887 Congress. In spite of the separatist tendencies of Muslim politics, they had always remained close to Mylapore. C. P. Ramaswami Iyer, for example, was the legal adviser of the Muslim Education Society, in which they were prominent, and the Calivalla brothers were among its patrons. The Badshas themselves also donated money to Hindu charities. *Hindu* 23 April 1908, 25 April 1912, 12 March 1918. They were organisers of the Madras Muslim League which, of course, supported Home Rule League–Congress agitation at this time.

for example, prominent Home Rule politicians picked up the issue of emigrant labour and called on the government to regulate more closely and, in some instances, stop completely the traffic.[18] These demands, although for different publicly stated reasons, were the same as those of a large number of Tanjore *mirasidars* who objected to emigration because it depleted their labour force and pushed wages above subsistence level. That the association of ideas between the League and this powerful landed interest was due to more than coincidence was made clear by the opposition of the League to government measures to weaken the physical control which *mirasidars* exercised over their labourers.[19] So seriously did Fort St George regard the threat of a tight combination of League politicians and Tanjore *mirasidars* that it reversed its emigration policy and legislated against the advice of its emigration experts.[20] The Home Rule League also developed political connections with economic interests in the important hide and skin trade, which was hit by the dislocation of communications,[21] with village officers who, as we saw, were under pressure from bureaucratic reform,[22] with Indian merchants who sought to break the financial privileges of European business houses,[23] and, later, even with native factory labour in the few European-owned industrial undertakings of the South.[24] These economic forces, when combined with the networks of religious revivalism which Mrs Besant, as a religious leader, was able to mobilise, gave the British every reason to see the Home Rule League as an extremely serious threat to the continued existence of the *raj*

But it was not only the empire – as a concept – which the strength of the movement suggested was under attack. Much of Mrs Besant's polemic, which stressed Indian religious and national revival, served to concentrate the agitation on the fact that the government, besides being unsatisfactory, was alien.[25] The British servants of Fort St

---

[18] *Madras Mail* 5 February 1917.   [19] *Hindu* 2 February, 3 and 9 April 1918.

[20] Home Political 'Deposit' April 1917, No. 61. *N.A.I.*

[21] Home Political 'Deposit' May 1917, No. 40. *N.A.I.*

[22] *Hindu* 23, 24 and 27 December 1919.

[23] *The Southern India Chamber of Commerce. Report. March 1918–February 1919* (Madras, 1920), pp. ix–xiv.

[24] B. Shiva Rao, *The Industrial Worker in India* (London, 1939), pp. 15–16; *Desabhaktan* 9 May 1918. *R.N.P.*; Home Political 'Deposit' September 1918, Nos 19–20. *N.A.I.*

[25] Chief Secretary, Government of Madras, to Secretary, Home Department, Government of India, in G.O. 1019 (Public) dated 10 August 1917. *T.N.A.*; Slater, *Southern India. Its Political and Economic Problems*, p. 266; *Madras Mail* 28 February 1917; Irschick, *Politics and Social Conflict in South India*, pp. 57–8.

George found themselves challenged as much for being British as for being servants. They were the more susceptible to this attack for they regarded themselves as a race apart from and superior to that of the indigenous population. Indeed, in many ways they constituted a separate caste in Madras society, which behaved in politics much more like a community than most Indian castes. I.C.S. men tended to see the League as a danger not only to the government for which they worked but also to themselves and their social position. From 1917, when the appointment of Edwin Montagu as Secretary of State for India produced in London and New Delhi a policy of conciliation towards the League,[26] many Madras civilians felt themselves betrayed as their superiors threatened to sacrifice them to Indian political sentiment. They did not relish the idea of having to share their offices and status with the men of Mylapore. The traditional battle between Fort St George and its London and New Delhi superiors took on a new facet, therefore, as the civilians of Fort St George began to fight for their personal survival. That this, rather than concern for the empire as a whole, was their main preoccupation became clear in 1920 when they rejected every clause of the Montagu–Chelmsford Report and threatened to resign *en masse* if the report were implemented, leaving India and the empire to its fate.[27]

The severe and deepening hostility to Mylapore and the Home Rule League of a small group of highly placed civilians – Cardew, H. F. W. Gillman, Sir Lionel Davidson and Sir Murray Hammick – was crucial to the development of politics between 1916 and 1920. In late 1916, faced with the growing strength of the Home Rule League crusade, they began to look around for elements which could be used in a counter-movement of loyalty.[28] At first, communalism alone was not central to their plans. They responded to the initiatives of a few *zamindars* who wished to oppose the League on a straight ticket of loyalty to the *raj*[29] and even found subsidies for one Brahman

---

[26] Montagu ordered Mrs Besant's release from internment, the Government of India withdrew its ban on students and semi-government employees, such as public prosecutors, participating in Home Rule agitation and, in December 1917, Montagu showed obvious favour to such Madras Home Rulers as C. P. Ramaswami Iyer when considering suggestions for the reforms he had promised. G.O. 1474 (Public) dated 22 December 1917. *T.N.A.*; Montagu, *An Indian Diary*, pp. 120–30.

[27] See P. & J. (Reforms) File 95. *I.O.L.*

[28] For discussions on the nature of this counter-movement or 'show' see notes of Sir Harold Stuart, H. F. W. Gillman and Sir Alexander Cardew in G.O. 447 (Home, Misc.) dated 8 May 1917 and G.O. 414 (Home, Misc.) dated 26 April 1917. *T.N.A.*

[29] *Madras Mail* 14 March, 8 May, 30 June and 2 July 1917.

newspaper editor who promised to denounce the League in his broad-sheet.[30] However, it was not long before the main thrust of their campaign turned to the non-Brahman category. In part, this was because the Madras Dravidian Association and the non-Brahman interest, which Cardew had been developing since 1912,[31] provided a ready-made organisation which would work for them in return for patronage. Cardew and Gillman offered this patronage: they were in correspondence with the M.D.A. leadership and attempted to bend the rules of service to allow government officials to join the South Indian People's Association (the first non-Brahman political associa-tion), and they knew of the founding of the S.I.P.A., several weeks before its inaugural meeting took place.[32] In 1917, they demonstrated clearly the nature of the S.I.P.A.'s official connection by manipulating the delegations which met Montagu in order to give loyalist non-Brahmans the maximum of representation and Congress non-Brah-mans the minimum.[33]

Undoubtedly, a second reason for the use which Madras civilians made of communalism lay in the way that London and Calcutta col-lected information for the reforms. A series of Montagu-appointed commissions arrived in Madras to hear evidence and to test public opinion. The civilians' own opposition to constitutional reform, and indeed that of the resident British business community, was unlikely to carry weight with commissioners who were concerned with the future of India as a whole. Moreover, the commissioners, if they had any experience of India at all, had received it in Northern India or at imperial headquarters, where political analyses tended to be

[30] Srinivasa Venkatachari of the *Hindu Nesan*. G.O. 414 (Home, Misc.) dated 26 April 1917, *T.N.A.*

[31] Since 1912, he had been using his personal influence to pass patronage to such non-Brahman service families as the Maddireddi. G.O. 1616 (Home, Misc.) dated 6 August 1917. He was instrumental in obtaining grants for separate caste hostels, as among the Sourashtras. *South Indian Mail* 30 April 1917. *R.N.P.* And also in twisting Education Department rules to aid the Kammas. Note signed A. Cardew dated 5 January 1918 in G.O. 102 (Home, Misc.) dated 31 January 1918. *T.N.A.* And also in campaigning for a revision of the rules of government employment to allow communal Indian Christian Associations to demonstrate against the Home Rule League. G.O. 970 (Home, Misc.) dated 6 August 1917. *T.N.A.*

[32] See Note signed H. F. W. Gillman dated 19 October 1916. in G.O. 447 (Home, Misc.) dated 8 May 1917. *T.N.A.*; also P. Thyagaraja Chetty to A. Cardew, 12 February 1917, in G.O. 147 (Home, Misc.) dated 15 February 1917. *T.N.A.*

[33] *Hindu* 11 February 1917; Proceedings of the Council of the Madras Muslim League, 30 November 1917, in 'Proceedings of the Madras Muslim League, 19 March 1917 to 21 February 1921'. Madras Mahajana Sabha Papers. *N.M.M.L.*; *Hindu* 15 November and 15 December 1917; G.O. 552 (Public, Confidential) dated 3 July 1918. *T.N.A.*

made in terms of community. The civilians, therefore, needed to find an argument, based on communal principles, with which to fend off the good intentions of their superiors. What better category could be thought of than the non-Brahmans, whose existence as a group could be shown in innumerable departmental statistics, who could be shown by examinations of education and public service employment (but not wealth or position in local bodies) to be weak and who numbered 98 per cent of the entire population? The non-Brahman category carried inside it the hopes and fears of the Madras I.C.S.

Of course, the thinking out of this strategy need not have been as coldly Machiavellian as we have supposed. Prior to 1916, many civilians had already classified the threat of Mylapore as the result of Brahman conspiracy, and so were already half-way to concluding that people who were not Brahmans were losing out. But certainly some explanation must be offered for the way that so much civilian evidence given to various commissions at this time was confused, and provided ill-conceived judgments on the basis of facts which were demonstrably wrong. For example, in spite of their evidence of . irrevocable cultural, social and political division between the Brahman and the non-Brahman, no civilian could tell Southborough why, only ten years before, the Madras Government had vehemently opposed the principle of communal representation on the grounds that communal divisions were not strong in Madras.[34] Or again, in London in 1919, Cardew and Hammick, carried away by the rectitude of their reasoning, told a Parliamentary Committee that not only would non-Brahmans be extinguished by a broadened constitution but that they were already extinct under the present Morley–Minto scheme. Unfortunately for them, while they were talking non-Brahmans were winning eleven of the fifteen seats in the Legislative Council election – a fact which they were unable to explain when asked.[35] A large part of the non-Brahman propaganda was written and performed by the

[34] Evidence of H. G. Stokes in *Evidence Taken before the Reform Committee (Franchise)*. Madras (Calcutta, 1919), II, 585. Stokes also admitted that the non-Brahman category, so vehemently defended by some of his colleagues as a concrete political entity, was no more than the result of rule-of-thumb definition: 'The constitution of the electorates proposed by Fort St George was based upon an identity of interests among the voters. As regards the non-Brahman community the interests of the different sub-castes might not be identical but government must draw the line somewhere owing to the necessity for keeping the Council within practical limits.' *Ibid.*, p. 586.

[35] See evidence of A. Cardew in *Joint Select Committee on the Government of India Bill*, II, 338. *P.P.* 1919, vol. IV.

leading Madras civilians; and it ought to be judged more by what it was meant to achieve than by what it appeared to say. The men who came forward to join the S.I.P.A. (and, later, the South Indian Liberal Federation and Justice Party) were drawn from the most diverse backgrounds. One of the main elements in the association, of course, was the professional 'non-Brahman' interest – the group of lawyers and bureaucrats who formed the Madras Dravidian Assocition. As we saw, it did not include non-Brahmans who were well-connected to Mylapore or, even, Egmore. Men like V. Masilamani Pillai, C. Sankara Nair and T. V. Gopalaswami Mudaliar[36] had no use for the S.I.P.A.'s mendicancy. It was composed only of the unsuccessful.

Behind this collection of career-seeking educated non-Brahmans, which extended to a host of journalists and petty publicists attracted to the S.I.P.A.'s patronage potential,[37] came a series of local magnates who had suffered from Mylapore's rise to power. Most prominent of these was Pitti Thyagaraja Chetty whose troubles in the Madras Corporation and Pachayappa's charities we have seen. Another was P. Ramarayaningar (later the Raja of Panagal), a member of a wealthy *zamindari* family from Chittoor. In spite of his petitions to P. S. Sivaswami Iyer, one of his local enemies had received important appointments in local self-government from the Secretariat.[38] In 1915, he had joined the Andhra movement, to protest at Mylapore's policies, but it did him little good for he lost a Council election in July 1916.[39] The new non-Brahman weapon was well suited to his old

---

[36] T. V. Gopalaswami Mudaliar, a celebrated lawyer and journalist, was an intimate of Kasturi Ranga Iyengar and associated with him throughout this period.

[37] Such, for example, as O. Kandaswami Chetty, editor of the *Social Reform Advocate* who, until 1916, had been on the payroll of the Brahman S. Srinivasa Iyengar, president of the Madras Social Reform Association, but then sought succour at the S.I.P.A. office. See *Hindu* (weekly) 29 April, 6 and 13 May 1926. And A. C. Parthasarathi Naidu, the editor of *Andhraprakasikha*, which had run into financial difficulties. After begging unsuccessfully from P. S. Sivaswami Iyer and Sir Alexander Cardew, he accepted an offer from P. Thyagaraja Chetty to make *Andhraprakasikha* the Telugu organ of the S.I.P.A. So ashamed was he of his new associates that he wrote to P. Kesava Pillai explaining that he did not really dislike Brahmans but had been forced to move with the times. A. C. Parthasarathi Naidu to P. S. Sivaswami Iyer, 14 September 1916. P. S. Sivaswami Iyer Papers, *N.A.I.*; G.O. 414 (Home, Misc.) dated 26 April 1917. *T.N.A.*; A. C. Parthasarathi Naidu to P. Kesava Pillai, 9 October 1917. P. Kesava Pillai Papers. *N.M.M.L.*

[38] P. Ramarayaningar to P. S. Sivaswami Iyer, 29 June 1912. P. S. Sivaswami Iyer Papers. *N.A.I.*

[39] Ramarayaningar was president of the 1915 Andhra conference. *Hindu* 12 May 1915. He was defeated in 1916 by the Trichinopoly *zamindar* K. V. Rangaswami

purposes. A third magnate who threw his weight behind the S.I.P.A. was the Raja of Pithapuram. For more than a decade he had been battling with Mylapore and its Andhra agents to retain control of his important college at Cocanada. In 1904, his choice for principal, R. Venkataratnam Naidu, had upset N. Subba Rao and V. Bashyam Iyengar, who wanted the place for V. S. Srinivasa Sastri (Krishnaswami Iyer's protege). Subba Rao had led an agitation against Venkataratnam Naidu on the issue of the new principal's advocacy of advanced social reform.[40] Discord between the raja and local Mylapore-oriented lawyers continued unabated for the next twelve years and in 1916, a few weeks before the foundation of the S.I.P.A., M. Ramachandra Rao had promoted a confrontation between the college students and the college administration in the hope of ousting Venkataratnam Naidu.[41] The raja was naturally drawn to the anti-Mylapore crusade, which had gathered in Madras city under the non-Brahman banner. Obviously, however, all three magnates, who were typical of a great many others who joined the S.I.P.A., were not enemies of Brahmans as such. Indeed, all three had been closely associated with some Brahmans in the past and saw no reason to break many of these contacts, even in their anti-Brahman period.[42] Their contention was with certain very specific Brahmans in Mylapore.

Iyengar in the landlords' Imperial Legislative Council election. Rangaswami Iyengar was the son of a previous Legislative Councillor, connected to the Dharmarakshana Sabha through the Srirangam temple and a Home Ruler. It did not escape contemporaries that four of the nascent S.I.P.A. leaders – Ramarayaningar, P. Thyagaraja Chetty, T. M. Nair and K. V. Reddi Naidu – all had been defeated in various Council elections in 1916 by men with Home Rule and Mylapore connections. *Prapanchamitran* 20 May 1917. *R.N.P.*

[40] 'Extract from the memoirs of Dr B. Pattabhisittaramayya' in *Brahmarishi Dr Sir Raghupathi Venkata Ratnam Naidu. Birth Centenary Souvenir, Mahavanavami, 1962* (n.p., n.d.), pp. 2–5.

[41] *Hindu* (weekly) 6, 20 and 27 April, 11 and 18 May, 1 June 1916.

[42] P. Thyagaraja Chetty had been involved in the 1880s Congress with Brahmans; in Corporation politics, he was allied to K. Desikachari; in his banking enterprises he was linked to Sir V. C. Desikachari; in private life he was intensely orthodox, would not eat food not prepared by a Brahman, and in 1915 joined C. P. Ramaswami Iyer in protesting about remarks made by a European Corporation official on the sanitary habits of Brahmans. P. Ramarayaningar possessed an M.A. in Sanskrit and had been educated in the house of C. V. Sundara Sastri, P. Ananda Charlu's adopted brother; in the Andhra movement he had been associated with almost nobody but Brahmans, and as we shall see, his term as Chief Minister of Madras was not characterised by communalism. One of Pithapuram's most powerful contacts, not to say representatives, in Godavari politics was D. Seshagiri Rao, for many years standing *vakil* to the estate and district board president 1917–20. Seshagiri Rao was a Brahman.

The S.I.P.A.'s initial appeal went out to various local interests which had been put under pressure by developments at the centre of government since 1910. It repeatedly petitioned against Dharma-rakshana Sabha activities in the temples and opposed all attempts at legislative interference in temple affairs;[43] it raised to the gaze of the province innumerable local examples of Mylapore's spoliation of school committees and charities;[44] its newspapers provided columns in which the latest scandal concerning Mylapore's control of appointments could be brought to public attention.[45] Its purpose was to compile all manner of grievances against Mylapore and the present political system, to wrap them in a communalist and loyalist flag and to beg the British for help.

The fact that, via Cardew, Gillman and others, it did obtain help and access to the Secretariat, however, meant that the S.I.P.A. rapidly became more than a mere sounding board for local and professional 'out' factions. By providing the S.I.P.A. with administrative influence, the Madras civilians helped to turn it into a patronage machine which rivalled that of Mylapore. In 1917, the non-Brahmans' two greatest publicity victories were due entirely to the fact that the S.I.P.A. leadership was able to offer, in Mylapore style, very concrete rewards from the Secretariat to its followers. At Cuddalore and Coimbatore, important Congress conferences were broken up by the action of two magnates who had no personal quarrel with Mylapore and who had been sympathetic to the Home Rule League at its foundation. But both needed the favour of the Secretariat for particular projects and both felt that, at that time, the S.I.P.A. connection was more favourable to their purposes.

At Cuddalore, A. Subbarayalu Reddiar, lawyer, landowner, municipal council and temple committee chairman and *taluk* board president, was instrumental in opposing the holding of the 1917 Congress Provincial Conference. He was, undoubtedly, the most powerful man in South Arcot. For many years he had been on the closest of terms with Mylapore[46] and, in mid-1916, he was chairman of the D.C.C. which asked Mrs Besant to preside at a proposed

---

[43] *Hindu* 13 March 1918; G.O. 175 (L and M, L) dated 7 February 1918; Home Judicial B February 1920, No. 17. *N.A.I.*; *Non-Brahman* 18 March and 29 April 1917. *R.N.P.*

[44] For example, the Pachayappa's affair, *Hindu* 6, 10 and 11 April, 21 May, 6 and 20 June 1918; the Tinnevelly College Committee, *Hindu* 17, 22, 24, 25 and 30 January and 15 February 1918; the Kallidaikurichi College, *Hindu* 5 November 1918.

[45] For examples, *Non-Brahman* 20 January 1917; *Justice* 13 August 1919. *R.N.P.*

[46] Sivaswami Iyer made him *taluk* board president. A Subbarayalu Reddiar to P. S. Sivaswami Iyer, 12 April 1912. P. S. Sivaswami Iyer Papers. *N.A.I.*

Provincial Conference the next year. After his invitation had been accepted, however, Mrs Besant had launched her League and had become *persona non grata* with the Secretariat civilians. The opening out of the institutions of local self-government and the real possibility, late in 1916, of a non-official district board president in South Arcot put Subbarayalu Reddiar in an acutely embarrassing position. He withdrew the invitation to Mrs Besant and was pushed out of the D.C.C. by his oldest local enemies.[47] He demonstrated his loyalty to the Secretariat civilians by agitating against the holding of the conference – although, it must be said, his agitation was more anti-Besantine than anti-Brahman.[48] His judicious change of political coat came at exactly the right time for his office aspirations; later in 1917 he became one of the first non-officials to be nominated to the presidency of a district board.

At Coimbatore, the fracas was created by T. A. Ramalingam Chetty, a lawyer and rich banker who, for many years, had been vice-president of the district board and a well-known Congressman. According to a local resident of Coimbatore, Ramalingam's switch from the Congress to the S.I.P.A. was the result of his failure to win an election to the Legislative Council in 1916. He had lost to the Salem lawyer, B. V. Narasimha Iyer, but Sir Harold Stuart, a senior member of the Secretariat, promised to hold an inquiry into the election, with a view to disqualifying Narasimha Iyer, a prominent Home Ruler. Stuart's terms were that Ramalingam arrange a hostile reception for Mrs Besant who had been made president of the forthcoming district conference.[49] At the time, the Coimbatore municipal chairmanship election was taking place and, by gathering together a party of councillors loyal to him or tied to S.I.P.A. interests in Madras city or opposed to particular Home Rulers,[50] Ramalingam was able to force

[47] The opposition to him was led by the Brahman lawyer V. Srinivasachari, who had stood against him in a Legislative Council election in July and a municipal chairmanship election in November 1916. Srinivasachari worked in front of the wealthy local Muslim Maracair interest which had long been opposed to Subbarayalu's power. Subbarayalu replied to his critics by accepting a resignation from the temple committee, which Srinivasachari had tendered during a previous dispute in 1914. In 1917, Subbarayalu drove the Maracairs off the district board. *Hindu* 7 June, 3 July, 11 September, 3 November, 13, 15 and 19 December 1916; *Hindu* 12 June 1918.

[48] *Hindu* (weekly) 11 and 18 May 1917.

[49] K. V. Srinivasa Iyer to P. S. Sivaswami Iyer, 18 June 1917. P. S. Sivaswami Papers. *N.A.I.*

[50] This alliance included C. S. Ratnasabhapati Mudaliar, a powerful landlord and banker who was an old factional opponent of C. V. Venkataramana Iyengar, a

the main candidate, M. Sambadam Mudaliar, a Theosophist who had actually formed the Coimbatore Home Rule League, to join him.[51] Ramalingam provided the British civilians with as fine a show of loyalty as they were ever to receive in Madras.

By offering hard rewards to the men who supported the S.I.P.A., British civilians in the Secretariat succeeded in turning the S.I.P.A. leadership into a Mylapore-like clique at the centre. The S.I.P.A. leaders, in the manner of the chief Mylaporeans, were able to use the new powers of government to make a series of person-to-person deals with the magnates of the locality. Wealthy and locally powerful men, who were drawing a blank in their appeals to Mylapore, could shift their attention to the newly prominent non-Brahmans and seek succour from them. The Nadar merchants and bankers of Ramnad, for example, who had been trying and failing since 1910 to obtain a seat in the Legislative Council for their caste association, were quick to see the possibilities of the new situation. They began to invite S.I.P.A. leaders instead of Mylapore Brahmans as the visiting presidents of their annual caste conferences.[52] In 1920, the S.I.P.A. leaders (as the Justice Party Ministry) granted the Nadar request for representation in the legislative.

The S.I.P.A. connection, then, began to form a viable alternative to Mylapore at the centre. Importantly, however, it did not destroy Mylapore, which still had many strings to pull. Neither A. Subbarayalu Reddiar nor T. A. Ramalingam Chetty, for example, were prepared to sever all contact with their former friends. Subbarayalu Reddiar did not resign from the Congress, refused to accept direction from the S.I.P.A. in Madras city[53] and was adjudged to have stood as a 'Moderate' rather than as a member of the Justice Party at the 1920 Legislative Council elections;[54] T. A. Ramalingam Chetty turned

---

lawyer and banker and the chairman of the conference reception committee, and V. Veruvada Chetty, P. Thyagaraja Chetty's relative and business agent in Coimbatore. However, it did not last for long. By July 1919, V. Veruvada Chetty, his commitment to its relation notwithstanding, had joined forces with the Brahman Home Ruler K. Narayana Sastri to hound C. S. Ratnasabhapati Mudaliar in the municipal council. *Hindu* 1 August 1919.

[51] K. V. Srinivasa Iyer to P. S. Sivaswami Iyer, 18 June 1917. P. S. Sivaswami Iyer Papers. *N.A.I.* For the creation of the Coimbatore Home Rule League see *Hindu* 23 November 1916.

[52] Hardgrave, *Nadars of Tamilnad*, pp. 174–5.

[53] Both the S.I.P.A. and the S.I.L.F. boycotted the Madras sittings of the South-borough Commission on Franchise reform but A. Subbarayalu Reddiar accepted nomination as a local member of the commission. *Justice* 16 October 1918. *R.N.P.*

[54] Reforms (Franchise) B March 1921, Nos 34–99. *N.A.I.*

away from non-Brahman politics during 1918 and 1919, became active in the Mylapore-dominated Moderate Conference and was appointed district board president of Coimbatore in 1920 through the exertions of R. Ramachandra Rao, the departmental Secretary who was part of the Mylapore network.[55]

What had happened was that two Indian political 'parties' were now standing at the Secretariat, both of which were, to some extent, in power at the same time. Of course, this greatly extended the scope of factional warfare. The magnate-based factions which inhabited almost every local institution – municipalities, rural boards and temple committees – previously had been faced with a choice of coming to terms with Mylapore or suffering. Now they could play with two provincial leaderships and take measures against local opponents who were 'in' with one by joining the other. All had an incentive to reach out to the capital. The result was that the non-Brahman communal and the Home Rule issues, which governed the provincial political debate, found themselves transplanted to an extraordinary environment which was conditioned by squabbles over taxation, bye-laws and contracts and the eternal struggle for local power. Naturally, there was little correlation between the principles of political organisation at the two levels. In Periyakulam town, Madura district, for example, a Jesuit priest began to further the cause of so-called Brahman dominion. Opposition to the municipal chairman, the *zamindar* of Doddapanayakanur, was coming from several groups: firstly, men alienated by the *zamindar's* administration of patronage; secondly, a group of young lawyers, newly established in this expanding town and eager to capture the municipality by pulling together diverse grievances in their Ratepayers' Association; and thirdly, Father Marie Louise, a Jesuit whose missionary school was suffering from competition with the *zamindar's* Hindu High School. The *zamindar's* own municipal party was no less complex than its opposition. It consisted of various interests integrated by his patronage and included one of the new lawyers, a Brahman, who had been bought off. Although the battle for municipal control dated back to 1904, when the *zamindar* had first become municipal chairman, between 1917 and 1920 the factions clothed their local animosities in the garb of provincial politics. The opposition, led in the council by Father Marie Louise, used Home Rule propaganda against the *zamindar* to demand more seats open to election and less filled by the chairman's nomination. Doddapanaya-

[55] See note signed Panagal dated 16 May 1923 in G.O. 1131 (L.S.G.) dated 17 May 1923. *T.N.A.*

kanur replied by joining the S.I.L.F. and relying on favourable decisions from Secretariat officials to keep the council closed. [56]

In Negapatam, Tanjore district, by contrast, the arrival of the provincial conflict saw an Arabic Muslim leading in the formation of associations to support the Dravidian peoples. He was Ahmed Thambi Maracair who, for many years, had been involved in a fight for local power with K. S. Venkatarama Iyer. Ahmed Thambi, a merchant and landowner, relied for his support in municipal politics on the prominent Maracair Muslim trading families of the Nagore suburb and on various local landlords. K. S. Venkatarama Iyer, a Brahman lawyer and *mirasidar*, was connected to Hindu 'Pillaima' (Vellala) merchants, who were the natural competitors of the Maracairs, and exercised a considerable independent influence through his membership of the notoriously corrupt Negapatam temple committee. Venkatarama Iyer was the first to bring provincial politics to the locality in 1917. Ahmed Thambi, then municipal chairman, was acutely embarrassed by the indentured labour issue. His constituency was split between merchants and shipowners, who wished labour migration to expand unchecked, and landowners who saw their cheap labour supply beginning to dwindle. Venkatarama Iyer, joining the Home Rule campaign for the abolition of indentured labour, led a local agitation against him, stole his landlord support and took the municipal chair. Ahmed Thambi replied, rationally enough, by consolidating his merchant support and winning over the Pillaimas to his cause. But to make this class confrontation acceptable in provincial politics and to win for the merchants a measure of Secretariat support, Ahmed Thambi had to shift his rhetoric to the caste vocabulary. Thus the merchant party became a non-Brahman party and Ahmed Thambi established a Dravidian Association among the Pillaimas. This move also had the virtue of providing a further barrier to Venkatarama Iyer should he ever try to win back the Pillaimas. [57]

In Erode town, Coimbatore district, perhaps most strangely of all, the importation of provincial political concepts put two brothers on opposite sides of the communal fence. They were the Muslims Sheikh Dawood and Kadir Sahib, who were the premier magnates of the locality, owning vast lands and urban properties and running huge

---

[56] Collector of Madura to Secretary, Local and Municipal Department, 11 February 1919 in G.O. 374 (L and M, M) dated 6 March 1919; also G.O. 1383 (L and M, M) dated 18 September 1919. *T.N.A.*

[57] See *Madras Mail*, 20 March and 28 April 1917; Note signed Collector of Tanjore dated 21 August 1918 in G.O. 1150 (L and M, L) dated 7 September 1918. *T.N.A.*; *Justice* 10 January 1921.

trading empires. Their hatred of each other had long split the town, and the two municipal factions, led respectively by the lawyer, T. Srinivasa Mudaliar, and the wholesale merchant, E. V. Ramaswami Naicker, were in many ways extensions of their feud. During the War, Ramaswami Naicker's scarcely disguised manipulation of elections led him into conflict with the Collector and the Local and Municipal Department. He was dismissed from the council chairmanship and formally banned from holding local office. Already possessing close familial contacts with the leading Home Rule lawyers of Salem (C. Vijayaraghavachari was a trustee of his father's school) and now having personal cause for taking an agitational stance, he was not slow to move to the Home Rule campaign and to take Sheikh Dawood with him. T. Srinivasa Mudaliar and Sheikh Kadir naturally looked to the favour of the Collector and Secretariat and set up a local branch of the S.I.L.F.[58] In Periyakulam, Negapatam and Erode, as indeed in every other locality, the great provincial debate flowed along channels cut for quite another purpose.

The political paradoxes created by this system of local factionalism appearing as ideology were made even greater when Montagu's initiatives raised the political stakes. Discussions at the capital then became not only about who was to do well under the old constitution but also who was to make the new one. The nature of representation before commissions and the Government of India forced politicians to form associations of communal interests, for it was only these which obtained a hearing. Consequently, between 1917 and 1919, frantic efforts were made all over the province, both by provincial leaders and their magnate supporters, to found associations based on class, caste and religion. Yet the real, factional basis of local political organisation broke through, for not only did all 'natural' associations – such as those of Muslims, Christians and specific castes – collapse as their members were pulled different ways by their more important cross-communal ties,[59] but both non-Brahman and Congress leaderships

---

[58] G.O. 1250 (L and M, M) dated 19 July 1916. *T.N.A.; Madras Mail* 17 September 1917; G.O. 817 (L and M, M) dated 22 May 1919; G.O. 1114 (L and M, M) dated 25 July 1919; G.O. 1482 (L.S.G.) dated 30 July 1921; G.O. 1717 (L.S.G.) dated 4 August 1923. *T.N.A.*

[59] For Muslims, see 'Proceedings of the Council of the Madras Muslim League, 30 November 1917' in 'Proceedings of the Madras Muslim League, 19 March 1917 to 21 February 1921,' Madras Mahajana Sabha Papers. *N.M.M.* For Indian Christians, see *Hindu* 28 and 29 January 1918; for Indian Catholics, see *Madras Mail* 20 August and 10 September 1917, and *Hindu* 10 October and 6 November 1917. Among caste associations, the Visvabrahmanas tried to send five different deputations to see Montagu, which recommended no less than three different

tried to organise class followings out of the same class groups – notably village officers, factory workers and urban tradesmen.[60]

By the summer of 1918, the observer of Madras would be forced to notice the deep divisions in political society yet, unless he were extremely careful, he would be bemused by the shapes and the causes of the conflicts. If we take the S.I.P.A. and Mylapore groups to be leaderships, each was connected to a series of similar supports. For example, Mylapore represented firstly, clientage ties, many of them personal, between Mylapore men and magnates, which had been established by conditions before 1916; secondly, various local institutional factions which sought Mylapore's aid either for direct gain or because opponents had gone to the S.I.P.A.; thirdly, various disturbed interests, such as village officers, Tanjore *mirasidars*, factory hands and unsuccessful students who were attracted by the anti-administration stance of the Home Rule League and by the hope that their own grievances would be carried by the agitation; and fourthly, a variety of sectarian organisations. The S.I.P.A. leadership was linked firstly, to magnates who had been driven into opposition to Mylapore by events prior to 1916; secondly, to various local factions seeking rewards from the centre or opposing Mylapore-connected enemies; thirdly, to various disturbed elements who regarded the condemnation of Mylapore Brahmans as a condemnation of the administration; and fourthly, to a further variety of sectarian associations, often of the same sect as Mylapore's own. Both 'parties' thus mobilised an extraordinary collection of forces, some of which were 'in' power in local and provincial institutions, some of which were 'out' of power and all of which hoped to be 'in' power in the promised but unknown future political system. Particular divisions and alliances were the result of personal connection, factional opposition and political guesswork. It is not surprising that the political combinations of these years were a trifle confusing.

Not the least casualties of the developments, which had produced two structurally identical 'parties' in Madras politics, were the initial ideological cleavages between the Home Rule League and its non-

and mutually exclusive programmes of reform. *Addresses presented in India to His Excellency the Viceroy and the Right Honourable Secretary of State*, p. 88. *P.P.* 1918. vol. xviii.

[60] For village officers, see *Hindu* 29 November 1919, 13 May and 18 June 1920; *Swadesamitran* 9 August 1920. *R.N.P.* For factory and urban workers, see Shiva Rao, *Industrial Worker in India*, pp. 15–16; *Hindu* 27 and 29 January 1920; G.O. 157 (Public) dated 8 March 1920. *T.N.A.*; *Hindu* 16, 19, 23, 27, 28, 29 and 30 August 1919; *Hindu* 20 February, 26 March and 7 December 1920.

Brahman opponents. The S.I.P.A. banner had been raised with the help of the civilians to campaign for no change in the constitutional system because of the fear of 'Brahman' domination. It had thus attracted support from groups which were already suffering from Mylapore's influence. However, as it became a more positive political force, its leaders were provided with the opportunity of picking up much more than the support of the weaker political elements. Indeed, unless they did so, their movement would count for very little in real terms of political control. Yet, clearly, they were hampered by a slogan which identified them to local magnates as a group which stood against Indians being given more power: few politicians would expect to gain popularity by offering the people less bread than their opponents. By mid-1917, several S.I.P.A. leaders were moving steadily away from 'no-change' to an acceptance of some reform providing non-Brahmans were protected by electoral safeguards.[61] But by this time, the Congress itself had accepted the principles of non-Brahman protection in order to weaken the appeal of the S.I.P.A.[62] Thus both parties stood for some reform and for the reservation of non-Brahman seats in the Legislative Council. Certainly, there remained differences over the amount of reform possible and the size and nature of the reservations but the issues of principle between them were dead. Not, of course, that there was any sign or any hope of a compromise being reached between the S.I.P.A. and Home Rule League. Indeed, as the issues between them disappeared, the acrimony increased.[63] The S.I.P.A. group had come to prominence and existed as a united force only in opposition to Mylapore. It had received vital support from British civilians only because it served to counter the activities of the Home Rule League. Quite simply, the S.I.P.A. could not consider a deal with Mylapore and the Home Rule League/Congress without compromising itself out of existence and losing a crucial source of its support.[64]

[61] For example, in April 1917, P. Thyagaraja Chetty made a thundering speech in which he demanded that control of the Indian economy should be placed entirely in Indian hands. *Hindu* 2 April 1917. At the Coimbatore non-Brahman conference in August 1917 several proposals for constitutional reform were debated and passed. *Kistnapatrika* 25 August 1917; *Andhrapatrika* 7 September 1917. *R.N.P.*

[62] *Hindu* 30 October 1917. In September 1917, non-Brahman Congressmen set up the Madras Presidency Association under P. Kesava Pillai. This demanded communal safeguards for non-Brahmans and received Mylapore's full approval.

[63] The S.I.P.A.–S.I.L.F. employed 'goondas' to break up the inaugural meeting of the Madras Presidency Association. *Madras Mail* 17 September 1917.

[64] In November 1917, the S.I.L.F. called an all-party non-Brahman conference at Bezwada in what appeared to be an attempt to come to agreement with the

Towards the end of 1918, Montagu's report initiated a period of further change in Madras politics: for the first time, politicians had concrete proposals on which to negotiate. Given the extraordinarily complicated structure of the non-Brahman and Home Rule movements, their respective leaderships were not under any particular pressure or in receipt of any specific mandate to guide their behaviour. They could do what they liked so long as the constitution which was created put them – as a small leadership group – into positions of central power: they were commanded only by the opportunities for the advancement of factions at the top of the provincial political system.

The attitude of the S.I.P.A. – or Justice Party as we might now more conveniently call it – leadership during the negotiations was exactly predictable. Under no circumstances could it reach agreement with Mylapore or the 'new' Congress leadership which had arisen alongside Mylapore in 1919. Its policy was one of continued opposition to everything the various Home Rule League and Congress elements demanded and of using its connections with British civilians (and their own Parliamentary contacts) to maintain its credibility.[65] It followed in reverse the political contortions which the Home Rule League and Congress were practising and, in the short space of eighteen months, managed to accept and reject the principles of Montagu's report twice.[66] On the central issue of communal representation, the decision of London to rule all question of separate electorates out of consideration, gave it a weapon perfectly tempered to its needs. Prior to this decision, it had vacillated endlessly over the terms of communal safeguards.[67] Now that it was impossible for the Congress to threaten it by agreeing to its request, it demanded separate electorates as a prerequisite for its acceptance of the reforms. Lord Willingdon, who had undertaken the improbable task of obtaining an agreed solution to the communal problem, was nearly driven to distraction by the Justice

M.P.A. However, it turned out to be no more than a clumsy ploy by the S.I.L.F. to destroy its Congress opposition. M.P.A. men were excluded from all offices at the conference and were allowed to negotiate only after they had resigned their Congress memberships. *Hindu* 14 November 1917. There were no other attempts at compromise before 1920.

[65] T. M. Nair tried to link up with Lord Sydenham who led the opposition to the Montagu–Chelmsford reforms in the House of Lords. Reforms (General, Franchise) A May 1920, Nos 31–43. *N.A.I.*

[66] See *Hindu* 21 April 1919.

[67] The S.I.L.F. had no official policy on the amount of communal safeguards it required. Various members, at various times, suggested proposals which would

Party leaders' determination to cling to a position which had been made untenable before the negotiations began.[68] During the course of two conferences called by Willingdon, the Justice Party men turned down offers from 'Brahman representatives' which would have given non-Brahmans a guarantee of 60 per cent of the seats in the Legislative Council and which were much more generous than the terms of settlement forced upon them by Lord Meston, the independent arbitrator of the final award.[69] Their real political interests lay not in any absurd mathematical division of seats in a hypothetical Council but in avoiding coming to any agreement at all. Meston's imposed award thus played into their hands, for they were still able to refuse to accept it and to continue campaigning on the communal issue as a separate leadership group.

The problems faced by the Justice Party leaders, however, were as nothing to those of the Home Rule leaders. Mylapore had joined the agitation to press the British for a further devolution of power. But many of Mylapore's enemies in provincial politics also had joined in order to break back into the Congress and provincial affairs, from which they had been excluded by Krishnaswami Iyer. During 1917, Mrs Besant had used her amalgam of opposites to work herself into a position of dominance in the Congress, and the Home Rule League itself had fallen into decay.[70] It had served its purpose which was to take her to the leadership of national politics. But the cracks between the segments of her support had never been satisfactorily cemented over. Montagu's report and the serious business of negotiating the reforms provided the occasion for the old conflict to reassert itself, dressed, no doubt, in the new language of representative democracy, but making all the same points as before.

Mylapore's position on the proposed reforms was quite straightforward. It wanted as much reform as it could conceivably obtain and it would push the British to go further than their initial proposals,

have allowed Brahmans to stand in anything between 3 and 15 of the 60 proposed seats. Some members proposed communal electorates, others were not opposed to simply reserving seats.

[68] 'The non-Brahmans are certainly the dirtiest and meanest devils I've ever come across, and again I say why the devil they should be allowed this most unfair advantage which they are most unfairly exploiting I can't think.' Willingdon to Montagu, 5 February 1920. Willingdon Papers. *I.O.L.*

[69] Reforms (Franchise) 'Deposit' February 1920, No. 4; Reforms (General, Franchise) A May 1920, Nos 31–43. *N.A.I.*

[70] By December 1917 Mrs Besant had become Congress president and C. P. Ramaswami Iyer Secretary-General of the All India Congress.

whatever they might be. But it would accept the reforms as they came for, in its mind and without the experience of post-1920 politics before it, any extension of power to Indians beyond the Morley–Minto constitution was likely to redound to its own benefit. The leading men of Mylapore, C. P. Ramaswami Iyer, G. A. Natesan, L. A. Govindaraghava Iyer and their connections, therefore, wished to use the Congress organisation as a responsible negotiating body. In so far as Mrs Besant, though conceptually independent, was most reliant on Mylapore for advice and support, this was her position as well. The enemies of Besant and Mylapore were thus presented with a golden opportunity of ousting them from Congress leadership and taking over for themselves the vital organ of provincial agitation by making the Congress too wild and too violent a body for it to accord with the purposes of responsible negotiation.[71]

The leadership of the group which planned the *putsch* of Mylapore passed naturally into the hands of Kasturi Ranga Iyengar, who had been fighting Mylapore's influence since the 1890s. As one of the leading press barons of his day and as a Madras city figure capable of forging widespread *mofussil* contacts, he was crucial to the successful organisation of the manoeuvre. It is clear that he, and his lieutenants S. Satyamurthi, T. V. Gopalaswami Mudaliar and V. O. Chidambaram Pillai (the Tuticorin agitator of 1908 who now lived in Madras city), perceived the way that the Mylaporeans would go during the reform negotiations rather before C. P. Ramaswami Iyer and Mrs Besant had made a move. By the spring of 1918, they had tightened their connections with those 'frustrated' politicians, mostly from the *mofussil*, who were outside all channels of Secretariat influence and provincial political importance. They rebuilt an exact replica of the 1906–8 Extremist alliance which had done battle with Krishnaswami Iyer. Indeed most of the men of 1918 were the same as those of 1906–8. Beside Kasturi Ranga Iyengar stood C. Vijaraghavachari, his protege C. Rajagopalachari, and N. K. Ramaswami Iyer; and the newer leaders – P. Varadarajulu Naidu, E. V. Ramaswami Naicker,

[71] The probability of tension between Mylapore and the wilder student elements which carried on its agitation was apparent as early as the summer of 1917 when calls had been made for a passive resistance movement to secure Mrs Besant's release from internment. C. P. Ramaswami Iyer and the Mylapore leaders had been extremely cautious over this proposal and had agreed to it only after they had arranged the wording of the resolution so that it did not commit them to any practical action. *Hindu* 15, 24 and 27 August 1917. For an interesting discussion of student politics and its relationship to national affairs at this time see, S. Ramanathan, *Gandhi and the Youth* (Bombay, 1947).

S. Satyamurthi and T. S. S. Rajan – had all been inducted into the political system through personal connection with the old.[72] For Kasturi Ranga Iyengar's immediate purposes, the alliance looked extremely promising. The 'frustrated' would be unwilling to end the agitation which had brought them back into provincial prominence and to settle for anything like the amount of constitutional reform which would suit Mylapore. As Mrs Besant herself had brought students and other disturbed elements into the Congress in order to heat her own campaign, the material which her opponents required to destroy her was ready to hand.

The first open breach in the Congress front came at the Conjeeveram Provincial Conference in April 1918. Mrs Besant and Mylapore were nearly defeated on a challenge offered by C. Rajagopalachari to their resolution promising aid for the war effort in return for constitutional reform.[73] A few weeks later the conflict was extended to the Madras P. C. C. The Besantine–Mylapore group noticed that its grip on the organisation was being weakened by the steady induction of members of the *mofussil* 'frustrated'. It responded by recruiting to the P.C.C. nearly all the residents of the Theosophical Society's grounds at Adyar, including European women and children.[74] To prevent this membership power from being converted into executive posts at the next elections, Kasturi Ranga Iyengar began his own recruiting drive and enrolled *en masse* supporters of himself and his allies.[75] The battle returned to the open stage at the Special Provincial Conference called in August to discuss the Montagu–Chelmsford reform proposals. Satyamurthi and N. K. Ramaswami Iyer organised an attack on the Besantine–Mylapore-dominated Subjects Committee. They attempted to replace the formal resolution rejecting the reform proposals with one which, though substantially the same, was worded to give the British the impression of much greater defiance.[76] The Besantine–Mylapore

---

[72] P. Varadarajulu Naidu, E. V. Ramaswami Naicker and T. S. S. Rajan all had close political connections with C. Rajagopalachari's Salem base. S. Satyamurthi worked for Kasturi Ranga Iyengar as a journalist on the *Hindu*.

[73] *Hindu* 9, 11, 13, 14, 15 and 16 May 1918; *New India* 20 May 1918; Home Political 'Deposit' August 1918, No. 28. *N.A.I.*

[74] 'Proceedings of the Executive Committee of the Madras Provincial Congress Committee, 23 June 1918'. Proceedings of the Madras Provincial Congress Committee 1918. Madras Mahajana Sabha Papers. *N.M.M.L.*

[75] *Ibid.*, 5 July 1918.

[76] The formal resolution rejected the proposals as a basis for negotiation until they

leaders clumsily tried to prevent the expression of views opposed to their own, and the conference ended in uproar.[77]

After this debacle, both sides went back into the committee room to build their followings for the forthcoming Special Congress session on the Montagu–Chelmsford report to be held at Bombay.[78] The decline of Mrs Besant in All India politics during 1918 and 1919 is well known. She, and the groups from other provinces, which were similar in ambition to Mylapore, found it impossible to control the Congress and turn it from a wild agitational organisation into one capable of rational discussion with the British. In even attempting this, she became the object of as much hate as she had once been of adulation. Her Mylapore-type supporters only risked their own careers by remaining within an institution which was in the hands of their enemies and committed to policies they could not accept. They withdrew from the Congress and formed a 'Moderate Conference' away from the turmoil of agitation.[79] Mrs Besant, herself, returned to Madras and attempted to revive her Home Rule League only to find that it too was in the hands of Kasturi Ranga Iyengar.[80] She formed a separate National Home Rule League but it never had a serious following.[81] By the middle of 1919 she was no longer of any consequence, and the institutions of the Madras Congress were firmly under Kasturi Ranga Iyengar's control. Indeed, by 1920, he had even forced Mylapore and the Besantines out of the relatively harmless Madras Mahajana Sabha.[82]

The problems facing the new leaders of the Madras Congress, how-

were brought into line with the Congress–League scheme; the amendment rejected the proposals because they were not the same as the Congress–League scheme.

[77] The Subjects Committee insisted that the resolution should be put from the chair, and not debated at all. *Hindu* 5, 9, 12, 13, 16, 18, 20, 23, 29 and 30 July, and 1, 3 and 5 August 1918.

[78] Once again this took the form of the two sides electing as many supporters as they could find. 'Proceedings of the General Body of the Madras Provincial Congress Committee, 20 August 1918'. Proceedings of the Madras Provincial Congress Committee, 1918. Madras Mahajana Sabha Papers. *N.M.M.L.*

[79] In Madras the main organiser of the Moderate Conference was Sir P. S. Sivaswami Iyer who, although never actually a member of the Home Rule League, was known to support Home Rule objects. *Hindu* 27 and 29 July 1918. Within a year most of the leading men of Mylapore had defected from the Congress to the Moderate Conference.'

[80] *The National Home Rule League. How Founded and Why* (Adyar, 1919), pp. 1–3.

[81] *Ibid.*

[82] *Hindu* 16 and 24 August 1920.

ever, were very similar to those facing the leaders who had just gone. The organisation had fed on years of agitation and had grown fat. It was a reasonable presupposition that, in the unknown era of politics about to commence, it was going to have a considerable influence. But it would have to moderate its tone and prepare itself for constitutional action. Yet in order to gain control of it, Kasturi Ranga Iyengar and his men had had to foster the more extreme elements in political life and to give a greater share of power to the *mofussil* frustrated, particularly C. Rajagopalachari,[83] who had nothing to gain by a return to constitutional activity. The tensions can be seen clearly in the response to Gandhi's call for a *hartal* and demonstration over the Rowlatt Acts in April 1919. C. Rajagopalachari and his extreme associates, using trades union and cultural as well as political linkages, which had been developed during the period of united Home Rule League–Congress agitation,[84] organised a show of force in Madras city on a scale never seen before. The police estimated that about one hundred thousand people attended lectures and parades on the beach.[85] Yet the Congress leadership – the Kasturi Ranga Iyengar group – so far from being delighted by Rajagopalachari's achievement was absolutely terrified.[86] For the next six months it made sure that scarcely a dog was heard to bark in the city and Congress public activity virtually dried up.

To the extremist group, now headed by C. Rajagopalachari, it became increasingly clear that the new Congress leadership was no great improvement on the old. During 1919 and 1920, Kasturi Ranga Iyengar demonstrated that he intended to use his control of the Congress organisation and the contacts he possessed with higher administrative officers – forged both through personal connections and through his role in the Congress – to exercise as tight and as closed a leadership as had Mylapore. The first overt manifestation of this came during the summer of 1919, when the Tamil newspaper *Desabhaktan*, of which Rajagopalachari and T. S. S. Rajan were directors, began to rival the circulation of the *Swadesamitran*, the Tamil organ

[83] By 1919, C. Rajagopalachari was a member of the executive committee of the Madras P.C.C. and vice-president of the Madras Mahajana Sabha. He had sold his possessions in Salem and set up house in the capital.

[84] During 1919, C. Rajagopalachari and other *mofussil* politicians (particularly the Salem barrister T. Audinarayana Chetty) fostered a series of labour organisations in Madras city. These provided them with a base for agitational politics in the capital. *Hindu* 6 and 7 December 1918 and 14 February 1920.

[85] G.O. 318 (Public) dated 2 June 1919. *T.N.A.*

[86] See T. V. Kalyanasundram Mudaliar, *Valkkai Kurippugal* (Madras, 1969), pp. 305–6 (Tamil).

of the *Hindu* complex. According to the Commissioner of the Madras city police, Kasturi Ranga Iyengar persuaded the Attorney-General, S. Srinivasa Iyengar (who had broken with Mylapore on personal grounds),[87] to raise *Desabhaktan*'s security deposit to a level which its directors could scarcely hope to meet. The newspaper was threatened with closure and was able to survive only through the intervention of C. P. Ramaswami Iyer and Mrs Besant who provided it with funds. While it may seem ideologically paradoxical for 'moderates' to support an 'extremist' journal, the move makes excellent sense if viewed from the standpoint of the political factions involved in the Congress fight.[88]

In the spring and summer of 1920, Kasturi Ranga Iyengar's activities announced that there would be no place for Rajagopalachari and his followers once Congress moved into the new Montagu–Chelmsford councils. At the Tinnevelly Provincial Conference in June, the Congress began its advance towards the elections and set up a committee to co-ordinate its campaign. It was essential now for the Congress leadership to work closely with important local magnates if it were to translate its agitational power into votes. The Raja of Ramnad, the *zamindar* of Kumaramangalam and the powerful Tinnevelly temple and local board politician N. A. V. Somasundram Pillai were drafted onto the committee. The only members of the Congress executive to be included, however, were Kasturi Ranga Iyengar himself and S. Srinivasa Iyengar, who had now resigned his post as Attorney-General and openly joined Kasturi Ranga Iyengar. None of Rajagopalachari's associates was considered initially for a place and it was only following a threat to refuse to recognise the committee that C. Vijayaraghavachari was begrudgingly brought in.[89] Later, at the beginning of August, the massive Tilak Memorial Fund was set up and again the Rajagopalachari group was squeezed out. The best any of its number could obtain was a minor office shared with the manager of the *Swadesamitran* press.[90]

[87] S. Srinivasa Iyengar was a member of the Vembakkam clan and a leading lawyer in the capital. His alienation from Mylapore dated from Krishnaswami Iyer's death, when he and L. A. Govindaraghava Iyer had fought over the University Legislative Council seat vacated by Sivaswami Iyer who moved onto the Executive Council to take up Krishnaswami Iyer's posts. Most of Mylapore preferred Govindaraghava Iyer who eventually won the election. *Hindu* 5 February 1914. See also V. S. Srinivasa Sastri to P. S. Sivaswami Iyer, 7 August 1916; S. Srinivasa Iyengar to P. S. Sivaswami Iyer, 18 February 1914. P. S. Sivaswami Iyer Papers. *N.A.I.*

[88] Report 422-D from Commissioner of Police, Madras City, dated 4 March 1919 in G.O. 230 (Public) dated 29 April 1919. *T.N.A.*

[89] *Hindu* 23 and 25 June 1920.

[90] *Hindu* 11 August 1920.

Nonetheless, before the middle of August 1920, Kasturi Ranga Iyengar's opponents in the Congress had no coherent plans for opposing him, least of all on the non-co-operation issue of boycotting the Legislative Councils. The position of Rajagopalachari and his 'party', no less than that of the 'old' and 'new' Congress leaderships, was defined by their proximity to the sources of power, which obviously were going to lie in the Legislative Council. Although they were an 'out' faction, they were still a faction and had no inclination to abandon the political game completely. They joined with Kasturi Ranga Iyengar in calling on Gandhi to wait for a Congress session before declaring non-co-operation.[91]

Their decision to back Gandhi followed only after considerable consultations with the Mahatma while he was campaigning in Madras in August 1920. Gandhi's tour coincided with a debate in the Madras P.C.C. on the question of non-co-operation. In the first session of discussions, Rajagopalachari was equivocal on the possibilities of the tactic. Gandhi arrived in the city just before the second session and, by the third, Rajagopalachari was a pronounced advocate of non-co-operation.[92] The Kasturi Ranga Iyengar group, of course, was bitterly opposed to the notion of Council boycott which would defeat the purpose of the previous two years' exercise.[93] Rajagopalachari's conversion, however, was not merely a ploy to embarrass his provincial opponents. Gandhi's movement made sense to his reasonable ambitions. He, and his associates, had risen to prominence only through the agitation of the 1916 to 1920 period. It was clear from Kasturi Ranga Iyengar's behaviour that, once the agitation died, they would sink back into obscurity. Gandhi, by promising to place the weight of the All-India Congress behind continued agitation, offered Rajagopalachari the one chance he had left of remaining a politician of significance. Until he had that promise, however, Council boycott itself meant nothing but consignment to an even greater obscurity.[94]

---

[91] Letter of P. Varadarajulu Naidu in *Hindu* 20 July 1920.

[92] *Hindu* 5, 6 and 25 August 1920.

[93] During the many conferences and discussions on non-co-operation which took place in 1920, the Madras leadership group had managed to maintain its ambiguous posture. It agreed to some kind of campaign but succeeded in preventing all attempts to define what that campaign should be. See S. Satyamurthi to Secretary, All India Congress Committee, 26 August 1920. All India Congress Committee Papers, File 13(2) of 1920. *N.M.M.L.* The only authoritative statement made on the matter was that 'the programme in no case shall include the boycotting of elections to the Reformed Councils'. *Hindu* 16 August 1920.

[94] This statement in no way denies Rajagopalachari's 'spiritual' conversion to the Gandhian cause, which was manifest by 1924. It is perfectly compatible with a

At the Calcutta Congress, Rajagopalachari led to Gandhi's cause a collection of students and Muslims disturbed by the Khilafat agitation.[95] Gandhi's victory destroyed Kasturi Ranga Iyengar's leadership of the Madras Congress. His important magnate supporters deserted the Congress for the Councils and the disturbed agitational groups naturally looked to Rajagopalachari rather than himself. He was left the nominal head of an organisation whose policies he disavowed and whose remaining supporters were his enemies. His involvement in non-co-operation was half-hearted to say the least. Logic was restored to the political situation after the Nagpur Congress when, using the new Congress constitution, Rajagopalachari was able to remove Kasturi Ranga Iyengar from the executive of the Tamil Nad C.C. and to switch Congress headquarters in the South from Madras city to Trichinopoly.[96] The stranglehold on Congress affairs, exercised for so long by a handful of men in the capital, had at last been broken and the frustrated *mofussil* politicians who had spent years hammering at the dominance of Madras city had finally obtained their own provincial institution.

The provincial leadership groups which we have been examining existed logically apart from any local support on which they might hope to draw. None can be seen as parties possessing disciplined followings or structures through which followers could inform leaders of their requirements. Each was rather a group of associated individuals jockeying for position in relation to and for influence over the new and unknown constitution. With the exception of C. Rajagopalachari, whose independence was asserted only at the expense of the new constitution, all three leadership groups appealed to exactly the same social material for support. As we saw, they tried to form organisations out of the same caste, class and religious interests and, above all, were concerned to attract the sympathy of various local magnates. The reasons for the battles at the centre of provincial politics are clear, but what did the magnates themselves make of these faction fights and on what grounds did they give their support?

Up to the time of Meston's communal award, there was little ideological difference between the three leadership groups. All three accepted the principle of some form of communal safeguard for the non-Brahmans, and all three, tacitly at least, had decided to work

---

'conversion' hypothesis and merely points out that, in the circumstances, spiritual and material factors both worked towards the same end.

[95] *Hindu* 2 and 6 September 1920.

[96] All India Congress Committee Papers, File 1 of 1921. *N.M.M.L.* Home Political A File 244 of 1921 *N.A.I.*

through the new constitution. It would be difficult, therefore, to see any of the leaderships winning support because of their principles. Of course, each group could count on particular magnates, tied by personal connections and by the connections of opponents with other groups. But that would only explain the behaviour of a handful of men. For most magnates of local power, the relevant question was which of the three groups was most likely to be successful and, given that the nature of political life in the new Councils was uncertain, the answer was impossible to calculate. A great many, therefore, kept their lines of contact open with several leaderships at the same time in order to play the odds. The ambivalent behaviour of A. Subbarayalu Reddiar and T. A. Ramalingam Chetty, which we noted earlier, set a general pattern. In Ellore, as early as 1917, the Mothey family had demonstrated overt Congress connections and had attended a non-Brahman conference with their lawyer K. V. Reddi Naidu;[97] later they tightened their Justice Party connections as Reddi Naidu climbed into the Justice leadership group but, through their Arya Vysya caste conference, they remained in touch also with the Congress.[98] In Tanjore, by 1918, two of the largest landowners, V. A. Vandayar of Pundi and T. Somasundram Mudaliar, could be found in both S.I.P.A. and Congress organisations.[99] In Ganjam, the local politician A. P. Patro was an organiser for both the Justice Party and the Mylapore-inspired Moderate Conference;[100] in Cocanada, K. Suryanarayanamurthi Naidu, a millionaire shipowner and landlord who had great influence in the town, held office in the local Justice Party and the Congress District Association;[101] in Salem, the banker S. Ellapa Chetty, a member of the Justice Party, presided at the local Congress meeting to pick candidates for the election.[102] As, in 1917, a separate Andhra P.C.C. had been created, the expulsion of Mylapore from the Madras P.C.C. did not necessarily affect many of Mylapore's closest contacts in the Andhra *mofussil*. Such men as N. Subba Rao, M. Ramachandra

---

[97] Subba Rao, *Life and Times of Sir K. V. Reddi Naidu*, p. 31. *Hindu* 30 November 1917.

[98] The Komati merchants of the Andhra delta towns, who ran the caste *sabha*, were strong supporters of the Congress and its local leaders, Konda Venkatappayya and A. Kaleswara Rao. *Hindu* 27 February 1920.

[99] *Hindu* 19 March, 2, 22 and 23 April 1918.

[100] *Hindu* 16 October 1918.

[101] In April 1920, the District Association gave its support to several candidates including K. Suryanarayanamurthi Naidu of the Justice Party and D. V. Prakasa Rao, a Congressman and later chief non-co-operator in the town. *Hindu* 23 April 1920.

[102] *Hindu* 1 June 1920.

Rao and the Nellore Mylapore contact, A. S. Krishna Rao, found it possible to remain members both of Mylapore's Moderate Conference and of the Andhra Congress.[103] Indeed, N. Subba Rao and M. Ramachandra Rao were members of the committee which selected Congress candidates for the election.[104] So desperately did some local figures feel the need for a multiplicity of connections at the centre that, at the Tinnevelly Provincial Congress Conference of 1920, S. T. Shanmugham Pillai and T. N. Sivagnana Pillai, the Tinnevelly politicians who had been most responsible for the spread of anti-Brahman and anti-Congress propaganda in the district, showed considerable interest in the affairs of the session.[105]

The contortions of the local magnates make it clear that they, the most important political forces in Madras, saw the provincial political conflict in terms of men not measures and patronage not principle. As the elections approached, however, events in the leadership groups made worse the near total chaos to which magnate floor-crossing had reduced provincial politics. One of the leadership groups, the 'new' Congress, dropped out of contention and left a number of magnates, who had close ties with it, floating uncertainly on the surface of political life. In Madras, no man of political substance who had a chance of election – not even S. Srinivasa Iyengar[106] – was prepared to entertain Gandhi's overtures and boycott the Councils. Further, the Justice Party, responding to the conservatism of Meston's Award, launched a desperate crusade which made nonsense of its avowed political position. It elaborated a campaign, based on Meston's reservation of only 28 seats, to secure the election of all non-Brahmans. It offered its ticket to any non-Brahman who stood for election, no matter what his political hue, his connections with Brahmans and his intentions in the new legislature.[107] Thus it threw its cloak over virtually everybody in the presidency and, as it demanded no return for its generosity, utterly obscured any differences between the majority of candidates. A great many local magnates and politicians stood at the polls as 'non-Brahmans' without showing the least sign of breaking with their Brahman friends. In Madras city, for example, Lodd

---

[103] *Hindu* 22 January 1920 and 19 February 1920.
[104] *Hindu* 23 June 1920. M. Ramachandra Rao even made an election pact with A. A Kaleswara Rao who later was a leader of non-co-operation. *Hindu* 26 June 1920.
[105] *Hindu* 28 May and 23 June 1920.
[106] Who temporarily dumped the Congress and won the University Legislative Council seat in 1920.
[107] *Hindu* 18 March, 23 and 26 April and 13 May 1920.

Govindoss, who had poured *lakhs* of rupees into the Congress and remained on the best of terms with Mylapore, accepted the support of Justice Party polemic.[108] In Salem, the banker and lawyer T. Audina-rayana Chetty, who had been a close ally of Rajagopalachari and was to return in 1926 as a Congress Swarajist, found that he too could accept Thyagaraja Chetty's blank cheque.[109] In Tanjore, V. A. Vandayar of Pundi stood for the Legislative Council as a specifically nominated Justice Party non-Brahman, while actively helping the Mylapore Brahman Sir. P. S. Sivaswami Iyer to win an election to the Central Legislative Assembly.[110]

Although the conduct of many candidates in this election may seem, to the outside observer, to be regulated by principles of mayhem, it was guided by an inner logic. The non-Brahman category allowed candidates in multi-member constituencies to exclude some of the individuals, namely Brahmans, who competed against them. Exclusion was so much in everybody's mind that the Governor, Lord Willingdon, was driven to distraction by the arrival of hundreds of petitions – many of them from election candidates – calling for separate caste and sub-caste constituencies, which, if acted upon, would have obviated the necessity for any competition at all.[111] Once beyond constituency boundaries, however, candidates were not committed to maintaining their hostility to other sub-castes or even to Brahmans. As might be expected in such a complicated polity, outside Madras city there was little evidence of systematic campaigning on any particular ticket and most candidates would have found it extremely difficult to say where they stood.[112]

---

[108] *Hindu* 29 April 1926.   [109] *Hindu* 13 May 1920.

[110] M. D. Subramanyam to P. S. Sivaswami Iyer, 8 June 1920. P. S. Sivaswami Iyer Papers. *N.A.I.*

[111] 'Oh this communal business. I am being bombarded by all sorts of sub-castes of the non-Brahmins for special representation, and as I believe there are some 250 of these, I am not likely to satisfy many in a council of 127. You're a nice fellow to have given me this job.' Willingdon to Montagu, 20 February 1920. Willingdon Papers *I.O.L.*

[112] 'As for an appeal or manifesto, I am afraid it may not be quite expedient at this stage to decide upon making one, as difficulties of all sorts are likely to be experienced in procuring the signatures of some prominent Non-Brahmin leaders. While they are quite willing to render every sort of help practically in promoting our cause, it is easy to understand that some at least among them feel it very delicate and inconvenient to be signatories in the appeal proposed to be published.' M. D. Subramanyam to P. S. Sivaswami Iyer, 8 June 1920. P. S. Sivaswami Iyer Papers. *N.A.I.* In the deltas of the Northern Circars, one of the few places in which candidates regularly made speeches, election addresses were concerned much more with the land revenue, Public Works Department and local matters than with provincial issues, such as the non-Brahman movement. See,

In fact, looking at the successful Legislative Councillors from a rather different angle, it is relevant to ask whether the enormities of the propaganda which filled the press had any direct impact on local political structures. Those who were elected were, to a man, important local magnates or the representatives of magnate interests. No district board president who stood for election failed to be returned; the vast majority of M.L.C.s held combinations of places in rural boards, municipalities, and temple, school and government advisory committees.[113] The few who did not, possessed equally concrete political resources in their control of various informal social institutions.[114] Every man elected was of substantial political power in his locality before the election – in most cases before the first whiff of polemic had spread across Madras in 1916. As the turn-out to the polls was extremely small and as the number of votes necessary to win election in the multi-member constituencies was minute,[115] it seems more than probable that factors of personal connection and control had been of dominant importance.

The one constituency in which there had been a systematic party campaign, at least by one party, was Madras city.[116] Not only had this been the headquarters of the Justice leadership group since 1916 but it was also one of the few constituencies which was physically small enough to be amenable to parades and polling organisation. Yet even here, the results would lend themselves to an interpretation which emphasised more local power than party or ideology. Two of the four Justice Party candidates were defeated, and the two who were victorious were P. Thyagaraja Chetty and O. Thanikachellam Chetty, both of

for example, P. Govindarow Naidu, *The Legislative Council Elections* (Cocanada, 1920).

[113] For brief biographies, see Reforms (Franchise) B March 1921, Nos 34–99. *N.A.I.*

[114] Such as A. Thangavelu Naicker of North Arcot, who was one of the richest *ryotwari* landlords in his district and came from a family commonly regarded as leaders among the locally dominant Palli caste; or T. C. Srinivasa Iyengar of Ramnad, who represented the interests of the enormously influential Nattukottai Chetty bankers of his district. *Ibid.*

[115] Although the district electorates varied in size from between 20,000 and 90,000 voters, candidates found that they needed only between 1000 and 5000 votes to be successful. *Hindu* 9 and 10 December 1920.

[116] It was a very violent campaign, aimed specifically at C. P. Ramaswami Iyer. M. Kothandavelu Mudaliar, a Sengunthair Vellala *dubash* who was acting as his election agent, was beaten and stoned by a mob and Ramaswami Iyer himself took to carrying loaded pistols to his election meetings. *Hindu* 6 October 1920; Prakash, *Sir C. P.*, p. 35. For Justice Party organisation, see *Hindu* 5, 9 and 16 October 1920.

whom held a multitude of local offices and were extremely influential in city affairs without reference to the Justice Party.[117] In spite of the fact that the electorate was predominantly non-Brahman, the two non-Justice Party winners were Brahmans. One was C. P. Ramaswami Iyer, whose local power in the city scarcely needs stressing. The other, Dr U. Rama Rao, was a Canarese 'foreigner' in the city who had been a municipal commissioner for several years – as the representative of the important Saraswat Brahman economic interest – and was influential in education circles through his place on the University Senate. He had taken virtually no part in the great debate of the previous four years.

The correspondence of Sir P. S. Sivaswami Iyer suggests a better way to explain the elections than grand but meaningless generalisations on the theme of ideology. Sivaswami Iyer stood in the Trichinopoly–Tanjore constituency for the Central Legislative Assembly. His campaign was based on two assumptions both of which, judging by his huge success, proved to be correct: firstly, that certain magnates, through their hold over a variety of local institutions, possessed 'blocs' of votes of a cross-communal character; and secondly, that although he possessed little direct power in the local arenas of Tanjore and Trichinopoly, he had influence in provincial and, by this time, national political circles and could use his position in these to forward the interests of the controllers of local blocs. His campaign workers consisted of relatives, friends, family networks put at his disposal by friends and the staff of a school of which he was president.[118] His first move was to gain the allegiance of the Kallar *zamindar* of Papanad whose landowning and banking activities were said to give him 800 votes, even on the restricted C.L.A. franchise.[119] Next came the *pandarasanidhis* of the *maths* at Thiruvadathorai and Dharmapuram, who were of equal importance.[120] Then he mobilised his Nattukottai Chetty connections, whose banking empire was far flung and who allowed him to use appointments at their college in Chidambaram

[117] O. Thanikachellam Chetty was a member of the Corporation and Pachayappa's Charities board; he was also a Beri Chetty, related to various leading members of the city's mercantile community and a founder member of the Beri Chetty Sangam.

[118] T. R. Venkatarama Sastri to P. S. Sivaswami Iyer, 23 May and 31 August 1920; P. S. Sivaswami Iyer to V. Guruswami Sastri, 8 and 22 May 1920. P. S. Sivaswami Iyer Papers *N.A.I.*

[119] M. D. Subramanyam to P. S. Sivaswami Iyer, 6 June and 7 September 1920 P. S. Sivaswami Iyer Papers. *N.A.I.*

[120] M. D. Subramanyam to P. S. Sivaswami Iyer, 14 May and 31 August 1920. P. S. Sivaswami Iyer Papers. *N.A.I.*

to reward his campaign staff.[121] Finally, his agents fanned out across the district contacting influential landlords and merchants, such as V. A. Vandayar of Pundi and a complex of Odayar families based on Mannargudi who controlled 200 votes.[122] By the date of the election, Sivaswami Iyer had pledged support from aristocrats, priests (in the case of the *maths*, priests of the supposedly anti-Brahman Saiva Siddhanta religious philosophy), bankers and rural-local leaders. Among the more eccentric elements of his following were Father Bertram (the influential principal of the Jesuit college at Trichinopoly), the cashier of the Negapatam branch of the Bank of Madras and a Reddi shipowner, whom he had met in Burma, who put his family trading network at Sivaswami Iyer's disposal. The whole structure was held together only by Sivaswami Iyer himself, whose influence had provided in the past and would continue to provide in the future services and rewards from higher political organisations for this variegated mass of local groupings.[123] The campaign provides us with a classic example of the provincially extended magnate network which was the most usual form of political organisation in Madras throughout our period.

Sivaswami Iyer's election, however, had been to the Central Legislative Assembly in New Delhi. His constituency covered two districts and was, therefore, similar in size to the constituencies under the Morley–Minto constitution. His political network, though of the same type, was more elongated than that used by most politicians to get into the Montagu–Chelmsford provincial Council, the constituencies of which covered only single districts. The new provincial Councillors, as we have seen, were men who could mobilise the political resources of district institutions. Before 1920, relatively few of them had appeared on the provincial political stage. Certainly some of them had been in contact with provincial political leaderships during the years

---

121 M. D. Subramanyam to P. S. Sivaswami Iyer, 14 May 1920. P. S. Sivaswami Iyer Papers. *N.A.I.*

122 T. R. Venkatarama Sastri to P. S. Sivaswami Iyer, 23 May 1920; G. Venkatesan to P. S. Sivaswami Iyer, 20 November 1920; M. D. Subramanyam to P. S. Sivaswami Iyer, 8 June 1920. P. S. Sivaswami Iyer Papers. *N.A.I.*

123 For example, Sivaswami's agents helped Papanad to a temple committee place. M. D. Subramanyam to P. S. Sivaswami Iyer, 8 June 1920. S. Parasurama Iyer, a rich *mirasidar*, offered 100 votes for help in fighting the impending revenue resettlement – help which Sivaswami Iyer was only too pleased to provide. S. Parasurama Iyer to P. S. Sivaswami Iyer, 26 November 1920, and Publicity Bureau to P. S. Sivaswami Iyer, 30 November 1920. R. P. Moorthy, a temple politician, expected a district board seat for his help. R. P. Moorthy to P. S. Sivaswami Iyer, 16 December 1920. P. S. Sivaswami Iyer Papers. *N.A.I.*

of agitation. But the connections between provincial and local politics were so tenuous and the conduct of local politicians in provincial parties was so ambivalent, that it would be impossible to describe the new M.L.C.s as the stalwarts of any party.

Lord Willingdon's decision to appoint a Justice Party Ministry was the result of a misinterpretation of the election returns. Under pressure from his civilians to favour the non-Brahman cause[124] and a witness to the Justice Party's only election campaign in Madras city, he deemed the election to have been a Justice Party victory because a majority of the victors were non-Brahmans. In fact, when information from the localities arrived at Fort St George, it was seen that only 15 of the 65 men elected from general constituencies had particularly close ties with Justice Party leadership. The rest were classified vaguely as 'Liberals', 'Moderates' or 'Independents'.[125] One newspaper, outraged by Willingdon's choice, pointed out that at least 35 general constituency M.L.C.s were 'progressives' having some, albeit loose, connection with the Congress or Mylapore and none at all with the party of the new Ministry.[126] It took Willingdon only a few weeks to realise that his invitation to the Justice Party to form a Ministry had been a mistake:

The present position as far as I have seen it here now that the budget debate is on, is that the Government is damned all round by everyone and the so-called followers of the ministry show no allegiance at all unless it is convenient. This is the more significant here for I definitely put in a non-Brahman ministry and they appear to have no hold over their followers. I have urged them to try and organise their party. I have appointed at their request council secretaries who shall act as whips but at present they are not very effective.[127]

Even the old war-cry of 'Down with the Brahman' failed to provide a basis for the unification of a Council majority. Not only were few of the new non-Brahman M.L.C.s antagonistic to Brahmans as a group but, with a Council of local power, the Ministry could no longer present the Brahman as a political threat, real or imagined. At the

---

[124] In 1919, the Chief Secretary, Sir Lionel Davidson, had argued that only the Justice Party represented the true interests of the non-Brahmans. Those non-Brahmans who sympathised with Congress aims (the majority of non-Brahmans returned in both 1919 and 1920 elections) were serving Brahman interests. G.O. 122 (L and M, Leg.) dated 17 October 1919. *T.N.A.*

[125] Reforms (Franchise) B March 1921, Nos 34–99. *N.A.I.*

[126] *Hindu* 15 December 1920. A considerable section of the press regarded Willingdon's decision as scandalous. See *Swadesamitran* 18 December 1920; *Venkatesapatrika* 25 December 1920. *R.N.P.*

[127] Willingdon to Montagu, 21 March 1921. Willingdon Papers. *I.O.L.*

election, the provisions of the meagre Meston Award had not needed to be invoked for, on the basis of local power, Brahmans were not in a position to swamp a single constituency.[128] Indeed, at no time under the Montagu–Chelmsford constitution was protection required. The communal issue was finally obvious for the hoax it had always been.

In its early days, the operation of the Legislative Council was characterised only by chaos. Most of the new M.L.C.s were local men whose previous contacts with the provincial level of politics had been mediated by one or other of the provincial leadership groups. Now they were placed at the provincial capital itself and, initially, had very little idea of what they were supposed to do. Gradually, however, the turbulence subsided as the Ministry became conscious of its position and of the necessities of its new job. Through the vigorous use of the considerable powers of patronage at its disposal, it bought itself a majority of the independent Councillors and thus kept itself in office. In the words of its chief whip, 'the party lived on patronage'.[129] The Ministry showed little interest in the antecedents of the men to whom it offered its favours. Patronage was always limited and the Chief Minister (between 1921 and 1926 P. Ramarayaningar, the Raja of Panagal) calculated its distribution to produce the strongest Council combination rather than to reward old friends. Many powerful local magnates and politicians, who, before 1920, had been associated with the Congress or Mylapore, became attached to the Ministry. Not the least of these were the three magnates whom Kasturi Ranga Iyengar had placed on the Congress election committee in June 1920. The Raja of Ramnad was supported in the district board of Ramnad,[130] the *zamindar* of Kumaramangalam was made a Council secretary and chief whip and N. A. V. Somasundram Pillai was allowed to help in the drafting of the Ministry's temple legislation.[131] All three supported the Ministry until its demise in 1926. Equally, Ramarayaningar found it politic to reward several Brahmans whose local position was strong

---

[128] Meston reached his award on the basis of seats held in the institutions of local self-government. The evidence showed so clearly that non-Brahmans – as a category – were not a threatened interest that he accepted C. P. Ramaswami Iyer's plan for communal safeguards in its entirety. Reforms (Franchise) 'Deposit' February 1920, No. 12, *N.A.I.*

[129] R. V. Krishna Ayyar, *In the Legislature of Those Days* (Madras, 1956), p. 45.

[130] The raja became district board president in 1921. For his role in breaking up anti-ministerial organisations see *Hindu* 24 August 1923.

[131] *Justice* 10 January 1921, cutting in G.O. 171 (Public) dated 26 March 1921. *T.N.A.*

and who could guarantee their own return to Council seats.[132] Those who particularly suffered as a result of the changing emphasis of Justice Party policy were the innumerable publicists and petty political organisers who had carried on the non-Brahman communal agitation but who had no secured local bases under them. When Ramarayaningar took office, they expected his support and patronage. Most were to find very quickly, however, that they were not to get it. In the age of Council politics, journalists and demagogues, such as O. Kandaswami Chetty and the educationist C. Ramalinga Reddy, and local party organisers, such as J. Ramanathan of Madura and C. Natesan of Madras city, were no longer necessary nor valuable.[133] By 1923, they had formed an anti-Ministerial Justice Party,[134] the existence of which demonstrates clearly the character of politics in Madras at this time. The basic cleavage in the Council was between followers and opponents of the Ministry, who were determined by the favours they received or failed to receive from the Ministry.

Once it had secured office, the Justice Party Ministry threw off the last vestiges of its guise as a party of local grievance against the centre, which, we saw, characterised its formation. Between 1917 and 1920, as it gained access to the centre and saw the prospect of power, it had steadily modified this image. Now the Ministry could abandon it completely and enjoy the fruits of its labours. Its opposition to the Dharmarakshana Sabha and temple reform gave way to the preparation of a bill to bring the temples under central – i.e. its own – control.[135] Its early antipathy to the interference of the Secretariat in local self-government appointments gave way to an aggressive use of local self-government patronage by comparison to which Mylapore's previous endeavours were mere tinkerings. Its views on the control of service appointments were revised. No longer did it wish the I.C.S.

[132] Notably, T. Desikachari of Trichinopoly, A. S. Krishna Rao of Nellore, N. Subba Rao of South Kanara and T. M. Narasimhacharlu of Cuddapah. The last two also had personal ties with the Ministry. *The Cult of Incompetence, being an impartial enquiry into the record of the First Madras Ministry* (Madras, 1923), pp. 37–9.

[133] Ramarayaningar ridiculed C. Ramalinga Reddy, C. Natesan and O. Kandaswami Chetty by exposing publicly their various personal demands for favour – which included district board presidencies, University Vice-Chancellorships, jobs for their relatives and council nominations. Kandaswami Chetty eventually sued Ramarayaningar for libel and won damages of one pie. *Hindu* (weekly) 7 and 17 February 1924 and 29 April 1926. *Madras Legislative Council Proceedings*, XVII (March 1924), 145.

[134] *Hindu* 26 February, 28 May and 13 June 1923.

[135] See Baker, 'Political Change in South India 1919–1937', pp. 127–8.

to retain a role of impartiality and to prevent one group of Indians from monopolising the entry and promotion points in the careers structure. It wanted full powers of appointment to be given to the Ministers.[136] The sympathy which some of its members, notably P. Ramarayaningar, had shown to the cause of Andhra separatism also evaporated.[137] Devolution meant less patronage.

Of course, Mylapore's own reaction to the new circumstances was precisely the opposite of the Ministry's and it came to take up many of the positions which the S.I.P.A. had occupied against it four years before. By 1920, it had lost many of its privileges and powers. The Local and Municipal Department had gone forever, the Dharmarak-shana Sabha was being made redundant by the Ministry's legislation and the University was in the process of being swamped by Ministerial appointees. Admittedly, all had not yet disappeared. Mylapore still dominated the legal profession and had a hand in one or two departments. But it had been replaced substantially at the centre and so was moved to obstruct the growth of central influence. It bitterly opposed the temple legislation which once had been its pet project;[138] it demanded the rapid decentralisation of local self-government powers, which once it had fought strongly to prevent;[139] and it even supported the retention of I.C.S. control of selection to the services, over which it had gone to war with the British in 1916.[140] Indeed, by the early 1920s Mylapore, the archfiend of the Home Rule League, had become the most loyal supporter of the continuation of the British connection. Intellectually, through such organisations as the Liberal League, it evinced policies which pleased the heart of every Secretary of State. And politically, it offered loyal service to the *raj*: in 1921, C. P. Ramaswami Iyer, the devil incarnate of 1916–18, was offered the portfolio of the Home Department – an office which had been reserved and considered too delicate and important to be transferred to the Justice Party. Many of the fears which the British had felt about relying over much on the collaboration of Mylapore were now passed on to the collaboration of the Ministry; and Mylapore, like the

---

[136] A. Ramaswami Mudaliar, *Mirror of the Year* (Madras, 1928), p. 209.

[137] See J. G. Leonard, 'Politics and Social Change in South India: A Study of the Andhra Movement' in *Journal of Commonwealth Political Studies*, v: 1 (1967).

[138] M. Ramachandra Rao to P. S. Sivaswami Iyer, 13 June 1923. P. S. Sivaswami Iyer Papers. *N.A.I.*

[139] For example, V. Krishnaswami Iyer, when an Executive Councillor, had been very heavy-handed with the local rights of municipalities; now Mylapore, in concert with all of the Ministry's opponents, stood out for local rights.

[140] P. S. Sivaswami Iyer to T. Sapru, 6 May 1922. P. S. Sivaswami Iyer Papers. *N.A.I.*

non-Brahmans of 1916, became to the British the sought-after alternative which required help. The world of provincial politics had been turned upside down.

1920, however, did not only mark the replacement of one clique by another in the offices of the capital. It also signified a change in the way that cliques were formed and hence an alteration in the structure of politics. Mylapore's position had rested on its ability to control the professional institutions of the law, education and bureaucracy which alone had comprised the channels of political communication between the local and provincial levels. After 1920, however, these channels were joined and largely replaced by those of election. As it realised before the 1920 election, when its members begged Willingdon to appoint them Ministers before the election had taken place, Mylapore could not compete in this new medium of politics in which local resources were all important. Its Home Rule campaign had been too successful for its own good, and franchise qualifications and constituency boundaries had been drawn too near the ground for its comfort. It was no longer of very much account.

In relation to the localities, the new Ministry found itself in a weaker position than Mylapore had been. As we have seen, Mylapore itself could not entirely mould local political situations to fit its own abstract designs. It did not have the wherewithal to invent magnates. But it could choose between magnates who were already present and intervene decisively in factional struggles to aid one side or another. And, importantly, local magnates who were injured by it had no real means of obtaining redress. Mylapore was appointed by the British and was not responsible to any institution or body of Indian opinion. If it added up its sums of patronage incorrectly it could not be dismissed.

The Ministry, however, was in a rather different boat. It too could only intervene in local situations and not create them. As the 1920 election proved, its nominations to the party ticket were not valuable in themselves. It had little control over the vast splay of economic sanctions and patronage incentives which enabled the local magnate to commandeer the votes of tenants, dependents and clients. Indeed, in some ways, its patronage powers were less than those which Mylapore had possessed. Before the Religious Endowments Act of 1926, it had no Dharmarakshana Sabha to give it entry to the temples; and the local self-government legislation of 1919 and 1920, while increasing the number of seats and executive positions which the Minister could fill by nomination, increased much faster the number which he could not and which were elective. The Justice Party Ministry was not well placed to dominate the localities. Yet the localities had gained greatly in their ability to influence the Ministry, for if the Ministry disregarded the opinions of those local magnates who sat in the new Legislative Council, they could bring it to its knees.

Ramarayaningar rapidly discovered the tenuousness of his position and was forced to give way to local pressure in the matter of several important nominations. In 1921, still flushed with the success of his recent appointment and eager to demonstrate to the British the reality of the non-Brahman cause, he tried to fill two vacancies on the district boards of Ramnad and Salem with 'professional' non-Brahman clients of his own and badly burnt his fingers. In Ramnad, the new district board president and recent convert to the Justice Party, the Raja of Ramnad, would have nothing to do with Ramarayaningar's man and insisted instead on the place being given to a Brahman lawyer of his acquaintance. After an exchange of several angry letters, the Minister backed down.[141] In Salem, the district board president, G. Foulkes, a European *zamindar* and erstwhile friend of the Justice Party, was no less emphatic. He refused to accept the Minister's choice of P. L. Ramaswami Naicker, an active non-Brahman party worker, and forced Ramarayaningar to appoint another Brahman lawyer. He also provided the Minister with the maxim which was to guide his remaining years in office: 'On general principles if Government is going to nominate members without reference to responsible local opinion, it is not going to be long before Government is going to land itself in difficulties.'[142] Ramarayaningar marked this sentence well and kept his role down to that of offering sweetmeats to the local men who mattered. He performed this task with some brilliance and held his place until 1926, constantly searching for more morsels with which to favour his magnate 'followers'. By 1926, however, even his cupboard was bare and the Ministry fell.

In essence, the Montagu–Chelmsford Councils represented a further 'localisation' of provincial politics. This development was to some extent implicit in the political functions which Mylapore had assumed after 1910. It brought provincial power to the locality on the terms of the locality, that is around the magnate. The narrowness of the place which Mylapore enjoyed at the centre, however, also opened some, be they only small, channels through which provincial issues could reach the locality. In 1916, when Mylapore and the non-Brahmans stood against each other in the province, their respective

[141] G.O. 545 (L.S.G.) dated 19 March 1921. *T.N.A.*
[142] G.O. 1295 (L.S.G.) dated 5 July 1921. *T.N.A.*

local followers dressed themselves, however poorly, in provincial cloth. Mylapore was not of the locality and it still retained an interest in the issue-orientated forms of provincial politics. After 1920, however, the extension of elective opportunities allowed the localities to swallow up the province. For six years, as the echoes of the communal controversy died away, there ceased to be any real difference between the way that local and provincial politics were run. Everything was dominated by the locality and by the need to make person-to-person transactions of power. In spite of the Swarajists' prodding in 1926, it was probably not until the economic and constitutional revolutions of the 1930s that even the rhetoric of the politics of issue and community re-entered the provincial arena in any significant manner.

Without issues to which the localities would respond, the Congress rapidly withered. After Gandhi had taken it into non-co-operation in 1920, the organisation lost the importance which it had attained in provincial politics in the three preceding years. It existed to put pressure on the British during periods of constitutional negotiation. But the early 1920s, like the mid-1890s, marked an interlude in negotiation and, at such periods, it was not clear what the Congress was supposed to do. The non-co-operation tactic did not prove a success in South India. On the one hand, in Malabar it raised a Moplah rebellion of savage fury which the Congress leadership soon disowned.[143] On the other, led in Tamilnad by C. Rajagopalachari and in Andhra by T. Prakasam and Konda Venkatappayya, it fanned agitation only intermittently until 1922. Rajagopalachari relied on Khilafat Muslims and local powers irritated by aspects of administrative advance for most of his support but his movement never took off. After the Tilak fund had run out, money became extremely short and activity had virtually ceased by 1921.[144] The Andhra leaders were able to use an autonomous crusade against the government by village officers in Guntur and Kistna, whose plight we noted earlier, and the financial and organisational support of Komati trading groups to whom they were personally connected, to raise a more impressive campaign.[145] But that too was more or less dead by February 1922 when Gandhi called off non-co-operation. While the Congress refused to act within the framework of institutional politics in Madras, it was irrelevant to most political interests. Rajagopalachari's apparent victory in 1920 proved to be hollow, for he had won an

[143] All India Congress Committee Papers, File 1, Part 6 of 1922. *N.M.M.L.*
[144] Baker, 'Political Change in South India 1919–1937', pp. 337–90.
[145] *Ibid.*; Venkatarangaiya, *Freedom Struggle in Andhra Pradesh* III, 20–60, 240–300.

organisation which nobody else wanted in its present form. Between 1923 and 1926, the old Kasturi Ranga Iyengar group, which had been in the wilderness, returned under the direction of S. Satyamurthi and S. Srinivasa Iyengar to stake its claim to the Congress again. As the Swarajya Party, it re-established its contacts with many of its old local magnates, who had been sitting as Independents in the Council, and fought the 1926 election as a leadership group with some success. Rajagopalachari was driven from the Tamil Nad C.C., and some of his non-Brahman allies, to show their disapproval at the return of the city, started their own anti-Brahman movement.[146] Later, Rajagopalachari himself returned to the fray to carry forward to the 1930s the struggle against city cliquism which had begun in the 1890s. The struggle ended perhaps only in 1937, when Satyamurthi, using the network of contacts available solely to an important Madras city politician, constructed the machine which was to take Congress to its great victory at the polls, only to find himself replaced in the centre of the organisation at the last minute by Rajagopalachari.[147]

[146] Baker, *The Politics of South India. 1920–1937*, ch. 4.
[147] *Ibid.*

Conclusion

By the 1830s, when their initial political settlement had been completed, the British had done much to alter the South Indian political system which they had found in 1800. They had established a new level of state authority over all the variegated territories which comprised their province and had liquidated the previous, more regional, warrior level of government. Even where the warriors had not been destroyed but transmogrified into *zamindars*, the right to use force, on which warrior/*zamindar* rule ultimately depended for its success, was steadily, albeit slowly, undermined. In place of warrior government, the British built the machinery of a centralised bureaucratic state. They promised to bring strong civil government to their province; to substitute the rule of law for that of force; to guarantee the possession of private property; to promote economic growth and social development within the framework of a new, larger and more unified state.

As we have seen, however, by 1870 the British had lived up to few of these promises. By liquidating the warriors, they had removed the old core around which political society had been organised. But whether or not they could provide a new and greater core depended very much on the volume and intensity of the political relationships which they could establish with the social elements freed by the dismantlement of the warrior regimes. Certainly in terms of revenue flow, the British developed for themselves a more important place in society than ever the warriors had possessed: even their loosely jointed tribute system guaranteed them a higher regular income.[1] But it is a serious mistake to regard revenue collection as the only, or even the main, connection between the Indian state and its society. In addition to linkages made through the extraction of revenue, there also must be linkages made through its redistribution and redeployment, through relationships of licensed force and through relationships of cultural sympathy. In comparison to the warriors, British rule was peculiarly deficient in these latter connections.

[1] Stein, 'Integration of the Agrarian System of South India' in Frykenberg (ed.), *Land Control and Social Structure in Indian History*, pp. 210–12.

Conclusion

Warriors spent most of the revenues which they had gathered on conspicuous consumption at their courts, on their armies and on religious and cultural patronage inside their territories. Indeed, if they were successful at looting, their local expenditures amounted to more than their local incomes. Warrior courts represented centres through which resources flowed both in and out and a variety of 'state-level' groups – priests, merchants, artisans, soldiers, administrators and poets – were organised around the outflow. Fort St George, however, as we have seen, was forced to export most of its revenue out of Madras and, consequently, had little left to reinvest in its province. Its educational expenditure nowhere near matched the warriors' support of Brahmans and literati; it endowed no new temples; it built far fewer palaces, and built them in a way which minimised involvement with local skills and the local economy; from the 1850s, it recruited ever smaller numbers of troops, for its overlord, the Government of India, preferred soldiers from the 'martial' races of the North; it even discarded elaborate court rituals and the patronage of a court culture.

Not only did the British fail to extend the activity of the state into society but, for ideological reasons, they also weakened many of the institutions of connection which the warriors had already built for them and which they had simply to maintain. Fort St George adopted economic policies which lessened (although did not destroy) its role as a commercial monopolist, and hence made national and international trade independent of it and of greater weight than service to the state. The intimate connections between, for example, Vijayanagar warriors and Telugu Komati merchants, which had spread over large tracts of the economy, were replicated only in miniature by the connections between the British government and Indian mercantile interests. The British also introduced the law of private property which altered the character of several important socio-economic institutions. Religious *inams*, for example, ceased to be franchises held at the discretion of the state and became private properties held in law independently of state interference. British attitudes towards religion and social life led to a further reduction of state influence. Formally by 1863, but in practice as early as 1840, the British had severed the relationship of their government to the institutions of religion and so had relinquished control of the vast economic and emotional resources of the temples. Although Fort St George did attempt to create a new series of ideological and cultural bonds with its subjects, these were never strong. Western education and court honorifics (Rao Bahadurships, knighthoods, etc.) penetrated to a far shallower level of society than had the religiously orientated political symbols of the warriors. Moreover, lack of patronage prevented the British from tying their honours and their culture to an important system of material rewards. The British were much less present in the society which they governed than had been their warrior predecessors: in many ways, they were 'absentee' rulers.

It would be true to say that the major connection between the British government and its subjects in the nineteenth century was through the formal administration and, particularly, through the processes by which revenue was extracted. This admission in itself suggests the likelihood that this government would be weak. As we have seen, the way in which the administration was organised turned the likelihood into fact. The British had brought no new service groups with them into Madras and so were unable to adopt the tried and tested tactics of South Indian statecraft. They had to find the material for their administration from within the existing structure of Madras society. But they greatly feared that, were they to use the socio-political connections which the warriors' administrators had developed and which were waiting for them, they would lock themselves out of their own government. In consequence, they came to anchor their administration to the dominant peasant elites of the South and to support their higher bureaucrats, who were supposed to relate the peasants to the *raj*, with very insufficient force. This policy contained an inherent contradiction, for the British had failed to perceive that while 'state-level' administrative groups at least had some points of interest in common with them (and, under the right circumstances, might be eager to build state power if only because it meant more power for themselves as well), the new peasant collaborators had none. The dominant peasant elites over most of South India were of local-level culture and used resources derived from within the locality to maintain their power. Connection to the government was important to them less because it drew them into a wider state structure than because it could be used to prevent the state from interfering in the locality. Local powers could block external influence at the boundaries of their localities and do what they pleased inside.

By 1870, the net results of British rule had been to fragment the political integrations achieved by the warriors and to bury effective political power deep in the localities from which the state had been all but completely excluded. Each temple, each 'rural locality', each section of a town became a potentially autonomous arena in which the disposition of internal forces determined the pattern of political dominance. The profound parochialism into which South India had

Conclusion

fallen was apparent everywhere in the political attitudes and behaviour of the period. It was reflected in the way that bureaucrats sold their authority to local magnates for bribes; it was reflected in the manner in which temple trustees personally appropriated the endowments of their temples and frequently allowed temple fabric and public ceremonial to run down; it was reflected in the process by which the intermediary institutions of clan political structures (in the few areas where these had retained a political significance into the nineteenth century) steadily became broken up; it was reflected in the success with which the rural-local boss arrogated to himself *de facto* powers of arbitration, revenue collection and police coercion over his local subjects. Perhaps the final and clearest indicator of the dominance of the locality over higher levels of political integration can be seen in the attitude of the British courts to questions of landed property. In the early nineteenth century, British legal policy had sought to bring western private property rights to the locality and to protect the landholdings of every peasant with the weight of a central legal system. Had this been accomplished, Fort St George would have been in a prime position to order the socio-political base of rural society. In practice, however, so dubiously did the courts view the relationship between the politically flexible village records of the *ryotwari* settlement and the problem of justice in apportioning village lands that they refused to accept *ryotwari* records as proof of the ownership of lands. As there was no order requiring the compulsory legal registration of landholdings, this meant that in most cases they refused to link village lands to the central legal grid. The courts stood off from local society and tacitly recognised its ability to come to its own arrangements about land.[2] External authorities at every level were permitted scant influence in the locality and consequently were unable to attract and pattern the political relationships of men who were their nominal inferiors. In mid-nineteenth-century Madras, all important politics had become local politics.

The process of rebuilding a greater political state began in earnest in the 1870s. In part it was accomplished simply by increasing the pressure of the bureaucratic centre on the periphery and by tightening up the existing administrative system. As Burton Stein has argued, at this time the promises of British administrative theory, which had been made in 1800 but had lain in abeyance for three-quarters of a century, started to be fulfilled.[3] But in much larger part, the process was accomplished through the development of new institutions and

---

[2] See my 'Law and Land in South India'. Unpublished paper read at Conference on Indian Economic History, University of Pennsylvania, 1975.
[3] Stein, 'Integration of the Agrarian System of South India', pp. 211–12.

the emergence of new political forces which had no counterpart in previous South Indian history and which produced not only a wider political integration but one of a qualitatively new kind. The expansion of the commercial economy and the creation of a new range of administrative institutions, as we have seen, lured the powers of the locality into participating in much broader politico-economic structures: they altered the dimensions of the local political arena. Moreover, from the 1910s, further institutional changes helped to bring the capital back into the localities and, thereby, to articulate a framework of provincial politics. What was so novel about these developments was that the local groups who were being drawn into the state system had never been fully integrated into any supra-local state system before.[4] They were largely groups of local-level culture whose relationships with the warrior regimes had been indirect and often antagonistic. Warrior rule had incorporated them by forcing groups of state-level culture on top of them; now they themselves were to play active roles in the operations of the new state. By the early 1920s, they dominated district-level government through the rural boards and other administrative committees and had begun to fill the seats in the Legislative Council – the 'court' of their provincial governor. Political and economic change began slowly but surely to forge great alterations in the elite sections of the local level: marriage circles expanded, literacy became more common, symbols of deference and defiance changed and new social and cultural perceptions emerged.[5] The peasant elites of the 1920s were structurally different from the rural-local bosses of the same peasant families who had dominated rural society in separate localities just sixty years before.

But the processes of unification did not only work their way up from the bottom of political society. As Fort St George became more competent at the state level so its influence and relevance spread across the province. This development had two important consequences. In the first place, administrative groups of state-level culture, whose loci of operations had been reduced almost to the district alone, were pulled back towards a larger state centre. They organised themselves around the provincial capital in order to extend themselves through the legal, educational and service networks of the whole presidency and to draw sustenance from the state-centre for their own cultural pursuits. Gradually, the growing intrusion of the

---

[4] Their pre-warrior political system was based on the clan and not the state.
[5] See my 'Country Politics: Madras 1880 to 1930'.

Government of India in the affairs of South India also pushed them into making connections with other service groups across the sub-continent. The province and the nation ceased to be abstract notions but became concrete political contexts in which they were forced to work. Moreover, the language and concepts through which Fort St George sought to govern its charge began to make their own impact. The interest groups and political communities which it defined as operating at the provincial level began to form and to fill the niches which had been cut for them in the political structure. In a strange way, British misconceptions about the relationships of Indian political society started to produce real relationships in the image of the misconceptions. Without arguing that it was only state action that created the politics of, particularly, the caste association (for many social and economic factors helped to determine the emergence of specific caste communities), it would be difficult to deny that state action played a major part.

Many of the changes which we have followed through from the 1870s and brought to a conclusion in 1920 helped to lay the foundations of politics in South India today. The old ways of force were slowly dying; the locality as a political notion was in decay; the province and the nation were beginning to have a political meaning in much wider circles. The Home Rule and non-Brahman movements of 1917 to 1920 attested to these profound changes. We have sought to explain the movements less by reference to the issues which divided them than by reference to the institutional context in which they arose. Ideas similar to those of the Home Rule League and non-Brahman leaders could be found in the minds of some, be it only a few, men at any time from the late 1870s and, in all probability, from long before that too. But what was so crucial about the movements was not the ideas alone but the way in which those ideas interacted with the new political context of 1917 to produce political relationships and political forces which would have been inconceivable a few years earlier. The Home Rule League and non-Brahman movements were the first manifestations of political division in the newly articulated provincial structure of politics. This structure was being wrought out of the material of centralised bureaucratic power, of franchises and elective institutions, of civil processes and the rule of law. It was beginning to look like the political structure which the Indian Republic inherited from the British in 1947 and has been obliged to work with ever since.

GLOSSARY

Abkari: *Liquor*
Anicut: *Dam*
Arrack: *Liquor*
Bania: *Moneylender/Merchant*
Bhadralok: *Bengali educated gentry*
Choultry: *Charitable institution*
Crore: *10,000,000*
Dallal: *Commercial broker*
Dharmakartha: *Temple trustee*
Diwan: *Prime Minister*
Dubash: *Agent*
Firka: *Part of a taluk*
Gumastah: *Clerk*
Guru: *Holy man*
Hartal: *Strike*
Hundis: *Cheques for transfers of funds*
Huzur: *Head office*
Huzur Sheristidar: *Head clerk*
Inam: *Land held at reduced assessment (usually in return for services)*
Jajmani: *Transactions between an inferior and superior in the caste system*
Jamabundi: *Revenue settlement*
Jati: *Caste (in the sense of an endogamous unit)*
Jenmi: *Holder of large landed property under* ryotwari *system in Malabar*
Jutka (-wallah): *Horse-drawn carriage (its operator)*
Kanomdar: *Holder of a privileged tenure from a* jenmi
Kazi: *Judge under Islamic law*
Kiramam: *Revenue village*
Kumbabishekham: *Purification ceremony*
Kurnam: *Village accountant*
Lakh: *100,000*
Madrassa: *Islamic school*
Mahant: *Principal of a monastery*
Math: *Monastery*
Mirasi (-dar): *Privileged land tenure under* ryotwari *system in areas of Coromandel (its holder)*
Mittadar: *Holder of a small property under permanent settlement*
Mofussil: *Provinces (as opposed to metropolis)*

Glossary

Mohurram: *Islamic festival*

Moplah: *Muslim peasant of upland Malabar*

Munsiff: *Magistrate*

Panchama: *Untouchable*

Panchayat: *Council (classically of five people)*

Pandarasanidhi: *Principal of a monastery*

Pariah: *Untouchable*

Patta (-dar): *Document giving right to hold land under* ryotwari *system (its holder)*

Patsala: *Sanskrit school*

Pattagar: *Traditional leader of Gounder Vellala community*

Poligar: *Small warrior chief of the eighteenth century*

Raj: *Rule (colloquially British rule)*

Ryot (wari): *Peasant (system by which each peasant is assessed separately for revenue)*

Sabha: *Association*

Sachimattam: *Bribe*

Samasthanam: *Estate (of a great lord)*

Sankarachariar (or -yar): *Religious leader*

Sirker: *State*

Satyagraha: *(Lit. soul-force; in practice, civil disobedience)*

Shrotriemdar: *Holder of a small property under permanent settlement*

Sowcar (or Sahukar): *Moneylender*

Swami: *Holy man*

Tahsil: *Division in revenue administration*

Tahsildar: *Officer in charge of a* tahsil

Takavi: *State-backed credit for long-term loans*

Taluk: *Equivalent of* tahsil

Thambiram: *Disciple in charge of a subordinate monastery*

Varna: *Four-caste system by which Hindu society is divided*

Zamindar: *Holder of a property under permanent settlement*

Zamorin: *Prince in Malabar*

BIBLIOGRAPHY

Government Records

The proceedings of the Secretary of State for India in the Public and Judicial Department. India Office Library.

The proceedings of the Government of India in the Home Department, branches of Education, Judicial, Police, Political, Public Departments. National Archives of India.

The proceedings of the Government of Madras in the Departments of Education, Home, Judicial, Legislative, and Revenue; and in the Board of Revenue. Tamil Nad Archives and State Archives, Hyderabad.

Official Publications

(1) Parliamentary Papers

Report of the Indian Famine Commission. 1880. Volume II, 1881. Volume LII. [Command. 2735].

Appendix to the Report of the Indian Famine Commission, 1898, being Minutes of Evidence, etc., Volume II. The Madras Presidency. 1889. Volume XXXII. [Command. 9253].

Minutes of Evidence taken before the Royal Commission upon Decentralization in India, Madras. 1908. Volume XLIV. [Command. 4361].

Royal Commission on the Public Services in India. Appendix to the Report of the Commissioners, Volume II. Minutes of Evidence Relating to the Indian Civil Services Taken in Madras from 8th to 18th January 1913. 1914. Volume XXI. [Command. 7293].

Addresses Presented in India to His Excellency the Viceroy and the Right Honorable the Secretary of State of India. 1918. Volume XVIII. [Command. 9178].

Report on Indian Constitutional Reform. 1918. Volume VIII. [Command. 9109].

Minutes of Evidence taken before the Indian Industrial Commission 1916–18. Volume II. 1919. Volume XIX. [Command. 235].

Report of the Committee appointed by the Secretary of State for India to enquire into questions connected with Franchise and other matters relating to constitutional reforms. Chairman Lord Southborough. 1919. Volume XVI. [Command. 141].

Joint Select Committee on the Government of India Bill. 1919. Volume IV.

Report of the Committee appointed by the Secretary of State for India to Advise on the Question of the Financial Relations between the Central and Provincial Governments in India. 1920. Volume XIV. [Command. 724].

338

Bibliography

(2) His Majesty's Stationery Office

Report of the Royal Commission on Agriculture in India. Appendix. Volume III. 1927; Volume XIV. 1928.

Indian Statutory Commission. Vol. VI. Memorandum Submitted by the Government of Madras. 1930.

(3) Government of India

Education Commission. Report by the Madras Provincial Committee. Calcutta, 1884.

Proceedings of the Public Service Commission. Volume V. Calcutta, 1887.

Indian Universities' Commission. Simla, 1902.

Evidence taken before the Reforms Committee (Franchise). Madras. Calcutta, 1919.

Indian Central Cotton Commission. General Report on Eight Investigations into the Finance and Marketing of Cultivators' Cotton. 1925–8. Bombay, n.d.

Memorandum on the Working of Representative Institutions in Local Self-Government. New Delhi, 1928.

Reports of the Provincial Banking Enquiry Committees, 1929–30. Calcutta, 1931.

Agriculture Statistics of British India. Calcutta, 1884–5 to 1920–1.

Prices and Wages in India. Calcutta, 1889 to 1921.

(4) Government of Madras – Special

Report of the Commissioners for the Investigation of Alleged Cases of Torture in the Madras Presidency. Madras, 1855.

Selections from the Madras Records. XXII. Madras, 1870.

Report of the Committee on Local Self-Government in Madras. 1882. Madras, 1883.

J. H. Garstin, *Report on the Revision of the Revenue Establishments in the Madras Presidency.* Madras, 1883.

H. S. Thomas, *Report on Tanjore Remissions in Fasli 1294 (A.D. 1884–5).* Madras, 1885.

II. S. Thomas, *Report on Mr Charles Stewart Crole. Collector of Madura.* Madras, 1886.

C. H. Benson, *An Account of the Kurnool District based on an Analysis of Statistical Information Relating Thereto and on Personal Observation.* Madras, 1889.

S. Srinivasa Raghavaiyangar, *Memorandum on the Progress of the Madras Presidency during the Last Forty Years of British Administration.* Madras, 1892.

C. H. Benson, *A Statistical Atlas of the Madras Presidency.* Madras, 1895. (Revised editions in 1908 and 1924.)

F. A. Nicholson, *Report regarding the possibilities of introducing Agricultural Banks into the Madras Presidency.* Madras, 1895–7.

Notes on the Working of Certain Departments of Government during the Administration of H. E. Lord Wenlock, with General Summary. Madras, 1896.

Statement of the Police Committee on the Administration of the District Police in the Madras Presidency. Madras, 1902.

W. S. Meyer, *Report on the Constitution of Additional Districts, Divisions and Taluks in the Madras Presidency, and on Other Connected Matters.* Madras, 1904.

Report on the Administration of His Excellency the Honourable Sir Arthur Lawley, G.C.S.I., G.C.I.E., K.C.M.G., Governor of Madras. Madras, 1912.

Report of the Forest Committee. 1913. Madras, 1913.
Madras Provincial Banking Enquiry Committee. Evidence. Madras, 1930.

(5) Government of Madras – Annual

Report on the Administration of the Abkari Revenue in the Presidency of Fort St George.
Report on the Administration of the Estates under the Court of Wards in the Madras Presidency.
Report on the Administration of the Income Tax under Act II of 1886.
Administration Report of the Forest Department of the Madras Presidency.
Report on the Administration of Civil Justice in the Madras Presidency.
Statistics of Criminal Courts in the Madras Presidency.
Report on the Settlement of the Land Revenue in the Districts of the Madras Presidency.
Report on the Administration of the Madras Presidency.
Report on the Administration of the Municipality of Madras.
Report on the Working of the District Municipalities in Madras Presidency.
Administration Report of the Madras Police.
Report on Public Instruction in the Madras Presidency.
Report of the Working of the Rural Boards in the Madras Presidency.
Annual Report of the Sanitary Commissioner for Madras.

(6) Census of India.

Census of India. 1881. Madras. Madras, 1882–3.
Census of India. 1891. Madras. Volume XIII to XV. Madras, 1893.
Census of India. 1901. Madras. Volumes XIV to XVI. Madras, 1902.
Census of India. 1911. Madras. Volume XII. Madras, 1912.
Census of India. 1921. Madras. Volume XIII. Madras, 1922.
Census of India. 1931. Madras. Volume XIII. Madras, 1933.

(7) Imperial Gazetteers

The Imperial Gazetteer of India. Volume IV. Oxford, 1907.

(8) Madras District Manuals and Gazetteers

Brackenbury, C. F. *Cuddapah.* Madras, 1916.
Crole, C. S. *A Chingleput District Manual.* Madras, 1879.
Dykes, J. W. B. *Salem, An Indian Collectorate.* London, 1853.
Francis, W. *Bellary.* Madras, 1904.
   Madura, Madras, 1906.
   The Nilgiris. Madras, 1908.
   South Arcot. Madras, 1906.
   Vizagapatam. Madras, 1907.
Gopalakrishnama Chetty, N. *A Manual of the Kurnool District.* Madras, 1886.
Gribble, J. D. B. *A Manual of the District of Cuddapah.* Madras, 1875.
Hall, J. F. *South Kanara,* Madras, 1938.
Hemingway, F. R. *Godaveri.* Madras, 1906.
   Tanjore. Madras, 1906.
   Trichinopoly. Madras, 1906.

Bibliography

Innes, C. A. *Malabar*. Madras, 1908.
Krishnaswami Ayyar, K. N. *Statistical Appendix, Together With a Supplement to the District Gazetteers (1917) for Tinnevelly District*. Madras, 1934.
Mackenzie, G. *A Manual of the Kistna District*. Madras, 1883.
Maltby, T. J. *The Ganjam District Manual*. Madras, 1882.
Nicholson, F. A. *The Coimbatore District Manual*. Madras, 1887.
    and H. Stuart, *Coimbatore*. Madras, 1898.
Pate, H. R. *Tinnevelly*. Madras, 1917.
Richards, F. J. *Salem*. Madras, 1918.

Private Papers

Ampthill Collection. India Office Library.
Cross Collection. India Office Library.
Kilbracken Collection. India Office Library
Montagu Collection. India Office Library.
Willingdon Collection. India Office Library.
Papers of V. Krishnaswami Iyer. National Archives of India.
Papers of G. A. Natesan. Nehru Memorial Museum Library.
Papers of P. Kesava Pillai. Nehru Memorial Museum Library.
Papers of V. S. Srinivasa Sastri. National Archives of India.
Papers of P. S. Sivaswami Iyer. National Archives of India.

Papers of Organisations

Papers of the All-India Congress Committee. Nehru Memorial Museum Library.
Papers of the Madras Mahajana Sabha. Nehru Memorial Museum Library.
Papers of the Theosophical Society (of Mrs Besant). Theosophical Society Archives, Adyar.

Newspapers

Reports on English Papers owned by Natives examined by the Criminal Investigations Department, Madras, and on Vernacular Papers Examined by the Translators to the Government of Madras. 1887–1921. (*R.N.P.*)
Hindu. Tri-weekly 1883–9, daily 1889–1921, weekly 1916–21.
Madras Mail. 1885–90 and 1916–20.
Madras Times. Daily 1888–91.
New India. Daily 1915–21.

Books, Pamphlets and Articles

Ananda Charlu, P. *The Madras Bar and How to Improve It*. Madras, 1893.
    The Six Fold Need of Indian Politics. Madras, 1895.
The First Andhra Conference held at Bapatla in 1913. Bezwada, n.d.
Sree Andhra Jatheeya Kala Sala Masulipatam. Work and Appreciations. 1907–1918. Masulipatam, 1918.

Anon. *The Ways and Means for the Amelioration of the Non-Brahman Races.* Bangalore, 1893.

Anuntha Row Pantulu, V. *An Old Man's Family Record and References.* Madras, 1916.

Appa Rao Naidu, K. *Communal Representation and Indian Constitutional Reforms.* Cocanada, 1918.

An Appeal Memorial of the Madras Landholders' Association Against the Madras Proprietary Estates Village Service Act II of 1894. Madras, 1894.

Arasu Pulavar, V. V. S. *Aiyer.* Madras, 1951. (Tamil).

Tiru, Vi. Kaliyanasundarana. Tirunelveli, 1961. (Tamil).

Arokiyasami, M. *The Kongu Country.* Madras, 1956.

The Asylum Press Almanack and Directory of Madras and Southern India. Madras, 1910, 1922, 1925, 1930.

Baden Powell, B. H. *The Land Systems of British India.* Volume III. Oxford, 1892.

Baker, C. J. *The Politics of South India 1920–1937.* Cambridge, 1976.

and Washbrook, D. A. (eds.), *South India: Political Institutions and Political Change.* New Delhi, 1975.

Balasubramaniam, K. M. *South Indian Celebrities.* Madras, Volume I, 1934; Volume II, 1939.

The Life of J. M. Nallaswami Pillai. Tiruchirapelle, 1965.

Baldwin, G. B. *Industrial Growth in South India.* Illinois, 1959.

Baliga, B. S. *Studies in Madras Administration.* Madras, 1960.

Bayly, C. A. 'Patrons and Politics in Northern India'. *Modern Asian Studies.* VII : 3 (1973).

Beaglehole, T. H. *Thomas Munro and the Development of Administrative Policy in Madras: 1792–1818.* Cambridge, 1966.

Beck, B. E. F. *Peasant Society in Konku.* Vancouver, 1972.

'The Right–Left Division of South Indian Society'. *Journal of Asian Studies.* XXIX : 4 (1970).

Besant, A. *The Birthplace of New India.* Adyar, 1917.

Dr Nair and Mrs Besant. Adyar, 1913.

Beteille, A. *Caste, Class and Power: Changing Patterns of Stratification in a Tanjore Village.* Berkeley and Los Angeles, 1965.

Bhargava, G. S. *V. V. Giri.* Bombay, 1969.

Bhaviah Chowdary, K. *A Brief History of the Kammas.* Sangamjagarlamudi, 1955.

Bhimasankara Rao, *The Indian National Congress – Then and Now.* Rajahmundry, 1929.

Boag, G. T. *The Madras Presidency 1881–1931.* Madras, 1933.

Bobbili, Maharaja of. *Bobbili Zamindari.* Madras, 1907.

Broomfield, J. H. *Elite Conflict in a Plural Society.* Berkeley and Los Angeles, 1968.

Brown, J. M. *Gandhi's Rise to Power.* Cambridge, 1972.

Chandrasekharan, K. *V. Krishnaswami Aiyer.* Masulipatam, 1963.

Chenchayya, Darsi. *Nenu Na Desamu.* Vijayawada, 1952. (Telegu – Myself and My Country).

Chiefs and Leading Families in the Madras Presidency. Madras, 1915.

Bibliography

'C.P.' by his Contemporaries. Madras, 1959.

The Cult of Incompetence, being an impartial enquiry into the record of the First Madras Ministry. Madras, 1923.

Das, R. K. The Temples of Tamilnad. Bombay, 1964.

Das Gupta, J. C. A National Biography for India. Dacca, 1911.

Directory of the Madras Legislature. Madras, 1938.

Dobbin, C. Urban Leadership in Western India. Politics and Communities in Bombay City 1840–1885. London, 1972.

Dumont, L. Homo Hierarchicus, London, 1970.

Hierarchy and Marriage Alliance in South Indian Kinship. London, 1957.

Une Sous-Caste de l'Inde du Sud: organisation sociale et religieuse des Pramalai Kallar. Paris, 1957.

Dupuis, J. Madras et le Nord du Coromandel. Etude des conditions de la vie indienne dans une cadre geographique. Paris, 1960.

Dutt, K. Iswara. Sparks and Fumes. Madras, 1929.

Firminger, W. F. (ed.), The Fifth Report of the Select Committee for the Affairs of the East India Company. 28 July 1812. Volume III. Calcutta, 1918.

For and Against the Andhra Province. Masulipatam, 1914.

Fox, R. G. From Zamindar to Ballot Box. New York, 1969.

'Varna Schemes and Ideological Integration in Indian Society.' Comparative Studies in Society and History. XI: 1 (1969).

'The Avatars of Indian Research?' Comparative Studies in Society and History. XII: 1 (1970).

Frykenberg, R. E. Guntur District 1788–1848. A History of Local Influence and Central Authority in South India. Oxford, 1965.

(ed.), Land Control and Social Structure in Indian History. Madison, Milwaukee and London, 1969.

Gopala Menon, N. A Short Sketch of the Life of Dr T. M. Nair. London, 1920.

Gopalaratnam, V. C. A Century Completed (The Madras High Court 1862–1962). Madras, n.d.

Gordon, L. A. Bengal: The Nationalist Movement 1870–1940. New York and London, 1974.

Gough, E. K. and Schneider, D. M. (eds.), Matrilineal Kinship. Berkeley and Los Angeles, 1961.

Govindarajan, S. A. G. Subramania Iyer. New Delhi, 1969.

Govindarow Naidu, P. The Legislative Council Elections. Rajahmundry, 1920.

Gurunatham, J. The Andhra Movement. Guntur, 1913.

Hamerow, T. S. Restoration, Revolution and Reaction. Princeton, 1958.

Hardgrave, R. L. The Dravidian Movement. Bombay, 1965.

The Nadars of Tamilnad, Berkeley and Los Angeles, 1969.

Harrison, S. S. India – The Most Dangerous Decades. Princeton, 1960.

Heimsath, C. Indian Nationalism and Hindu Social Reform. Princeton, 1964.

Heroes of the Hour. Madras, 1918.

Hilton Brown, J. Parry's of Madras: A Story of British Enterprise in India. Madras, 1954.

The Civilian's South India. London, 1921.

Hjelje, B. 'Slavery and Agricultural Bondage in the Nineteenth Century'. *Scandinavian Economic History Review.* xv: 1 and 2 (1967).

Organization of the Home Rule League. Passed at the First Meeting of the Council. October 8th, 1916. Madras, n.d.

The National Home Rule League. How Founded and Why. Adyar, 1919.

Report of the Third Indian National Congress held at Madras on 27th, 28th, 29th and 30th December 1887. London, 1888.

Report of the Tenth Indian National Congress held at Madras on the 26th, 27th, 28th and 29th December 1894. Madras, 1895.

Report of the Fourteenth Indian National Congress held at Madras on the 29th, 30th and 31st December 1898. Madras, 1899.

Report on the Proceedings of the Nineteenth Indian National Congress held at Madras on the 28th, 29th and 30th December 1903. Madras, 1904.

Report on the Twenty-Fourth Indian National Congress held at Madras on the 28th, 29th and 30th December 1908. Madras, 1909.

Indian Statesmen. Dewans and Prime Ministers. Madras, n.d.

Indian Year Book and Who's Who 1934–35. Bombay, 1935.

Irschick, E. F. *Politics and Social Conflict in South India.* Berkeley and Los Angeles, 1969.

Johnson, G. *Provincial Politics and Indian Nationalism.* Cambridge, 1973.

Justice Party Golden Jubilee Souvenir. Madras, 1968.

The Justice Year Book, 1929. Madras, n.d.

Kaleswara Rao, A. *Na Jivita Katha-Navya Andhramu.* Vijavawada, 1959. (Telugu – My Life and the New Andhra).

Kalyanasundra Mudaliar, T. V. *Valkkai Kurippugal.* Madras, 1969. (Tamil – Autobiography).

Kamesvara Aiyar, B. V. *Sir A. Shashiah Sastri. K.C.S.I. An Indian Statesman.* Madras, 1902.

Kandaswami Pillai, V. *Tiruvavadathurai Kurisanam.* Madras, 1921. (Tamil – A Visit to Tiruvandathorai).

Kannappar, J. S. *Suttirargal Yar?* Madras, 1926. (Tamil – Who are the Sudras?)

Kasipathi, K. *Tryst with Destiny.* Hyderabad, 1970.

Kausikan, *Rajaji.* Madras, 1968. (Tamil).

Kessinger, T. G. *Vilyatpur 1848–1968.* Berkeley, Los Angeles and London, 1974.

Kodanda Rao, P. *The Right Honourable V. S. Srinivasa Sastri: A Political Biography.* London, 1963.

Kothari, R. (ed.), *Caste in Indian Politics.* New Delhi, 1970.

Krishna Ayyar, R. V. *In the Legislature of Those Days.* Madras, 1956.

Krishnamurthi Mudaliar, C. *Life and Activities of K. Chidambaranatha Mudaliar.* Shiyali, 1938.

Sir Alladi Krishnaswami Iyer Shastyabdapoorthi Souvenir Volume. Madras, 1943.

The Hon'ble V. Krishnaswami Iyer. A Sketch. Trichinopoly, 1911.

Keraliyan, *The Father of Political Agitation in Travancore. G. Parameswaram Pillai.* Trivandrum, 1948.

Kumar, D. *Land and Caste in South India. Agricultural labour in the Madras Presidency during the nineteenth century.* Cambridge, 1965.

Bibliography

Leach, E. R. (ed.), *Aspects of Caste in South India, Ceylon and Northwest Pakistan.* Cambridge, 1960.

Leonard, J. G. 'Politics and Social Change in South India: A Study of the Andhra Movement'. *Journal of Commonwealth Political Studies.* v: 1 (1967).

'Urban Government under the Raj'. *Modern Asian Studies.* vii: 2 (1973).

Lingamurthy, V. 'Elections in Andhra'. *Indian Journal of Political Sciences.* xvi: 2. (April–June 1955).

Biography of Sriraman Lodd Govindas Maharaj, The Hindu Hero. Madras, 1942.

Low, D. A. (ed.), *Soundings in Modern South Asian History.* London, 1968.

Madhavaiah, A. *Thillai Govindan.* London, 1916.

Madhavan Nair, C. *A Short Life of Sir C. Sankaran Nair.* Madras, n.d.

Mahadevan, P. *Subramania Bharati: Poet and Patriot.* Madras, 1957.

The Madras Mahajana Sabha Annual Report for 1885–86. Madras, 1886.

Madras Mahajana Sabha Diamond Jubilee Souvenir. Madras, 1946.

Proceedings of the Madras Native Association on the Resolution of the Government of India on Local Self Government. Madras, 1883.

Report of the Executive Committee of the Madras Provincial Congress Committee for the year ending 31st December 1915. Madras, 1916

The Madras Year Book. Madras, 1924.

McPherson, K. 'The Social Background and Politics of the Muslims of Tamilnad 1901–1937'. *Indian Social and Economic History Review.* vi: 4 (1969).

Marriott, M. *Village India.* Chicago, 1955.

Mehrotra, S. M. *The Emergence of the Indian National Congress.* New Delhi, 1917.

Menon, K. P. S. *Many Worlds: An Autobiography.* London, 1965.

C. Sankaran Nair. New Delhi, 1967.

Misra, B. B. *The Indian Middle Classes.* Oxford, 1961.

The Administrative History of India, 1834–1947. Bombay, 1970.

Mitra, N. N. *Indian Annual Register.* Calcutta, annual.

Molony, J. C. *A Book of South India.* London, 1926.

Montagu, E. S. *An Indian Diary.* London, 1930.

Morris, M. D. 'Economic Change and Agriculture in Nineteenth Century India'. *Indian Economic and Social History Review.* iii: 2 (1966).

Mukherjee, N. *The Ryotwari System in Madras.* Calcutta, 1962.

Murton, B. J. 'Key People in the Countryside: Decision Makers in Interior Tamilnad in the late eighteenth century.' *Indian Economic and Social History Review.* x: 2 (1973).

Musgrave, P. J. 'Landlords and Lords of the Land: estate management and social control in Uttar Pradesh 1860–1920'. *Modern Asian Studies.* vi: 3 (1972).

Nair, B. N. *The Dynamic Brahman.* Bombay, 1959.

Nair, T. M. *The Evolution of Mrs Besant.* Madras, 1918.

Nancharayya, B. V. *Biography of Zamindar Lodd Govindas Varu.* Madras, 1942.

Narain, D. *Impact of Price Movements on Areas under Selected Crops in India, 1900–1939.* Cambridge, 1965.

Narasimhan, K. L. *Madras city – a history.* Madras, 1968.

Kasturi Ranga Iyengar. New Delhi, 1963.

Kasturi Srinivasan. Bombay, 1969.

Narayanaswami Naidu, B. V. (ed.), *Rajah Sir Annamalai Chettiar Commemoration Volume.* Chidambaram, 1941.

Nathan, T. A. V. (ed.), *The Justice Year Book, 1929.* n.p., n.d.

Nethercott, A. H. *The First Five Lives of Annie Besant.* Chicago, 1960.

The Last Four Lives of Annie Besant. (Chicago, 1963).

Nilakanta Sastri, K. A. (ed.), *A Great Liberal. Speeches and Writings of Sir P. S. Sivaswami Aiyar.* Bombay, 1965.

Note on the Past and Present Administration of the Raja's Chattram in the Tanjore and Madura Districts. Tanjore, 1908.

Padmanabha Iyer, K. V. *A History of Sourashtras in South India by the Sourashtra Literary Societies of Madras and Madura.* Madura, 1942.

Parameswaran Pillai, G. *Representative Men of Southern India.* Madras, 1896.

Representative Indians. London, 1902.

Parthasarathi, R. T. *The Dawn and Achievement of Indian Freedom.* Salem, 1953.

Patro, A. P. 'The Justice Movement in India'. *Asiatic Review.* XXVIII (1932).

Pattabhisitaramayya, B. *The History of the Indian National Congress.* Volume I, Madras, 1935; Volume II, Bombay, 1947.

Pentland, Lady *The Right Honourable John Sinclair: Lord Pentland G.C.S.I.* London, 1918.

Perumal, N. *Two Important Men: A Biographical Record.* Madras, 1938.

Jamal Mahommed. Madras, 1936.

Rajaji. Madras, 1953.

Talented Tamils. Madras, 1957.

Pillai, K. K. *History of Local Self-Government in the Madras Presidency 1850–1919.* Bombay, 1953.

Prakasam, T. *Na Jivita Yatra.* Rajahmundry, 1957. (Telugu – My Life's Path).

Prakash, A. *Sir C. P.* Madras, 1939.

Purnalingam Pillai M. S. *Tamil India.* Tinnevelly, 1945.

Raghavan, T. S. *Makers of Modern Tamil.* Tirunelveli, 1965.

Raghavayya Chowdary, S. *Brahmanettara Sangha Dharasyam.* Bapatla, 1927. (Telugu – Aims of the Non-Brahman Association).

Raj, V. P. *Dr Sir R. Venkataratnam. Part I – His Life.* Madras, 1929.

Rajagopalachari, C. *Rajaji's Jail Life: A Day to Day Record of Sri C. Rajagopalachariar's Life in Vellore Jail in 1920.* Madras, 1941.

Chats behind Bars. Madras, 1931.

Cuttantirap Por. Madras, 1931. (Tamil – War of Independence).

Raja Rama Rao, S. M. *Sir Subramania Aiyer. K.C.I.E., D.L.* Trichinopoly, 1914.

Ramachandra Chettiar, C. M. *Konku Natu Varalaru.* Annamalai, 1954. (Tamil – History of Konkunad).

Ramachandra Rao, D. S. *Dhannavada Anantamu 1850–1949.* Calcutta, 1956. (Telugu – History of the Dhannavada family).

Ramadas, V. *Memorandum on Andhra Province.* Madras, 1939.

Raman Rao, A. V. *Economic Development of Andhra Pradesh. 1766–1957.* Bombay, 1958.

Bibliography

Ramanatha Iyer, P. *Madras Hindu Religious Endowments Act (Act II of 1927)*. Madras, 1946.

Ramanathan, S. *Gandhi and the Youth*. Bombay, 1947.

Ramanathan Chettiar, L. P. K. *Annamalai Aracar*. Madras, 1965. (Tamil – Raja Annamalai).

Rama Rao, R. V. M. G. *Of Men, Matters and Me*. London, 1961.

Ramaswami Aiyar, C. P. *Biographical Vistas*. Bombay, 1968.

Ramaswami Mudaliar, A. *Mirror of the Year: Being a Collection of the Leading Articles in Justice 1927*. Madras, 1928.

Ramaswami Sastri, K. S. *Professor Sunderama Ayyar*. Srirangam, n.d.

Vita Sua. Madras, n.d.

Ramaswami Sastri, V. S. and Dhurta Swamin, *The Brahmins*. Madras, 1929.

Ranga, N. G. *Fight for Freedom*. New Delhi, 1968.

The Modern Indian Peasant. Madras, 1936.

Rangachari, K. *Sri Vaishnava Brahmins*. Madras, 1931.

Dewan Bahadur T. Rangachariar, B.A., B.L., C.I.E., A Life Sketch. Madras, n.d.

Richards, F. J. 'Cross-Cousin Marriage in South India', *Man*. 97 (1914).

Robinson, F. C. R. 'Consultation and Control: The United Province's government and its allies, 1860–1906'. *Modern Asian Studies*. v: 4 (1971).

'Municipal Government and Muslim Separatism in the United Provinces, 1883–1916'. *Modern Asian Studies*. VII: 3 (1973).

Separatism among Indian Muslims. Cambridge, 1975.

Row, C. S. *The Confessions of a Bogus Patriot*. Madras, 1923.

Rudloph, S. H. and L. I. *The Modernity of Tradition: Political Development in India*. Chicago, 1967.

Sambanda Mudaliar, P. *En Suyasarithai*. Madras, 1963. (Tamil–Autobiography.)

Sankaran Nair, C. *Gandhi and Anarchy*. Madras, n.d.

The Autobiography of Sir C. Sankaran Nair. Madras, 1966.

Sastri, V. L. (ed.), *Encyclopaedia of the Madras Presidency and the Adjacent States*. Cocanada, 1920.

Sastry, K. R. R. *The Madura Sourashtra Community: A Study in Applied Economics*. Bangalore, 1927.

'Satabisha', *Rashtrapathi Dr Pattabhi*. Madras, 1948.

Satyamurthi, S. *A Prize Essay on Loyalty to the British*. Madras, 1911.

Seal, A. *The Emergence of Indian Nationalism*. Cambridge, 1968.

Shiva Rao, B. *The Industrial Worker in India*. London, 1939.

Silverberg, J. (ed.), *Social Mobility in the Caste System in India*. The Hague, 1968.

Singer, M. and Cohn, B. (eds.), *Structure and Change in Indian Society*. Chicago, 1968.

Sivakolundu Mudaliar, A. *A Short Brochure on the Kallars*. Tanjore, 1926.

S. K. N. *Non-Brahmin Letters*. Madras, 1915.

Slater, G. Southern India. Its Political and Economic Problems. London, 1936.

Some South Indian Villages. Oxford, 1918.

347

Spate, O. H. K. *India and Pakistan. A General and Regional Geography.* London, 1954.

Spencer, G. W. 'Religious Networks and Royal Influence in Eleventh Century South India' in *Journal of the Economic and Social History of the Orient.* XII: pp. 42–56.

'Royal Initiative under Rajaraja I'. *Indian Social and Economic History Review.* VII: 4 (1970).

Somasundram Chetty, P. *Memoirs.* Madras, 1889.

Somasundram Pillai, S. A. *Dr T. M. Nair, M.D.* Madura, 1920.

Some Madras Leaders. Allahabad, 1922.

Second Supplement to the Life of Coopoo Soobraya Velu Chetty. Madras, 1919.

Third Supplement to the Life of Coopoo Soobraya Velu Chetty. Madras, 1922.

Southern India Chamber of Commerce. Annual Report. Madras, 1911–21.

South Indian Maharashtrians, issued by the Mahratta Education Fund. Madras, as its Silver Jubilee Souvenir. Madras, 1937.

Spratt, P. *D.M.K. in Power.* Bombay, 1970.

Srinivas, M. N. *Caste in Modern India and Other Essays.* Bombay, 1962.
  Social Change in Modern India. Berkeley and Los Angeles, 1966.

Srinivasa Aiyangar, K. R. *S. Srinivasa Aiyangar: The Story of a Decade in Indian Politics.* Mangalore, 1939.

Srinivasa Rao, K. *Papers on Social Reform.* Kurnool, 1906.

Stein, B. 'Economic Functions of a Medieval South Indian Temple' in *Journal of Asian Studies.* IX: 2 (1960).

Subba Rao, G. V. *The Life and Times of Sir K. V. Reddi Naidu.* Rajahmundry, 1957.
  Sree Gopalakrishnayya. Amalapuram, 1935.

Subba Rao, K. *Revived Memories.* Madras, 1933.

Subramaniam, S. *Dr A. Ramaswami Mudaliar and Dr A. Lakshmanaswami Mudaliar Eighty-First Birthday Commemoration Volume.* Madras, 1967.

A Brief Life Sketch of M. R. Ry P. Subramanyam Chettiar Avl. Madras, n.d.

Sundararaja Iyengar, S. *Land Tenures in the Madras Presidency.* Madras, 1922

Sunthralingam, R. *Politics and Nationalist Awakening in South India, 1852–1891.* Arizona, 1974.

Suryanarayana, K. *Sir R. Venkataratnam.* Rajahmundry, 1952.

Thacker's Indian Directory. 1909. Calcutta, 1909.

Thomas, P. J. *The Growth of Federal Finance in India.* Oxford, 1939.

Thurston, E. *Castes and Tribes of Southern India.* Madras, 1909.

Tinker, H. *The Foundations of Local Self-Government in India, Pakistan and Burma.* London, 1954.

Tiruvenkataswami, V. (ed.), *Pachaiyappa's College Centenary Commemoration Book. 1842–1942.* Madras, 1942.

Vadivelu, A. *The Aristocracy of Southern India. Volume II.* Madras, 1907.
  Ruling Chiefs, Nobles and Zamindars of India. Madras, 1915.

Varadarajan, *Tiru Vi Ka.* Madras, 1968. (Tamil).

Dr P. Varadarajulu Naidu Commemoration Volume. Madras, 1955.

Bibliography

The National Dharma: Speeches and Writings of Dr. P. Varadarajulu Naidu. Madras, 1934.

Venkatappayya, K. *Sviya Caritra.* (Vijayawada), Volume I, 1952; Volume II, 1955. (Telugu – Autobiography).

The Andhra Movement. (n.p., n.d.)

Venkata Raja, A. K. D. *A Brief Life Sketch of P. S. Kumaraswamy Raja.* Rajapalaiyam, 1964.

Venkataramana Iyengar, C. V. 'The Mill Industry in Coimbatore'. *The Journal of the Madras Geographical Association.* Volume V.

Venkatarangaiya, M. *The Freedom Struggle in Andhra Pradesh (Andhra).* Hyderabad, Volume I, 1965; Volume II, 1968; Volume III, 1965.

The Development of Local Boards in the Madras Presidency. Bombay, 1939.

Venkata Rao, V. *A Hundred Years of Local Self Government in the Andhra and Madras States. 1850–1950.* Bombay, 1960.

Venkataratnam, M. *The Reform of the Brahmins.* Madras, 1924.

The Non-Brahmin Origin of the Brahmins. Madras, 1922.

Brahmarshi Dr Sir Raghupathi Venkata Ratnam Naidu Birth Centenary Souvenir. 'Maharnavami' 1962. n.p., n.d.

Venkateswara Rao, K. *Tanguturi Prakasam.* Tanuku, 1958. (Telugu).

Viraraghavachari, M. 'The Hindu. Its Origin and History' in *The Hindu Golden Jubilee 1878–1928.* Madras, 1936.

Viresalingam, K. *The Autobiography of Rao Bahadur Kandukuri Viresalingam Pantulu.* Madras, 1911. (Telugu).

Visvanatha Sastri, C. V. *Biographies of a Grandfather and His Grandson.* Madras, 1939.

Waley, S. D. *Edwin Montagu.* London, 1964.

Washbrook, D. A. 'Country Politics: Madras 1880 to 1930' in *Modern Asian Studies.* VII: 3 (1973).

Who's Who in Madras 1935. Cochin, 1935.

Unpublished dissertations and manuscripts

Baker, C. J. 'Political Change in South India, 1919–1937'. Fellowship dissertation, Queens' College, Cambridge, 1972.

Bayly, C. A. 'The Development of Political Organisation in the Allahabad Locality, 1880–1925'. D.Phil. thesis, Oxford University, 1970.

Cohn, B. S. 'The Census, Social Structure and Objectification in South Asia'. Paper read at Second European Conference on Modern South Asia. Copenhagen

Gordon, R. A. 'Aspects in the history of the Indian National Congress, with special reference to the Swarajya Party, 1919 to 1927'. D.Phil. thesis, Oxford University, 1970.

Inden, R. 'Social Mobility in Pre-Modern Bengal'. Paper read at Study Conference on Tradition in Indian Politics and Society. University of London, 1–3 July 1969.

Leonard, J. G. 'Kandukuri Viresalingam: A Biography of an Indian Social Reformer, 1848–1919'. Ph.d. dissertation, University of Wisconsin, 1970.

McAlpin, M. B. 'The Impact of Railroads on Agriculture in India, 1860–1900: A Case Study of Cotton'. Ph.d. dissertation, University of Wisconsin, 1973.

Manor, J. 'The Evolution of Political Areas and Units of Social Organization: the Lingayats and Vokkaligas of Princely Mysore'. Privately circulated paper, 1972.

Ray, R. K. 'Social Conflict and Political Unrest in Bengal, 1875 to 1925'. Ph.d. dissertation, Cambridge University, 1972.

Washbrook, D. A. 'Political Change in the Madras Presidency 1880–1921', Fellowship dissertation, Trinity College, Cambridge, 1971.

'Law and Land in South India,' paper read at Conference on Indian Economic History, University of Pennsylvania, 1975.

INDEX

Index

Index

Kanara, South, 33, 37
Kandaswami Chetty, O., 324
Karvetnagar, Raja of, 96, 98, 280
Kasturi Ranga Iyengar, S., 214, 240, 241, 246, 247, 252, 253, 289, 291, 309–11, 314, 315, 323, 329
Kasu family, 156
Kesava Pillai, P., 171, 231, 285
Khilafat movement, 315
Kistna district, 11, 14, 19, 37, 47, 67, 68, 90–2, 156, 162, 176–8, 183, 242, 243, 328
Kistnapatrika, 243
Komati (caste), 18, 32, 92, 95, 101, 107, 109, 111, 113, 120, 123, 124, 128, 139–41, 142–4, 196, 199, 201, 203, 208, 214, 225, 328
Konkunad, 21
Kotaswami Thevar, 30, 31
Krishna Rao, D., 37
Krishna Rao, M., 243, 244
Krishnaswami Iyengar, N., 200
Krishnaswami Iyer, Sir V., 212, 220, 230, 236, 241
Kshatriya, 126–8, 131
Kumaramangalam, *zamindar* of, 99, 313, 323
Kumaraswami Sastri, C. V., 236, 237
Kumbakonam town, 102, 103, 106, 115, 145, 200, 219; Sankarachariar of 186, 225
Kurukula Vanisha (community), 202.

Land revenue settlement: theory of 26–7; practice of 32–4, 150–1, 177–8; attempts to change 52.
Latchmana Rao, H., 169
Legislative Council, 141, 156, 169, 200, 210, 222, 223, 228, 229, 230, 232, 235, 241, 244, 245, 248, 251, 254, 257, 271, 273, 285, 296, 300, 301, 306, 308, 314, 318, 323, 327, 334
Leonard, John, 193
Liberal League, 325
Lingamalee Subbaya, V., 140, 141
Lingayats, 147, 226
Local-level, political culture: definition 15–22; economic change and 84–5, 332–4; in Tanjore and Malabar 88–9; in Kistna and Godavari deltas 94–6; and pre-British state 147–50; and administrative change 172–3,

332–4; in non-Brahman movement 278–9
Local Self-Government; development 61–3, 223, 255–7; in towns 109, 190–200; in rural areas 166–73, 175–6, 180–1; in Madras city 200–14; and provincial politics 258–60, 298–304, 323–4
Lodd Govindoss, 123, 162, 214, 230, 292, 317

McAlpin, M., 74
Macleane, Collector, 32, 37, 270
Madras city, 14, 23, 26, 56, 58, 60, 65, 118, 124, 137–40, 143, 159, 172, 181, 190, 200, 207, 208, 215, 218, 220–3, 227, 235, 237–9, 241, 244–6, 251, 253, 254, 256, 280, 290, 298, 301, 309, 313, 315, 317, 318, 322, 329
Madras Dravidian Association, 295
Madras Mahajana Sabha, 209, 211, 222, 225, 231, 245, 246, 311
Madras Municipal Corporation, 201–12, 214, 242, 292
Madras Native Association, 222
Madras P. C. C., 248, 310, 314, 316
Madura district, 11, 30, 31, 33, 132; town, 110, 114, 128, 137, 138, 142, 185–7, 189, 190, 198, 261
Madura Tamil Sangam, 124
Mahdavaiah, 168
Mahadeva Chetty, G., 224
Mahalinga Chetty, 186
Mahommed Bazlullah, 60, 211
Majeti family, 113, 117, 118, 123
Malabar district, 11, 14, 16, 19, 20, 40, 46, 55, 85, 89, 90, 95, 102, 107, 108, 110, 130, 139, 174–6, 182, 200, 220, 221, 235, 261, 275, 328
Mangalore town, 12
Mannargudi town, 321
Maracair (Muslims) 113, 192
Maratha Brahmans, 16, 45
Maravar (caste), 16, 98, 130–2, 142, 157, 188
Marie Louise, Father, 302
Marwari (caste), 92, 116
Masilamani Pillai, V., 297
Masulipatam town, 95, 102, 109, 118, 177, 243
Mayavaram town, 176, 189

354

Index

Index

Index